Late Innings

Late Innings

A DOCUMENTARY HISTORY

OF BASEBALL, 1945–1972

COMPILED AND EDITED BY

DEAN A. SULLIVAN

UNIVERSITY OF NEBRASKA PRESS

LINCOLN & LONDON

Acknowledgments appear on pages 285–86, which constitutes an extension of the copyright page.

© 2002 by the University of Nebraska Press
All rights reserved
Manufactured in the United States of America

☉

Library of Congress
Cataloging-in-Publication Data
Late innings : a documentary history of baseball, 1945–1972 / compiled and edited by Dean A. Sullivan.
    p. cm.
Includes bibliographical references and index.
ISBN 0-8032-9285-6 (pbk. : alk. paper)
1. Baseball—United States—History—20th century—Sources. I. Title: Documentary history of baseball, 1945–1972. II. Sullivan, Dean A., 1963–
GV863.A1 L28   2002
796.357′0973′09045—dc21   2001043063

Contents

CHAPTER 6. BASEBALL CONFRONTS MODERNITY

CHAPTER 7. THE ERA OF LABOR UNREST BEGINS

Shortly after his election, Chandler was advised by owners that his duty was to endorse the positions they adopted without interference—regardless of the legality of the action. Chandler bristled at the suggestion that he subordinate himself to other baseball officials, but in his view they could not believe that he would defy them. In his first year in office Chandler's insistence on his independence was expressed in his public acceptance of the signing of Jackie Robinson by the Dodgers, in spite of a secret report on the "race question" in which owners made clear their opposition to integration. Other major decisions, like his suspension of Dodgers manager Leo Durocher for the 1947 season and his approval of a $5 million television contract with Gillette after failing to obtain a vote of confidence in 1949, offended many owners and baseball writers alike. Chandler was not allowed to serve a complete term in office, but in his brief service he addressed issues that would haunt future commissioners for years to come.

The impact of the reintegration of professional baseball was immediate and far-reaching. Major league owners feared that many players, fans, and even broadcast sponsors would rebel against the abandonment of segregation, but the reaction did not give them an excuse to halt "the great experiment." The clubs also claimed that integration would result in the collapse of the Negro Leagues, costing them thousands of dollars per season in rental fees, but they and their minor league affiliates would benefit monetarily from the gradual erasure of the color line. Nevertheless, Robinson and other African American players faced considerable opposition from abusive bigots in the stands and in the opposing dugouts.

The most serious incident—even worse than the torrent of racial slurs hurled at Robinson at the direction of Philadelphia Phillies manager Ben Chapman early in his rookie season—was the alleged threat of several St. Louis Cardinals players to boycott their scheduled games with Brooklyn rather than share the field with Robinson. Although then–National League president Ford Frick downplayed the event in his autobiography, reporter Stanley Woodward published his findings on May 9 in banner headlines just after the Cardinals-Dodgers series had concluded without controversy.

No definitive evidence that the conspiracy was a reality has surfaced, but the significance of Woodward's article stems not from its allegations, but from its publication. Baseball journalists had chronicled some of the crude treatment Robinson had received in the first month of the season, but they attributed it to unenlightened southern ballplayers taking the tradition of harassing rookies too far. The notion of a racist conspiracy among a number of Cardinal players and other sympathetic National Leaguers was ridiculed by most reporters, but they were forced to address the uncomfortable reality that baseball was not as democratic an institution as they indicated in their writings. Furthermore, baseball officials who were still shaken by the threat symbolized by the players who jumped to the Mexican League were compelled to defend the integrity of organized baseball by publicly standing behind the one player whose image they least wanted to represent the national pastime.

Introduction

Major league baseball owners faced a dilemma after the death of Commissioner Kenesaw Mountain Landis in November 1944. Following the shock of the Black Sox scandal of 1919, the owners hired Landis as the sport's first commissioner. They endowed his office with vast power and for the next quarter-century watched in silent horror as Landis wielded his authority with fierce abandon. Landis's death afforded owners an opportunity to reorganize the administrative structure of baseball to protect and enhance their influence while ensuring the prosperity of the game.

The owners realized that this opportunity arrived at a most propitious time. With the end of the war in sight, both players and fans would soon be returning en masse, restrictions on travel and on material used to construct top-quality balls and bats would be lifted, and the tension permeating American society would be replaced by euphoria. Baseball officials hoped their sport would serve as a primary recreational outlet for the nation. In order to capitalize on the situation, however, they had to act quickly to elect a new commissioner who would agree to assume Landis's office without Landis's power.

Landis's successor would be unable to unilaterally enact or reverse baseball policy based on his interpretation of "baseball's best interests," as Landis had on numerous occasions. The owners redefined this clause to indicate those decisions and strategies agreed to by a majority of owners. A successful commissioner would have to petition the owners to gain their approval on any particular issue. He would also have to earn at least three-quarters of the votes, rather than a simple majority, to retain his office. Post-Landis commissioners would have to be consummate politicians in order to survive, and their primary constituency would not be the baseball fan, but the ownership.

Given these conditions and their newfound power, the owners opted to award the commissionership to a career politician known for his personal eccentricities—U.S. senator Albert "Happy" Chandler. A detailed memo by Dodgers president Branch Rickey revealed the mistrust among the owners as the opportunity they had awaited for years finally presented itself. A primary source of resentment was the initial reluctance of the committee empowered with selecting candidates to reveal their top choices to the rest of the owners. According to Rickey, Rickey himself took the lead in gaining the release of the candidate list, only to see his accomplishment overshadowed by Yankees president Larry MacPhail, who nominated Chandler for the position and persuaded the others to vote for him.

acted on my request for the incorporation papers of the Association of National Baseball League Umpires. I would also like to thank the contributors to the list-servs of the Society of American Baseball Research and the North American Society for Sport History for inspiring me to pursue my love of baseball history.

In addition, I want to thank my entire family for supporting my efforts. In particular I want to express my appreciation to my niece Megan Theresa Sullivan, who, despite her tender age (three weeks at this writing), has reminded me of the wonder of life.

Preface

My earliest memories of baseball date from the 1971 World Series. As an eight-year-old living in northern Virginia, I could not understand why my older brother and sister were supporting the Pittsburgh Pirates rather than the Baltimore Orioles, a local team. Their explanation that the Orioles were the rivals of their beloved Washington Senators and that they were left with no choice but to root against the Orioles made no sense to me. Nor did I understand that I would never have a chance to cheer on the Senators, since the club had already announced its plans to abandon the nation's capital for greener pastures in Arlington, Texas. Nevertheless, a lifetime love affair with baseball had been ignited. Since that time I have learned to embrace the Orioles, though I still harbor hopes that in the near future I will be able to experience the joy of living and dying with a home team, either in Virginia or in Washington.

In the meantime I have invested my time researching the history of baseball through a study of pertinent documents, including newspaper and magazine articles, evidence presented before Congress, private letters, official league communications, legal decisions and law journal articles, and countless books. I have spent hundreds of hours at the Library of Congress, made frequent trips to the National Baseball Hall of Fame Library, and examined more than half a dozen collections of papers. As in my previous two books, *Early Innings* and *Middle Innings,* I have worked hard to discover documents that collectively depict a portrait of professional baseball, with this volume focusing on the period between the end of World War II and the conclusion of the Curt Flood legal saga.

I would like to thank the staffs of the libraries and archives who assisted me, including the Library of Congress; the Hagley Museum and Library in Greenville, Delaware; the University of Wisconsin–Milwaukee Area Research Center in Milwaukee; and the State Historical Society of Wisconsin in Madison, Wisconsin. William Gamson, Reynolds Farley, Phillip Converse, Jay Demarath, James McDonald, and Ernie Harwell helped me pin down the origins of the Baseball Seminar—a game they pioneered in the early 1960s—and demonstrate that it was a direct predecessor to Rotisserie Baseball. F. X. Flinn also provided me with information on the early history of Rotisserie Baseball. Bob Bailey and Tim Wiles (the director of research at the National Baseball Hall of Fame Library) contributed documents for the book, and Lyle K. Wilson sent me copies of several of his articles on African Americans in baseball. The Office of the Secretary of State of Illinois promptly

In the late 1940s major league baseball faced several antitrust lawsuits by Mexican League exiles whose requests for reinstatement had been denied. After an initial victory by the major leagues, a panel of three federal judges overturned the decision after concluding that baseball's antitrust exemption was no longer valid because its distribution nationwide through radio and television transformed it into an interstate business. Only after another judge ruled in a separate case that baseball was not obligated to reinstate Danny Gardella, Max Lanier, or Fred Martin did Commissioner Chandler offer amnesty to all Mexican League jumpers. Of the eighteen active major leaguers who played in the Mexican League, thirteen returned to the majors. The only player who achieved any success following reinstatement was New York Giants pitcher Sal Maglie.

The resolution of the Mexican League problem did not halt the flow of antitrust suits. A number of disgruntled minor league players (including New York Yankees farmhand George Toolson) and executives challenged the exemption in court. Toolson's case, after being combined with several others, progressed to the Supreme Court in 1953, when the justices refused to reconsider the exemption while acknowledging its apparent illogic. Baseball owners could hardly rejoice, however, because the exemption was also being examined by Congress and the Justice Department.

Throughout the 1950s and early 1960s, committees led by Representative Emanuel Celler (D-NY) and Senator Estes Kefauver (D-TN) exhaustively investigated the business practices of organized baseball and considered several bills designed to amend or abolish the exemption. Intense lobbying efforts by the major leagues, led by attorney Paul Porter, succeeded in preserving the status quo. Porter and Frick made clear to the owners the importance of aggressively defending their institution. The success of their efforts instilled in baseball executives a belief that the antitrust exemption would not be eliminated by Congress or overturned by the courts. In time their overconfidence would damage their attempts to maintain their position of strength.

This did not mean that the threat no longer existed. Starting in the late 1940s, the Justice Department challenged the television policy of major league baseball with regard to the minor leagues. The government concluded that Rule 1 (d), which established territorial boundaries around each city with a professional team and required the permission of one team prior to allowing the radio or television transmission of another game into its territory, violated antitrust laws. Both the major and minor leagues argued that the rule was necessary in order to protect the minor leagues, but in October 1951, Rule 1 (d) was withdrawn. The minor leagues held television primarily responsible for the near-collapse of the system in the 1950s and 1960s, but other factors—including overexpansion and poor management—also contributed. Minor league officials also resented the failure of their major league counterparts to fight harder for their position, but the immense profits of television overrode any consideration for the minor leagues.

On the field the major leagues enjoyed what sportswriter Roger Kahn described simply as "the era." From the late 1940s through the early 1960s baseball was dominated by three franchises, all based in New York—the Yankees, the Giants, and the Dodgers. While the imperial Yankees simply extended their longtime domination of the American League, the Giants and Dodgers earned their elite status only after years of struggle. They also took advantage of integration by signing stars like Jackie Robinson, Don Newcombe, and Willie Mays. The refusal of the Yankees to sign African American players prior to Elston Howard in 1955 generated resentment among local politicians and fans, some of whom protested outside Yankee Stadium. The majority of baseball fans, however, were satisfied with the progress of integration and the excitement the new players brought to the game.

Other new players, and a few previously obscure ones, helped generate excitement for major league fans. New Yorkers were treated to a hometown debate on the relative merits of three young centerfielders—Mays, Mickey Mantle, and Duke Snider. Mantle won the Triple Crown in 1956, the same year his journeyman teammate Don Larsen pitched a perfect game in the World Series. The following two seasons, the Milwaukee Braves—the first franchise in half a century to move to a different city—were led to the Series by Henry Aaron, one of the last Negro League players to make the majors. Another former Negro Leaguer, Ernie Banks, won consecutive Most Valuable Player Awards for the Chicago Cubs, but he never made the World Series.

The arrival of Aaron and Banks in the majors masked the deterioration of the Negro American League, which after years of operating in the red finally collapsed in 1963. Ironically, the integration of the major leagues, which was the foremost cause of the Negro Leagues' collapse, was far from complete. Historians Jules Tygiel and Bruce Adelson have chronicled in detail the trials of African American players who integrated different minor leagues in the South throughout the 1950s, and they concluded that the struggle—an antecedent of the Civil Rights movement of the 1960s—remained an arduous one. In many cases the profits realized by the signing of a black player and the increase in attendance by African Americans was a greater factor in breaking down racial barriers than any degree of racial enlightenment. Evidence of that process can be seen in Birmingham and Montgomery, Alabama, where segregation in sport was enforced by statutes that were revoked, reinstated, and finally revoked again within a decade.

Aside from integration, the primary transformation in major league baseball in the postwar era was westward expansion. The Boston Braves started the trend by moving to Milwaukee, displacing its top minor league club and occupying its new stadium, whose value was enhanced by access to a major highway and thousands of parking spaces. When the Braves earned extraordinary profits immediately after the move, other teams paid attention. The Braves' formula for success was taken to heart by owners of the St. Louis Browns and the Philadelphia Athletics, who moved their clubs to municipally built stadiums in Baltimore (1954) and Kansas City (1955), respectively.

It also intrigued Dodgers owner Walter O'Malley, who was failing in his efforts to get New York City officials to acquire land on which he would construct a new ballpark in Brooklyn. During these negotiations, O'Malley and Giants owner Horace Stoneham were in contact with officials in California. Although New Yorkers were given advance warning about a possible move, the news that the Dodgers and Giants were leaving for the West Coast for the 1958 season stunned them. New York mayor Robert Wagner, blamed by some for the abrupt departure, responded by forming a baseball committee authorized to develop a plan to attract another major league team to the city.

The Mayor's Baseball Committee of the City of New York, formed in late November 1957, was headed by lawyer William Shea. Shea and his committee pursued the possibility of enticing a National League club to move to New York, but they quickly realized that another strategy would be required. Aware that even after the recent franchise moves many large North American cities remained without representation in any major sports league, Shea worked behind the scenes to assemble a group of wealthy investors in cities like Houston, Denver, Toronto, and Minneapolis. He announced plans to form a third major league—to be called the Continental League (CL)—in July 1959, two months after a meeting in which major league and CL officials agreed on a list of conditions the CL had to meet in order to earn recognition by the majors.

In spite of a tacit pledge from the major leagues not to obstruct the formation of the CL, conflict ensued. Lawyers and lobbyists from the major leagues worked to defeat congressional efforts to modify the antitrust exemption in ways that would allow the CL to stock their teams by drafting major league players. Minor league clubs in prospective CL cities demanded exorbitant relocation payments, apparently at the direction of the parent teams. In addition, AL and NL officials negotiated with some CL investors to persuade them to accept expansion franchises in their leagues instead. In August 1960, Shea and CL president Branch Rickey dismantled the CL on the promise that each major league would grant franchises to two CL cities. The NL kept its promise by placing expansion franchises in New York—which would play in a stadium named for Shea—and Houston. However, the AL reneged by moving into Washington (replacing the Senators, which moved into Minneapolis—a CL city) and Los Angeles.

The expansion of the AL in 1961 resulted in the lengthening of the season from 154 to 162 games, which had a totally unexpected impact on baseball history—despite the efforts of Commissioner Frick. The defending AL MVP, Yankees right fielder Roger Maris, led teammate Mickey Mantle in a race to break Babe Ruth's single-season home run record. After Mantle was injured late in the season, Maris shrugged off immense pressure applied in part by resentful fans and reporters who were rooting for Mantle and passed Ruth in the 163rd and final game of the season (including one tie game). However, according to Frick—a friend of Ruth's in his days as a sportswriter—Maris's achievement was to be distinguished from Ruth's with a "distinctive mark" since he failed to surpass the record prior to the Yankees'

155th game. Frick did not ask that any qualification be placed next to any other record established during the extended portion of the season.

The Yankees won the 1961 World Series and appeared in the following three Series, continuing an incredible streak of excellence dating back to the early 1920s. However, starting with the loss of the 1964 Series to the St. Louis Cardinals, the fabled Bronx Bombers finally fell into disrepair. The Yankees struggled to play .500 ball for most of the next dozen years, not winning another pennant until 1976. In a sense the collapse of baseball's most storied team symbolized the entry of the major leagues into a more modern age. Although offensive statistics during the mid-1960s were reminiscent of the Dead Ball Era of the early twentieth century, the game was experiencing significant changes.

The Houston Astros responded to the challenge of playing in the Deep South by constructing the first domed, air-conditioned stadium—a decade after Walter O'Malley proposed building a similar stadium in Brooklyn—in 1965. The Astro-dome's glass panels, essential for the survival of the grass field, created a such a blinding glare that the management was forced to paint them over, killing the grass in the process. The club experimented with a plastic, grasslike covering quickly dubbed Astroturf. The following year the Atlanta Braves (whose transfer from Milwaukee had been delayed for a year by an antitrust suit) proved that a traditional stadium would have sufficed, but the audacity represented by the Astro-dome made clear in more ways than one that baseball was breaking from its past.

Perhaps the development with the greatest impact on baseball's future was the hiring of Marvin Miller as the executive director of the Major League Baseball Players' Association (MLBPA) in 1966. In the dozen years of its existence the MLBPA had achieved a few minor victories, but it was largely an undercapitalized organization completely dominated by the owners. Judge Robert Cannon, Miller's predecessor, frequently expressed the view that the players were lucky to have the few benefits they had and should not be so rude as to ask for more. In sharp contrast, Miller—an experienced labor official with the United Steelworkers of America—would challenge the owners at every opportunity on behalf of the players, whom he described as one of the most oppressed groups of workers he had ever encountered.

In the first three years of Miller's term, his counterpart was Commissioner William Eckert, a retired U.S. Air Force general who was ridiculed from the moment his surprising election was announced in November 1965. It is possible that the owners—who knew of Eckert's many weaknesses—selected him because the previous year they had restored the commissioner's power to act unilaterally in the "best interests of baseball." Although Frick—who urged the owners to make the change—had willingly acted on behalf of the owners, he admitted after his retirement that his inability to act in this regard was a "nuisance." Even though several noteworthy developments, including the signing of the first Basic Agreement between the majors and the MLBPA and the reorganization of the majors into four divisions, occurred during Eckert's term, he proved such an embarrassment that the owners relieved him of duty after only three years.

The owners fought among themselves for months during their search for a replacement. In desperation they made an interim choice in Bowie Kuhn, a NL lawyer, in February 1969. Even before his appointment was made permanent in August, Kuhn made clear that he was to be an activist commissioner by intervening in several disputes between players and clubs in the first several months of his administration. One case in which Kuhn did not involve himself was the refusal of St. Louis Cardinal center fielder Curt Flood to report to the team to which he had been traded. Flood's threats to retire and, later, to sue baseball were widely ignored as the rantings of a disgruntled player. Kuhn and the owners would soon discover that Flood and his adviser, Marvin Miller, were extremely serious about their quest for their vision of justice.

Late Innings

1

Baseball in the Post-Landis Era

The death of Kenesaw Mountain Landis in November 1944 ended a quarter-century of autocratic rule during which the owners had little say in baseball affairs. Within a month of his passing, the owners weakened the powers of the commissioner's office and, soon after, hired as their new commissioner a man who, they believed, understood that his role was to enforce the owners' will. To their surprise, Albert "Happy" Chandler demonstrated his independence on numerous occasions, especially when he supported Brooklyn Dodgers president Branch Rickey's decision to sign Jackie Robinson and acted behind the scenes to protect his right to play in the majors. On other issues, such as the suspension of Mexican League jumpers and their subsequent reinstatement three years later, Chandler carried out the owners' wishes.

Chandler was not responsible for the increase in popularity of the game in both the major and minor leagues immediately following World War II. Helping baseball's resurgence was a succession of exciting pennant races, starting with the first playoff games in major league history in 1946 and culminating in down-to-the-last-day finishes in 1948 and 1949. Many of these games were telecast nationwide as people fell victim to the television craze which, some argued, threatened the prosperity of the minor leagues. Another factor in the attendance surge—the slow integration of the sport— had a devastating effect on the Negro Leagues, which started to collapse as its fans changed allegiance to follow pathbreakers like Robinson, Larry Doby, and Don Newcombe in all levels of organized baseball. Major league officials had every reason to be optimistic about the immediate future of their sport.

Commissioner's Powers Diminished after Landis's Death (1945)

SOURCE: *Official Baseball 1945*, ed. Leslie M. O'Connor (New York: A. S. Barnes, 1945), pp. 219–21

Barely two weeks after the death of Kenesaw Mountain Landis, baseball owners met in New York to plan for the future and redefine the office of commissioner. Not only was the office vacant, but the Major League Agreement currently in force, written at the beginning of Landis's reign, was due to expire in 1946. The owners seized the opportunity to amend the agreement in their favor by weakening the power of the commissioner to act when he identified "conduct detrimental to baseball." Landis, upon accepting the post, had insisted on the power to unilaterally identify and punish such conduct. In the new agreement, signed on February 3, 1945, the owners declared that no rule or decision passed by the majority of owners could be construed as "detrimental to baseball." Moreover, the vote required to elect a new commissioner was changed from a majority to a three-quarters majority, soon amended to three-quarters in each league. Future czars of baseball would know that actions deemed "detrimental" by as few as three owners in either league could result in termination.

Ford Frick, in testimony before Congress in 1958, briefly discussed these changes. See Subcommittee on Antitrust and Monopoly, Organized Professional Team Sports, *85th Cong., 2nd sess., 1958, 148.*

MAJOR LEAGUE AGREEMENT

ARTICLE I

THE COMMISSIONER

Sec. 1. The Office of Commissioner, created by the Major League Agreement of January 12, 1921, is hereby continued for the period of this agreement.

Sec. 2. The functions of the Commissioner shall be as follows:

(a) To investigate, either upon complaint or upon his own initiative, any act, transaction or practice charged, alleged or suspected to be detrimental to the best interests of the national game of baseball, with authority to summon persons and to order the production of documents, and, in case of refusal to appear or produce, to impose such penalties as are hereinafter provided.

(b) To determine, after investigation, what preventive, remedial or punitive action is appropriate in the premises, and to take such action either against Major Leagues, Major League clubs or individuals, as the case may be.

(c) To hear and determine finally any dispute between the Major Leagues which may be certified to him for determination by the President of either Major League.

(d) To hear and determine finally any dispute to which a player is a party, or any dispute concerning a player, which may be certified to him by either or any of the disputants.

(e) To formulate, and from time to time announce, the rules of procedure to be observed by the Commissioner and all other parties in connection with the discharge of his duties. Such rules shall always recognize the right of any party in interest to appear before the Commissioner and be heard and the right of the Presidents of the two Major Leagues to appear and be heard upon any matter affecting the interests of the Major Leagues, or either of them.

Sec. 3. In the case of conduct detrimental to baseball by Major Leagues, Major League clubs, officers, employees, or players, punitive action by the Commissioner may in any case take the form of a public reprimand. In the case of a Major League or club, the Commissioner may impose a fine not exceeding Five Thousand Dollars ($5,000.00) for any one offense. In the case of a Major League club, punishment may extend to temporary deprivation of representation in joint meetings held under this agreement. In the case of any official or employee of a Major League or of any Major League club, punishment may extend to suspension or removal. For such conduct, a player may be declared by the Commissioner temporarily or permanently ineligible to play for any club which is a party to this agreement.

No Major League rule or other joint action of the two Major Leagues and no act or procedure taken in compliance with any such Major League rule or joint action of the two Major Leagues shall be considered or construed to be detrimental to baseball. If in the judgment of the Commissioner, any Major League rule or any joint action of the two Major Leagues becomes in its operation impracticable or disadvantageous to baseball, either by reason of changed conditions or otherwise, the Commissioner shall send a notice to the President of each Major League stating his judgment and the reasons therefore, and noticing such rule or joint action for reconsideration at the next regular joint meeting of the Major Leagues, or at a special joint meeting of the Major Leagues called by the Commissioner for the purpose of such reconsideration. At such regular or special joint meeting, such rule or joint action shall be voted upon as would be done if it were being initially proposed. During such period of reconsideration, such rule or joint action of the Leagues shall be in full force and effect.

Sec. 4. In the case of conduct detrimental to baseball by organizations not parties to this agreement, or by individuals not connected with any of the parties hereto, the Commissioner may pursue appropriate legal remedies, advocate remedial legislation and take such other steps as he may deem necessary and proper in the interests of the morale of the players and the honor of the game.

Sec. 5. The Commissioner shall hold office for seven (7) years and shall be eligible to succeed himself. His compensation shall be Fifty Thousand Dollars ($50,000.00) per annum.

Sec. 6. The election of any Commissioner hereunder shall be at a joint meeting of the two Major Leagues; the vote shall be by clubs; and to elect shall require the affirmative vote of twelve (12) of the sixteen clubs signatory hereto. During any vacancy in the office of Commissioner due to the resignation, death, or incapacity of any Commissioner during his term, or due to the failure to elect a Commissioner upon the expiration of a Commissioner's term, all the powers and duties of the Commissioner and the Advisory Council, as provided in the Major League Agreement, shall be conferred upon and thenceforth exercised by a Major League Advisory Council to consist of the President of the National League, the President of the American League and a third member to be selected by the two League presidents. Such Major League Advisory Council shall continue to exercise the powers and duties of the office of Commissioner under this agreement until a new Commissioner of Baseball has been elected as herein set forth. The decision of a majority of such Major League Advisory Council shall be controlling; provided that any case involving a player's claim against a club or League shall be decided solely by the third member of the Council.

2

Branch Rickey on Selection of Happy Chandler as Commissioner (1945)

SOURCE: "Memorandum of Meeting at Cleveland Ohio on April 24," April 25, 1945, Branch Rickey Papers, Box 35, Folder 9, Manuscript Division, Library of Congress

Diminishing the authority of the commissioner's office was a simple matter compared to the task of selecting a man capable of handling the position's power and willing to accept its limitations, both written and implied. The following memorandum by Brooklyn Dodgers president Branch Rickey is the only firsthand account of the stormy meeting that concluded unexpectedly with the election of Senator A. B. "Happy" Chandler as baseball's second commissioner. According to Rickey, Yankees president Larry MacPhail orchestrated Chandler's nomination after members of the committee empowered to identify candidates revealed, with great reluctance, that they had failed to settle on a suitable choice. After Chandler was accepted as a candidate, the lack of strong support for any of the others helped him win the necessary twelve votes on the third ballot.

Baseball historian William Marshall noted in Baseball's Pivotal Era: 1945–1951 *(Lexington: University Press of Kentucky, 1999) that the owners had many good reasons to believe Chandler would be a suitable commissioner. In addition to his legal and legislative experience, Chandler won the admiration of baseball executives in 1945 with his outspoken advocacy of the continuation of professional baseball in the face of threats to activate all but the most disabled players for military service. The senator's credentials as a baseball fan and as a politician accustomed to backroom compromises seemed tailor-made for the type of commissioner sought by the owners.*

However, Chandler soon made it clear that he would speak his mind and assert his independence when necessary. In his autobiography (written with Vance Trimble) Heroes, Plain Folks, and Skunks: The Life and Times of Happy Chandler *(Chicago: Bonus Books, 1989), Chandler stated that owners openly informed him that they vio-*

lated baseball rules and expected him to ignore such transgressions. His refusal to bypass the powers of his office, coupled with his support of the signing of Jackie Robinson, hastened his demise. On December 11, 1950, the owners declined to renew Chandler's contract.

Rickey concluded his memorandum by mentioning that after the election he held a meeting "with the boys of the United States Baseball League (USBL), a negro organization." On May 7, 1945, Rickey publicly revealed that he had established this organization as a better-organized alternative to the Negro Leagues. However, historian Jules Tygiel concluded that the USBL, first and foremost, was a diversion intended to obscure Rickey's search for a suitable candidate to integrate the major leagues. The USBL was launched in 1946, but it quietly collapsed at the end of the season.

APRIL 25TH 1945.
MEMORANDUM OF MEETING AT CLEVELAND OHIO ON APRIL 24TH.

At 11:00 A.M. Tuesday, April 24th, the American and National Leagues met at the Cleveland Hotel in Cleveland, Ohio. Secretary O'Connor presided. The meeting adjourned about 12:45 to reconvene at 2:00 P.M.. During this 1¾ hours, several matters were discussed including the War Bond exhibition games and negro baseball, most of the time being given to the latter subject. At 2:00 P.M., Mr. O'Connor read the notice calling the meeting, giving its purpose namely to receive the report of a Committee which had been appointed previously by joint action of the leagues to investigate and report upon candidates for the Commissionership. . . .

This report recited that the Committee had conducted considerable correspondence, telephone calls and conferences and that several hundred names had been submitted to the Committee for its consideration; that they had reduced the number to "about six" who in their judgment were qualified for the Commissionership. The report then went on to say that the Committee had not approached any of these qualified persons as to their availability; that because of their lack of knowledge of availability they had decided to recommend to the leagues that a temporary Commissioner should be appointed to perform the various duties of the Commissionership until such time as a permanent Commissioner could be found. The report did not name any of the persons who, in the opinion of the Committee, were qualified for the Commissionership. As soon as Mr. [Alva] Bradley had finished reading, he said that they had in mind that a temporary Commissioner could easily be found and he believed that baseball was in such need of a Commissioner that they should elect this temporary Commissioner at this meeting, indicating several of the needs.

Mr. [Donald] Barnes then stated, in support of the report, that the Committee had in mind Mr. [Joseph] Hostetler, the attorney for the American League as a man properly qualified to take over the Commissionership and that he would be willing to do the job until such time as a Commissioner would be elected. Neither Mr. [Sam] Breadon nor Mr. [Philip] Wrigley made any supporting statements.

The first speaker following the report of the Committee was Mr. [William]

Benswanger, President of the Pittsburgh Club, who said that the reasons given by Mr. Bradley showing the urgency for the election of a temporary Commissioner were very good reasons why there should be elected at this time a permanent Commissioner, and he stated that he was not at all in favor of the election of a temporary Commissioner. Mr. Giles of the Cincinnati Club, then stated, with a good deal of vehemence, that he did not know of anyone who was both qualified and available; that there just wasn't anyone now, in his judgment, whom he would care to vote for. . . .

I then asked for a copy of the report. Mr. Bradley then said that I could have his copy and that they had a number of the reports made out and he would get them. He left the table to go over to the corner desk where he had been occupied with his stenographer some time previously, and I believe he returned with several papers but they were not distributed. I took the report and said that I wished to read the fourth paragraph, which I then proceeded to do. This paragraph related to the statement that the Committee had interviewed, phoned, and had conferences with a great number of people and had received some hundreds of references, etc., but had decided only "about six" were qualified for consideration. After reading this paragraph I remarked, first, that it was gratifying to me that the Committee had been able to find "about six" who were, in their judgment, qualified for the Commissionership, and I asked this question, "Is it the judgment of the Committee that the six names, more or less whom they have decided upon as qualified, should not be named to this executive session of the two Major Leagues?" The answer from Mr. Bradley, which was quite apparently assented to by the other three members of the Committee was, "Yes," and Mr. Bradley said "because they did not feel that publicity was fair to themselves or persons considered when they did not know about availability." I then said that it was true, of course, that the Committee was not empowered to hire a Commissioner and pointed out that if we were in the position of having qualified persons found for us but to be left secretly in the hands of the Committee with no power whatever for the Committee to approach such persons, it seemed that we had reached the end of any possibility of ever finding a Commissioner through the Committee's work; that if the Committee was correct in saying that the other twelve men should not have the information which the four men had acquired, then the only thing the two leagues could do was simply to empower the four-man Committee to hire the Commissioner without the twelve knowing in the remotest fashion whom the Committee had in mind or whom they would hire, and indeed, without giving the two leagues any chance whatever even so much as to limit the Committee's selection to a list of names. And even if that was to be the procedure, I insisted, most certainly the other twelve members of the two leagues were entitled to know who the six men were out of which the Committee would select the Commissioner. And I closed by saying that I felt that we were entitled to have the information which the Committee had gathered; that was the purpose of the Committee's appointment and I felt that we should know the names of those to whom they had given favorable consideration.

Then Mr. MacPhail cut in with a good deal of vigor, and he resented the withholding of these names because, said he, "it seems that the four men feel that one or more of the other twelve cannot be trusted," and that whether they could be trusted or not, they were entitled to such information as the Committee held; that he felt that the Committee had no right to withhold the names; that that was the purpose for the Committee's appointment. MacPhail was pretty sharp and pointed in his remarks and immediately Mr. Benswanger said that he felt that they ought to be given the names and two or three others remarked, very quickly, and in such words as "so do I." . . .

About this time Mr. Bradley returned to the table with a quite heavy file. He began mentioning names, and immediately names of people who were obviously too old, or in ill health, or most patently unavailable. I asked the question about one of these names if, in the judgment of any one of the Committee, such person was within the possibility of availability and the answer was a definite "no." "Then," I said, "I don't believe that we need to hear the names of such persons and we don't want them. We want the 'about six' referred to in your report." That position was supported by Mr. MacPhail and others and Mr. Bradley then said he would come to those whom they had agreed were qualified, looking about into the faces of his Committee, apparently for assent. That statement met with approval on all sides.

Within what I judged to be about twenty minutes, he completed a list of eleven names. These eleven names were

[Frederick] Vinson
[Paul] McNutt
[J. Edgar] Hoover
[William] Douglas
[Governor Frank J.] Lausche
[Ford] Frick
[James A.] Farley
[Robert] Hannegan
[Thomas] Dewey
[John] Bricker

and a Judge of the Federal Court in Chicago whose name I did not get distinctly. He stated that this completed the list of those whom the Committee felt satisfied to recommend.

Several remarks were made about several of these men. For example, somebody said "Of course, Dewey is out of it," and I then asked the question as to whether it was likely that Governor Lausche of Ohio could accept. It was also remarked that two or three of the names mentioned, on account of their government jobs, would most certainly not be available.

After about ten minutes, certainly not more than that, of general remarks and discussions about this list of eleven, Mr. MacPhail said that he thought that a name that had not been mentioned by the Committee might be given consideration; that he knew the person was available and that he personally felt that the person was highly qualified for the job. He made two or three other complimentary introductory statements and then said "I refer to Senator Chandler of Kentucky." He then followed, giving a very brief biographical sketch of Sen. Chandler. I then said that I wished to make a statement which I was hopeful might be helpful in the immediate selection of a Commissioner. I then made this statement: "The Committee has g[iv]en us eleven names, and Mr. MacPhail has added one more which I accept in the making of my statement. I will be the twelfth vote (and it took 12 to elect) on any one of the twelve names now before us and I will gladly cast the first vote for a number of men on that list. In other words, if there are eleven men in this room who can make a similar statement, then we can elect a man from that list today, and I don't know of anything I would rather not do than leave this room without the election of a Commissioner."

Mr. MacPhail then referred to a letter which had come to his attention, having been written by Mr. Robert Carpenter, President of the Philadelphia National League Club, addressed to the two leagues, which he thought it was appropriate should be read at that time. Mr. Herb Pennock, who represented the Philadelphia Club at the meeting, produced the letter. Several in the room had seen it, but not all. Mr. MacPhail took the letter and handed it to me and asked me to read it. I handed it back to him and said "No, you read it, but read it distinctly. It's a good letter."

Mr. MacPhail then read Mr. Carpenter's letter which had several good points in it, but briefly, first, his belief that baseball should produce its own Commissioner, and second, and with much effect, that failure to elect a Commissioner at this meeting would not only be bad in the field of public relations but a perfectly silly and terribly weak position for baseball to take. This letter was a very conclusive answer to the previous remarks of Mr. Giles and a very strong attack upon the position of the Committee recommending delay. . . .

Now, Mr. Carpenter's letter had, in my judgment, very definite effect, particularly on the point of the advisability, if not necessity, of electing a Commissioner at that particular meeting. It seemed to me that it had special effect upon the mental processes of Sam Breadon, who, among others, spoke right away upon the advisability of our voting for a limited number of these twelve names, just to see how we stood. Discussion followed this suggestion, and it was finally agreed that we would reduce the twelve to five; that we would cast secret ballots without our names being written on them for not to exceed five of the twelve names. Then we would at least find out who the five leading candidates were. This ballot was to be taken without any commitment upon the part of anybody as a final vote. In fact, it was to be not at all significant, other than possibly to enable us to reduce, for further consideration, the number of names not to exceed five. While this was being discussed, the meeting digressed again to a discussion of various names and biographies were produced. The Committee showed that it had done a good deal of work in this direction. . . .

The whole discussion, as well as the recommendations of the Committee and the biographies read, and various remarks, lead [*sic*] me then to believe that the candidate of Mr. Bradley and Mr. Wrigley was Gov. Lausche, and the candidate of Mr. Breadon and Mr. Barnes was Bob Hannegan, and I believed, further, and I believe now, that the reason the Committee did not wish to give any names was because of its own disagreement on a candidate.

We then took up the matter of the proposed ballot, and the result of this first ballot, which was to be unlimited as to name but limited in number to five, resulted in part as follows:

	First	Second	Third	Fourth	Fifth
Frick	2	1		2	
Lausche	3	3	7	1	1
Farley	2	1	2	3	1
Chandler	5	6	1	3	1 (?)
Hannegan	4	3	5	1	1

Most of the others among the twelve received one or more votes in the balloting for some of the five positions. However, these five above received the 16 first votes. Therefore all 16 clubs cast its first vote for someone of these five and indeed, these five lead the rest of the field very substantially. There is a question mark above on the fifth vote for Mr. Chandler. I am sure he received this vote, but my markings are not clear on it. The results of this ballot were discussed at some length and the proposal was made that we should proceed to ballot on the three highest. This aroused some opposition on the part of Mr. Giles who was for delay and his position was supported by Mr. Barnes with some vigor. Mr. Breadon had had a complete change of heart. He now stated that he believed we could elect a man today and if so, we should do it; that he had come to the meeting with the idea that the report of the Committee stated the correct position but that he had now changed his mind. He thought we ought to stay right on the job and complete the election and he believed we could do it. He advocated another ballot on which we should be limited to voting on three men, namely, Chandler, Hannegan and Lausche. That was supported by Mr. Benswanger and by Mr. [Tom] Yawkey and others. Mr. Bradley then stated the conditions of the ballot. They were not to be signed; that they were not to commit anybody finally; that the ballot was simply to help us find out whether or not we could get anywhere at that particular meeting. He stated it was the view of the majority that we should proceed to the next ballot. There was no objection and accordingly another ballot was taken. A further condition of this ballot was that each club was to vote for only two of the three men. The result of this second ballot was as follows:

	First	Second
Chandler	8	5
Lausche	3	5
Hannegan	5	6

This ballot showed that all 16 clubs had voted both for first and second choice. The discussion then became a bit heated, lead by Mr. Barnes who opposed another ballot. The two ballots showed that Mr. Chandler had gained three first place votes; that Mr. Hannegan had simply held the five votes he received on the first ballot. Likewise, Mr. Lausche had held the first choice votes of the first ballot. Mr. Barnes showed considerable heat in his opposition to another ballot, stressing the importance of what we were doing, the years of regret if we made a mistake, etc., etc. Mr. Giles made what I would call an anti-Chandler talk referring to his singing proclivities and the fact that in his political campaigns he had his children singing from the public platform and some reference was made to some kind of a scandal that had something or other to do with a swimming pool. Mr. Breadon got quite a laugh out of the singing references and the point about Mr. Chandler's political cleanliness was answered satisfactorily. Mr. Giles insisted that he did not know enough about Mr. Chandler to vote for him today and that he would like to know more about a man for the Commissionership than he knew about Chandler. I remarked that this person had been in the public eye long enough for us to know about him pretty thoroughly and that a month or many months would not enable us to know much more about Chandler than we knew right then. Mr. MacPhail two or three different times made very effective points supporting Chandler. Speeches were made for Hannegan. Lausche had no open supporters but had great strength in the mind of everybody, I am sure. Mr. Breadon vigorously supported the taking of another ballot, was quite exercised about it, spoke again of not only the possibility of our making an election but seemed to be sure about it, and I then felt that he would go for Chandler on the next ballot. He lead the insistence upon another ballot on which we should be limited to voting for two men, namely the two leaders on the last ballot, and these were Chandler and Hannegan. This position got general support and I felt that if a final vote had been taken on the proposal for another ballot it would have received 14 votes, indeed all the votes except Mr. Barnes and Mr. Giles, Barnes for Hannegan and Giles for nobody.

Mr. Wrigley then proposed that if either person were to receive 12 votes then there was to be a definite understanding on the part of all of us that the vote was to stick. Mr. Breadon said "Yes, this ballot is to count." Considerable discussion followed and the sentiment finally prevailed that if either man received 12 votes, the ballot was not only to stick but the election was to be made unanimous. Mr. Bradley took a fine part, as I saw it, in this discussion. He was splendid. He spoke highly favorable to Chandler, about Mrs. Chandler and the family, etc., etc. He also took a strong part in stating the nature of the next ballot and said very clearly, in his summary of the whole discussion, that the ballot was to be determinative and that if 12 votes were cast for either candidate (either of whom, we were assured, would accept if elected), we would immediately get the successful candidate on the telephone and have quick acceptance or rejection. Giles at this point suffered terribly but privately, thinking that if Chandler were elected and refused to accept it might mean the election of Hannegan and he just could not go for him. I understood his position and his reasons for it.

With everything understood about the next ballot, it was taken. The first five votes called out by Harry Grabiner, the teller throughout the meeting, were for Chandler. Then followed two votes for Hannegan, then three for Chandler and one for Hannegan. And the vote stood 11–4. There was a few seconds delay on the reading of the last ballot that seemed to me an awfully long time. It was for Chandler, making 12 votes and the election. Mr. Bradley immediately suggested that, as there was no telephone in our meeting room, we should go to his room on the third floor of the hotel where we would call Chandler on the phone and that we would all talk to him as soon as he had accepted, which acceptance seemed quite assured. The question was then raised that if we went out through the lobby, 16 of us at one time, with the writers in the lobby, it would be known that we had come to a decision and we could not have anything known until we had gotten in touch with Sen. Chandler. Mr. Bradley suggested that we did not need to go through the lobby; that we could go out of the other entrance to his room. On the way out of the room we were immediately in front of a very large service elevator which stood open, and the operator apparently idle. Someone inquired if it went to the third floor, and when the operator said it did, everybody piled in. He took us to the third floor and we went to Mr. Bradley's parlor. Mr. MacPhail knew Chandler's whereabouts and after about fifteen minutes of continuous effort, calling two or three other people besides Chandler in Washington, he got the Senator on the telephone. He accepted very quickly and all of us talked to him. Mr. Bradley was last, stating the terms, $50,000. for seven years and also stating that it would be necessary to give spot release on publicity. We then returned to our meeting room where we took formal action in electing Senator Chandler unanimously, and immediately thereafter Mr. Frick drew the statement for newspaper release which was amended, here and there, and the reporters were called in and the statement was read by Mr. O'Connor.

I then went to my room for a conference with the boys of the United States Baseball League, a negro organization.

3

Rickey, O'Malley Purchase Half-Interest in Dodgers (1945)

SOURCE: *Brooklyn Eagle*, August 14, 1945

Following the deaths of Charles Ebbets and co-owner Ed McKeever in April 1925, different factions within the Brooklyn Dodgers vied for control of the club. The hiring of Larry MacPhail in the winter of 1937 helped make the Dodgers successful on the field, but his free spending all but erased the expected dividends. MacPhail was replaced in 1943 by Branch Rickey, famed for his talent for "putting a dollar sign on a muscle." The following year, Rickey, seeing an opportunity for increased power and profit, purchased a 25 percent share along with John L. Smith, a pharmaceutical executive, and Walter O'Malley, a lawyer with the Brooklyn Trust Company, which had managed the team through its possession of the Ebbets family stock. In August 1945 the three men acquired the Ebbets stock to give them 75 percent of Dodger stock. The following article focuses on Rickey while almost ignoring O'Malley—a mistake few would repeat in the future.

For a discussion on this transaction, see Lee Lowenfish, "The Two Titans and the Mystery Man: Branch Rickey, Walter O'Malley, and John L. Smith as Brooklyn Dodgers Partners, 1944–1950," in Jackie Robinson: Race, Sport, and the American Dream, *ed. Joseph Dorinson and Joram Warmund (Armonk NY: M. E. Sharpe, 1998): 165–78.*

PENICILLIN MAKER GIVES RICKEY, CLUB FINANCIAL "SHOT"

John L. Smith, Angel of Deal, Hands Branch Full Control of Dodgers—Stars May Stride on Block Now
By Harold C. Burr

President Branch Rickey really moved into Brooklyn yesterday and is going to stay here for a long, long while. The Mahatma's purchase, with two associates, of the 50 percent Ebbets' Estate holdings gives him absolute control of the Dodgers, to run as he pleases. It's believed that the three-man syndicate, consisting of Rickey, Walter F. O'Malley, an attorney, and John L. Smith, president of the Pfizer Company, paid $750,000 for the Ebbets' stock.

The Dodgers actually received a shot in the arm. Mr. Smith is the manufacturer of penicillin and is the angel of the group. The Rickey crowd has been gunning for the stock for some time. Last June Surrogate Francis D. McGarey turned down their bid of $650,000. Rickey previously had bought out the Ed McKeery heirs, who owned 25 percent of the stock, for an estimated $250,000, with a fourth associate, Andrew Schmitz, who doesn't figure in the latest venture and has retired from the arena.

If those figures are correct then it took a cool million dollars for Branch to climb into the driver's seat. He doesn't need the remaining 25 percent now held so steadfastly by Dearie McKeever, daughter of Judge McKeever and wife of James A. Mulvey, moving picture executive.

AIDS FINANCING

The Brooklyn Trust Company is no longer executor but has agreed to help out in the financing. A substantial deposit has been made to bind the sale and the transaction will be completed in a few days, according to Harold F. Klein, spokesman for the bank. Thus the name of Charles Ebbets passes out of baseball except for Ebbets Field that bears his name. Joseph A. Gilleandeau and Grace Slade Ebbets were co-executors.

Rickey, here on a five-year contract at $25,000 in straight salary, and a bonus clause based on attendance, is enjoying his biggest year. It's expected that the

Dodgers will play to a million fans before the end of the campaign. The gate is already well over 800,000 and big Sunday turnouts still to come with the Cubs and Giants in town.

MAY SELL STARS

What the Deacon's policy will be in regard to spending money for players is conjecture. The best guess is that he will operate with a modest payroll in the future as was his practice in St. Louis. He doesn't expect to win this year or next year, but 1947, he predicts, will be a different story and is building up a youthful ball club toward that praiseworthy end. He may sell some of his high priced stars while they have market value, another of his Missouri customs. The Dodgers are no million-dollar toy to him. He intends to make them pay.

Undoubtedly, Rickey will get the ball club out of the red, but he won't spend money like Larry MacPhail, who paid off some of the mortgage held by the Brooklyn Trust and left the club with a $300,000 bank balance.

Charley Ebbets once said that baseball was still in its infancy but it's growing up rapidly in Flatbush under Rickey.

4

Report of the Mayor's Committee on Baseball (1945)

SOURCE: "Integration" file, National Baseball Hall of Fame Library

In response to pressure brought on major league baseball in New York City to integrate, the league presidents acceded to a suggestion by New York mayor Fiorello LaGuardia to establish a Committee on Baseball to study the problem. Appointed as baseball's representatives to the committee were Branch Rickey and Yankee general manager Larry MacPhail, whose opposition to the integration of the major leagues was well known. Rickey's biographer, Murray Polner, stated that Rickey was horrified at the political nature of the committee, but Jules Tygiel countered that Rickey himself acted behind the scenes to create the committee. Formed in late August, the committee issued its final report on October 31, just eight days after Rickey's Dodgers announced the signing of Jackie Robinson to a minor league contract. Interestingly, Rickey resigned from the committee two days after Robinson's signing.

A "Tentative Proposal" for the final report, dated September 28, differed in some important respects from its successor. The draft's author, sociologist and Rickey associate Dan W. Dodson, claimed that even scouts could not determine "whether the players are good 'baseball' players or simply good 'Negro' baseball players." He also placed greater emphasis on anticipated resistance from white southern players and hotel keepers, and suggested that the onus was on the black players to adjust to the situation. Dodson proposed that organized baseball form minor leagues for black players in the South while integrating minor league teams in the North, and that it admit the Negro Leagues as minor leagues subject to the authority of the commissioner's office. This proposal was not included in the final report, and other seemingly offensive comments were watered down or eliminated. The proposal can be found in the Arthur Mann Papers, Box 3, Manuscript Division, Library of Congress.

REPORT OF THE MAYOR'S COMMITTEE ON BASEBALL

THE EQUITY OF NEGRO BASEBALL

The Committee also examined the status of the Negro Leagues. It is estimated that they do a $2,000,000 a year business and the New York Yankee management points out that last year, Negro teams paid $100,000 in rentals and concessions for their four parks in New York, Kansas City, Newark and Norfolk.

This equity cannot be overlooked and yet any major social advance must inevitably run up against such vested interests. It has been pointed out that organized Negro baseball would not have been necessary had Negroes been integrated into the system the same as other minority groups.

Yet, many familiar with Negro baseball feel that Negro teams meet a need among Negroes which would not be met even if their players were integrated into the profession. The Negro baseball game is an attraction within the local Negro community and no doubt will continue to draw local patronage. The contention has been made by some that the Negro players are under contract or reservation to clubs in Negro leagues and that this contractual relationship could not be violated and that the signing of the better Negro players in the major leagues would destroy the interest of Negro teams. . . .

If the equity of Negro professional baseball clubs were never to be disturbed, the reform could never be accomplished and the onus of present Jim Crow practices would be placed on Negroes themselves. Thus the practice which arose because of an evil would become the reason for its perpetuation. Most people admit that the Negro leagues, under present arrangements, can never produce players qualified for big league competition. These Negro leagues are powerless to bring themselves into organized baseball and no one from within the profession has seen fit to organize them into leagues capable of participating in such competition.

QUALIFICATION OF NEGRO PLAYERS
FOR BIG LEAGUE PARTICIPATION

The next problem examined was that of whether the Negro players possess abilities to make them worthy of major league participation.

At this point, the entire field of sports other than baseball serves as an illustration. The exploits of Negroes in boxing, football, basketball and track are too well known to reenumerate. We have not found a single individual who would admit that Negroes do not possess potential physical capacities which would make them worthy of major league competition.

The Committee does not contend that there should be any other standards for participation in organized baseball for Negroes than there is for whites but that the sole formula be that of skill. No one should be taken because of color nor excluded because of color. There is no more exacting sport where merit counts than in baseball and we are merely asking that the Negro players be given their chance to compete on an equal basis and that ability to perform be the single determining factor. This would provide:

1. Equality of opportunity for all and

2. Would be a great benefit for Negroes in amateur sports because the professional opportunities opened to them would encourage them to participate.

SUMMATION

In summary, we should like to set forth the following principles which seem to us valid:

1. That there is no difference between the potential ability of Negro and white youths. We all admit that the reason Negroes are excluded from organized baseball is sheer prejudice and tradition.

2. Negro youths have demonstrated their abilities both to perform and cooperate with other players in team-work in practically every other sport, leaving organized baseball as one of the last to square itself with the ideals of democracy. In sports where even more intimate team-work is needed and more physical contact found such as in football and basketball, there has been demonstrated the fact that Negroes and whites play together as a team without any difficulty.

3. That good sportsmanship alone as well as the moral principles involved, would demand that they not be excluded.

4. Inasmuch as Commissioner Landis said within the past year that there was no rule in organized baseball whereby a Negro could not be accepted on a team, it becomes clear then that their exclusion is due to segregation. While it is true that there is no such rule, the fact that Negroes have been excluded for these seventy years indicates that something more is needed if this barrier is to be hurdled. Consequently, organized baseball has a responsibility of taking positive, aggressive action rather than remaining passively complacent.

5. This only leaves then the matter of timing the move. Here, one would be forced to say that the time is never ripe for social reform. The argument as to the ill-timed pattern, is one that has been offered by every industry which has been called upon to meet this situation. It has been pointed out that major league baseball draws 35% of its players from traditionally prejudiced Southern communities and that these players would not care to play with Negroes. Yet, it is to be recognized that there is scarcely a city in which major league baseball operates that could be classified as a traditionally Southern city and aspiring youths who come from Southern sections of the country are expected to recognize and respect other customs and laws of the sections into which they migrate. An exception could hardly be made for organized baseball.

If Southern youths expect to come to Northern cities and compete for the honors which such communities have to bestow, it is only fair and right that they allow other youths, many of whom have no relation to these Southern backgrounds but happen to have a different color of skin, the same right to compete for these selfsame honors and we know that the major portion of the population in these Northern cities are impatient of any low order of sportsmanship which refuses to recognize this request.

6. We should hope that a way would be found to bring the Negro leagues into organized baseball with some sort of arrangements made whereby they could continue to service local needs within our larger communities and at the same time could offer opportunities for the development of Negro players but, in the last analysis, it is not the responsibility of the Negroes to prepare players to participate in major league competition any more than it is the responsibility of the Jews or Italians or the Cubans to accept such responsibilities for their groups. We believe that the only equitable solution to this problem is that individuals be treated alike and with relation to their abilities throughout organized baseball.

In conclusion, it need only be said that the move by the Brooklyn club, we believe, meets this responsibility and paves the way for others to follow. How the process of integration is to be consummated is a problem for each club to undertake individually but a problem which can no longer be deferred or avoided. We would like to ask lastly that the Committee be continued to extend the work started.

5

Major League Baseball Addresses the "Race Question" (1946)

SOURCE: House Judiciary Committee, *Study of Monopoly Power, Part 6: Organized Baseball,* 82nd Cong., 1st sess., 1952, 474–88*

Baseball owners staged a historic meeting in Chicago in late August 1946. The meeting, which was the first at which players were represented, is described in document 6. A topic of discussion that was not reported in the press was the "race question." The signing of Jackie Robinson by the Dodgers the previous October brought to the surface a controversy that the owners—save, of course, the newly empowered Branch Rickey—had hoped to keep buried. A special steering committee discussed race and other baseball issues— organization, legality of structure, player relationship, public relations problems, and operational problems—at meetings held in July and August. Their final report was presented at the owners' meeting on August 27. The committee hoped to recommend

*Hereafter *Study of Monopoly Power, Part 6: Organized Baseball* will be cited as *Organized Baseball.*

"methods to protect baseball from charges that it is fostering unfair discrimination against the Negro by reason of his race and color," but instead commented on the damage "the individual action of any one club" could have on the viability of the Negro Leagues, and its financial relationship with different major league clubs.

The committee's recommendations on the "race question," taken from pages 483–85, also appear in The Jackie Robinson Reader, *ed. Jules Tygiel (New York: Dutton, 1997), pp. 129–33.*

REPORT OF MAJOR LEAGUE STEERING COMMITTED FOR SUBMISSION TO THE NATIONAL AND AMERICAN LEAGUES AT THEIR MEETINGS IN CHICAGO

II. FOREWORD

Baseball, as a game, provides pleasure and relaxation to millions who see it played, and to countless millions who follow it through the printed page and radio. The time is not far distant when more millions will relax at home or in a theater and see and hear the game wherever it may be being played.

Professional baseball, however, is more than a game. It is BIG BUSINESS—A $100,000,000 industry—actively engaged in providing the American public with its greatest and, next to the movies, its cheapest entertainment buy. . . .

Today, however, baseball faces its most critical period in all its history. It is under attack as an illegal monopoly. Its right to survive as it always has existed is being challenged by rapidly changing conditions and new economic and political forces. What the future holds none can foretell, but certain it is that the character of American baseball for many years to come will be determined in large measure by its ability to withstand the pressures of today. At no time in the history of professional baseball has there been greater need for intelligent management and procedures to determine the common ends toward which efforts shall be directed and to maintain coordination and cooperation between the various components of the baseball structure.

We have an important job to do. In the opinion of your committee, now is the time to do it. . . .

E. RACE QUESTION

The appeal of baseball is not limited to any racial group. The Negro takes great interest in baseball and is, and always has been, among the most loyal supporters of professional baseball.

The American people are primarily concerned with the excellence and performance in sport rather than the color, race, or creed of the performer. The history of American sport has been enriched by the performance of great Negro athletes who have attained the mythical all-American team in football; who have won world championships in boxing; and who have helped carry America to track and field victories in the Olympic Games. Fifty-four Negro players served with the Armed Forces in this war—one player was killed and several wounded in combat.

Baseball will jeopardize its leadership in professional sport if it fails to give full appreciation to the fact that the Negro fan and the Negro player are part and parcel of the game. Certain groups in this country, including political and social-minded drum-beaters, are conducting pressure campaigns in an attempt to force major league clubs to sign Negro players. Members of these groups are not primarily interested in professional baseball. They are not campaigning to provide better opportunity for thousands of Negro boys who want to play baseball. They are not even particularly interested in improving the lot of Negro players who are already employed. They know little about baseball—and nothing about the business end of its operation. They single out professional baseball for attack because it offers a good publicity medium.

These people who charge that baseball is flying a Jim Crow flag at its mast-head—or that racial discrimination is the basic reason for failure of the major leagues to give employment to Negroes—are simply talking through their individual or collective hats. Professional baseball is a private business enterprise. It has to depend on profits for its existence, just like any business. It is a business in which Negroes, as well as whites, have substantial investments in parks, franchises, and player contracts. Professional baseball, both Negro and white, has grown and prospered over a period of many years on the basis of separate leagues. The employment of a Negro on one AAA League club in 1946 resulted in a tremendous increase in Negro attendance at all games in which the player appeared. The percentage of Negro attendance at some games at Newark and Baltimore was in excess of 50 percent. The situation might be presented, if Negroes participate in major-league games, in which the preponderance of Negro attendance in parks such as Yankee Stadium, the Polo Grounds, and Comiskey Park could conceivably threaten the value of the major league franchises owned by these clubs.

The thousands of Negro boys of ability who aspire to careers in professional baseball should have a better opportunity. Every American boy, without regard to his race or his color or his creed, should have a fair chance in baseball. Jobs for half a dozen good Negro players now employed in the Negro leagues is relatively unimportant. Signing a few Negro players for the major leagues would be a gesture—but it would contribute little or nothing toward a solution of the real problem. Let's look at the facts:

(1) A major-league baseball player must have something besides great natural ability. He must possess the technique, the coordination, the competitive attitude, and the discipline which is usually acquired only after years of training in the minor leagues. The minor-league experience of players on the major-league rosters, for instance, averages 7 years. The young Negro player never has had a good chance in baseball. Comparatively few good young Negro players are being developed. This is the reason that there are not more players who meet major-league standards in the big Negro leagues. Sam Lacy, sports editor of the Afro-American newspapers, says, "I am reluctant to say that we haven't a single man in the ranks of colored baseball who could step into the major-

league uniform and disport himself after the fashion of a big leaguer. There are those among our league players who might possibly excel in the matter of hitting or fielding or base running. But for the most part, the fellows who could hold their own in more than one of these phases of the game are few and far between—perhaps nil."† Mr. Lacy's opinions are shared by almost everyone, Negro or white, competent to appraise the qualifications of Negro players.

(2) About 400 Negro professionals are under contract to the 24 clubs in four Negro leagues. Negro leagues have made substantial progress in recent years. Negro baseball is now a $2,000,000 business. One club, the Kansas City Monarchs, drew over 300,000 people to its home and road games in 1944 and 1945. Over 50,000 people paid $72,000 to witness the east-west game at the White Sox Stadium in Chicago. A Negro-league game established the all-time attendance record at Griffith Stadium in Washington. The average attendance at Negro games in the Yankee Stadium is over 10,000 per game.

These Negro leagues cannot exist without good players. If they cannot field good teams, they will not continue to attract the fans who click the turnstiles. Continued prosperity depends upon improving standards of play. If the major leagues and the big minors of professional baseball raid these leagues and take their best players—the Negro leagues will eventually fold up—and a lot of professional Negro players will lose their jobs. The Negroes who own and operate these clubs do not want to part with their outstanding players—no one accuses them of racial discrimination.

(3) The Negro leagues rent their parks in many cities from clubs in organized baseball. Many major and minor league clubs derive substantial revenue from these rentals. (The Yankee organization, for instance, nets nearly $100,000 a year from rentals and concessions in connection with Negro league games at the Yankee Stadium in New York—and in Newark, Kansas City, and Norfolk.) Club owners in the major leagues are reluctant to give up revenues amounting to hundreds of thousands of dollars every year. They naturally want the Negro leagues to continue. They do not sign, and cannot properly sign, players under contracts to Negro clubs. This is not racial discrimination. It's simply respecting the contractual relationship between the Negro leagues and their players.

Summary: Your committee believes that the relationship of the Negro player, and/or the existing Negro leagues to professional baseball is a real problem—one that affects all baseball—and one that should have serious consideration by an executive council.

There are many factors in this problem and many difficulties which will have to be solved before any generally satisfactory solution can be worked out. The individual action of any one club may exert tremendous pressures upon the whole

---

†This quotation was taken by an article by Sam Lacy, "Will Our Boys Make Big League Grade?," which appeared after the 1944 season in the *Negro Baseball Pictorial Year Book*. The article is reprinted in *Middle Innings: A Documentary History of Baseball, 1900–1948*, ed. Dean A. Sullivan (Lincoln: University of Nebraska Press, 1998), pp. 188–91.

structure of professional baseball, and could conceivably result in lessening the value of several major league franchises.

Your committee does not desire to question the motives of any organization or individual who sincerely opposes segregation or who believes that such a policy is detrimental in the best interests of professional baseball.

Your committee wishes to go on record as feeling that this is an over-all problem which vitally affects each and every one of us—and that effort should be made to arrive at a fair and just solution—compatible with good business judgment and the principles of good sportsmanship.

6

Players, Owners Agree on Changes in Contracts, Game (1946)

SOURCE: *Organized Baseball*, pp. 500–503

The threat posed to the major leagues by the Mexican League and the newly formed American Baseball Guild forced owners to make a number of concessions to players at the Chicago meeting. Players were guaranteed a minimum salary of $5,000, a weekly stipend of $25 during spring training (referred to as "Murphy money" in honor of guild organizer Robert Murphy), representation before owners through inclusion on an advisory committee, and a minimum salary reduction of 25 percent. In addition, owners promised to begin formulating the first pension plan in American sports history, which started on April 1, 1947. The Major League Baseball Players Annuity and Insurance Plan is reprinted in Organized Baseball, *pages 269–77. Owners also agreed to expand the season to 168 games, but they abandoned this plan by mid-September. Many of these changes were ironed out in the Major League Steering Committee meeting on August 27. They were officially implemented in a meeting in Chicago the following day.*

ARTICLE IV. UNIFORM RULES

B. PLAYER RELATIONSHIP

Your committee considered it desirable, from a standpoint of both employee and public relations, that the new contract should be regarded as a contract in the players' interest, as well as the club owners. If this was to be accomplished, it was necessary to ascertain the players' views.

Your committee therefore requested the commissioner to call meetings of the players of each major league club in order that player representatives from each club would elect league committees authorized to represent the players in negotiations for a new contract.

As a result of this request players' meetings were held, player representatives from each club selected, a committee of three from each league elected. Players Herman, Walker, and Marion were elected to represent the National League players; Murphy, Harder, and Kuhel the American League players. Your committee met in conference with the players' committee in New York on August 5.

The New York meeting provided opportunity for a frank and friendly exchange of ideas and viewpoints. We were impressed with the fine attitude of the players' representatives, with their desire to work matters out for our mutual benefit, with their concern for the best interests of the game as a whole.

Every request or suggestion offered by the players was discussed. We were also impressed with the soundness of the opinions and position of the players on many of their proposals. We believe the players' representatives, in turn, were convinced of our sincerity and our desire to reach mutually satisfactory understandings. There was a certain amount of "give and take" in evidence and the concessions were not entirely one-sided.

An important development, in our opinion, was the expressed willingness of the players' representatives to cooperate in defending baseball against attacks upon the reserve clause.

Many of the matters which were discussed with the players' representatives pertain to the proposed new uniform players' contract. Consideration was also given to modification or revision of the major league rules, as they affect club and player relationships.

As a result of its deliberations, both before and after the meeting with player representatives, your committee recommends the following:

1. *REVISIONS IN UNIFORM PLAYERS' CONTRACT*

(a) *Termination*—Revise the present clause covering contract termination to include specification of the causes which would give both clubs and players the right to terminate. In the event the club elects to terminate the contract on account of the failure of the player, in the opinion of club management, to exhibit sufficient skill or competitive ability to qualify or continue as a member of the club's team, provide that the player shall be entitled to receive 30 days' instead of 10 days' separation pay with transportation to his home.

In the event a club desires to release a player unconditionally, establish a waiver price of $1 instead of $7,500, and provide that in the event the player is claimed on such waiver request he shall have the option either of accepting assignment to the claiming club or accepting his unconditional release. . . .

(e) *Spring training period and expenses.*—Provide in the regulations for an allowance of $25 per week payable in advance, in addition to housing, meals, and transportation, to all major league players, to cover all incidental expenses of the player during spring training. Provide for limitation of the period in which players are required to report for spring training to a period beginning not earlier than February 15 in 1947 and not earlier than March 1 in 1948 and subsequent years. . . .

2. REVISIONS IN MAJOR LEAGUE RULES
AFFECTING PLAYER-CLUB RELATIONSHIPS

(a) *Minimum salary*—Amend the major league rules to provide for a minimum major league payment at the rate of $5,000 per year.

(b) *Barnstorming*—Amend major league rule 18 (b) to permit players to engage in postseason exhibition games, with the written consent of the commissioner, for 30 days after the close of the major league championship season. Provide that player conduct on and off the field in connection with such post-season exhibition games shall be subject to the discipline of the commissioner and that the commissioner shall not approve participation in any such games of more than three players of any one club.

(c) *Player representation*—In connection with the proposed creation of a major league executive council (and, if concurrence of the minors is secured, a major-minor league executive council), include provision for the representation of players (to be elected annually by the players of each major league and, in the case of major-minor league executive council, to be elected annually by the players of each major league and the national association) for consideration of all matters which concern the standard form of player contract or its provisions and regulations, or other matters of club-player relationship.

Provide further that at the third quarter meeting of such executive council all matters of player grievance, player relationships, and contractual matters affecting players should be considered by the council with representatives of the players.

3. SECURITY OR PENSION FUND

Your committee was informed by the representatives of the players that major league players are more vitally interested and concerned in the establishment of some form of security or pension fund than in any other matter involved in player-club relationships.

The players, your committee, and various major league clubs have given considerable thought and study to the feasibility of establishing pension or security benefits and/or group insurance and/or hospitalization insurance, etc., for the benefit of players under some plan whereby the players and clubs would both contribute, and other funds be raised through the medium of world series, all-star, or interleague games.

It seems to be the opinion of the players that—

(a) Player participation in such a fund would begin after 5 years' service; (b) at that point players would be permitted to choose whether or not they desired to come under the plan and, if so, would be required to contribute covering the previous 5 years' service; (c) contribution by players would probably amount to 5 percent of the proposed minimum, or $250 per year; (d) club owners would contribute in like amount with players; (e) the total amount raised annually by contributions of players and club owners would approximate $250,000; (f) a further sum of approximately $150,000 per year would be added from receipts of the world series, all-star, or interleague games; (g) total contributions would approximate $400,000 per year and the fund would be built up, in a period of 10 years, to approximately $4,000,000; (h) this sum would be sufficient to provide payments to retired players beginning at age 50 for a period of approximately 10 years of service of between $50 and $100 per month, based upon length of service.

Without further conference and discussions with the players' committee, and until their proposals can be studied by actuaries, it is impossible to determine whether or not any such plan or fund is feasible.

Your committee favors the general principle of some sort of pension fund, security benefits, and/or group insurance and/or hospitalization insurance for the deferred benefit of major league players with long service records, and recommends the matter be referred to the executive council, if established, with request that they confer with the players, obtain reports from actuaries as to the feasibility of such plans as they may desire to consider, and report their conclusions, when practicable, to the National and American Leagues.

7

Minor Leagues Prepare for Future (1946)

SOURCE: *Sporting News*, December 11, 1946

At its annual meeting, the National Association, governing body of the minor leagues, celebrated two milestones. First, after six years of failure, a new Major-Minor League Agreement, signed on January 12, 1947, and effective for five years, was drafted. The minors won additional protection against major league incursions into their territory, but this protection, to the disappointment of the Pacific Coast League, did not include a requirement that the minors "agree and consent" to the transfer of a major league franchise to its designated region. In addition, a "bonus player" was defined for the first time. Second, the association replaced President William G. Bramham, who retired, with George M. Trautman. Trautman would preside over the rapid growth of the minors over the next five years, celebrated in the book The Story of Minor League Baseball *(Columbus OH: National Association of Professional Baseball Leagues, 1953), and the precipitous decline of the minors, which continued past Trautman's death in 1963 through the late 1970s.*

NAMED TO 5-YEAR TERM; RETIRING CHIEF HONORED

Unanimous Election Dispels Rumors of Fight Over Post; New President to Move Headquarters to Columbus; Former Leader Voted $10,000 Life Salary
By Edgar G. Brands

LOS ANGELES, Calif.—After 14 years under the administration of William G. Bramham, who became president at the 1932 meeting in Columbus, O., following the reorganization of the minors the year before, the National Association launched its forty-fifth season under a new president and a new agreement with the majors. The 56-year-old George M. Trautman, executive vice-president of the Detroit Tigers, succeeded the 72-year-old retiring head of the minors at the same salary of $25,000 and for a five-year term by a unanimous vote that harmoniously wound up the forty-fifth annual convention here.

For days there had been the threat of a bitter fight over the presidency and as many as 12 candidates had been mentioned, but Trautman held the lead all the way and as league after league swung behind him, all other aspirants withdrew and made his election unanimous. Some resentment had been expressed because his boom had been started by major league farm clubs and dictatorship was charged, but all recriminations were forgotten in a desire to unite on one man. . . .

ACCEPT NEW AGREEMENT IN TOTO

In moving toward the acceptance of new pacts with the majors, the National Association accepted in toto a Major-Minor League Agreement to replace the old document, which expired in 1940 but had been renewed from year to year. The minors also approved the new Major-Minor League Rules, submitted by the revision committee, with a number of changes made from the floor of the convention by the committee and by individual leagues.

Since none of the amendments previously had been submitted to the majors, their acceptance was dependent upon action of the big leagues. Both pacts were accepted by the big leagues, with the exceptions noted on Page 3 of this issue.

Instead of the old rule with reference to the protection of territory from major league encroachment, which the revision committee originally had recommended be retained, and the amendment submitted by the Syracuse club of the International League, the convention adopted the proposal made by the Pacific Coast League. The old rule provided that no minor league city could be taken over by the majors unless the big league paid the invaded circuit $5,000 and paid to the club affected reasonable compensation for damage to its assets, as determined by agreement or fixed by the commissioner.

As requested by the Pacific Coast League, the minors proposed that no such territory can be invaded unless the minor league and its club "shall agree and consent" (but the majors killed the quoted words) and are paid such compensation as shall be mutually agreed upon as just as reasonable. In case of a disagreement on compensation, the major league desiring to occupy the territory is to notify the commissioner and request the amount to be determined by a board of arbitration to consist of seven men, appointed by him. The board is to be made up of a representative of the minor league involved, of the major league, of the minor and major league club, the president of the National Association, the commissioner and a seventh to be agreed upon by the six. The commissioner is to designate the time and place of the meeting, to be held within 30 days of receipt of the request by the commissioner. The findings of the board are to be final and within ten days after the decision has been compiled with the territory will be considered belonging to the major league club. . . .

Following the lead for protection of minor league territory from invasion from the majors, incorporated in an amendment to the Major-Minor League Rules, the minors set up safeguards within their own organization under the following provisions:

"By notice to the president of the National Association, which must be filed between October 1 and December 1 of each year, if a league in any class selects a city in which a club of lower classification is located, the league and club making such selection shall pay to the league and club of lower classification such compensation as shall be mutually agreed upon as just as reasonable compensation for such action; payment thereof to be made within 30 days of agreement.

"In event of disagreement for such action, the selecting league desiring to occupy the territory shall notify the president of the National Association of their desire and request that the just and reasonable compensation required to be paid to be determined by a board of arbitration" named by the minors' head to include a representative from each league and club as four members, with the four to name the fifth, and failing to agree, the president of the National Association appoints the fifth. A meeting must be heard within 20 days and making the arbitration board's decisions final. It is required that the findings must be complied with and the territory given to the selecting league within ten days.

8

Reporter Alleges Strike Threat against Jackie Robinson (1947)

SOURCE: *New York Herald Tribune,* May 9, 1947

Stanley Woodward, longtime sports editor of the New York Herald Tribune, *was one of the most respected men in the business. In several years he would write* Sports Page *(New York: Simon and Schuster, 1949), still one of the best accounts of the behind-the-scenes workings of a newspaper sports department. The most acclaimed story of his career (it won the Best Sports Story of 1947 award), it cemented his reputation among his peers.*

Woodward, acting on a tip from Herald Tribune *sportswriter Rud Rennie, alleged that several members of the St. Louis Cardinals had told owner Sam Breadon that they would go on strike rather than share the playing field with Robinson. He stated that Breadon and National League president Ford Frick, at the last minute, crushed the threatened revolt. However, by the time this copyrighted article was published, the Cardinals and Dodgers, with Robinson in the lineup, had already played several games. Frick, in his book* Games, Asterisks, and People: Memoirs of a Lucky Fan *(New York: Crown, 1973), confirmed the threat and Breadon's role in the affair, but noted that the* incident had occurred six weeks earlier, and that Woodward should have known this. *Another* Herald Tribune *writer, Roger Kahn, wrote in* The Era, 1947–1957: When the Yankees, the Giants, and the Dodgers Ruled the World *(New York: Ticknor and Fields, 1993) that the strike was originally planned to start in Brooklyn but was later switched to St. Louis, a fact Woodward noted at the end of his article.*

Woodward's readers had reason to question the seriousness of his charges. Much of the racist treatment accorded Robinson on and off the field was not reported, though fans were aware of certain problems Robinson faced. Robinson's experience against the Philadelphia Phillies, orchestrated by manager Ben Chapman, was well documented. Nevertheless, the incident remains clouded in mystery and controversy because the Cardinals players—including popular figures like Stan Musial and Joe Garagiola—have consistently denied planning a strike or any other actions against Robinson. Readers may question Kahn's assessment of the article as "the sports scoop of the century," but they should not doubt the significance of the article.

NATIONAL LEAGUE AVERTS STRIKE OF CARDINALS AGAINST ROBINSON'S PRESENCE IN BASEBALL

Frick, Breadon Together Quash Anti-Negro Action
Quick Retribution Promised by President of Loop Even If It Wrecks Senior Circuit; General League Walkout Planned by Instigators
By Stanley Woodward

A National League players' strike, instigated by some of the St. Louis Cardinals against the presence in the league of Jackie Robinson, Brooklyn's Negro first baseman, has been averted temporarily and perhaps permanently quashed. In recent days Ford Frick, president of the National League, and Sam Breadon, president of the St. Louis club, have been conferring with St. Louis players in the Hotel New Yorker. Mr. Breadon flew East when he heard of the projected strike. The story that he came to consult with Eddie Dyer, manager, about the lowly state of the St. Louis club was fictitious. He came on a much more serious errand.

The strike plan, formulated by certain St. Louis players, was instigated by a member of the Brooklyn Dodgers who has since recanted. The original plan was for a St. Louis club strike on the occasion of the first game in Brooklyn, May 6, in other words last Tuesday. Subsequently the St. Louis players conceived the idea of a general strike within the National League on a certain date. That is what Frick and Breadon have been combatting in the last few days.

FRICK TAKES FIRM STAND

It is understood that Frick addressed the players, in effect, as follows:

If you do this you will be suspended from the league. You will find that the friends you think you have in the press box will not support you, that you will be outcasts. I do not care if half the league strikes. Those who do it will encounter quick retribution. All will be suspended and I don't care if it wrecks the National League for five years. This is the United States of America and one citizen has as much right to play as another. The National League will go down the line with Robinson whatever the consequences. You will find if you go through with your intention that you have been guilty of complete madness.

Several anticipatory protests against the transfer of Robinson to the Brooklyn club were forthcoming during spring training when he was still a member of the Montreal Royals, Brooklyn farm. Prejudice has been subsequently curbed except on one occasion when Ben Chapman, manager of the Phillies, undertook to ride Robinson from the bench in a particularly vicious manner.

It is understood that Frick took this matter up with the Philadelphia management and that Chapman has been advised to keep his bench comments above the belt.

It is understood that the players involved—and the recalcitrants are not all Cardinals—will say, if they decide to carry out their strike, that their object is to gain the right to have a say on who shall be eligible to play in the major leagues. As far as is known the move so far is confined entirely to the National League. Ringleaders apparently have not solicited the cooperation of American League players.

CHANDLER NOT CALLED ON

In view of this fact it is understood that Frick will not call the matter to the attention of Happy Chandler, the commissioner. So far, it is believed, Frick has operated with the sole aid of Breadon. Other National League club owners apparently know nothing about it.

The New York Herald Tribune prints this story in part as a public service. It is factual and thoroughly substantiated. The St. Louis players involved unquestionably will deny it. We doubt, however, that Frick or Breadon will go that far. A return of "No comment" from either or both will serve as confirmation. On our own authority we can say that both of them were present at long conferences with the ringleaders and that both probably now feel that the overt act has been averted. . . .

It is understood the St. Louis players recently have been talking about staging the strike on the day that Brooklyn plays its first game in St. Louis. Publicity probably will render the move abortive.

9

"Pitch Spahn and Sain, Then Pray for Rain" (1948)

SOURCE: *Boston Post*, September 14, 1948

As the 1948 National League pennant race wound to a close the Boston Braves held first place, but several members of their pitching staff were injured or had recently been ineffective. Manager Billy Southworth opted to rely on his best starters, Warren Spahn and Johnny Sain, to pitch for the remainder of the season on two days' rest each. Southworth's plan worked, but the Braves lost to the Cleveland Indians in the World Series four games to two. Both Spahn and Sain took care to mention that the famous poem (usually misquoted) did not acknowledge the substantial contributions of pitchers Bill Voiselle and Vern Bickford, who between them won twenty-four games.

BRAVES BOAST TWO-MAN STAFF

Pitch Spahn and Sain, Then Pray for Rain— But Every Day Is a Dark Day for Tribe

By Gerry Hern

> First we'll use Spahn, then we'll use Sain,
> Then an off day, followed by rain.
> Back will come Spahn, followed by Sain
> And followed, we hope, by two days of rain.
> From the collected writings of W. Southworth, 1948.

It would have been easier for the poet laureate of the Braves to produce this ode if he had decided to use Barrett and Shoun to fill in the other lines, but yesterday Mr. Southworth said he had made up his mind. From here on he will rotate his pitching staff. Spahn on one day, Sain the next. That's really rotation. In fact, that is almost spinning.

The schedule is working for the Braves in one respect. They at least have some off-days scattered through the remaining program. On the other hand, they are playing at home, which is an advantage to most clubs but not the Boston Nationals. Their natural modesty has kept them from showing off in front of the home folks.

The time for showing off has come. It is no secret that the Braves will win, or fail to win the National league pennant in the next 11 games, all of which are scheduled for Braves Field. The belief here is that they will win it or choke off the opposition until it runs out of games during the stretch.

10

Indians, Bearden Win Playoff Game to Claim American League Pennant (1948)

SOURCE: *Cleveland Plain Dealer, October 5, 1948*

After a furious pennant race that involved four teams for the majority of the season, the Cleveland Indians and the Boston Red Sox were deadlocked. First place would be decided by a single playoff game in Boston. Rookie Gene Bearden, pitching on one day's rest, was the surprise choice of Indians manager Lou Boudreau. His counterpart, the legendary Joe McCarthy, made an even more stunning decision, selecting journeyman Denny Galehouse to pitch the pivotal match. Bearden won an 8–3 decision, and the Indians proceeded to beat the other Boston club in the World Series. This would be the only good season for Bearden. He pitched only five more years in the majors, totaling twenty-five victories in that span.

The best book on the 1948 campaign is David Kaiser, Epic Season: The 1948 American League Pennant Race *(Amherst: University of Massachusetts Press, 1998).*

ROOKIE PERFORMS "IMPOSSIBLE" TASK

Boudreau Withholds Name of Starting Pitcher to Give Southpaw Chance to Rest

By Gordon Cobbledick
Plain Dealer Sports Editor

BOSTON, Oct. 4—People were saying in Boston tonight that Lou Boudreau was certainly the greatest ball player of his generation. It was true, of course, but it wasn't news to us of Cleveland. We know and have known for a time what the finest competitor in the whole world of sport can do when the chips are down.

But people were also saying in Boston tonight that Gene Bearden was something extra special, and that was a realization that is just beginning to hit with full impact on the consciousness of those whose pleasure or business is to observe and evaluate and analyze the performances of the Boudreaus and Beardens.

The lean Purple Heart veteran was given an impossible assignment today, and the manner in which he carried it through assured him of a place in the annals of Cleveland baseball along with Speaker and Lajoie and Coveleski and a few others whose names are posted in our own Hall of Fame.

MAGNIFICENT TRIBUTE
Boudreau himself paid Bearden a magnificent tribute a few minutes after the Indians had been humiliated by Hal Newhouser and the Detroit Tigers in Cleveland yesterday, necessitating a play-off of their tie with the Boston Red Sox.

In a club house meeting after that defeat, Boudreau announced his pitcher for today—the sudden-death encounter with a team that has been all but unbeatable in its own park.

He said that Gene Bearden, the fellow who had shut out the Tigers only the day before, would be his man. He said he realized Bearden would go into the most important assignment of his career with only one day's rest. He said he knew the Red Sox had the reputation of being poison to left-handed pitchers. He said he knew there would be no other chance if the Indians blew this one.

And he still said Bearden would pitch.

It was a well-guessed secret. A quarter of an hour before the game today the fans were still guessing and most of them were guessing that the job would go to Bob Lemon, who had pitched Friday and so had two days in which to recuperate. Some even guessed he would shoot the works on Bob Feller, who had started against Detroit yesterday and lasted less than three innings.

But few were guessing Bearden.

Boudreau said he hadn't wanted it known that the slender southpaw would do the pitching because he hadn't wanted him to be a target for photographers on the train last night and for interviewers in Boston this morning.

"I didn't want him to do anything but rest," said Lou, "and I didn't want him to worry. I should have known him better. He could have posed all night for photographers and still won today. He's got what it takes."

What Bearden had this afternoon was complete confidence in himself and his teammates, and the courage to get out there and battle the mightiest batting team in baseball on its home grounds, in his own way. . . .

And so the Indians have climaxed the bitterest fight in baseball history by winning their first pennant since 1920.

Lou Boudreau was terrific, and in the later stages of the game the disappointed Boston fans were applauding him for what he is—the greatest of them all. Ken Keltner was a big man, too, for his home run with two on in the fourth inning was the blow that gave the Indians all the runs they needed. Larry Doby came through with two well stroked doubles and the rest of the boys were great.

But in the last analysis the major hero was Bearden. Everyone knew the Indians had a chance if they got a well pitched game. But there aren't many well pitched games against the Red Sox in Boston.

A good one in any circumstances is notable. Such a one as Bearden threw today with a pennant at stake must be accounted one of the gems of all time.

The Indians' victory was a popular one among visitors. As one New York writer put it before the game: "Unless the Indians are in it the world series will be an anticlimax to this season. Who is going to get excited about a series between the best team in the National League and the second best in the American?"

11

Negro National League Disintegrates (1948)

SOURCE: *Newark Evening News,* November 9, 1948

As the members of the Major League Steering Committee had predicted in the summer of 1946, the integration of the major leagues had a devastating impact on the Negro Leagues. Black fans were abandoning the Negro Leagues in order to see Jackie Robinson, Larry Doby, and other African American stars display their talents in the majors. The pain caused by this exodus was increased by the refusal of several major league teams, most notably Branch Rickey's Dodgers, to purchase the contracts of their new stars.

The following article details the fate of the Newark Eagles, a club noted primarily for its colorful owner, Effa Manley. Later in the month the New York Black Yankees and the Homestead Grays would also disband. On November 28 the Negro American League (NAL) absorbed the Baltimore Elite Giants, the New York Cubans, and the Philadelphia Stars while awarding an expansion franchise to Houston, which was in reality the transferred Newark club. This did not mark the death knell for the Negro Leagues; several other leagues, including the NAL, survived this turbulent period. The NAL continued into the 1960s before expiring in 1963.

NEWARK EAGLES WILL DISBAND

Can't Go on Manleys Say in Quitting Negro Baseball Loop

Disbanding of the Newark Eagles, this city's representative in the Negro National Baseball League since 1935, was revealed today by Mr. and Mrs. Abraham Manley, co-owners of the club. The Eagles, first operated in Brooklyn, came to Newark in 1935 and have since then annually played their home games at the Bears Stadium.

Some of the outstanding figures in Negro baseball have been developed and played for the Eagles under the Manleys' management. The most publicized has been Larry Doby of Paterson, who in mid-season of 1947 was sold for $15,000 by the club to the Cleveland Indians and was a star in this year's World Series.

"We are not quitters," Mrs. Manley said this morning, "but it is just impossible for us to continue." Negro baseball has had some good years, she said, but added that the Eagles had suffered financially during the last two seasons. The club won the league championship in 1946.

"RICH MAN'S HOBBY"

"Baseball has become a rich man's hobby and we aren't rich," she continued. Mrs. Manley traced the first real blow which has led to the disbandment of the Eagles to the signing by Brooklyn Dodgers of Jackie Robinson. Dropping off of attendance in 1947, Robby's first year at Ebbets Field, was immediately noticeable at local games.

She emphasized that she does not expect other clubs in the league to quit, adding that owners in the South, where segregation at baseball games still exists, are doing all right.

HITS RICKEY, NEGRO FANS

Always bitter at Rickey for the manner in which she believes he took Robinson from the Negro league, she again assailed him for "trying to wreck Negro baseball" and "the gullibility and stupidity of the Negro baseball fans themselves into believing that he has been interested in anything more than the clicking of the turnstiles."

12

Chandler Reinstates Mexican League Jumpers (1949)

SOURCE: *Organized Baseball*, pp. 343–44 (also 1587–88)

The Mexican League was no longer a threat to the major leagues by 1949, but some owners still felt that the blacklisting of defecting players needed to be maintained indefinitely. Several affected players, most notably Danny Gardella and George Toolson, fought back through the court system. Although the courts initially supported the right of baseball to ban these players, on February 9, 1949, the U.S. Court of Appeals overturned a previous decision against Gardella. In the ruling, Judge Jerome Frank expressed contempt toward the position and behavior of baseball, concluding that "the answer is that the public's pleasure does not authorize the courts to condone illegality, and that no court should strive ingeniously to legalize a private (even if benevolent) dictatorship." The decision left considerable doubt as to whether baseball's antitrust exemption would be preserved. Nevertheless, in Toolson v. New York Yankees, *reached on November 9, 1953, the Supreme Court upheld the exemption.*

Fear among baseball officials was strong enough in 1949, however, that Commissioner Chandler officially reinstated the eighteen defectors on June 5.

The decisions in the Gardella and Toolson cases are reprinted in Baseball and the American Legal Mind, *ed. Spencer Weber Waller, Neil B. Cohen, and Paul Finkelman (New York: Garland, 1995), pp. 82–97.*

In 1946 when our players were being induced to break their contracts and jump to Mexico by glowing promises and enormous cash bonuses, I announced that I would suspend for 5 years those players who violated their player contracts by jumping to Mexico and who did not return to their clubs before the beginning of the season.

In Habana [*sic*], Cuba, in March, I personally told those players who had jumped to come back to the majors and report to their clubs or they would be suspended.

This action (suspension for five years) was then necessary in order to make these young men fully realize the serious nature of their contractual obligations and because of the threat to the integrity of the game resulting from their wrongful action.

Some 18 men in all were nevertheless persuaded to break their contracts and to play baseball in the Mexican league, and I accordingly notified each of these men that he would be placed on the ineligible list for 5 years. Shortly afterward, major-league rule 15 (A) was enacted to make compulsory the 5-year ineligibility of players who jumped their contracts after that time. No more did so.

Following the failure of the Mexican league to live up to the glowing promises made for it, many of these men petitioned me for reinstatement. In fairness to those players who had, in spite of large cash offers, remained with their clubs and carried out their obligations, I refused to reinstate them at that time. I always intended to give consideration for their reinstatement at a later date, after I had become convinced that the seriousness of their action in disregarding solemn obligations had been sufficiently brought home.

In October 1947, however, the Gardella suit was filed for the purpose, among others, of forcing the reinstatement of these players on the ground that baseball's contracts, and in fact its entire structure, was an illegal violation of the antitrust laws. Another action was later filed by [Fred] Martin and [Max] Lanier.

If these suits had been successful in compelling the immediate reinstatement of these players, my authority, as commissioner, to enforce rules designed to preserve the honesty and integrity of the game would have been seriously impaired, if not destroyed. I have been confident throughout that no court would order the immediate reinstatement of these players, who have properly been declared ineligible for contract violation.

While this question was still before the courts and could be interpreted as a threat, however, I could not even consider taking such action voluntarily. Baseball will not ever submit to threats of force, and it cannot afford to take action which could be interpreted as such a surrender.

The attempt to force immediate reinstatement through the courts has now failed. In denying the plaintiffs this relief in April, Judge Conger pointed out that to compel reinstatement of these players "would restore them to positions they resigned voluntarily." On appeal the circuit court of appeals last Thursday unanimously affirmed this decision. This is a definite determination that baseball cannot be compelled to reinstate these players now, and it accordingly appears to remove the possibility that a court will order any change in their status during the term of the 5-year ineligibility period originally ordered.

The threat of compulsion by a court order having been ended, I feel justified in tempering justice with mercy in dealing with all these players. They have been ineligible for more than 3 years, and nearly all of them have admitted their original mistake and have expressed regret at their submission to temptation to violate their contracts. In addition, the president of the Mexican League has met with me in Cincinnati, and satisfactory relations have been established which should end the efforts of that league to induce our players to break their contracts.

In the interest, therefore, of fair play to all and in the hope that the misguided young men who once so lightly disregarded their obligations will now be able to make a fresh start, I have decided to permit them to be restored, on application, to the eligible list.

13

Jackie Robinson v. Paul Robeson (1949)

SOURCE: *Washington Evening Star,* July 18, 1949

By the late 1940s the Cold War seemed anything but cold. The House Un-American Activities Committee (HUAC), formed in 1938, had kept busy in recent years investigat-

ing Alger Hiss and Communists in Hollywood, and it would soon be occupied by the avalanche of accusations by Senator Joseph McCarthy. When Paul Robeson—world-famous actor, singer, and former All-American and professional football star—stated that African Americans would refuse to take part in a war against the Soviet Union because of racial discrimination, the HUAC immediately invited prominent African Americans, including Jackie Robinson, to denounce him. As Ronald A. Smith explained in "The Paul Robeson–Jackie Robinson Saga and a Political Collision" (Journal of Sport History 6 [Summer 1979]: 5–27), Robinson was presented with a dilemma. If he refused to testify he risked being branded a Communist sympathizer, and if he testified his words could be twisted by segregationists to deny the reality of discrimination in America. Robinson commented at length on racism, but the press focused almost exclusively on his repudiation of Robeson.

NEGROES ARE WILLING TO FIGHT FOR U.S., ROBINSON TESTIFIES

Robeson Has Right to Sound "Silly" If He Wants, Athlete Says

By Chris Mathisen

Jackie Robinson, Brooklyn Dodgers second baseman, assured the House Committee on Un-American Activities today that Negroes would fight willingly to defend the United States in the event of a war with Russia—despite Singer Paul Robeson's statement to the contrary.

He emphasized, however, that this did not mean the bulk of the colored population is not determined to end racial discrimination in this country.

The star infielder, first member of his race to break into the major leagues, testified as the committee brought to a close its open hearing intended to give Negro leaders opportunity to contradict the Robeson statement.

Newsreel cameras whirred and a cluster of youthful autograph seekers waited in the corridor as the ball player made his statement to the committee. He prefaced it by commenting:

"It isn't very pleasant for me to find myself in the middle of a public argument that has nothing to do with the standing of the Dodgers in the pennant race—or even the pay raise I'm going to ask Mr. Branch Rickey for next year."

Of Mr. Robeson's declaration that American Negroes had too much affection for Russia ever to fight her, he said:

"I haven't any comment to make except that the statement, if Mr. Robeson actually made it, sounds very silly to me. But he has a right to his personal views, and if he wants to sound silly when he expresses them in public that's his business and not mine. He's still a famous ex-athlete and a great singer and actor.

"I understand that there are some few Negroes who are members of the Communist party, and in event of war with Russia they'd probably act just as any other Communist would. And most Negroes—and Italians and Irish and Jews and Swedes and Slavs and other Americans—would act just as all these groups did in the last war.

"They would do their best to keep their country out of war; if unsuccessful, they would do their best to help their country win the war—against Russia or any other enemy that threatened us.

"I and other Americans of many races and faiths have too much invested in our country's welfare for any of us to throw it away because of a siren song sung in bass."

He went on to say, however, that white citizens should realize Negroes resent "slurs and discrimination."

"Just because Communists kick up a big fuss over racial discrimination when it suits their purposes, a lot of people try to pretend that the whole issue in [*sic*] a creation of Communist imagination," Mr. Robinson said. "But they are not fooling any one with this kind of pretense, and talk about 'Communists stirring up Negroes to protest' only makes the present misunderstanding worse than ever."

WAS URGED NOT TO TESTIFY.

"Negroes were stirred up long before there was a Communist Party," he added, "and they will stay stirred up long after the party has disappeared—unless Jim Crow has disappeared by then as well."

Mr. Robinson said he had received a number of messages urging him not to show up at the hearing—some of them "from people from whom I have a lot of respect and who are just as opposed to Communism methods as I am."

He explained these apparently were sent because "some of the policies of this committee have become political issues." He said he decided to appear, however, out "of a sense of responsibility."

While not pretending to be an expert on communism, he told the committee, "you can put me down as an expert on being a colored American."

SAYS JOB IS UNFINISHED.

"I'm not fooled because I've had a chance open to very few Negro Americans," he continued. "It's true that I've been the laboratory specimen in a great change in organized baseball. I'm proud that I've made good on my assignment to the point where other colored players will find it easier to enter the game and go to the top. But I'm well aware that even this limited job isn't finished yet. There are only three major league teams with only seven colored players signed up, out of close to 400 major league players on 16 clubs.

"But a start has been made, and progress goes on, and Southern as well as Northern fans, are showing that they like the way things are working. And as long as the fans approve, we're going to keep on making progress, until we go the rest of the way in wiping Jim Crow out of American sports."

Mr. Robinson's wife sat near the witness table as he testified. When he was finished members of the committee complimented him on his statement. Representative Harrison, Democrat, of Virginia, assured him that the committee had no doubt as to the loyalty of the bulk of the colored population.

14

Yankees Win Pennant in Dramatic Fashion (1949)

SOURCE: *New York Herald Tribune,* October 3, 1949

David Halberstam, in Summer of '49 (New York: William Morrow, 1989), portrayed the 1949 season in the American League as one of the most exciting in baseball history. His argument is difficult to dispute. New York and Boston, who just missed winning the pennant in a thrilling race with Cleveland the previous season, entered the season's final game with identical records. The Yankees, led by first-year manager Casey Stengel, survived the absence of Joe DiMaggio for half the season and injuries to seemingly every other Yankee (whose starters, aside from Phil Rizzuto, missed an average of forty-two games) to earn a tie with the mighty Red Sox. Boston, in contrast, suffered no significant injuries and enjoyed spectacular seasons from sluggers Ted Williams and Vern Stephens, along with pitchers Mel Parnell and Ellis Kinder. Even though the final game of the season was played at Yankee Stadium, the Red Sox were expected to triumph. Yet as Halberstam and other writers have noted, destiny seemed to be on the side of the club that had won fifteen of the last twenty-eight American League pennants.

YANKEES WIN A.L. PENNANT AS RASCHI CONQUERS RED SOX

4 Runs in the 8th Offset Boston 3-Run Rally in 9th
Coleman's Double Scores 3 and Gives New Yorkers 16th Title;
Parnell, Dobson* Fail in Relief
By Ed Sinclair

Casey Stengel, the man they ridiculed last winter when he became manager of the Yankees, and his patchwork ball club, a far cry from the Yankees of old and quite often the butt of jibes and jokes over the campaign, confounded their detractors and delighted their defenders before 68,055 at the Stadium yesterday afternoon.

Deadlocked with their toughest opponents for first place in the pennant fight after 153 games, the battered Bombers pulled themselves together for one all-out effort and crushed the mighty Red Sox, 5 to 3, to become 1949 champions of the American League.

The climactic victory, made possible by one run in the first inning, a savage four-run attack in the eighth and a desperate ninth-inning stand, brought the New York team its sixteenth and perhaps sweetest title in its history.

NOTHING EASY IN TRIUMPH

For Stengel, called a clown who would try to win the pennant with laughs instead of players, it brought surcease from a bitter six-months struggle in which

*Should read "Hughson"—Ed.

he had to cope with a seemingly endless string of injuries to key players and it fulfilled his lifetime dream of leading an entry into the major league winner's circle.

There was nothing easy about the decisive triumph. The Yankees were up against the team which had overcome a late start in the final week in the campaign. They had beaten the Sox on Saturday to draw even in the standings and now they had to beat them again in the absolute last opportunity.

The Yankees squeezed a run from Ellis Kinder, the Boston right-hander, in the first. They took another from Mel Parnell, the league's best left-hander, in the eighth on Tommy Henrich's twenty-fourth home run of the year and they finished with three more runs off Tex Hughson in the same inning.

INVINCIBLE FOR 8 INNINGS

Even so, Vic Raschi, New York's finest pitcher in the first half of the season and a mysterious failure over most of the second half, had to be right against the Red Sox sluggers and right he was. For eight tight innings he shut them out, allowing only two hits and one of them scratchy.

With his twenty-first victory and the most important of them all so near in the ninth, he weakened just a little but held out to complete his performance. His path through the final inning was a perilous one, for the Boston bats suddenly found the range.

The strapping Yankee right-hander had retired Johnny Pesky on a foul to Yogi Berra when Ted Williams, the great hitter and the only man to commit an error in the series, walked and took second base on a wild pitch. Vern Stephens followed with a sinking single into centerfield on a 3-and-2 pitch, putting runners on first and third.

Bobby Doerr immediately slugged a first pitch into deep center. Joe DiMaggio, weakened by a two-week siege of a virus infection, tried for the catch, but the ball sailed over his head and carried to the bleacher wall for a two-run triple.

DIMAGGIO LEAVES GAME

The effort took so much out of the famous Clipper that he became dizzy and took himself out of the game. Rearranging his forces, Stengel shifted Cliff Mapes from right field to center, moved Hank Bauer from left field to right and send Gene Woodling into left.

Al Zarilla then drove a fly ball into right center which Mapes played beautifully, throwing home with such accuracy that Berra caught the ball beside the plate a foot up the third base path, holding Doerr to third.

Although there now were two out, Raschi had yet to reach the end of the trail. Billy Goodman slashed a wicked liner between the Yankee pitcher's legs and bounded over second base to score Doerr. The next batter, Birdie Tebbetts, represented the tying run, but Raschi used only two pitches on him, inducing him to foul out to Henrich beside first base.

The final out precipitated a demonstration on the part of the audience which included the use of firecrackers among many other sorts of didoes.† Perhaps it was fitting, for the Yankees had completed a job which will always be remembered as one of the finest accomplishments in baseball history.

SECOND BITTER DEFEAT

By the same token, Boston's bitter defeat on the last day of the season will always be recalled as the second in a row the Red Sox and McCarthy suffered in that manner. Last year the Sox tied the Cleveland Indians on the final day of the season, only to lose out in the first play-off game in the league's history.

Phil Rizzuto, the little sparkplug of the team, led off the home half of the first with a drive into extreme left field. Williams played the ball as if he were afraid it would bite him and, by the time he got around to returning it to the infield, the Scooter was sliding into third with a triple.

The little fellow immediately scored on Henrich's grounder to Doerr. Although DiMaggio tripled out of Zarilla's cruising range in right field after there were two out in that inning, and John Lindell walked, there was no further scoring. As a matter of fact, Kinder had held the Yankees hitless from there to the fifth.

Rizzuto singled with two away in that inning, and Henrich walked, but Berra lined out to Dom DiMaggio. In the sixth Billy Johnson singled with two out and died on first as Kinder threw out Mapes.

As the innings passed by, however, the one run assumed larger and larger proportions in the might of Raschi's airtight work. Finally, in the eighth after Kinder had stepped down for a pinch batter, the Bombers went out and got the insurance runs.

HENRICH CLOUTS HOMER

Henrich, the first batter to face Parnell, Kinder's successor, who came a cropper against the Yankees on Saturday, accepted his second service and drove it into the lower stands in rightfield. Berra added a single to the homer and Hughson came on from the Boston bullpen.

The Red Sox right-hander was successful with Joe DiMaggio, getting him to hit into a double play, but Lindell singled to center and Bauer was sent to run for him. Johnson lashed a single into left and Bauer made third on Williams's bobble of the ball.

Then Mapes walked to fill the paths and Jerry Coleman sliced a curving shot into short rightfield. Zarilla attempted a diving catch and missed and, by the time Doerr had recovered the ball and started the relay, all runners had scored and Coleman was heading for third.

Even though the Yankee second baseman was out at third on Goodman's relay to Pesky, the Yankees had the necessary runs to last out the game.

---

†A "dido" is a mischievous act—Ed.

BOSTON (A.L.)	AB	R	H	PO	A		NEW YORK (A.L.)	AB	R	H	PO	A
D. DiMaggio, CF	4	0	0	5	0		Rizzuto, SS	4	1	2	1	7
Pesky, 2B	3	0	0	1	0		Henrich, 1B	3	1	1	10	0
Williams, LF	2	1	0	0	0		Berra, C	4	0	1	5	0
Stephens, SS	4	1	1	2	3		J. DiMaggio, CF	4	0	1	3	0
Doerr, 2B	4	1	2	0	6		Woodling, LF	0	0	0	0	0
Zarilla, RF	4	0	1	1	0		Lindell, LF	2	0	1	1	0
Goodman, 1B	3	0	1	9	1		Bauer, LF-RF	0	1	0	0	0
Tebbetts, C	4	0	0	6	0		Johnson, 3B	4	1	2	0	0
Kinder, P	2	0	0	0	2		Mapes, RF-CF	3	1	0	3	0
¹Wright	0	0	0	0	0		Coleman, 2B	4	0	1	3	1
Parnell, P	0	0	0	0	0		Raschi, P	3	0	0	1	0
Hughson, P	0	0	0	0	0							
Totals	30	3	5	24	12		Totals	31	5	9	27	8

¹Walked for Kinder in eighth.

```
Boston ......    0  0  0    0  0  0    0  0  3—3
New York ....    1  0  0    0  0  0    0  4  x—5
```

E—Williams. RBI—Henrich 2, Coleman 3, Doerr 2, Goodman. 2B—Coleman. 3B—Rizzuto, DiMaggio, Doerr. HR—Henrich. SB—Goodman, Lindell. DP— Coleman and Henrich; Rizzuto and Henrich; Doerr, Stephens, and Goodman. Left—Boston 5, New York 6. BB—Off Raschi 5, Kinder 3, Hughson 1. SO—By Raschi 4, Kinder 5. HO—Kinder, 4 in 7 innings; Parnell, 2 in 0 (pitched to two batters); Hughson, 3 in 1. WP—Raschi. PB—Berra. Winner—Raschi (21–10). Loser—Kinder (23–6). U—Hubbard, Rommel, Berry, Summers, Honochick, and Hurley. T—2:30. A—68,055 (paid).

Controversies over Antitrust, Airwaves

One of Commissioner Chandler's primary reasons for reinstating players who had jumped to the Mexican League was to prevent baseball from becoming entangled in federal lawsuits that could threaten the sport's antitrust exemption. Chandler was successful, but he could not forestall future legal action against the reserve clause. In some cases threats to the exemption came from unexpected sources. Shortly after organized baseball passed Rule 1 (d), which was designed to regulate telecasts of major league contests as a means of protecting the territorial rights of minor league clubs, the Justice Department threatened a lawsuit based on its conclusion that the restrictions violated antitrust law. Again, major league officials backed down in order to protect their greater interests. The withdrawal of Rule 1 (d) on October 8, 1951—just five days after Bobby Thomson hit one of the most dramatic home runs in baseball history—was one of several factors that led to the near-collapse of the minor leagues in the 1950s and to the first of several investigations of organized baseball by Congress.

Although the game on the field was unaffected by these problems, the pressures were mounting. For the first time in a half-century a franchise was permitted to move to another city, as the Boston Braves shifted westward to Milwaukee. Race continued to be an issue, as advocates for both integration and segregation in baseball lobbied players, fans, and officials alike. Even after earning another validation of the antitrust exemption with the Supreme Court's *Toolson* decision in November 1953, baseball leaders—including new commissioner Ford Frick—did not rest easy.

15

Organized Baseball, Government Quarrel over Broadcast Regulations (1949)

SOURCE: Subcommittee of the Committee on Interstate and Foreign Commerce, *Broadcasting and Televising Baseball Games*, 83rd Cong., 1st sess., 1953, 13–15.

On December 6, 1946, the major leagues adopted Rule 1 (d) to govern the circumstances under which major league clubs granted rights to local radio stations and television stations to air their games. In short, major league clubs were required to obtain the consent of other teams—especially minor league teams—before granting broadcast or telecast rights to outlets in the vicinity of that team's home city. The intent was to respect the territory of minor league clubs by effectively preventing local fans from watching or listening to other games—which, minor league officials feared, would result in the inevitable loss of spectators.

However, the Justice Department objected to these restrictions as possible violations of antitrust legislation. Fearing another federal lawsuit (after related cases brought by Danny Gardella and George Toolson), the majors amended Rule 1 (d) effective October 15, 1949. Less than two weeks later, the Justice Department issued a press release in which it stated its intent to continue the investigation. Commissioner Chandler, in response, issued to his owners a memo on November 3 entitled "Radio Broadcasting and Television Illustrations of Application of Amended Major League Rule 1 (d)," available in the "Television" file at the National Baseball Hall of Fame Library and Archive.

Although they disagreed with the government's position, baseball officials gave in and repealed Rule 1 (d) on October 8, 1951. The absence of restrictions on baseball broadcasts and telecasts, compounded by the end of a Federal Communications Commission–imposed freeze on the granting of new television licenses in late 1952, greatly accelerated the incursion of major league contests into minor league airspace, and the competition was a significant factor in the minors' near-collapse in the 1950s. Congress would devote much time to the nature of sports broadcasting over the next decade.

AMENDED MAJOR LEAGUE RULE 1 (D)
Adopted October 4, 1949

Resolved, That major league rule 1 (d) be amended so that, as amended, the same shall read as follows:

"(d) (1) Broadcasting: Each major league club shall have the exclusive right freely to authorize a broadcast (including rebroadcast and network broadcast) of games played in its home park, except that a major league club shall not authorize a broadcast of such games to be made from a station located outside its home territory and within the home territory of another major or minor league club during the time that such other club is playing a home game, unless such other club has prior thereto consented to the broadcast of said game or of any game of another major league club during such time from a station located within its home territory.

"(2) Telecasting: Each major league club shall have the exclusive right freely to authorize a telecast (including retelecast and network telecast) of games played in its home park, except that a major league club shall not authorize a telecast of such games to be made from a station located outside its home territory and within the home territory of another major or minor league club during the time that (a) a home game of such other club is being played or (b) its away-from-home game is being telecast from any television station or stations located within the home territory of such other club, unless such other club has prior thereto consented to the telecast of said game or of any game of another major league club during such time from a station located within its home territory.

"(3) Nothing contained in paragraphs (1) and (2) shall be deemed to limit the right of each major league club to authorize a broadcast or telecast of any or all of both its home and away-from-home games at any time from any station or stations located within its home territory.

"(4) Where any consent is required under paragraphs (1) or (2), the major league club or major league authorizing the broadcast or telecast must secure such consent. No club giving such consent shall be entitled to limit its consent to any particular station or sponsor or to the games of any particular club or grant any rights (exclusive or otherwise) in respect of the broadcasting or telecasting within its home territory of any games of any other club; but such club may limit its consent to a particular date or dates.

"(5) The words 'home territory' shall mean and include, with respect to any baseball club, the territory included within the circumference of a circle having a radius of 50 miles, with its center at the baseball park of such baseball club.

"For the purposes of this rule, the phrase 'during the time,' as applied to the playing of a home game or the telecast of an away-from-home game, shall mean a period of time commencing 30 minutes before the commencement of such game and continuing for $3\frac{1}{2}$ hours in the case of a single game, and for $5\frac{1}{2}$ hours in the case of a doubleheader.

"(6) Nothing contained in this rule shall be deemed to affect or limit the ownership by each major league club or all right, title and interest in and to its games, including the news thereof, or to affect or limit (except to the extent set forth in paragraph (1) and (2) of this rule 1 (d)) its exclusive right and privilege to sell, license, control, regulate and terminate the publication or dissemination by radio, television, or otherwise of any news, reports, descriptions and accounts of any game or any part thereof, both within and outside its home territory."

OCTOBER 27, 1949 PRESS RELEASE, DEPARTMENT OF JUSTICE

Attorney General J. Howard McGrath today announced that the Department of Justice was suspending further action in its investigation of alleged restraints in the broadcasting and telecasting of major league baseball games until such time as the situation can be evaluated as it will exist under new major league rules recently adopted by baseball. Substantial changes in the major league broadcasting and telecasting rules were adopted by representatives of the two major leagues in an effort to eliminate the causes of complaints which led to the Department's investigation. The Department is informed that these changes are being put into effect immediately.

Herbert A. Bergson, Assistant Attorney General in charge of the Antitrust Division, in commenting on the matter, stated that the investigation which has been in progress by the Department was instituted following complaints concerning alleged restrictions imposed by the major leagues upon the play-by-play broadcasting and telecasting of their games. He said that the Department's investigation has been directed toward determining whether unreasonable restraints have been imposed by the major leagues which would deny to radio and television stations reasonable access to the broadcasting and telecasting of the games of major league clubs wherever the individual major league club is itself willing to grant or sell those rights. . . .

Complaints received by the Department of Justice over a period of time were directed principally against a major league rule requiring each major league club to refuse to permit the broadcast or telecast of its own games at any time from a station located within 50 miles of the ball park of another major or minor league baseball club without the consent of the other baseball club. This area was known as the local club's "home territory." The Department was informed that many baseball clubs used this veto power completely to prevent the broadcast in their home territories of baseball games played by other clubs.

Some baseball clubs in the minor leagues required local radio stations to pay them for the privilege of broadcasting games played by other teams. Some clubs granted limited consents to the broadcast of games of other teams which, in effect, gave the exclusive right to broadcast all baseball games in the area to a single sponsor or single local radio station, and denied this right to all other sponsors and local stations. Complainants had also asserted that the contract between the commissioner of baseball, the Mutual Broadcasting System, and the sponsor of the world series games denied many people the opportunity to hear these games because no Mutual station happened to be located in their particular areas. . . .

Under the new rule the local club will have no power to object to the broadcasting or telecasting of the major league games of other clubs in its home territory at any other time. The local club will have no power to sell its consent to a broadcast or telecast of the game of another club even within this period. It will not be necessary for a station to pay the local baseball club for the right to broadcast or telecast games played by other clubs. In addition, the Department has been informed that the local major or minor league clubs will no longer be permitted to give a local radio station or sponsor the exclusive right to broadcast the games of other clubs in its home territory, or to designate the station that will broadcast or telecast such game. . . .

Attorney General J. Howard McGrath stated: "Baseball is accurately referred to as the great American game. It is also an important commercial enterprise upon which thousands of Americans depend for their livelihood. Both the fans who desire to hear or see baseball broadcasts or telecasts, and the businessmen engaged directly or indirectly in bringing these broadcasts and telecasts to the public, are entitled to freedom from unreasonable restraints. It is hoped that the changes which have been put into effect as a result of the Department's investigation will have this effect."

16

The Effect of Television on Minor League Baseball Attendance (1951)

SOURCES: Undated letter from Robert C. Sprague, "Television" file, National Baseball Hall of Fame Library; Jerry N. Jordan, *The Long Range Effects of Television and Other Factors on Sports Attendance,* (Washington DC: Radio-Television Manufacturers Association, 1951).

Many baseball officials, particularly in the minor leagues, worried that the unfettered telecasting of major league games could substantially reduce attendance in their parks. Jerry N. Jordan, a graduate student in psychology at the University of Pennsylvania, conducted an in-depth study of the problem and concluded that while new television owners were less likely than before to attend a baseball game, after the first year of ownership—by which time the novelty of owning a TV had presumably worn off—their rate of attendance rose above that of non-TV owners. It should not be surprising to learn that these conclusions were embraced by the Radio-Television Manufacturers Association (RTMA), which published the thesis and promoted it through the mailing of letters such as that reprinted below, or that Jordan was the son of the vice-president of an advertising agency with several large sports accounts.

It is unclear what impact Jordan's study had on baseball officials or members of Congress. Jordan's research was first published in a three-part series in Television Magazine *between May and July 1950, during the period when the Justice Department was pressuring the majors to amend or drop Rule 1 (d). Peter Craig, author of the influential thesis "Organized Baseball: An Industry Study of a $100 Million Spectator Sport" (B.A., Oberlin College, 1950), who served as a researcher on the Celler Committee during its investigation of baseball, cited Jordan's work approvingly. In addition, it is likely that the* RTMA *arranged for copies of Jordan's book to be sent to people in positions to influence the future of baseball telecasting. The end result of the television controversy was that minor league attendance plummeted and many teams folded, belying Jordan's conclusion that television's effect on minor league attendance was only marginally negative, and only on those clubs in close proximity to a major league team.*

The RTMA letter appears first, followed by excerpts from Jordan's chapter "Baseball Attendance—And Television," pages 46–65. I have deleted all references to graphs and figures in the text.

The best book on the relationship between baseball and television is Benjamin Rader, In Its Own Image: How Television Has Transformed Sports (New York: Free Press, 1984).

Dear Sir:

The enclosed complimentary copy of "The Long-Range Effect of Television and Other Factors on Sports Attendance" is being sent to you because of your present or possible future interest in an answer to the question, "Does television reduce attendance at sports events?"

We believe that this carefully documented study does answer the question currently and, in the long run, negatively. It certainly is the most careful and complete analysis of the problem to date.

The study was neither initiated nor financed by the Radio-Television Manufacturers Association. It was made by a young university student, Mr. Jerry N. Jordan, in connection with his academic pursuits at Princeton and the University of Pennsylvania without any commercial influences or considerations.

RTMA did not enter the picture until after the study had been completed and the results announced. Then our Board of Directors provided funds for its publication and distribution because of the considerable light it casts on a complex and controversial issue.

We respectfully suggest that you or the appropriate persons within your organization take time to read this pamphlet carefully. It will be time well spent.

Cordially yours,

Robert C. Sprague, President

Radio-Television Manufacturers Association

BASEBALL ATTENDANCE—AND TELEVISION
MINOR LEAGUES

Baseball's concern over television has been greater in the minors than in the majors. Very few big league owners appear to be worried about [the effect of] TV on their own gates. Nearly all of them join a host of writers and minor league officials in grave concern over what it may do to the smaller teams nearby.

We were urged, in all our discussions with baseball men, to make a specific study on this subject. With the help and cooperation of Mr. R. R. M. Carpenter (owner of both the Phillies and Wilmington), we selected Wilmington, Del., as a good place to make this study. . . .

The basic theory of *length of ownership* held true in Wilmington, just as it has everywhere. A higher percentage of long-term owners (65%) went out to see the Wilmington Blue Rocks in 1949 than did short-term owners (58%).

The main difference in Wilmington was that a higher percentage of TV owners of less than one year went out to see the Blue Rocks than did non-owners (44%).

Wilmington, being newer to widespread television than Philadelphia, still has a higher concentration of sets in the hands of people who are sports fans. . . . [A] higher percentage of both long- and short-term owners had been to see the Blue Rocks play in the past than had non-owners. Their higher attendance rate in 1949 was only to be expected.

In Wilmington, as in Philadelphia, long-term owners went to more games and took their families with them more often than short-term owners. There was just one big difference. This special study left no doubt that televising the Philadelphia teams did hurt the attendance at Blue Rocks games.

In answer to the question: Which would you rather do—see the Wilmington Blue Rocks play at the park or see the A's or Phillies over television?—53% of the men covered preferred to see the big league team via TV.

Many stated frankly that the big league games, even over TV, had greater interest than the actual playing of the home-town team.

Television did hurt—but do not forget that the big harm done to nearby minor league attendance *came when the majors started playing a lot of night games.* Before that time, the major league clubs did not compete with the minors for the sports audience at night. The big crowds drawn to major league night games (much larger than day games) are composed partially of fans who formerly spent the evenings watching nearby minor league games.

That is a much more powerful factor even than television. When the sports fans in Jersey City or Newark found that they had the choice, within easy travel distance, of seeing the Yankees, Giants or Dodgers—or the Jersey City Giants or Newark Bears play at night—what did they do?

About one-third of the men interviewed in Wilmington had been to Shibe Park at least once during the 1949 season—only 13% lower than the percentage of Philadelphians. Many of these people referred to the A's or Phillies as their "home teams" just as they spoke of the Blue Rocks.

This was particularly true of the Phillies. Mr. R. R. M. Carpenter owned the Wilmington Blue Rocks before he bought the Phillies. The allegiance of many Wilmington fans moved to Philadelphia with him. Also, some of the outstanding young "bonus" players, who had been farmed out to the Blue Rocks, were brought up to the parent club. These reasons were mentioned frequently in our interviews.

Individual personalities play a huge part in sports. Players, managers and owners have strong personal followings. When they move from a minor league club to a nearby major league club, the allegiance of many of the fans moves with them. With or without television, Wilmington would have been hard hit by this situation. Undoubtedly, TV has accentuated it.

17

Baseball Asked to Reinstate Joe Jackson (1951)

SOURCE: *The State* (Columbia SC), February 22, 1951

Although he and seven teammates had been banished from baseball for thirty years, Joe Jackson remained a respected and popular figure in his home state. After Jackson had suffered several heart attacks, the South Carolina House of Representatives passed a resolution asking baseball to reinstate him. Their call went unanswered, and Jackson died in December of that year.

HOUSE ASKS BASEBALL TO REINSTATE JACKSON

The South Carolina House of Representatives wants "Shoeless Joe" Jackson reinstated as a member in good standing in organized baseball.

It adopted yesterday and sent to the Senate a resolution asking Baseball Commissioner A. P. Chandler to reinstate Jackson, star outfielder with the Chicago White Sox who figured in the 1919 "Black Sox" world series with Cincinnati. Jackson was banned from baseball for life after the scandal broke.

Jackson, who lives in Greenville, S.C., is recovering from the third of a series of heart attacks.

He was acquitted of bribery charges in a criminal court trial. Later he sued the Chicago team for his salary of the unfinished contract and was awarded a verdict which the judge set aside.

Jackson has maintained his innocence through the years of any part of a conspiracy with other Chicago players to throw games in the series with Cincinnati. "The Supreme Being is my judge and not any man in baseball," he once said.

Text of the resolution, authored by Reps. Snow of Williamsburg and Eppes of Greenville:

"Whereas, nearly 32 years have elapsed since the scandal of the 1919 World Series; and

"Whereas, though the story has frequently seen print, fact and fancy have been so confused that today it is still not known what actually took place; and

"Whereas, Joe Jackson was acquitted of all charges of conspiracy by a jury of 'twelve good men and true'; and

"Whereas, though set aside by the judge, a jury verdict against the Chicago White Sox was awarded him for the balance of his contract; and

"Whereas the fact that his fielding average for the series of 1919 was perfect and the fact that in that series he set a record of 12 hits for a World Series (a record that still stands though once tied) offer strong evidence that he was no party to a conspiracy to 'throw' the Series; and

"Whereas, he has suffered lifelong ignominy as a result of the scandal of 1919 and his subsequent banishment from organized baseball; and

"Whereas, persons actually convicted of crimes are not barred from the pursuit of their trades and professions upon their return to private life; and

"Whereas, 32 years is far too long for any man to be penalized for an act as to which strong evidence exists that it was never committed by him; and

"Whereas, Joe Jackson has been active in civic matters, particularly in programs for the benefit of young boys, since his return to private life; and

"Whereas, the General Assembly of South Carolina believes him to have been innocent of any conspiracy to 'throw' the World Series of 1919; and

"Whereas, though he is now too old to participate in baseball, the General Assembly feels that he should be exonerated by baseball as he was exonerated by juries in both criminal and civil courts; now therefore,

"Be it resolved by the House of Representatives, the Senate concurring:

"Section 1. The Commissioner of Baseball is memorialized to reinstate "Shoeless Joe" Jackson as a member in good standing in organized baseball.

"Section 2. The clerk of the House of Representatives is directed to send copies of this resolution to the Commissioner of Baseball, the President of the American baseball league, the President of the National baseball league, and Joe Jackson."

18

Willie Mays Joins the New York Giants (1951)

SOURCE: *New York Herald Tribune*, May 25, 1951

Even in the midst of the "bonus baby" era, few rookies were awaited with such anticipation as Willie Mays. Mays earned the acclaim with his spectacular performance in Minnesota, the Giants' top minor league club, including a "preposterous" batting average of .477 in the first thirty-five games of the American Association season. Giants manager Leo Durocher immediately announced that Mays would be his starting center fielder, and stuck with him even when Mays got off to a rocky start.

ROOKIE PHENOM JOINS NEW YORK CLUB TONIGHT

Minneapolis Centerfielder Batting .477 in 35 Games; Wilson Is Optioned Out
By Bob Cooke

Willie Mays, a preposterous rookie outfielder, reputed to be so skilled that his play may make Leo Durocher forget about the frailties of an umpire, was acquired by the Giants yesterday.

While the Giants were en route home from Chicago early yesterday morning, Horace Stoneham, club president, notified New York's Minneapolis farm that Mays was to report immediately. To make room for the allegedly incredible athlete, who had been hitting .477 in the American Association, the Giants optioned Artie Wilson, an infielder, to Ottawa, of the International League. Mays is due to play centerfield tonight against the Phillies.

The announcement regarding the purchase of Mays was made at a spontaneous press conference in the Giant downtown offices. Needless to report, adjectives regarding the twenty-year-old phenomenon were spilling over the carpeted floor as reporters arrived.

"AS GOOD AS ANY"

For Giant fans, who have spent a dreary season thus far trying to root their club above the .500 mark, an introduction to Mays should not be made by any one so base as a mere baseball writer. So let's listen to Tom Heath, Minneapolis manager, who has been chaperoning the remarkable fellow this spring.

"Mays is as good as any ball player in the country," says Heath conservatively.

Heath repeated the above information over the phone to Durocher during the press conference. He added:

"You're breaking my heart, taking him away, Leo. If Willie can't help you, then we all better pack up."

Durocher, obviously overjoyed by reports regarding his latest outfielder, immediately revealed that the Giants would present a new outfield threesome when they meet the Phillies tonight in Philadelphia.

DUROCHER'S NEW OUTFIELD

"It'll be Mays in center, Bobby Thomson in left and Monte Irvin in right," said Leo.

Durocher, however, was counting on the efficiency of an airline to accommodate him. As this was written, Mays had no knowledge that he was en route to the majors, but Giant executives were trying to contact officials in order that the newest Giant might be rerouted to the majors.

Salient facts about Mays include (a) he weighs 170; (b) he bats and throws right-handed; (c) he lives in Fairfield, Ala.; (d) he made seventy-one hits in 149 times at bat with Minneapolis this year, including eighteen doubles, three triples and eight homers; (e) after graduating from high school last year he hit .353 with Trenton; (f) he was signed when a member of the Birmingham Black Barons by Ed Montague, a Giants scout, who was actually looking for a first baseman; (g) he has a nice disposition.

It was Durocher who told reporters that Mays was a nice guy, all of which made some of them wonder whether he would help the club at all in view of Leo's annual prediction that "nice guys finish last."

Be that as it may, the new Giant centerfielder is Willie Mays. His Polo Grounds debut is scheduled for Monday evening when the New Yorkers entertain the Braves.

19

Celler Committee Begins Investigation
of Antitrust Exemption (1951)

SOURCE: *Washington Evening Star*, July 29, 1951

Disturbed by the number of lawsuits pending against baseball, including the Toolson case discussed earlier, New York representative Emanuel Celler convened a hearing in the House Judiciary Committee to study the feasibility of abolishing or amending baseball's exemption from federal antitrust laws. The exemption resulted from a 1922 Supreme Court decision, upholding an appellate court decision, which held that baseball games were exhibitions of skill—not products—between clubs belonging to the same league and therefore did not constitute commercial transactions covered under the Sherman Antitrust Act and subsequent legislation. The cases facing baseball in the 1940s and 1950s, however, involved individuals, not teams or leagues as in 1922, so the exemption attracted the interest of Congress. After a lengthy hearing in which scores of players and officials testified and dozens of documents were examined, Celler concluded that baseball should resolve the problem itself and Congress should exempt itself from that process. Nevertheless, Celler's committee would reconvene in future years, and baseball continued to face further congressional inquiry on antitrust and other issues.

HOUSE INQUIRY INTO BASEBALL'S "RESERVE CLAUSE" STARTS TOMORROW

Ty Cobb First Witness At Hearings to Study Anti-Trust Question
By Miriam Ottenburg

The House Monopoly subcommittee sets out tomorrow to determine whether organized baseball violates anti-trust laws.

With Ty Cobb, one of baseball's immortals, as the first witness—but without benefit of television—the subcommittee will hold hearings for two weeks and then adjourn until after the World Series.

Principal question in the investigation is baseball's "reserve clause," a combination of contract provisions and league rules that binds a player to a club owner for his baseball life or as long as that owner wants him.

Chairman Celler, a Dodger fan, says he wants to do what's best for baseball. He considers the suits now pending against organized baseball because of the "reserve clause" a sword of Damocles hanging over the national pastime.

COULD ASK EXEMPTION

One idea behind the congressional inquiry is that the courts would decide only whether the "reserve clause" is legal or not whereas the subcommittee, if it finds the "reserve clause" illegal but good for baseball, could recommend exempting the game from the anti-trust laws. Four bills to that effect already have been introduced and will be discussed during the hearings.

It's because of the pending suits that the subcommittee voted to bar on-the-spot radio and television broadcasts as well as newsreels. Some of the issues to be discussed at the hearings are also raised in the legal actions and the subcommittee doesn't want to influence prospective jurors.

Cobb is expected to testify only briefly. He is coming here from California to recall his experiences.

LEGAL DISCUSSION NEXT

After Cobb, the subcommittee will get down to legal technicalities involving baseball's history and structure, the relationship and agreements between the major and minors, the draft system and the farm clubs, the role of the high commissioner and the financial angles of the game.

Ford Frick, National League president, is expected to go into these details in a long statement. He will be the second witness tomorrow and Tuesday's session also has been reserved for his testimony. . . .

The fall hearings are expected to feature major league players as well as sports writers. The players' representatives at their meeting before the All-Star game approved a resolution backing up the "reserve clause." Sports writers across the Nation were polled to find out how they feel about it but the subcommittee has not announced results of the poll.

20

Robinson's Heroics Put Dodgers in Playoff (1951)

SOURCE: *Brooklyn Eagle,* October 1, 1951

After losing a lead of thirteen and one-half games over the New York Giants in the season's final two months, the Brooklyn Dodgers had to win the season finale against Philadelphia—which had defeated the Dodgers under similar circumstances to win the pennant the previous year—to clinch a tie with the Giants. When the Dodgers fell five runs behind after three innings, the task seemed nearly impossible. However, Jackie Robinson, in arguably the greatest performance in his career, led the Dodgers back with his offense and defense, and in the fourteenth inning he hit a game-winning home run off reliever Robin Roberts to earn a place in the third playoff in baseball history—and the third in the last six years.

ROBINSON DRAMA KEEPS FLOCK ON STAGE

Jackie Hero of Philly Story—Durocher Praises Giants
Home Run Clout Brings Victory in 14th Frame
By Harold C. Burr

Another chapter was added yesterday at Shibe Park, Philadelphia, to the Jackie Robinson story. Always the great showman, Robinson was never more dramatic than in the Dodgers' thrill-packed 9-to-8 triumph over the Phillies that threw the National League race into a Brooklyn playoff with the Giants.

He overcame a couple of bad early innings. He hit into a double play in the first and was called out on strikes in the fourth. He allowed Richie Ashburn's dubious infield hit to spurt out of his glove in the second for a pair of Philadelphia runs.

But his triple to right in the fifth put the Dodgers back in the ball game. Then, as the Flatbushers fought up to a deadlocked score from a five-run deficit and the tense struggle went into extra rounds, Robinson came up with a catch on Eddie Waitkus with the bases loaded and two out in the 12th inning.

It was a low liner toward second. Jackie grabbed it in the act of falling and his right elbow came up to hit him in the stomach, and knock the wind out of him. Robinson tossed the ball away as he collapsed. But it was a catch that kept the Dodgers fighting for their life.

Jackie remained in the game. He was dizzy and felt sick, but two innings later and with two out hit a home run into the left field stands to win the game. It was No. 18 for Robinson.

FANS GO WILD

The crowd of 31,755 went wild as Clarence Podbielan, the seventh Dodger pitcher, retired the last two Philadelphia batters with the tying run on second to receive credit for his second win of the year. They poured out on the field, dancing and yelling madly—Jackie Robinson's public hitting the hallelujah trail.

Preacher Roe started with two days' rest. He got by the first frame, but in the second Tommy Brown started a four-run rally with a home run. Ralph Branca came in to retire the side, but the tall and willowy Violet was wild and Bubba Church hit him for a two-run single.

Clyde King gave up two additional tallies in the fifth, made possible when Granny Hamner's ordinary single took a high hop over Carl Furillo's head for a fluke triple. That was a low ebb in the Dodger fortunes.

Clem Labine and Carl Erskine came on, but went out for pinch hitters, and Don Newcombe, with the score tied on Rube Walker's pinch double, became the seventh [sic] Flock flinger. Richie Ashburn, the first batter to face Newcombe, singled solidly to center. That was the lone safety off Newcombe. He worked one putout short of six innings. But he gave up seven bases on balls.

It was a terrific ball game that consumed four hours and 30 minutes to play. Just how much it took out of the winded Dodgers the next few days will tell. Perhaps it's what the doctor ordered. Long ago in St. Louis they got their second wind. This might be their third—the old championship club of June and July born again.

The Dodger future might hinge on the pulled muscle in Roy Campanella's right leg, sustained yesterday while running out a triple. If the big workhorse catcher is able to climb into his mask, mitt and windpad today in the first of the playoff games, Brooklyn, except for pitching, would be ready to keep up the good fight.

21

Bobby Thomson Home Run Clinches Miracle Pennant for Giants (1951)

SOURCE: *Brooklyn Eagle,* October 4, 1951

The third and final playoff game of the 1951 National League season has inspired as much prose, praise, and sorrow as any game in baseball history. Most sports fans have heard the frenzied radio call of Russ Hodges, and many have read Red Smith's classic account of the contest. Both men justifiably celebrated Thomson's feat and congratulated the Giants for successfully completing their comeback from a double-digit deficit in the pennant race. Dodger fans, though cognizant of the meaning of New York's victory, were more interested in consolation and explanations. Columnist Tommy Holmes attempted to address their shock in the following article.

Tommy Holmes

IT JUST WASN'T MEANT FOR DODGERS TO WIN

LIGHTS GO OUT—All the hopes and dreams of the 1951 Brooklyn Dodgers and their more or less loyal constituents ended in the last half of the ninth inning at the Polo Grounds yesterday. Ralph Branca threw a fast ball where Bobby Thomson was swinging his bat and a three-run homer landed in the lap of a lady in the left-field stands. The lady's name is unofficially reported to be Helen Gawn.

This was a dynamic melodramatic climax in a great season that has no parallel in the entire history of major league baseball. The finish was unbelievable, Giant fans went wild with enthusiasm and the Dodger rooters who all but died in their seats had to settle for the scant solace—they had seen their ball club go down to defeat in what certainly must have been one of the greatest ball games ever played.

It was a spectacle utterly without precedent. Here were two ball clubs infused with a traditional interborough rivalry for decades. Here were the Dodgers, who had been far in the lead. Here were the Giants, who had lost 11 straight games in the early stages of the season and had come from way back to finish the season schedule in a tie. And here were the two teams all tied up after two games of a playoff. And the Dodgers leading by 4 to 1 moving into the last of the ninth and the Giants winning out by 5 to 4.

MAKE MINE POISON—Don't make mine vanilla on this round, I'll settle for cyanide and there must be thousands of people in our fair and happy town who feel about the same, as the Giants moved into action against the Yankees in the first game of the World Series today.

This really was a rough one if you're the type to grow emotional over the game of baseball and are a fan of Dodger persuasion.

But it seems to be rough, year after year.

The Dodgers lost the pennant last season in the tenth inning of their 154th scheduled game.

The year before they won the pennant in the tenth inning of their 154th scheduled game. And so, this becomes the third year in succession that the Brooklyn club has figured in a photo finish.

The second-guessers are at work, of course, today. Why did Charley Dressen take Don Newcombe out in the ninth and substitute big Branca? Branca threw exactly two pitches and Thomson hit the second to win the jackpot for the Giants.

A second guess is a wonderful thing. The fellow who does it can't miss. He's got to be right. To baseball men, the reason for Newcombe's removal must be obvious. The big fellow was really weary.

ONE BAD BREAK—He had been terrific pitching the eighth and this was after the Giants had tied the score at 1 to 1 in the last of the seventh. The break of the ball game and the madcap pennant race, in the opinion of this corner, was the base hit of Al Dark which led off the New York ninth.

Newcombe fooled Dark on three successive power pitches. The third was an outside pitch on which the Giant captain was caught leaning. A right-handed hitter whose greatest power is a pulled ball to left field, Dark slapped this pitch through the right side of the infield. Hodges dove for it, deflected the ball toward Robinson, but the thing squirted through and that was the break the Giants needed and got.

Don Mueller slashed a much more legitimate single to right and Dark steamed into third. For a moment, it seemed that Newcombe would get out of the jam. He forced Monte Irvin to pop a high foul to Hodges. But then Whitey Lockman doubled to left. It was another case of Newcombe forcing a batter to hit to the opposite field. But one run scored, making the score 4 to 2, and now a home run would win the game and a single would tie it up. Here was Lockman on second and Mueller being carried off the field on a stretcher after spraining an ankle racing from first to third.

Now Branca came in. Here the opinion must be that Charley Dressen made a wise choice although it must be admitted that this is a difficult notion to sell. The situation called for a power pitcher, which Branca is. The other fellows available to Dressen aren't really strong-arm guys.

KISS THE FLAG GOODBYE—So Ralph came in. He opened up with a sharp-breaking inside curve for one strike on Thomson. He wheeled and threw again and the roof of the Polo Grounds fell in so far as the Dodgers and their followers are concerned. It was a fast ball inside and perhaps a trifle high. There wasn't a moment of doubt with the crack of the bat. The game and the pennant were lost.

Big Newcombe and Sal Maglie of the Giants had pitched a remarkable duel for a couple of hours. Newcombe up until the fatal ninth, pitched with greater success. Surprisingly, at least to this observer, was that Newcombe's pitching poise seemed to hold up better than the more mature, more phlegmatic and methodical Maglie. Wildness on Maglie's part initiated the first-inning Brooklyn run, which kept the Dodgers in front until the last of the seventh, and a wild pitch by Maglie was an important factor in the three-run rally in the top of the eighth.

But it must be admitted that big Newcombe had fielding support that was simply out of this world. Billy Cox played a game at third base, the like of which has never been seen before. He was a glove-man virtuoso. Peewee Reese came close to matching Cox's brilliance and so did Robinson and Hodges.

DODGERS DAZED—There was every reason to understand at the finish why the Dodgers stood there stunned, dead in their tracks standing up when Thomson's smash brought them to the end of the line. In the closing days of a tough and rugged fight, they had picked themselves up off the floor and fought so hard and well.

The Giants richly deserve the congratulations they received. But this was the roughest possible kind of a defeat to take. It was the first pennant for the Giants in 17 years, but you had to come out of a daze and congratulate them with sincerity. I suppose that is why baseball is the game it is.

22

The Responsibilities of a Team Statistician (1952)

SOURCE: *Baseball Is Their Business,* ed. Harold Rosenthal (New York: Random House, 1952), pp. 134–44.

Allan Roth was perhaps the first statistician hired by a baseball team to create and maintain statistics with the goal of improving strategies and performance. In 1946, Roth, formerly employed by the Montreal Canadiens, convinced Branch Rickey that the Dodgers could benefit from his services. Roth remained with the Dodgers until 1964, and he helped scout Andy High draft a scouting report on the New York Yankees for the 1951 World Series which was so compelling that Life *published it following the Series. In time he moved to* NBC, *where he worked on the Saturday Game of the Week.*

In the following excerpt, Roth describes the sorts of statistics he gathered and the ways in which the Dodgers used them.

Editor Harold Rosenthal, a sportswriter for the New York Herald Tribune, *interviewed nine other baseball men for this fascinating book, including a television producer of baseball games, umpire Charles Berry, writer Dick Young, announcer Ernie Harwell, and Dodgers first baseman Gil Hodges.*

Being a baseball team statistician has one unusual advantage over any other job in baseball. They can't compare you and your work to any predecessors in the "good old days," because in the "good old days," there weren't any baseball team statisticians. Like all new jobs the possibilities are largely unexplored. . . .

He is virtually a "confidential aide" to the important people in the front office. Frequently, by noting the information requested of him and the time at which such a request is made, he can surmise pretty well the way things are going. He may be able to guess who is being ticketed for the minors, what the front office thinks it needs in the way of replacements, etc.

Furthermore, the club statistician is in a position to prove an invaluable adjunct to his ball club. It gives him a good feeling to know that the figures he shepherds into his ledgers might some day decide a pennant, or even a World Series. . . .

During a normal baseball season I see 154 games, give or take a dozen to include play-offs, exhibitions, and other events. Usually I don't go to Spring training because there's nothing for me to do there. The managers, coaches, and front-office people are using my figures from the previous year at that time to help them make their decisions.

But during the season I see a lot of baseball. I once figured out that I mark down on paper, for future analysis, 40,000 pitches a year. That's just the initial entry at the ball park. Later these are collated, entered into other books, and then re-entered a third time.

At a ball game, practically every one in the park, even the manager, can relax for a moment. The statistician is the exception. I can't go out to buy a hot dog, or get a drink, and I'd better not blow my nose while the pitcher is on the mound.

Every statistician looks for his own particular figures and at the end of the year he breaks them down according to the needs of his club. This is usually in the form of a top-secret report to the Number 1 man of the club, usually the club's president or general manager.

Every statistician looks for a different set of figures, but generally I'm concerned with the following:

Performance, home and away, day and night, team vs. team, individual vs.
    individual (pitcher vs. hitter and hitter vs. pitcher), team progress during
    the season
Performance against left-handed and right-handed pitching
Direction of hitting (degree of "pulling" the ball)
Type of hit (ground ball, etc.)
Power (number of bases stemming from one hit and percentage of extra bases)
Getting-on-base ability (including number of walks)
Batter's performance (when ahead or behind in the balls-and-strikes count)
Bunting performances and percentages
Individual clutch performances (hitting with runners on base, and runs-
    batted-in percentages).

Pitching also calls for a separate set of statistics. My final report has a very important comparison showing a player's performance against that of his previous year. . . .

When I first approached Branch Rickey, then president of the Brooklyn club, we spoke for a while. I soon discovered that one of the things he liked best in my presentation was an opinion of the value of runs-batted-in. He said that he didn't think they were important and hardly ever looked at them. I told him I didn't think they were important either unless there were other figures presented along-side them.

I emphasized the fact that runs-batted-in meant nothing statistically, unless the *opportunity* for runs-batted-in was offered along with the original information. In other words, a club owner or manager certainly wouldn't be interested in how many base hits a fellow got in a season unless he knew how many times the fellow had gone to bat. So it was, ran my argument, with runs-batted-in—in from where, and under what circumstances? One particular player may have batted in more runs than the next fellow, but how many additional opportunities did he have? . . .

Let's put it this way. The job of the team statistician is to analyze the individual performance rather than offer an over-all average. Sometimes these analyses turn up startling information, like .350 hitters batting one hundred percentage points lower against certain pitchers. It's the job of the statistician to get information like this to the manager.

When he does so, he has figures to back him up and nothing talks in quite so impressive a voice as figures. I give the manager the information, black on white, furnish him with the percentages involved, and then let him make up his mind. Some managers depend upon your figures more than others, but that's a difference in personalities. Once every possible angle has been called to the manager's atten-tion, the statistician's job is done—until the next game when he has to be back there behind home plate again with his graph paper and sharpened pencils.

23

Minor Leaguer Fans Twenty-Seven in Nine-Inning Game (1952)

SOURCE: *Sporting News*, May 21, 1952

In an era when the most talented young baseball players received large bonuses and considerable publicity but seldom delivered as promised, news that an unheralded nineteen-year-old pitcher for the Bristol (Virginia) Twins named Ron Necciai had fanned twenty-seven players in a regulation Class D game on May 13 took the nation by storm. The Pittsburgh Pirates, Bristol's parent club, sought to deflect attention from their woeful season—in 1952 they lost 112 games—by hustling Necciai to the majors. It also served the purpose of justifying Pirate general manager Branch Rickey's extravagance in the bonus market, which had yet to lift the Pirates out of the second division. Unfortu-

nately for Necciai and the Pirates, the fireballer was unprepared for the promotion. In his only major league season, Necciai went 1-6 with an 7.08 ERA.

NECCIAI WHIFFS 27 IN BRISTOL NO-HITTER

Four Batters Reach Base; Bucco Farmhand, 19, in Second Year of Pro Ball
By Frank Weirich

BRISTOL, Va.—Never before in the history of the minors has there been such a sensational pitching feat as the record performance of a 19-year-old Pittsburgh Pirate farmhand, Ron Necciai, who struck out 27 batters in nine innings when he hurled a no-hit game in the Class D Appalachian League May 13.

Rocket Ron turned in his amazing strikeout record as he pitched the Bristol Twins to a 7 to 0 victory over the Welch Miners in a regulation game. It was not a perfect game, however, four players reaching base safely.

Third Sacker Joe Giel was safe in the third inning when Shortstop Don Deveau bobbled his grounder; First Baseman Mickey Shelton was hit by a pitched ball in the fourth frame; Bob Ganung drew a walk in the seventh, and Bobby Hammond reached first in the ninth when Necciai's strikeout pitch got away from Catcher Harry Dunlop.

Necciai's string of strikeouts was a freak, in a way.

With two out in the ninth inning, Necciai had struck out 25 batters, one having grounded out to first base in the fourth inning—Ganung bouncing out to Phil Filiatrault.

CATCHER MUFFS THIRD STRIKE

Necciai was pitching to Hammond, Welch center fielder. Hammond swung at a third strike in the dirt and Dunlop muffed the catch, Hammond going to first safely.

That gave Necciai his twenty-sixth strikeout, although his catcher missed making the putout. Ordinarily that putout would have ended the game and Necciai would not have had an opportunity to fan a twenty-seventh batter.

Bob Kendrick, Welch left fielder, provided Necciai with the next and final strikeout which brought the 1,853 spectators to their feet in a tremendous round of applause.

Necciai entered pro ball with Salisbury of the North Carolina State League in 1951 as a first baseman. His manager there, as at Bristol this year, was George Detore.

It was Detore who first discovered Necciai's amazing speed while the youth was taking infield practice with the Salisbury club last year. His powerful throws to the shortstop on first-short-first double plays were almost knocking the shortfielder out into left field. Detore decided then and there to make a pitcher out of him.

Necciai lost his first seven games as a pitcher for Salisbury. Then he turned in a one-hitter his eighth time out and fanned 17 batters. That was his start. He finished the season with the New Orleans Pelicans of the Southern Association with a 1-4 mark.

IN CLASS D AT OWN REQUEST

Necciai is playing in Class D ball again this year at his own request.

"I've got a lot of years in baseball ahead of me and I want to be prepared when the time comes to move along," he said. "Detore started me out pitching and brought me a long way despite my faulty control. I still have a lot of kinks in my delivery and I want Detore to help me straighten them out.

"I asked Mr. Rickey to allow me to work with Detore and he has been swell to permit me to do so. Maybe I'll be worth a lot more to the Pirates and myself in a few years because of it."

24

Minor League Head Forbids Signing of Female Players (1952)

SOURCE: NAPBL Bulletin No. 639, June 24, 1952, "Women in Baseball" file, National Baseball Hall of Fame Library

When the national media spread the word that the Harrisburg Senators of the Class B Interstate League had signed a female player—twenty-four-year-old Eleanor Engle— National Association of Professional Baseball Leagues president George M. Trautman was outraged. Three days later he distributed the following memo, in which he declared that all such contracts in the future would be invalidated (though he denied the validity of the report that prompted the memo). Given that many minor league clubs—especially last-place clubs like Harrisburg—were suffering greatly in the early 1950s and that minor league teams had a long history of flamboyant promotional stunts, the serious tone of Trautman's memo is somewhat surprising.

SIGNING OF WOMEN PLAYERS

Following press reports that the Harrisburg Club, of the Interstate League, had entered into a contract with a woman player, this office contacted that club and has been informed that no such contract has been executed nor has any woman player ever appeared in a game of the Harrisburg Club.

So as to remove any possible doubt as to the attitude of the National Association office toward any such contract, I am notifying all Minor League clubs that no such contract will be approved and that any club which undertakes to enter into such a contract, will be subject to severe disciplinary action. I have consulted Commissioner Frick on this matter and he has asked me to express his concurrence in the view that it just is not in the best interests of professional baseball that such travesties be tolerated.

25

New Bonus Rule Enacted (1952)

SOURCE: *Sporting News*, December 10, 1952

Ever since Branch Rickey's idea of the farm system began to catch on in the 1930s, major league teams often committed tens of thousands of dollars in order to sign the most promising amateur players. Commissioner Landis, a foe of the farm system, periodically granted free agency to minor league players whom he believed had been signed illegally (see Sullivan, Middle Innings, *pp. 178–79, for one example). Following Landis's death, the surge in baseball's financial fortunes and in the number of minor league teams accelerated the creation of "bonus babies." In July 1946 the problem was first addressed with the drafting of Rule 3-A, which defined bonus players as those who received in excess of $5,000 for their initial season with a major league club and placed restrictions on the signing of such players. The rule is described in* Organized Baseball, *pp. 485–87.*

After years of complaints from the minor leagues, Rule 3-A was repealed in 1950, but the situation continued to get out of hand as dozens of unproven players were signed to large contracts only to fail to achieve their potential. During the winter meetings in 1952 major and minor league officials amended the rule once more, with disastrous results. Under the new bonus rule, major league teams were required to keep bonus players on the active roster for a minimum of two years or they would become free agents. Rather than deter teams from making these investments, the rule, according to some historians, ruined many promising careers by preventing players from developing in the minor leagues. Instead, all but a handful of bonus players rotted at the end of the bench, receiving no playing time and gaining no experience. The rule was repealed in January 1958, but the controversial practice continued. Only with the institution of the amateur free agent draft in 1965 did the payment of bonuses end.

The most complete account of the bonus baby phenomenon is Brent Kelley, Baseball's Biggest Blunder: The Bonus Rule of 1953–1957 *(Lanham MD: Scarecrow Press, 1997).*

MINORS REJECT MOVES TO LOOSEN MAJOR TIES
VEECK'S SURPRISE PROPOSALS CREATE CONVENTION TUMULT

Bonus Rule and Curb on Recalls Voted
Big League Teams Barred From Pulling Back
Their Optionees After July 31
By Edgar G. Brands

PHOENIX, Ariz.—Attempts to loosen the ties held on the minor leagues by the majors were defeated at nearly every turn in the fifty-first annual convention of the National Association held here, December 3–5. Only two amendments designed to restrict the big leagues—a new bonus rule and a ban on recall of optioned players after July 31—survived and both were recommended by the Major-Minor League Executive Committee.

Efforts of the Dallas (Texas) club to force a consideration of abrogation of the major-minor league agreement were snowed under. Bill Veeck, president of the Browns, dropped a bombshell into the convention with proposals that the majors be forbidden the right to sign free agents without previous professional experience and to give the lower minors the first right to draft ahead of the higher minors and the majors, but he met a similar defeat. . . .

NEW BONUS RATING UNOPPOSED

The new bonus rule providing for the designation as bonus players of those who receive payments in excess of certain amounts was unopposed in the vote, but many misgivings were voiced as to how it would work.

Arthur Ehlers, general manager of the Athletics, declared it did not safeguard against promising a player signed within the limits prescribed that he would be moved up to the majors the following year at a salary of $25,000 for example.

[Leslie] O'Connor, a member of the Major-Minor League Executive Committee that drew up the rule, confessed the regulation had weaknesses because investigations were required to ascertain violations, but he said the language clearly put enforcement up to the commissioner.

President Warren Giles of the National League asked [George] Trautman what his interpretation would be of the example cited by Ehlers, but Trautman replied that it was a matter for the commissioner.

The rule as adopted makes a bonus player of any free agent signed for more than $4,000 by the major league club ($5,000 if the player is retained in the majors), $4,000 by clubs higher than Class B and $3,000 by B, C and D. Such player in the minors must pass through a draft period before he can be transferred in any manner, except by outright release, and a major bonus player must be retained for two years unless waivers are asked for his unconditional release. Such waivers are imposed for violations.

A Kansas City proposal that would have made a bonus player retain that status for life, placed the top figure at $6,000 before the bonus tag would apply and banned his assignment outright to lower classification unless waivers were secured, was withdrawn following passage of the other rule.

26

O'Malley Promotes Pay Television (1953)

SOURCES: *New York World-Telegram and Sun,* January 27, 1953; letter from Ted Leitzell in "Television" file, National Baseball Hall of Fame Library

After the major leagues rescinded Rule 1 (d) in October 1951, there was no effective television policy in baseball. Each team sought the most lucrative contracts while deciding how many home games it could air without diminishing attendance receipts. Dodger

president Walter O'Malley thought that if his team's games could be telecast over a closed circuit to those who had paid specifically for the privilege, his profit margin would increase considerably. In 1957, while testifying before Congress, he acknowledged his interest in pay TV. O'Malley did not mention that the prospect of subscriber-based TV was one of the major reasons behind his move to Los Angeles the following year. An initiative passed in California placed restrictions on the spread of pay television. However, in 1964 the Dodgers and Giants experimented with coverage provided by Subscription TeleVision, Inc., but soon abandoned it.

Unfortunately for O'Malley, the technology necessary to make pay TV profitable was not available in the 1950s, so the scheme he describes in the following article never materialized. Nevertheless, Ted Leitzell, an executive with Zenith, was sufficiently intrigued with the article that he wrote O'Malley and suggested that the Dodger owner testify before Congress on behalf of pay television. Hearings on telecasting baseball games were held in May 1953, but O'Malley did not testify.

O'MALLEY WANTS TO TEST PAY-AT-HOME BASEBALL TV

Urges Majors To Try One Area
By Joe King

Walter O'Malley proposes that pay-in-the-home TV be tried out in one major league territory in the coming season.

The Brooklyn Dodgers president claims this would be the first logical valuable step toward a solution of baseball's manifold problems.

O'Malley also allows that with metered TV, but not until then, he might see a point in Fred Saigh's demand that a visiting club be cut in [on] the air receipts.

Frank Shaughnessy, chairman of the recently formed committee to study the entire radio and TV structure of organized baseball, also views the ultimate remedy as pay-in-the-home.

The International League president will open hearings here Thursday, and while he admits countless considerations may come before his group, he does not expect success until the fan pays directly for the air game, just as he does at the gate.

THREE SYSTEMS

"In the past two years," Shaughnessy expounded, "we have had three systems demonstrated to us. One worked with cards, another with coins and a third was billed on the phone service. Surely one of the three must be ready to operate on a large scale."

O'Malley believes it would be practical to equip an entire area with meters if the promoters were guaranteed "programming."

He explained: "There is no point in meters until the operators have something attractive to offer. Baseball might be the inducement to get them going.

"Baseball provided the first boost for sponsored television. Shortly after the Dodgers, for instance, took the air, purchases of sets leaped in this area. It could be the same with the meters, or whatever system may be used."

Pittsburgh, which does not televise, might be interested. Maybe Cincinnati or Detroit, which have limited TV schedules, could give the coin machines a tryout.

SAIGH OUT OF LUCK

O'Malley says home-paid TV would create a new set of circumstances for the plan of Saigh, president of the Cardinals.

"With meters, it would be possible for every city to sell its product on a comparable footing," he outlined, "and these machines also would report the exact drawing power of any visiting team, as a basis for any payoff scheme."

But right now Saigh seems out of luck, at least in Brooklyn.

"Some have said baseball teams should share in the TV receipts of a game just as two boxers in the ring cut into the pot.

"Unfortunately, there is no parallel. Boxers go into the ring with approximately equal expenses, or overhead. Baseball teams do not.

"One club may hire a park for $40,000 or $50,000," he concluded, obviously meaning the Cardinals, "while the Dodgers, Giants and Yankees own and run their own parks at expenses which run from $250,000 to $350,000 a year. With that disparity, something must make up the difference, and our air revenue does."

ZENITH RADIO CORPORATION

OFFICE OF TED LEITZELL

January 29, 1953

Dear Mr. O'Malley:

We have just read in the *World-Telegram and Sun* your interesting proposal that subscription telecasting of major league baseball be tried out this summer.

If it were possible, we should certainly like to see your suggestion put into effect, because we would like to see it provided that subscription television can provide a solution to baseball box office problems.

Unfortunately, subscription television has not been authorized by the Federal Communications Commission. We have petitioned for hearings on the subject and hope they will be scheduled this year, but I doubt that anything can be done to put your suggestion into effect during the 1953 season.

If [the] Federal Communications Commission authorizes subscription television, it will be because this new service is in the public interest. One thing that affects public interest is the availability of good sports programs, many of which are now leaving the air because advertisers can't pay enough for sponsoring rights to offset television caused losses of gate attendance. It would, therefore, seem that organized baseball should be prepared to appear at Federal Communications Commission hearings on subscription television to tell the story of what television has done to baseball, and what subscription television can do to make baseball telecasts generally available to the public.

May I have your reaction to this suggestion?

27

Boston Braves Move to Milwaukee (1953)

SOURCES: Resolutions by Richard S. Falk and C. R. Dineen, Box 6, Folder 6, Walter H. Bender Papers, Milwaukee Urban Archives

In his book America Needs Four Major Leagues *(Bakersfield CA: Western Technical Press, 1947), H. D. Robins advocated the expansion of the major leagues to thirty-two teams in four leagues, to be accomplished primarily through the creation of new clubs but also including the transfer of unprofitable teams to new cities, including, among many others, Milwaukee and Baltimore. Robins identified the St. Louis Browns as a club that should be moved, but he suggested that the Boston Braves—then a strong club— should remain in place. At the time Robins's book was published, his ideas, however logically argued, may have seemed unrealistic and far-fetched.*

As it turned out, however, Robins's recommendations were often followed in future decades. The first step in this direction was taken on March 18, 1953, when National League owners unanimously approved the transfer of the Braves to Milwaukee, two days after the American League denied Bill Veeck's Browns permission to move to Baltimore. The AL reversed itself the next year, probably after noticing the phenomenal success of what came to be called the "Milwaukee miracle." Then the floodgates opened. By 1961 six of the original sixteen major league teams had moved, and by 1971 ten franchise transfers—including two each by the Braves and Athletics—had been completed.

The initial franchise transfer served as a model for future moves. On March 14, 1953, officials of the Braves contacted the Milwaukee County Park Commission, which controlled the new County Stadium, and informed them that they had less than two hours to craft a contract sufficiently attractive to lure the Braves to abandon Boston. The resolutions printed below indicate some of the conditions the commissioners placed in the short-term contract. In future contract negotiations following the 1957 and 1962 seasons, the Park Commission aggressively sought to rewrite the contract to maximize its profit, aggravating the Braves, who wanted to maintain the original, lopsided contract. When city officials could not meet the demands of the Braves, they moved to Atlanta— which, like Milwaukee a dozen years earlier, agreed to a lopsided contract. Major league officials learned the benefits of hardball negotiating tactics—or blackmail—in part from the experience of the Braves.

A RESOLUTION

Introduced by MR. RICHARD S. FALK, Park Commissioner:

WHEREAS, The owners of the BOSTON BRAVES baseball team have agreed to transfer their franchise to Milwaukee and to make use of the Milwaukee County

Stadium upon the condition that it be brought up to the standards usually accepted in Major League baseball; and

WHEREAS, MILWAUKEE COUNTY, in the planning for the construction of its Stadium, included in its program in that respect a complete plant to conform with such standards; and,

WHEREAS, the MILWAUKEE COUNTY STADIUM is now lacking in certain respects, because the completion of the original plans were delayed until the County was assured that a Major League Baseball Club would be transferred to Milwaukee; now, therefore,

BE IT RESOLVED BY THE MILWAUKEE COUNTY PARK COMMISSION, That, in the furtherance of the plan to bring the BOSTON BRAVES to Milwaukee, the following items on the Stadium be completed:

1) Provide additional lighting as quickly as possible to conform to Major League standards.

2) Erect additional permanent seats sufficient to meet the reasonable requirements of the League.

3) Provide additional office space and concession stands as shown in the original plans.

BE IT FURTHER RESOLVED, That the COUNTY BOARD OF SUPERVISORS OF MILWAUKEE COUNTY be asked to provide the additional funds for the accomplishment of this program and that the Director of Public Works for the County of Milwaukee be requested to arrange, as promptly as possible, to do all the necessary things to expedite the carrying out of this program; and

BE IT FURTHER RESOLVED, That this matter be brought to the attention of the County Board through its COMMITTEE ON PARKS & RECREATION at the earliest possible moment.

Upon motion be Mr. Falk, seconded by Mr. Dineen, the foregoing resolution was unanimously ADOPTED at Special Meeting of the Milwaukee County Park Commission, held March 14, 1953.

A RESOLUTION

Introduced by MR. C. R. DINEEN, Park Commissioner;

WHEREAS, The transfer of the BOSTON BRAVES to Milwaukee and the use of the County Stadium was presented to the Milwaukee County Park Commission, including the matter of cancellation or revision of the contract now existing with the Milwaukee Baseball Club;* now, therefore,

BE IT RESOLVED, That, in view of the offer of the owners of THE MILWAUKEE BASEBALL CLUB to cancel, by mutual consent, their contract with the COUNTY OF

*The Milwaukee Brewers were a farm club of the Braves in the International League. For the 1953 season they were transferred to Toledo.—Ed.

MILWAUKEE relative to the use of the County Stadium and substitute the use of the Stadium by the BOSTON BRAVES, the MILWAUKEE COUNTY PARK COMMISSION agrees to permit the BOSTON BRAVES to have use of the County Stadium for a period of two (2) years at an annual rental of One Thousand Dollars ($1,000.00), and to have a contract for an additional period of three (3) years upon the basis whereby they shall pay the County of Milwaukee five percent (5%) of the gross receipts from tickets and concessions, subject to the provision that there shall be a review of the contract at the end of the initial five (5) years of operation for the purpose of determining the returns to the ball club and a reopening of the contract to permit of increases in amounts to be paid to the County based upon such returns; and,

BE IT FURTHER RESOLVED, That the Boston Braves Baseball Club is to have, during said initial five-year term, all revenue from Radio and Television and from the returns thereon to be included as part of the total revenue to be subject to review at the end of such term, and that the details of the remaining portion of the contract shall conform generally, so far as may be practicable, to the existing contract with the Milwaukee Baseball Club.

Upon motion by Mr. Dineen, seconded by Mr. Falk, the foregoing resolution was unanimously ADOPTED by the Milwaukee County Park Commission at Special Meeting held March 14, 1953.

28

Community Organization Pressures Yankees to Integrate (1953)

SOURCE: Bronx County Labor Youth League flyer distributed at Yankee Stadium in April 1953, "Integration" file, National Baseball Hall of Fame Library.

By the beginning of the 1953 season only six of the sixteen major league teams had signed African American players (twenty-seven in all), but two of those clubs were the Brooklyn Dodgers and the New York Giants, both of which had won pennants in large part because of the contributions of black stars like Jackie Robinson, Don Newcombe, and Willie Mays. In contrast, the failure of the third New York team, the Yankees, to sign a black player was conspicuous to local activists, including the Communist Party and organizations sympathetic to the party. The Communists had campaigned for baseball's integration as far back as 1937, when its paper the Daily Worker *published an interview with Satchel Paige. Six years later it arranged a meeting between Commissioner Landis and several black leaders, including Paul Robeson. On several occasions Communists picketed major league ballparks—including Yankee Stadium on the opening day of the 1945 season—or distributed handbills urging fans to pressure their team to sign black players.*

Printed below is the text of a flyer distributed at Yankee Stadium in April 1953 by the

Bronx County Labor Youth League. In that same month the Labor Youth League was one of a dozen groups ordered by Attorney General Herbert Brownell to register with the federal government as a front group for the Communist Party, and Robeson published in Freedom, *a periodical supportive of the Communists, an open letter to Jackie Robinson reminding him that the integration of baseball was in part due to the pressure applied on owners by Robeson, black leaders, and Communist Party members. The article can be found in* Paul Robeson Speaks: Writings, Speeches, Interviews, 1918–1974, *ed. Philip S. Foner (New York: Brunner/Mazel, 1978), pp. 342–44.*

Predictably, the Yankees ignored the flyer. They did not use an African American player until 1955, when Elston Howard was signed.

STRIKE OUT DISCRIMINATION

How Can We Get Greater Democracy on the Yankees?

To this date, there has never been a Negro ballplayer on the Yankees. While the Yanks are World Champs they still fall behind many other ball clubs who today are the real representatives of Democracy in baseball!

Many have spoken out against the Yankee policy of discrimination—among them the noted Dodger star, JACKIE ROBINSON.

The various sandlot, PAL,* Church and other ball leagues of the Bronx are made up of young ball players Negro and white. Why can't the Yankees represent this democratic atmosphere? We are sure the fans will enjoy seeing a greater and better quality of baseball. More democracy by the hiring of Negro ballplayers will ensure better quality of baseball.

The Dodgers, Giants, Cleveland Indians and some others have take[n] a great step forward. The Yankee Management could once and for *all* bring up Negro ballplayers. This would make more democracy!

HERE——IS——WHAT——YOU——CAN——DO——

WRITE TO: MR. DAN TOPPING of the Yankee office urge him to hire the many talented Negro ballplayers who are waiting and ready to play top ball.

Bronx County Labor Youth League—1029 East 163rd Street

29

Umpires Accused of Showing Off on Television (1953)

SOURCES: *TV Guide*, April 17, 1953, p. 22; *Congressional Record*, 83rd Cong., 1st sess., 1953, 99, pt. 5:6125–26.

The increasing frequency of televising baseball games changed the way the game and its participants were perceived by fans and players alike. For decades, umpires like Bill

*Police Athletic League—Ed.

McGowan and his mentor, legendary minor league umpire Harry "Steamboat" Johnson, were noted for their distinctive, colorful styles. Although umpires were advised by league officials to tone down their acts, certain umpires on all levels of baseball retained their originality. However, in the late 1940s and early 1950s commentators like Red Smith complained about umpires who sought to overshadow the players during televised games. According to David Halberstam in Summer of '49, Smith wrote an article on this subject in 1949, and he addressed it again in the column below, the third he had written for TV Guide. James M. Kahn, in The Umpire Story (New York: Putnam, 1953), also noted that many complained about umpires' flamboyance on television, though the umpires he talked to refuted the accusations. Even a member of Congress, Representative Joseph Matthews (D-FL), commented on the apparent trend. His remarks, reprinted after Smith's column, were made on June 5.

SPORTS

"Out . . . "—*Macbeth*, Act V, Scene 1

When the Giants were converting an airfield into a baseball training camp in Sanford, Fla., the half-completed base was used as a school for rookie umpires. One day John Lombert, who was directing construction of the playing fields, spied from an upstairs barracks window upon the student body at classwork.

A bag had been set down on an unmarked plain to represent first base. As phantom runners raced for the bag and non-existent infielders hurled and caught an imaginary ball, the scholars practiced calling decisions. A student would crouch tensely over the bag, wait one portentous moment then straighten to full height, brandishing a thumb aloft with a sweeping, full-arm gesture.

"He's out—" each bellowed in turn. "He's out—He's out—He's out—"

NO ONE EVER SAFE

Mr. Lombert watched and waited. At last he cupped his hands and shouted.

"Hey—don't you bums ever call *anybody* safe?"

Mr. Lombert did not appreciate the importance of this labor-story work. He thought the apprentice umpires were supposed to be sharpening their judgment. Actually, they were concerned with something much more vital to their trade. They were rehearsing for starring roles on television.

Of all the capital crimes for which the inventors of the cathode ray tube must some day answer, possibly the most grievous is the part they have played in bringing out the ham latent in umpires. Now that a new baseball season has begun, the blue-clad Barrymores are with us again.

There was a time when a man could qualify as an umpire if he possessed integrity, keen eyesight, sound judgment, an understanding of the rules, a degree of physical agility, courage, some discretion in the exercise of authority, and a skull thick enough to bear the impact of an occasional pop bottle.

Today these qualities are as nothing unless he is also gifted with stage presence. Aware that the television camera's all-seeing eye is upon them, umpires no longer simply call balls and strikes. They render decisions.

They move in an aura of conscious grandeur. They are imperious, majestic. The simple fact that a pitch went through the strike zone or a runner has been retired at second is announced with gestures that must set Francois Delsarte* spinning in his grave.

"I never called one wrong," the late Bill Klem testified, and when player or manager rushed up to contradict him, Mr. Klem would scratch a mark on the earth with his shoe. One step across that line sent the trespasser off the premises, and the game would go briskly forward.

Today, a small difference of opinion calls forth a performance worthy of Booth—and I mean John Wilkes. Assuming his stance in dead center of the camera's focus, the umpire swells with wrath like an affronted blowfish. Kingly scorn darkens his brow. His eyes flash.

"I am Sir Oracle" he declaims. "And when I open my lips, let no dog bark— (that's Shakespeare, ya bum ya—'The Merchant of Venice,' Act 1, Scene 1)."

CONGRESSIONAL BASEBALL GAME

Mr. MATTHEWS. Mr. Speaker, I ask unanimous consent to address the House for 1 minute and to revise and extend my remarks.

The SPEAKER. Is there objection to the request of the gentleman from Florida? There was no objection.

Mr. MATTHEWS. Mr. Speaker, I have tried unsuccessfully to make the Democratic baseball team, even though I have gone out and offered my services to the manager of that team who comes from the great State of Florida. I do believe, however, I am well qualified to be an umpire. I have not had the backing of either party but I want to say that I cannot see well enough to play and I think that qualifies me most admirably to be selected. I do not know whether my great desire to be an umpire is because of television or because of my love of the game, but if an umpire does not show up I will be glad to be a substitute.

Mr. Speaker, I promise to wipe my glasses before every Republican play, and give impartial justice from the Democratic point of view.

30

Mantle Hits Tape-Measure Home Run in Washington (1953)

SOURCE: *Washington Evening Star*, April 18, 1953

Mickey Mantle made this otherwise meaningless early season game with the Washington Senators memorable by hitting one of the longest home runs in major league

*A nineteenth-century French singing teacher who invented a system of bodily movements designed to improve grace—Ed.

history. As the following article states, one reason why Mantle's tape-measure shot is so well known is because of the efforts of Yankee public relations director Arthur Patterson to label it a historic achievement. It is not known whether or not the home run actually traveled 565 feet—indeed, even at the turn of the twenty-first century the measurement of home runs is more of an art than a science—but since it was hit by Mantle, it will retain its position as one of the most famous home runs ever hit.

MANTLE'S HOMER HAILED AS YARDSTICK FOR GRIFFITH STADIUM CLOUTS

Harris Is Dumbstruck By Force of Wallop; Red Sox Here Tonight

By Burton Hawkins

Mickey Mantle, the Yankees' switch-hitting slugger, has left an indelible imprint on Griffith Stadium. Henceforth all homers of considerable distance here will be gauged by the monumental clout Mickey blasted over the bleachers yesterday while batting righthanded.

Bucky Harris, the Nats' pilot, was so amazed at Mantle's hitting feat that he couldn't comprehend it an hour after Mickey became the first player in history to clear the structure. "I just wouldn't have believed a ball could be hit that hard," Harris declared. "I've never seen anything like it." Bucky was so astonished at the mighty blow that the Nats' 7–3 defeat was shunted to the background.

Clark Griffith, the Nats' 83-year-old boss, who has seen some tremendous homers, said the high wind blowing at the time of Mantle's homer didn't detract from the towering smash, delivered off Chuck Stobbs with two out in the fifth inning after Yogi Berra walked.

GRIFF DISCOUNTS WIND.

"Wind or no wind," Griffith said, "nobody ever hit a ball that hard here before. I don't know if it would have cleared the bleachers without the wind, but let's put it this way—nobody ever hit one that would have come closer to clearing the bleachers under any circumstances. It's simply remarkable."

Mantle's unforgettable blow hit about 6 feet up on the center field side of the beer sign—The Star's football scoreboard during the fall. The ball struck at the end of the sign and caromed out of the park. Estimates of its distance varied from 565 to 595 feet, with the most conservative having the ball hit the sign at a point 481 feet from the plate before it left the park.

The ball sailed over the bleachers at the 391-foot mark. The bleachers are 36 feet deep, according to Groundkeeper Jimmy Ritchie. The wall at the rear of the bleachers is 55 feet high according to Ritchie, 48 feet high according to Secretary Eddie Eynon. And the ball hit at least 6 feet above the top of the wall.

MANTLE HAS THE BALL.

Arthur Patterson, alert public relations director of the Yankees, retrieved the ball from Donald Dunaway, colored youngster who recovered it originally. Patterson said Dunaway took him to the spot where the boy found the ball. Patterson measured the distance from the base of the wall to that spot and announced it as 105 feet. Dunaway told Patterson that the ball cleared Fifth street behind the bleachers, but there are skeptics.

By any measurement it was one of the longest home runs ever hit, if not the super-stroke of all time, and Mantle has the ball to place among his souvenirs. Patterson paid Dunaway for his prize and turned the ball over to Mickey after the game.

Jimmy Foxx probably came closer to clearing the bleachers than any player before the Mantle when he hit a homer several rows from the top of the stands in left field against the Nats' Rene Monteagudo 15 years ago. That smash was hit against the wind.

Larry Doby, Cleveland outfielder, hit one homer into the megaphones atop the centerfield and another one over them, but Mickey Vernon and Walter Masterson of the Nats agreed that Doby's most terrific homer here was a shot over the signboard by 20 feet and still seemed to be rising when it left the park.

PITTSBURGH HOMER A "BUNT."

Less than 10 days ago Mantle became the third player in history to hit a home run over the right field roof at Forbes Field in Pittsburgh during an exhibition game with the Pirates. Babe Ruth and Ted Beard had been the only previous players to accomplish that feat, but writers with the Yankees said his Pittsburgh poke was a bunt compared with yesterday's achievement.

31

Robinson's Interracial Barnstorming Team
Banned by Bull Connor (1953)

SOURCE: *Chicago Defender*, October 17, 1953

In the early 1930s, the popular radio announcer for the Birmingham Barons quit his job in order to run for public office. According to his biographer, his initial political victory was due primarily to his fame as a baseball broadcaster. Some twenty years later, Birmingham police commissioner Eugene "Bull" Connor, who would become one of the most notorious figures in the Civil Rights movement, reentered the baseball world by forbidding Jackie Robinson's barnstorming club from playing in the city on October 18 because it included three white players. Robinson opted to play both games without taking his white teammates into the cities mentioned. The ordinance, passed originally in September 1950 in response to an exhibition game featuring the Detroit Lions and its

African American star Wally Triplett, was overturned in January 1954, which led directly to the brief integration of the Southern Association that season. Connor's enforcement of the ordinance was not mentioned in Birmingham's major newspaper, and the game received only scant coverage.

For a more detailed examination of the integration of baseball in the South during the 1950s see Bruce Adelson, Brushing Back Jim Crow: The Integration of Minor-League Baseball in the American South (Charlottesville: University Press of Virginia, 1999).

DIXIE BARS JACKIE'S ALL-STAR TEAM

Law Bans Mixed 9 In Birmingham

BIRMINGHAM, Ala.—Public Safety Commissioner Eugene "Bull" Connor said this week that Jackie Robinson's All-Stars, which include several white players, will not be allowed to play in Birmingham Oct. 18.

"There is a city ordinance that forbids mixed athletic events," Connor said.

Formerly Robinson toured the country with an all-Negro team, but this year he has signed up several white players.

Connor said he had called Birmingham Baron Manager Eddie Glennon Friday morning about the proposed game in Birmingham. Glennon had informed him that Robinson was informed of the Birmingham ordinance.

Several weeks ago the Birmingham city commission failed to consider an expected repeal of the local racial segregation law, which would have permitted Negro and white athletes to play together.

The expected repeal was designed primarily to permit the Birmingham Barons to meet partly Negro teams in the Dixie series if the Barons should have won out in the Southern association play off against Nashville.

Birmingham was eliminated from the playoffs, so the city commission did not discuss the projected measure.

32

Supreme Court Upholds Baseball's Antitrust Exemption (1953)

SOURCE: Washington Evening Star, November 9, 1953

In Toolson v. New York Yankees the Supreme Court refused to overturn its 1922 ruling in the Federal Baseball case, in which baseball was declared a sport, not a business, and therefore exempt from antitrust laws. The brief ruling, reproduced in Baseball and the American Legal Mind, ed. Spencer Weber Waller, Neil B. Cohen, and Paul Finkleman (New York: Garland, 1995), pp. 96–97, made clear that it was up to Congress to eliminate the exemption. However, the central argument in the case was refuted by Justice

Harold Burton, who noted in his dissenting opinion that changes in baseball over the previous thirty-one years, especially its expansive farm system and the growing television and radio coverage of the sport, made clear that baseball was indeed involved in interstate commerce. Nevertheless, despite frequent attempts in Congress, the antitrust exemption remained in place until October 28, 1998, when President Clinton signed the Curt Flood Act of 1998.

SUPREME COURT HOLDS BASEBALL ONLY A SPORT

7–2 Decision Rules Game Isn't Subject To Anti-Trust Laws
By Robert K. Walsh

The Supreme Court today upheld a 31-year-old decision that organized baseball is a sport and hence is not subject to the Federal anti-trust laws.

The 7-to-2 decision, from which Justices Burton and Reed dissented, left the legal status of baseball, together with its controversial "reserve clause," exactly where it has been since the late Justice Oliver Wendell Holmes read the tribunal's decision in 1922 that baseball is essentially a game and is not engaged in interstate trade or commerce.

The court's opinion today was a "per curiam" pronouncement in that it was unsigned and was merely read by Chief Justice Warren.

ACCLAIMED BY GRIFFITH.

Clark Griffith, president of the Washington Baseball Club, greeted the Supreme Court's decision enthusiastically when awakened from his customary mid-day nap at the ball park.

"That's wonderful," Mr. Griffith said. "I thought they'd do that. We wouldn't have baseball without the reserve clause. I hope this will end all of those nonsensical suits against baseball."

Recalling the 1922 decision, the court noted that congressional committees in recent years have looked into the question of whether organized baseball should be brought within anti-trust laws.

"But Congress has not seen fit to bring such business under these laws by legislation having prospective effect," the opinion continued. "The business has thus been left for 30 years to develop on the understanding that it was not subject to existing anti-trust legislation. The present cases ask us to overrule the prior decision and without retrospective effect, hold the legislation applicable.

LEGISLATION SUGGESTED.

"We think that if there are evils in this field which now warrant application to it of the anti-trust laws, it should be by legislation. Without re-examination of the underlying issues, the judgments (of the courts below) are affirmed on the authority of Federal Baseball Club of Baltimore vs. National League of Professional

League of Baseball Clubs (the 1922 decision) so far as that decision determines that Congress had no intention of including the business of baseball within the scope of the Federal anti-trust laws."

The opinion today came less than a month after the court heard arguments on three cases contending that professional baseball should be subject to the anti-trust laws and that the "reserve clause" violated the constitutional rights of players.

Under the reserve clause—included in all baseball contracts—a player is the property of a club with which he signs a contract and remains so until released or sold by the club.

TRIPLE DAMAGES SOUGHT

The suits were filed by two players who were with farm clubs of the New York Yankees and the Brooklyn Dodgers, and by the former owner of the El Paso (Tex.) baseball club. The two former players asked triple damages because they said they were unable to play or to advance in baseball because of the reserve clause provisions. The El Paso man asked damages on the ground that he was prevented from hiring several Mexican players.

All three suits were dismissed by the lower courts on the basis of the 1922 Holmes decision.

Attorneys for the major and minor leagues warned that a Supreme Court reversal of the 1922 decision would necessitate an almost complete overhauling of the organized baseball setup, and possibly would wreck the system as it operates today.

They insisted that baseball is essentially a sport which is exempt from the anti-trust laws and that its status has not been essentially changed because of the development of radio and television programs.

3

Baseball Moves West

During the mid-1950s five major league teams moved to different cities. Each of the first three—the Boston Braves, the St. Louis Browns, and the Philadelphia Athletics—was overshadowed by another team in its own city and had been losing money (and games) for years. When the Brooklyn Dodgers and the New York Giants announced plans to relocate to California for the 1958 season, the rationale for their decision, in spite of the uproar it generated, was substantially similar to that of their predecessors. In each case, the new city promised the club it would build (or provide the land for) a modern ballpark with ample parking space located near major highways but away from the central cities, whose population consisted of growing numbers of minorities seen as undesirable by baseball owners. In addition, the new markets provided a willing audience for expanded television coverage, which in turn inspired visionaries like Brooklyn's (and Los Angeles's) Walter O'Malley to consider the possibilities of pay television.

Fans enjoying major league baseball for the first time thanks to television were fortunate to witness the blossoming of extraordinary new stars like Mickey Mantle and Willie Mays, and to see historic achievements like Don Larsen's perfect game in the 1956 World Series. They could not watch the frustration of their heroes as their newly won pension plan was threatened and as they responded by forming a new union, since baseball executives were more interested in highlighting its stars with new prizes like the Cy Young Award than in encouraging objective reporting on the sport's weaknesses. As traditions like the geographic configuration of the major leagues, the stability of the minor leagues, and even the humble box score were threatened, baseball continued to successfully promote itself as an institution representative of an era that outwardly celebrated conformity but which was in fact a period of cultural transformation.

33

Major League Owners Consider Ending Player Pension Plan (1953)

SOURCE: *New York Journal-American*, December 10, 1953

Almost three years after then-commissioner Happy Chandler signed a $6 million contract with Gillette to televise the next six World Series, with the money intended to finance the new pension plan for the players, baseball owners started to reconsider their part of the deal. The players realized that in the future money from television contracts would increase dramatically, and they wanted to ensure that the entire proceeds from All-Star and World Series television pacts would continue to be applied to their pensions. Their concerns were justified and supported by Chandler, who in January 1953 commented that the owners, in attempting to reduce or eliminate their contributions, were doing "a horrible thing to the players." In August the players hired lawyer J. Norman Lewis to represent them, but the owners refused to meet with him. The dispute was soon resolved, but the players, meeting in Atlanta after the owners refused to admit Lewis to their meeting in New York, informally organized the Major League Baseball Players' Association (MLBPA). The union became official when it drafted its constitution eight months later.

COLOR, COIN BOX TV LOOT TARGETS

Pension Brawl Not In Game's Interests
Owners Committee Studies End of Plan—But Are They Serious?
By Michael Gaven

How much will the color television rights for the all-star game and world series be worth to sponsors after 1955 when baseball will write a new contract?

Or if we have coin box TV in 1956 how many of the anticipated 50,000,000 set owners will drop a quarter in the slot to see Pee Wee Reese's Dodgers battle Phil Rizzuto's Yankees?

If you know the answer you also know exactly what the major league owners, the players and their owners are fighting about.

Meanwhile you might try the $64,000,000 question? Does the all-star and world series television and radio receipts belong to the owners or the players?

Pending a definite answer to that one, both owners and players are taking desperate measures in their efforts to make the first pitch for millions that aren't even minted.

Baseball can only lose prestige and good will by the highhanded methods employed by both sides to strike the best possible bargain when they know a compromise is inevitable.

The players, encouraged by the deposed commissioner, Happy Chandler, started by asking for all the television and radio monies but most of them admitted they were only punching for a fair share after the owners threw their Sunday punch yesterday.

OWNERS INSINCERE?

Obviously, the owners cannot be sincere in their threat to terminate the pension plan with the 1955 season. They cannot let down the players who have already earned their pensions.

The owners' ulterior aim is hidden in the wordy resolution which was passed at the joint meeting and supposedly set up the machinery for scrapping the pension plan. It concluded as follows:

"—and to submit proposals providing, in the event of the termination of the plan, for distributing under Major League Rule 45 a portion of the receipts from the sale of world series radio and television rights."

SPECIFIES MANNER.

Major League Rule 45 specifies the manner in which the world series gate receipts shall be distributed. In other words the owners would like to split the television loot on the same basis with 70 per cent of the proceeds of the first four games going to the players and the balance to the clubs, leagues and commissioner's office.

It was on this basis that the radio receipts were split prior to the establishment of the pension plan when all concerned agreed to donate their shares to the fund. This fact might be used to contradict the claims made by both sides.

"All proceeds from the sale of world series radio and television rights and all-star game proceeds belong to the major league clubs" said the owners in their official statement.

"The TV and broadcast funds belong to the players" said J. Norman Lewis, lawyer for the players.

Lewis, who was charged by the owners with misrepresenting the facts to the players as well as the press, said that his clients were not going to take this lying down. However, he indicated that a fair share plan would not be harmful "if the players can get that one and a half million dollars from the world series and all-star television and divide it as they see fit."

"We have a definite course of action," said the lawyer, "can't say what it is. That announcement will have to come from Allie Reynolds and Ralph Kiner, the players' representatives."

SEES SOLUTION.

Kiner, when told that the owners' action was in retaliation for "excessive" demands by the players, said, "We only requested them to give us a decision that when there was an excess of money, that the money would go into the pension fund."

"I still maintain a feeling this problem can be worked out on an equitable basis for all concerned," said Reynolds in part.

Thus did it seem today that all concerned were pulling in their horns at least just a little with Hank Greenberg striking a more conciliatory note on behalf of the owners.

Greenberg, named along with John Galbreath, Pittsburgh owner, to the committee to "study procedure for terminating the plan," said that he considered himself a mediator.

FRIENDS OF KINER.

"As I see it, it is our job to get both sides together and patch up the differences," said the Pittsburgh general manager.

It might be no coincident [sic] that Greenberg and Galbreath are personal friends of Kiner, the acknowledged player leader.

Greenberg indicated that he and Galbreath planned to meet with Kiner and Reynolds in the very near future. Meanwhile, except for Commissioner Ford Frick's strange hands-off attitude when leadership is badly needed, Larry Jansen seemed to tell the entire story.

"The trouble is that 90 per cent of the players don't know what it's all about," said the Giant pitcher.

34

Minor League President Warns of Slow Games (1954)

SOURCE: "Three I League" file: Manager Memos, Box 2, Folder 3, National Baseball Hall of Fame Library

Many of the baseball officials and fans of the 1990s who were concerned with increasingly lengthy games would be shocked to learn that their worries have been shared by some of their counterparts throughout the entirety of baseball history. The minor leagues—and some of the weaker major league teams—were waging a losing fight against television, and perhaps the fast pace of the new medium, in the eyes of contemporaries, made a two-hour baseball game seem plodding by comparison. A poll taken for Commissioner Frick in 1955 revealed that 80 percent of sportswriters believed spectators wanted faster-paced games. In 1956 the Sporting News *printed a front-page article on the problem posed by long games. Two years earlier, however, Three I League president Hal Totten identified several steps clubs should take to quicken the speed of play. His suggestions were hardly radical: making sure players were ready to bat and relievers prepared to enter the game without delay, and ensuring that disputes with umpires were dealt with quickly and quietly. Nevertheless, Totten issued a second memo on the same subject just six weeks later. It is not known if the average game time had actually increased significantly by 1954, or if it decreased after Totten issued his memos.*

THREE I LEAGUE

Memorandum to Managers, May 20, 1954

Conduct of the games throughout the league this season has been better than average, and a great deal of the credit goes to your gentlemen and your control of your players. Even the times of the games have been faster than ordinarily could be expected, considering the extreme weather conditions. I commend you for this generally-good condition and your important parts in it.

However, now that better weather seems to have arrived, and the pennant race takes shape, we must all guard against any relaxation of this situation. So I'm calling a few matters to your attention and asking your cooperation in seeing that they are observed—for the good of all concerned.

In the interest of speeding up the game, please see that:

If your club uses safety helmets while at bat, there are sufficient protective devices available so that there is no delay while a player at bat must wait for one after the preceding batsman has reached base or has been retired.

Get your relief pitchers into the game quickly; have pitchers await their turn at bat in the circle, as other players do, or if the weather is extreme, see that he is ready with the right bat and proceeds to the plate at once when it is his turn, if he waits on the bench.

Managers are responsible for the conduct of their players during games, and will be held responsible if players, especially on the bench, become unruly. Rule 4.06 will be enforced strictly.

Remember that the umpires are the representatives of Baseball, the National Association, and the League. Cooperate at all times, even in the matter of information requested by them. This includes identification of players for any purpose.

Players replaced in a game, or removed from it, are permitted to enter the stands after changing clothes. THEY MUST REFRAIN FROM POINTED COMMENT WHILE THERE. This permission is entirely a matter for your convenience.

There has been too much strong language, especially near the bench. A player is not to cuss, even at himself, if he pops up or fans.

Managers, as well as players, who are removed from the game are out of it completely. There shall be no contact, especially in directing play, with the field. Rule 4.07 applies and will be enforced literally.
Good luck to you all.
Hal Totten
President

35

Major League Baseball Players' Association Formed (1954)

SOURCE: House Subcommittee on Antitrust and Monopoly, *Organized Professional Team Sports*, 85th Cong., 2nd sess., 1958, 674–76.

After the baseball owners refused to meet with lawyer J. Norman Lewis in December 1953 (see document 33) to discuss the future of the players' pension plan, disgruntled players gathered in Atlanta. At that meeting the players agreed on the outlines of an organization—the Major League Baseball Players' Association—that would become, in time, a worthy adversary to the baseball ownership. The issue that precipitated the formation of the MLBPA—pensions—was in fact settled shortly after July 12, the date on which the association's constitution became effective.

Bob Feller, president of the MLBPA, described—in controversial language—the Atlanta meeting and his feelings about how owners viewed players during testimony before the House Antitrust Subcommittee, chaired by Representative Emanuel Celler, on June 25, 1957. His testimony is published in House Antitrust Subcommittee, Organized Professional Team Sports, 85th Cong., 1st sess., 1957, 1309–31 (see document 48).

**MAJOR LEAGUE BASEBALL PLAYERS' ASSOCIATION
CONSTITUTION, BYLAWS, AND ARTICLES OF ASSOCIATION**

ARTICLE I. NAME AND OBJECTIVES
SECTION 1. There shall be constituted an association to be called Major League Baseball Players' Association.
SEC. 2. The purposes of said Association shall be:
(a) To promote and foster the best interests of baseball.
(b) To promote, foster and protect the best interests of major league baseball players.
(c) To promote and foster fellowship and mutual consideration among major league baseball players.

(d) To promote and foster improvements of economic, physical, and security conditions of major league baseball players, including pension arrangements.

ARTICLE II. MEMBERSHIP

SECTION 1. Every player who shall hold a signed contract with a club in the American League or in the National League shall be eligible for membership in this Association.

SEC. 2. Membership of any member may be terminated at any time by the majority vote of the 16 player representatives referred in article III hereof.

ARTICLE III. ELECTION OF PLAYER REPRESENTATIVES

SECTION 1. Each major league club shall elect a club player representative and alternate club player representative who shall be active players on the said club. The election for each shall be by vote of a majority of the active players on the club.

SEC. 2. Each club player representative and alternate club player representative shall be elected for a term of 2 years, commencing July 1; except that if it be necessary to elect a replacement club player representative, his term shall extend only until the July 1 date for the next general election of club player representatives.

SEC. 3. The first general election of club player representatives and alternate club player representatives shall take place on July 1, 1955, and subsequent general elections shall take place every 2 years thereafter. All club player representatives shall remain in office until the next general election, except where circumstances, such as change of clubs, retirement, or resignation make it impossible for such club player representative to continue in office.

SEC. 4. The election of a club player representative and alternate club representative by the players of each club shall be by secret ballot. At least 24 hours' notice shall be given before such election posted on the clubhouse bulletin board. A majority of the players on the roster of each club must be present at the time that the election is held. In the event of the termination of office of the club player representative prior to the expiration of his 2-year term, another election, as set forth in this article, shall be held within 3 days after the vacancy occurs. In the event that the office becomes vacant between the end of the playing season and the opening of the new season, then the election shall take place as soon as possible after the beginning of spring training.

SEC. 5. The alternate club representative, in the absence or disability of the club player representative, shall perform duties and have powers of the club player representative. . . .

ARTICLE VII. DUTIES OF CLUB PLAYER REPRESENTATIVES

SECTION 1. The duties of club player representatives shall be—

(a) To confer with the players of their respective clubs from time to time but at least 1 week before each of the first 3 club player representative meetings and to transmit players' suggestions for the betterment of interests of players and of baseball, to league player representatives;

(b) To confer on at least four occasions during the year with other club player representatives at regular meetings;

(c) To confer and consult with counsel for such advice, information, and interpretations as may be required;

(d) To authorize and direct league player representatives and pension committee player representatives as to steps and positions to be taken in matters affecting players, and the players' pension;

(e) To consider, and to ratify and approve, or reject and disapprove, or modify, acts of league player representatives and pension committee player representatives;

(f) To consider and authorize expenditures permitted to be made by league player representatives and pension committee player representatives;

(g) To consider and authorize the hiring and compensation of legal, actuarial, or auditing assistance by league player representatives and pension committee representatives;

(h) To report to players of their respective clubs after each meeting of club player representatives, and to report from time to time to said players concerning any new developments;

(i) To select 2 pension committee player representatives to serve on the 4- man pension committee with the pension committee owner representatives, the terms of such pension committee player representatives to be for 2 years; and other arrangements regarding such representatives to be decided by the 16 player representatives;

(j) To determine eligibility of all applicants for membership in this association. . . .

ARTICLE IX. APPOINTMENT OF COUNSEL

SECTION 1. The counsel shall be appointed by the club player representatives for such term as they shall decide. He shall be the legal advisor of the Association, of the club player representatives, of the league player representatives, and of the pension committee player representatives, and of any committees that may be created by this association. He shall have supervision of all matters involving legal questions, and shall appear for the Association in all actions or proceedings where requested by club player representatives. His compensation shall be fixed by vote of the 16 club player representatives.

36

Mays, Rhodes Lead Giants to Victory in Series Opener (1954)

SOURCE: *New York Herald Tribune,* September 30, 1954

The Cleveland Indians have participated in only four World Series in their history, but they figured in three of the most memorable Series games. The fifth game of the 1920

Series featured three firsts—the first grand slam, the first home run by a pitcher, and the first (and thus far the only) unassisted triple play—all of which helped Cleveland win the game and the series. The otherwise forgettable 1997 Series was partially redeemed by the dramatic seventh game, which the Indians lost to the Florida Marlins in extra innings. The first game of the 1954 Series, described below, featured two remarkable plays. In the eighth inning, Willie Mays made one of the most famous catches in baseball history (though, by many accounts, not the best of his career) to squelch an Indians rally and help send the game to extra innings. Two innings later, journeyman Dusty Rhodes, pinch-hitting for Monte Irvin, hit a three-run home run off starter Bob Lemon to lead the New York Giants to a 5–2 win over the heavily favored Indians, coming off an American League–record 111-win regular season. The Giants proceeded to sweep the Indians in four games for their first Series title in twenty-one years. Rhodes hit a second home run and batted .667 (4-6), while Mays contributed with a .286 average.

GIANTS BEAT INDIANS, 5 TO 2, ON RHODES' HOMER IN 10TH

Mays' Catch Saves Opener in 8th Before Record 52,751
By Rud Rennie

The Giants did a magnificent job defensively in the first game of the World Series yesterday and capped the exciting type of play with a three-run, pinch-hit homer by Dusty Rhodes in the tenth inning, defeating Bob Lemon and the Cleveland Indians, 5 to 2.

Five times the Indians had a man on third base after they had scored two runs in the first inning. Twice they had their farthest runner on second. And in one of these situations, they had the bases loaded with one out after a spectacular catch by Willie Mays which kept the Indians from scoring in the eighth inning and winning the game in nine.

THEY SHALL NOT PASS!

Such was the determination and excellence of the Giants' defense, despite three errors, two by Don Mueller and one by Monte Irvin, that the American League champions had thirteen men left on bases.

Lemon, a righthander and a twenty-three-game winner this season, had limited the Giants to three hits after they tied the score, 2–2, in the third inning. Mueller was the only man to hit him safely in the five innings preceding the tenth.

In the tenth, Lemon fanned Mueller, the first man to face him. It was Lemon's sixth strikeout.

But he walked Mays, and Willie stole second on a pitch to Hank Thompson. Mickey Grasso was catching at the time, having just come into the game because Bill Glynn had batted for Jim Hegan in the Cleveland half of the tenth. Grasso's throw was in the dirt and Sam Dente, the current shortstop, did well to stop it.

After Willie stole second, Lemon passed Thompson purposely. And then Leo Durocher, the Giants' manager, used his only pinch-hitter in the game.

Al Lopez, the Cleveland manager, had sent three pinch-hitters up to bat. Two had struck out, one with the bases loaded, and the other with men on first and third.

Durocher had better luck. His pinch-hitters during the season had been the best in the league in coming through with homers for him. Rhodes was one of these pinch-hitters. Leo told him to get a bat and go up to hit for Irvin.

It turned out to be a happy selection. Rhodes lifted the first pitch into the air, and it came slanting down not far from the foul line, just over the wall into the stands. The ball bounced out of the stands back onto the playing field almost before the crowd of 52,751 persons was aware that it had gone in. It was not until Larry Napp, the right field umpire, waved his arm in circles indicating a home run that the biggest crowd ever to see a World Series game in the Polo Grounds realized that it was a homer and the Giants had won.

TEAM GREETS RHODES

Mays led the parade of winning runners, just as he had led the victory parade up Broadway on Monday. He paused at third, to wave for Thompson to slow down and take it easy. It was as if he wanted every one to come home together. And that's what they did. Mays, Thompson and Rhodes trotted across the plate, one close behind the other to be greeted by the entire team.

Until yesterday, only three pinch-hit homers ever had been hit in World Series competition. Rhodes was the fourth and it got the Giants away in front in their quest for the world championship.

It was a tough game for Lemon to lose, because in seven of the ten innings, the Indians had men in scoring position and in any one of these innings a timely hit would have won for them. If they had hit timely in every inning in which they had a chance to score, they would have murdered the Giants.

MAYS SAVES GAME

But that is where Sal Maglie, their starter, and Marvin Grissom did such a beautiful job. It can't be said that Don Liddle, who relieved Maglie in the eighth, did wonderfully, because Vic Wertz, who made four of Cleveland's eight hits, belted the ball over Mays' head to the rightfield bleachers at a time when there were two men on bases. But Mays, running with his back to the plate, caught the ball. His cap flew off and he fell to his knees after making the catch. But he hung on to the ball and saved the game. It was far and away the most spectacular play of the game.

Maglie, the Giants' best righthander, had a wobbly start. The Indians made two runs off him in the first inning. He hit Al Smith, the first man to face him, with a pitched ball. Bob Avila, the American League's leading hitter, singled over Davey Williams' head and reached second when Mueller fumbled the ball.

Maglie got the next two men to hit harmlessly into the air but with two away, Wertz, a .256 hitter acquired in June from the Orioles, tripled off the distant rightfield wall scoring Smith and Avila.

This was the beginning of a great day for Wertz, but it also saw the beginning of a defensive job by the Giants which foiled this and six more chances to score more runs.

Maglie got Dave Philley to hit a fly to Mueller, leaving Wertz on third. He settled down in the next two innings and then in their half of the third, the Giants tied the score.

Whitey Lockman started the rally with a single to right. Al Dark slashed a single past Lemon, sending Lockman to third. Mueller forced Dark, but Lockman scored, then Lemon walked Mays. Now, as later, the passing of Mays hurt him because Thompson came through with a single, scoring Mueller.

LEMON FANS IRVIN

The Giants had two runs in and men on first and third, but Lemon fanned Irvin and got Williams to rap a grounder to George Strickland.

Wertz got his second hit in the fourth and was on second when Maglie got out of the inning. Lemon stopped Mueller in the Giants' half, leaving them with men on first and third. That was the last real Giant threat until the tenth when Rhodes made it real.

But Maglie was in trouble in the fifth when the Indians had men on first and third and Al Rosen up with two out. Rosen, however, like so many of the Indians yesterday, did not come through with a hit when it would have meant a run batted in.

MAGLIE TIRES

Maglie was having to pitch much longer innings than Lemon and he was tiring. He had to be taken out in the eighth when the Indians looked as if they simply could not fail to score and break the tie.

Maglie walked Larry Doby, the first man up. Rosen hit a grounder to Dark's right where the Giant shortstop got it in his bare hand but could not hold it. The Indians had men on first and second with none out.

Fred Fitzsimmons, Durocher's emissary, walked to the mound and told Maglie he was through and called Liddle, a lefthander, from the bull pen.

It was then that the Giants got Wertz out for the only time in the game. It took a hair-raising catch by Mays to do it, and Doby moved to third, but Rosen was held at first after the catch.

LOPEZ MAKES MOVE

Then Lopez made his move to break the tie with pinch hitters. He sent Hank Majeski, a righthanded batsman to bat for Philley, knowing full well that Durocher would take out Liddle and come in with Grissom. And when Leo did this, Lopez sent Dale Mitchell, a lefthanded batter, to bat for Majeski.

Grissom gave Mitchell nothing good to hit at and walked him, filling the bases. The crowd buzzed in expectation of a score because there was only one out.

Lopez sent Dave Pope, a lefthanded batter, to hit for Strickland. The count went to two and two. Then Grissom slid a third strike past Pope and the crowd roared.

Hegan, up with two out, hit a long fly to left which, for a moment, looked as if it might fall into the stands, but the breeze held it back and it fell into Irvin's hands for the third out.

That was the Indians' biggest opportunity of an afternoon filled with opportunities to walk away with the game. The crowd applauded Grissom as he walked to the bench.

The Giants had a chance in their half of the eighth when Thompson walked and Irvin sacrificed and Lemon made a wild pitch which let Thompson reach third. But Williams was thrown out at first by Rosen on a close play on which Thompson held his base. Then Wes Westrum, who had got off to a good start with two singles, lined to Doby for the third out.

WILD PITCH BY LEMON

Grissom was in trouble with two out in the ninth after Irvin dropped a short fly hit by Avila for a two-base error. But he walked Doby purposely and got Rosen to lift a fly to Irvin. Irvin handled every ball that was hit in this inning.

In the tenth Grissom was in a jam again. Wertz made his fourth hit, a double to deep left-center. Rudy Regalado ran for him and reached third when Dente sacrificed. But Grissom passed Pope purposely, fanned Bill Glynn, a pinch hitter, and was out of trouble when Lemon, up with a chance to win his own game, lined to Lockman.

Lopez did not have any luck with his pinch hitters, or with the men who came to bat with men on bases.

And so, in the last of the tenth, Durocher's one move beat him. Rhodes, the only pinch hitter he used, came through with a home run on the first pitch to him.

It was a warm, sunny day and the crowd filled every seat. Fans stood four deep in back, and sat and kneeled on the runways. Jimmy Barbieri, captain of the world champion Little League Schenectady team threw out the first ball, and the old barnstorming partners went at each other for the first time in a World Series and the Giants won with the flair and last-minute explosive force which served them so often and well during the regular season.

Today it will be Johnny Antonelli, the Giants' brilliant young lefthander against Early Wynn in the second game of the series and the last in the Polo Grounds before it moves to Cleveland for the next three games.

<table>
<tr><td colspan="6" align="center">CLEVELAND (A)</td></tr>
<tr><td></td><td>AB</td><td>R</td><td>H</td><td>PO</td><td>A</td></tr>
<tr><td>Smith, LF</td><td>4</td><td>1</td><td>1</td><td>1</td><td>0</td></tr>
<tr><td>Avila, 2B</td><td>5</td><td>1</td><td>1</td><td>2</td><td>3</td></tr>
<tr><td>Doby, CF</td><td>3</td><td>0</td><td>1</td><td>3</td><td>0</td></tr>
<tr><td>Rosen, 3B</td><td>5</td><td>0</td><td>1</td><td>1</td><td>3</td></tr>
<tr><td>Wertz, 1B</td><td>5</td><td>0</td><td>4</td><td>11</td><td>1</td></tr>
<tr><td>[1]Regalado</td><td>0</td><td>0</td><td>0</td><td>0</td><td>0</td></tr>
<tr><td>Grasso, C</td><td>0</td><td>0</td><td>0</td><td>1</td><td>0</td></tr>
<tr><td>Philley, RF</td><td>3</td><td>0</td><td>0</td><td>0</td><td>0</td></tr>
<tr><td>[2]Majeski</td><td>0</td><td>0</td><td>0</td><td>0</td><td>0</td></tr>
<tr><td>[3]Mitchell</td><td>0</td><td>0</td><td>0</td><td>0</td><td>0</td></tr>
<tr><td>Dente, SS</td><td>0</td><td>0</td><td>0</td><td>0</td><td>0</td></tr>
<tr><td>Strickland, SS</td><td>3</td><td>0</td><td>0</td><td>2</td><td>3</td></tr>
<tr><td>[4]Pope, RF</td><td>1</td><td>0</td><td>0</td><td>0</td><td>0</td></tr>
<tr><td>Hegan, C</td><td>4</td><td>0</td><td>0</td><td>6</td><td>1</td></tr>
<tr><td>[5]Glynn, 1B</td><td>1</td><td>0</td><td>0</td><td>0</td><td>0</td></tr>
<tr><td>Lemon, P</td><td>4</td><td>0</td><td>0</td><td>1</td><td>1</td></tr>
<tr><td>Totals</td><td>38</td><td>2</td><td>8</td><td>[6]28</td><td>12</td></tr>
</table>

<table>
<tr><td colspan="6" align="center">NEW YORK (N)</td></tr>
<tr><td></td><td>AB</td><td>R</td><td>H</td><td>PO</td><td>A</td></tr>
<tr><td>Lockman, 1B</td><td>5</td><td>1</td><td>1</td><td>9</td><td>0</td></tr>
<tr><td>Dark, SS</td><td>4</td><td>0</td><td>2</td><td>3</td><td>2</td></tr>
<tr><td>Mueller, RF</td><td>5</td><td>1</td><td>2</td><td>2</td><td>0</td></tr>
<tr><td>Mays, CF</td><td>3</td><td>1</td><td>0</td><td>2</td><td>0</td></tr>
<tr><td>Thompson, 3B</td><td>3</td><td>1</td><td>1</td><td>3</td><td>3</td></tr>
<tr><td>Irvin, LF</td><td>3</td><td>0</td><td>0</td><td>5</td><td>0</td></tr>
<tr><td>[7]Rhodes</td><td>1</td><td>1</td><td>1</td><td>0</td><td>0</td></tr>
<tr><td>Williams, 2B</td><td>4</td><td>0</td><td>0</td><td>1</td><td>1</td></tr>
<tr><td>Westrum, C</td><td>4</td><td>0</td><td>2</td><td>5</td><td>0</td></tr>
<tr><td>Maglie, P</td><td>3</td><td>0</td><td>0</td><td>0</td><td>2</td></tr>
<tr><td>Liddle, P</td><td>0</td><td>0</td><td>0</td><td>0</td><td>0</td></tr>
<tr><td>Grissom, P</td><td>1</td><td>0</td><td>0</td><td>0</td><td>0</td></tr>
<tr><td>Totals</td><td>36</td><td>5</td><td>9</td><td>30</td><td>8</td></tr>
</table>

[1]Ran for Wertz in 10th.
[2]Announced as batter for Philley in 8th.
[3]Walked for Majeski in 8th.
[4]Called out on strikes for Strickland in 8th.
[5]Struck out for Hegan in 10th.
[6]One out when winning run scored.
[7]Hit home run for Irvin in 10th.

| Cleveland (A) | 2 | 0 | 0 | 0 | 0 | 0 | 0 | 0 | 0 | 2—3 |
| New York (N) | 0 | 0 | 2 | 0 | 0 | 0 | 0 | 0 | 0 | 3—5 |

E—Mueller 2, Irvin. RBI—Wertz 2, Mueller, Thompson, Rhodes 3. 2B—Wertz. 3B—Wertz. HR—Rhodes. SB—Mays. S—Irvin, Dente. Left—Cleveland (A) 13, New York (N) 9. BB—Lemon 5 (Dark, Mays 2, Thompson 2), Maglie 2 (Lemon, Doby), Grissom 3 (Mitchell, Doby, Pope). SO—Maglie 2 (Strickland, Smith), Grissom 2 (Pope Glynn), Lemon 6 (Maglie 2, Irvin, Thompson, Grissom, Mueller). HO—Maglie 7 in 7 (none out in 8th), Liddle 0 in 1/3, Grissom 1 in 2 2/3. R & ER—Maglie 2-2, Liddle 0-0, Grissom 0-0, Lemon 5-5. HBP—Maglie (Smith). WP—Lemon. Winner—Grissom. Loser—Lemon. U—Al Barlick (N) plate, Charlie Berry (A) first base, Jocko Conlan (N) second base, John Stevens (A) third base, Lon Warneke (N) left field, Larry Napp (A) right field. T—3:11. A—52,751 (paid). Receipts (net)—$316,957.25.

37

Frick Updates Owners on Recent
Baseball Litigation (1955)

SOURCE: March 3, 1955, memo in "Litigation" file, National Baseball Hall of Fame Library

For the previous decade, baseball owners had been dealing with a crush of antitrust lawsuits. Not only had some courts supported claims that the reserve clause was illegal, but some members of Congress were making efforts to overturn baseball's historic antitrust exemption. Furthermore, baseball and Congress continued to tangle over the regulation of television coverage. Commissioner Ford Frick, in the following memo, reminded his owners that baseball had won nearly every case, and had received damages in several. The costs of defending the status quo, Frick argued, were justified by the benefits that future judicial victories would bring to the sport.

Baseball's success in court and in Congress may have had its own costs. The attitude expressed by Frick below, and by Organized Baseball attorney Paul Porter in 1961 (see document 66), was one of growing overconfidence. They believed that when baseball was challenged justice would ultimately prevail, and that they and other baseball officials were the foremost defenders of justice. As long as they took their opposition seriously, they would triumph in the end. In the mid-1960s they encountered Marvin Miller, who was able to exploit their assuredness to the advantage of players.

MARCH 3, 1955
BASEBALL LITIGATION

The New York Giants' victory on February 28th in their suit to stop piracy of their broadcasts and telecasts is another demonstration that Baseball has been willing and ready to go into court to assert and defend its rights and has repeatedly fought the cases to successful final decisions. The Giants carried through their suit against Martin Fass in spite of countercharges of monopoly and illegal player contracts which the trial court threw out.

During Ford Frick's term as Commissioner, Organized Baseball has been in court in 15 cases, of which 9 have been decided in Baseball's favor, 1 was settled on a nuisance value basis and 5 are undecided.

PLAYER CASES

Seven cases attacking the player contract and the reserve clause have been brought against Baseball during the period 1951 to date. Five of these cases, in which it was claimed that Organized Baseball violated the federal antitrust laws, were won by Baseball in 1953 and 1954. These included the Toolson, Kowalski and Corbett cases decided by the U.S. Supreme Court in November, 1953; Prendergast v. Syracuse Baseball Club, Ford Frick and others, dismissed by the Federal Court in Syracuse in December, 1953; and Tepler v. Frick and others, dismissal by the Federal District Court being upheld by the Court of Appeals of the Second Circuit in May, 1953.

Two player cases are now pending in the New York State courts claiming that the player contracts violate the common law of New York. One of these, Tepler v. Sheehan, Frick and others, was dismissed in May, 1954, by the New York County Supreme Court, after which Tepler filed a notice of appeal which he has not prosecuted. The other case (Prendergast v. Frick and the Syracuse Club) is still pending, the baseball defendants having filed motions to dismiss.

In the course of these seven player cases in trial and appellate courts, thirteen courts have thus far held in Baseball's favor, none has held against Baseball.

BROADCASTING CASES

Since 1951, Baseball has been in court in 8 broadcasting cases, in 5 of them as defendant and in 3 as plaintiff.

Three suits are now pending in the Federal Courts against Baseball defendants which charge that rules and agreements regarding broadcasting of baseball games violate the federal antitrust laws. These are Tri-City Broadcasting Company v. Cincinnati and other Clubs, filed in the Federal Court in Cincinnati in 1951; Tri-City Broadcasting Company v. Mutual Broadcasting System and the Cincinnati Club, filed in the Federal Court in New York in 1954; and Fass v. Frick, New York Giants and others, filed in the Federal Court in New York in 1954 in retaliation for the Giants' successful suit to stop piracy of Giants' games by Fass. None of these cases has yet been reached for trial on the court calendars. The radio suits by Liberty Broadcasting System against 13 Major League Clubs in the Federal Court in Chicago was dismissed on February 8, 1955, under a settlement which cost the Baseball defendants less than it would have cost to prepare and try the case. The settlement was initiated by Liberty and was a nuisance value settlement so far as Baseball is concerned.

In another case, the Portsmouth Baseball Corporation is suing Commissioner Frick, the Major Leagues and the 16 Major League Clubs in the Federal Court in New York on the grounds that broadcasting and telecasting of Major League games into Portsmouth's territory is a violation of Portsmouth's territorial rights. This case is still in the preliminary pleading stage.

Despite threats that they would be met with countercharges of antitrust law violations and the like, Baseball Clubs in 1954 brought three suits to enjoin piracy of broadcasts of their games. In the Federal Court in San Francisco, the Chicago Cubs obtained a permanent injunction against Radio Station KYA. In New York, the Brooklyn Dodgers got an injunction against a baseball news service which was furnishing unauthorized play-by-play descriptions of Dodger games to out of town radio stations. The New York Giants, last summer, obtained a temporary injunction against Martin Fass who was teletyping descriptions of Giant games to unauthorized radio stations in the southwest and the far west. The Giants' request to make the injunction permanent and to require Fass to pay over his receipts to the Giants was granted on February 28th by Mr. Justice Edgar J. Nathan of the Supreme Court, New York County.

38

Ted Williams Fined $5,000 for Spitting (1956)

SOURCE: *Boston Post*, August 8, 1956

Ted Williams and the "knights of the keyboards" (his sarcastic term for the baseball reporters of Boston) had a complicated relationship. Williams's exploits on the field provided the writers with abundant material, both positive and negative, and he often complained that the writers emphasized the latter at the expense of the former, thus causing the fans to turn against him. The column below could be considered evidence that Williams was correct, but not entirely innocent.

On July 17 Williams hit his four hundredth career home run and commemorated the moment by making a spitting gesture toward the press box as he crossed the plate. Understandably, the reporters attacked him afterward. The star's anger built over the next few weeks, culminating in the events of August 7. With two out in the eleventh inning of a scoreless game with the Yankees, Williams dropped a simple fly ball off the bat of Mickey Mantle, and the Boston fans booed. When Williams responded by making a fine catch to end the inning minutes later, the fans booed again. Williams spat toward the crowd behind the dugout, and then spat again in the direction of left field. Williams won the game in the bottom of the inning with a bases-loaded walk, but he was not received as a hero by the fans or the writers.

In the column below, Gerry Hern applauded Red Sox owner Tom Yawkey for the stiff fine he levied immediately after the game, but stated that Williams should have been punished long before for his behavior. Appropriate discipline, administered early in his career, "would have helped him become the great player he should have been." Given the undisputed brilliance of Williams's career, it is easy to understand why he resented Boston writers for holding him responsible for not leading the Sox to more pennants over dominant Yankee teams. At the same time, however, the writers were correct to hold Williams accountable for his actions, and not to ignore his behavior and explicit lack of contrition.

CITY, STATE, REGION, BASEBALL EVENTUALLY WILL APPLAUD YAWKEY

By Gerry Hern

Was the $5000 fine too much and too late? Should the Red Sox have slapped down on the young man in 1939, or a year earlier, and thus have done the greatest favor that could have been done for one of the truly great and genuine baseball talents ever known? And will the severe fine make him a martyr to the fans who applaud every gesture he makes?

Those are some of the questions that follow the move by the Red Sox yesterday in fining the hero of the crowds the sum of $5000 for "misconduct on the field."

It's possible, and, more than possible, it's likely—that a tough fine slapped on

Theodore Samuel Williams in 1939 would have helped him become the great player he should have been.

With the equipment he had, Ted Williams should have led the Red Sox to the greatest triumphs of baseball history. The post-war Red Sox should have been what the Yankees became. But they weren't. The Red Sox were always the team Ted Williams played for. They were never the all-conquering Red Sox, the product of the most expensive selection process the game has known. They were never big enough to absorb Williams.

TAX SITUATION WILL COUNT

What will Williams do now? No one knows for sure. Certainly he will look into the tax situation on the fine. Is it a loss of income or a casualty loss? Is it like a hurricane or a flood? Those business factors have to be considered in the financial doings of a man with his income.

More important than the personal effect on Williams is the effect on Boston baseball. The belief here is that this is the most notable move ever made by Tom Yawkey during his ownership of the Boston franchise.

Yawkey ceased being an indulgent owner yesterday and suddenly developed into the clubowner who could break the Yankees' hold on the American league. For what he did, the city and State and region will eventually be grateful.

Many baseball observers thought last night that the fine would be secretly eased by a post-season addition of salary for next year's contract, but the belief here is that Yawkey is a man of purpose, a long suffering one, but a firm one when he makes up his mind. The thought here is that the fine will stick and that the Red Sox will benefit by it.

The size of the fine will probably make Williams a hero. That is traditional. If, and when, he goes on the field tomorrow night, men, women and children will applaud until their hands are sore. Every pop-foul he hits, if he shows up, will be greeted with the attention reserved for a visiting dignitary. His very appearance on the field will be like the arrival of Colonel Nasser in Cairo.

YAWKEY SPOKE FOR GAME

Is a fine of $5000 the answer to Williams? Nobody knows, especially this agent, who has long known of the personal affection the owner, Tom Yawkey, feels for his greatest gate attraction. But the opinion is growing that Yawkey also respects the feelings of the manager he selected and brought here, Mike Higgins.

Yawkey spoke yesterday for the game and the manager he respects. If nothing had been done, Yawkey would be condoning Williams' actions. He would, therefore, be brushing off his manager, a strong man with the courage to make his decisions fairly and honorably. Williams has never really had a manager. Williams never had to, because he always had Yawkey in his corner. Even Joe McCarthy, the greatest of them, recognized and accepted that. It was part of his coming to Boston.

The essence of the disciplinary action is that Williams' greatest admirer, Tom Yawkey, was the one who fined him. He fined him after hearing Mel Allen broadcast the spitting incident to the New York audience.

He fined him after warning him three weeks ago that his actions on the field reflected on the Red Sox.

Have the Red Sox absorbed Williams finally? The answer will take days to discover, but at least the move was made.

39

Don Larsen Pitches Perfect World Series Game (1956)

SOURCE: *New York Daily News,* October 9, 1956

One of the greatest challenges for any reporter for a daily newspaper is to capture the significance of a historic event with no time for reflection. The best sportswriters of the 1950s, like Red Smith of the New York Herald Tribune *and Shirley Povich of the* Washington Post, *met that challenge with their memorable accounts of one of baseball's most electrifying achievements: Don Larsen's perfect game in the 1956 World Series. Less acclaimed, but still remembered by aficionados, was the story by veteran writer Joe Trimble. Trimble framed the drama on the ballfield with the unlikelihood that such a game was pitched by a erratic journeyman like Larsen. The first sentence of the article captured the irony perfectly: "The unperfect man pitched a perfect game yesterday." Although* New York Daily News *reporter Bill Gallo revealed in an October 6, 1996, column that this sentence was actually composed by Trimble's colleague Dick Young, the rest of the article—aside from his error regarding the number of perfect games predating Larsen's (five, not one)—exhibits the quality of Trimble's prose under pressure.*

HISTORY IS MADE IN SERIES CLASSIC; LARSEN HURLS PERFECT GAME, WINS 2–0
By Joe Trimble

The unperfect man pitched a perfect game yesterday. Don Larsen, a free soul who loves the gay life, retired all 27 Dodgers in the classic pitching performance of all time as the Yankees won the fifth game, 2–0, at the Stadium and took a 3–2 edge in the set. In this first perfect World Series game, he made but 97 pitches, threw three balls to only one batter, and fanned seven. A man must be lucky as well as good to reach such an incredible height and Don got four breaks, a "foul homer" which missed being fair by inches and three superb fielding plays on line drives.

This was only the second perfect game ever pitched in the majors, the other by righthander Charley Robertson of the White Sox against Detroit on April 30, 1922. Larsen's was the first series no-hitter, of course. There have been three one-hitters.

Don, an affable, nerveless man who laughs his way through life, doesn't know how to worry. And that was his greatest asset in the pressure cauldron that was the big Bronx ball park in the late innings, with the crowd of 64,519 adding to the mounting tension with swelling roars and cheers as one grim-faced Dodger after another failed to break through his serves.

With the tension tearing at their nerves and sweat breaking out on the palms of the onlookers, Larsen seemed to be the calmest man in the place. He knew he had a perfect game and was determined to get it. In the ninth inning, though inwardly tense, he kept perfect control of himself and the ball. Only when pinch-hitter Dale Mitchell was called out on strikes to become the 27th dead Dodger, did Larsen show emotion.

A grin broke across his face as Yogi Berra dashed up to him. Berra jumped wildly into Don's arms, the pitcher grabbing and carrying the catcher like a baby for a few strides. Then the entire Yankee bench engolfed [*sic*] the pair of them and ushers and cops ushered the ball players off the field and into the safety of the dugout before the crowd could get at them.

The Yankee fielders ran up to shake his hand and Don had a special hug for Mickey Mantle, whose fourth-inning homer had given him a lead and whose great catch of a liner by Gil Hodges had saved things in the fifth.

Andy Carey, who has been the sloppiest man in the Series afield, also helped on two plays. The third baseman deflected Jack Robinson's liner in the second inning, leaping and pawing the ball to shortstop Gil McDougald who made the throw to first in time. The play wasn't close.

Carey's other contribution came in the eighth when the pressure was on everybody. Hodges was the hitter then, too. Gil took a half swing and hit a low liner which Andy gloved one-hand, bobbled a bit and then held while on the run.

The other nod from Lady Luck didn't involve a fielder. In the fifth inning, Sandy Amoros drove a screaming liner into the right-field stands. But it veered to the right side of the foul pole, missing by about four inches. Larsen then got the little Dodger to ground out to Billy Martin and end the inning.

The party of the second part in this incredible sizzler was the man who may have been pitching his last World Series game, Sal Maglie. The 39-year-old right-hander, who had won the opener of the series, pitched a handsome game himself. . . .

The crowd gave Larsen a tremendous hand when he came up to bat in the eighth, standing up to applaud. Then, after the Yankees were retired, he went back to the mound to get the last three outs—the three men who stood between him and baseball immortality.

The Dodgers, still trying to win, dug in. Carl Furillo fouled off a couple and then flied to Hank Bauer in right field. Campy belted a long drive into the upper left-field seats but it was foul by many yards, then grounded weakly to Martin. Mitchell then came up to bat for Maglie and the Stadium rocked with roars of anticipation.

(Fifth Game)

DODGERS

	[1]B AV	AB	R	H	2B	3B	HR	TB	BB	SO	RBI	PO	A	E	[2]B AV
Gilliam, 2B	.300	3	0	0	0	0	0	0	0	1	0	2	0	0	.059
Reese, ss	.257	3	0	0	0	0	0	0	0	1	0	4	2	0	.256
Snider, CF	.292	3	0	0	0	0	0	0	0	1	0	1	0	0	.235
Robinson, 3B ..	.275	3	0	0	0	0	0	0	0	0	0	2	4	0	.294
Hodges, 1B	.265	3	0	0	0	0	0	0	0	1	0	5	1	0	.412
Amoros, LF	.260	3	0	0	0	0	0	0	0	0	0	3	0	0	.077
Furillo, RF	.289	3	0	0	0	0	0	0	0	0	0	0	0	0	.273
Campanella, C ..	.219	3	0	0	0	0	0	0	0	1	0	7	2	0	.267
Maglie, P	13-5	2	0	0	0	0	0	0	0	1	0	0	1	0	.000
[3]Mitchell	.292	1	0	0	0	0	0	0	0	1	0	0	0	0	.000
Team Totals		27	0	0	0	0	0	0	0	7	0	24	10	0	

[1]Season's batting average.
[2]Series batting average.
[3]Struck out for Maglie in 9th.

YANKEES

	[1]B AV	AB	R	H	2B	3B	HR	TB	BB	SO	RBI	PO	A	E	[2]B AV
Bauer, RF	.241	4	0	1	0	0	0	1	0	1	1	4	0	0	.273
Collins, 1B	.225	4	0	1	0	0	0	1	0	2	0	7	0	0	.133
Mantle, CF	.353	3	1	1	0	0	1	4	0	0	1	4	0	0	.294
Berra, C	.298	3	0	0	0	0	0	0	0	0	0	7	0	0	.273
Slaughter, LF ...	.281	2	0	0	0	0	0	0	1	0	0	1	0	0	.412
Martin, 2B	.264	3	0	1	0	0	0	1	0	1	0	3	4	0	.273
McDougald, ss	.311	2	0	0	0	0	0	0	1	0	0	0	2	0	.154
Carey, 3B	.236	3	1	1	0	0	0	1	0	0	0	1	1	0	.250
Larsen, P	11-5	2	0	0	0	0	0	0	0	1	0	0	1	0	.333
Team Totals		26	2	5	0	0	1	8	2	5	2	27	8	0	

[1]Season's batting average.
[2]Series batting average.

Dodgers	0	0	0		0	0	0		0 0 0—0
Yankees	0	0	0		1	0	1		0 0 0—2

Earned runs—All. Home run—Mantle. Sacrifice—Larsen. Double plays—Dodgers 2 (Reese-Hodges; Hodges-Campanella-Robinson). Left on bases—Dodgers 0, Yankees 3. Bases on balls—off Maglie 2 (Slaughter, McDougald). Struck out—by Larsen 7 (Gilliam, Reese, Hodges, Campanella, Snider, Maglie, Mitchell), Maglie 5 (Collins 2, Martin, Larsen, Bauer). Winning pitcher—Larsen. Losing pitcher—Maglie. Time—2:04. Umpires—Pinelli (NL), Soar (AL), Boggess (NL), Napp (AL), Gorman (NL), Runge (AL). Attendance—64,519.

The first pitch to the left-swinger was a fast one which was on the outside, high. Then Don got a low curve over for a strike. Then another fast ball which Mitchell swung at and missed.

Now, for the first time, Larsen was visibly affected. There he stood, one strike away from the most amazing feat in Series history. Don stepped off the mound, turned around to look at the outfielders and took off his hat. Then he threw another curve that Mitch fouled.

Casey Stengel then moved two of the outfielders, Mantle and Bauer, a few feet to the left. Mitchell, a slap hitter, seldom pulls the ball to right. Besides, Berra was going to call for a fast ball.

Don, who pitches without a windup, then made his next throw, a fast ball letter-high and as Pinelli's right hand went up, the whole baseball world exploded.

The fans at radio and TV sets all over the nation knew it was a perfect game all the way. Announcers Vince Scully and Mel Allen didn't try to disguise it in that silly superstition that to talk about it would jinx the pitcher.

So, an incredible character who laughs at training rules, reads comic books, and describes himself as "the nightrider," has become the classic pitcher in all baseball legend. His has been a fantastic season.

He started it with an escapade in St. Petersburg during spring training, when he drove his car into an electric light pole, after falling asleep at the wheel at five o'clock in the morning. Instead of fining him, Stengel used psychology and named Don as opening day pitcher. He won, beating Washington.

Then Don went bad and had to be removed from the starting rotation. He showed some flashes as a reliever and was reinstated as a starter in the last two months of the season. Over the last month, Larsen was the Yankee's best pitcher, with two four-hitters and a three-hitter, as well as a string of four victories to the finish.

He started the second game of the Series Friday at Ebbets Field and helped blow the 6–0 lead in the second inning. So, in his up-and-down way of life, he came back with the first perfect Series game.

40

Review of *The Fireside Book of Baseball* (1956)

SOURCE: *Wall Street Journal*, October 22, 1956

Baseball fans who are believers in fate will no doubt find their belief strengthened upon learning that on the same day baseball's most historic pitching performance was reported, the New York Times *published the first review of Charles Einstein's anthology* The Fireside Book of Baseball *(New York: Simon and Schuster, 1956). Two weeks later, the* Wall Street Journal *published its own rave review, which appears below.*

Einstein, a veteran baseball writer on the Giants beat, edited what has become one of the most beloved baseball books ever published—a collection of reportage, fiction, car-

toons, historical sketches, and other examples of baseball writing. Einstein acted quickly to improve the book by adding a play-by-play account of Larsen's masterpiece to his own after the first twenty thousand copies had been printed. He published three subsequent Fireside *volumes in the next thirty years. Despite their undisputed status as books essential to any baseball library, none of the volumes currently is in print.*

READING FOR PLEASURE

Grand Slam

"The Fireside Book of Baseball," edited by Charles Einstein, is one more reminder that some of the most flavorsome writing of our times appears on the sports pages. It is also a reminder that the sports sections develop more and better magazine writers than other departments in the paper.

Maybe this should be taken as a commentary on modern journalism as it is practiced on many papers. Or maybe it merely constitutes an admission that sports events are too trivial to be bound by ordinary standards of discretion, charity and courtesy. Whatever the reason, we may be thankful that Mr. Einstein was interested in collecting baseball yarns, not an anthology of diplomatic doings which would exhibit John Foster Dulles, say, in a perpetual scoreless tie.

What Mr. Einstein set out to do was to "spread-eagle the sport from Frank Merriwell to the kitchen sink." He has accomplished his task so well that both Mr. Merriwell and the sink got pushed out of the book on grounds of comparative dullness. What remains is enough to burst the seams of the biggest pantry at the Waldorf. There are sports writers going all the way back to Henry Chadwick, who invented the box score, and Charlie Dryden, who pioneered the art of applying the personal touch to spot reporting of games. There are pieces by baseball players, sometimes heavily ghosted, sometimes not. There are profiles and nonsense columns, satire and philosophy, poems and a bit on the etymology of the Charley horse. Finally, there is fiction—and what fiction it is.

Let's begin with the fiction. It is not just that Mr. Einstein is sufficiently well-read to have spotted and lifted the tale of the fabled Nebraska Crane from Thomas Wolfe's "You Can't Go Home Again." It is not just that he has uncovered an old baseball story by Zane Grey, the writer of westerns, about three red-headed outfielders. (Incidentally, one of Zane Grey's better novels is something called "The Shortstop.") And it is not just that he has picked an adolescent's dream about baseball from the works of James T. Farrell.

No, the real measure of Mr. Einstein's ability as an anthologist is the inclusion of a hitherto unpublished yarn by Paul Fisher called "The Spitter." Mr. Fisher, an executive of the United Aircraft Corporation, wrote this for the private amusement of Charles Lindbergh, General Hoyt Vandenberg and other friends, and somehow Mr. Einstein got hold of it. It's probably the funniest tall tale to achieve print since Mark Twain joined his Jumping Frog on the other side of the Styx, assuming that's where they both went.

The fiction also includes James Thurber's classic about the manager who hired a midget to pinch hit for his team at a crucial moment when the bases were full. Since this bit of fiction eventually became true when Bill Veeck of the St. Louis Browns sent a midget to bat against the Detroit Tigers on August 19, 1951, it will serve as a bridge to the more factual pieces in the anthology. The facts, as brought out by Mr. Einstein, are very seldom prosaic, for the world of baseball, it seems, is heavily populated by mugs at one extreme of the human spectrum and by philosophers at the other.

41

Don Newcombe Wins the First Cy Young Award (1956)

SOURCE: *New York Herald Tribune,* November 29, 1956

On July 6, 1956, Commissioner Ford Frick announced that the Baseball Writers Association of America (BWAA) would reward the best pitcher in the major leagues with the Cy Young Award. Only one Cy Young Award per year was presented until 1967. Although Frick mentioned that a primary reason for the creation of the new award was to ensure that pitchers received acclaim for outstanding performances, over 20 percent of the MVPs selected since 1931 (when the BWAA took over the awards) had been pitchers. That percentage increased in 1956, when Newcombe was presented with the National League MVP prior to winning the Cy Young Award.

BIG NEWK WINS AWARD AS MAJORS' TOP PITCHER
By Tommy Holmes

Tributes are hurled fast and furiously at the dead [*sic*] of large Donald Newcombe, who, when last seen on the co-axial cable, was trudging disconsolately toward the Dodger dugout, flattened in the deciding game of the World Series by the triumphant Yankees.

Since that dark day for Flatbush, big Newk's only pitching efforts have consisted of two starts in Hawaii and Japan and he was knocked out of the box in both of those faraway lands.

Still, he continues to cash in on the twenty-seven victories during the season which formed such a large chunk of the Brooklyn team's pennant-winning total.

Last week, he was elected most valuable National League player for 1956. Yesterday, he was elected the winner of the first Cy Young Memorial Award as the outstanding major league pitcher of the year.

This surely can come as no surprise. If he was the pitching stickout of the National League, he was the top pitcher of all baseball, for no hurler in the American League approximated his season record.

Newcombe received ten votes from a special committee of sixteen baseball writers, representing eight from each major league. As in the case of the most valuable player balloting, Don's tally was most closely approached by the score of his Dodger teammate, thirty-nine-year-old Sal Maglie.

Four of the selectors preferred Maglie, whose pitching after the Dodgers acquired him from Cleveland in May, gave the Brooklyn team a tremendous lift. The other two votes went to Warren Spahn, of the Braves, and Whitey Ford, of the Yankees.

Since Newcombe has an appointment with Buzy [*sic*] Bavasi at the Dodger offices today, Don's second distinction might be regarded as extra ammunition in a drive for more material rewards in his 1957 contract.

Actually, the probability is strong that Don and the Dodger vice-president in charge of salaries have already reached or almost reached an understanding.

"He will be paid on the basis of his twenty-seven victories," said Bavasi last week.

Chances are that Newk will get a $5,000 raise to the $30,000 he bargained for but did not get last winter.

42

DeWitt Named Administrator of "Save the Minors" Fund (1956)

SOURCE: *Sporting News,* December 12, 1956

Between the 1952 and 1956 seasons the number of minor leagues dropped from forty-three to twenty-seven, resulting in the dissolution of more than one hundred clubs. Alarmed by this sudden decline, Commissioner Ford Frick announced on August 2 the establishment of the "Save the Minors" committee. The stated purpose of the committee was to use the $500,000 fund it controlled to stabilize the situation. Bill DeWitt, the assistant general manager of the Yankees, was named to head the committee on December 3.

The committee did not succeed in saving the minors. It survived until 1959, when it was replaced by the Player Development and Promotion Program, which had $1 million at its disposal. By this time the minors were down to twenty-one leagues. The major leagues soon realized that the problem was intractable and, on May 18, 1962, eliminated the lowest three minor league classes (to be replaced by the "A" classification), assuring minimum payments to clubs who completed each season. The decline ended, but the minors did not claim to have been saved.

DEWITT SEES MINORS' FUND JOB AS "CHALLENGE"

Named as Administrator of $500,000 Aid Project
Leaves Post as Yank Official for New Assignment;
Bill to be "On Call" From St. Louis Headquarters

By Lowell Reidenbaugh

JACKSONVILLE, Fla.—"Let's get rid of all this negative thinking in baseball. Let's talk about what's right with this game and quit harping on what's wrong."

With those words of affirmative approach, Bill DeWitt, one of the game's top executives, resigned from his post as assistant general manager of the Yankees and took a new and "challenging" job as administrator of the $500,000 fund to stabilize minor league baseball.

"They have called this a 'Save the Minors' Fund,' said DeWitt. "It isn't a question of saving minor league ball, it is a question of stabilizing it and helping the fellows who really deserve help."

DeWitt, who will take over his new duties immediately, will make his headquarters in St. Louis, a city with a rich baseball background. . . .

Though he was reported to be receiving in the neighborhood of $50,000 annually, Bill took the new job as baseball co-ordinator at an annual stipend of $30,000 because of the terrific opportunities it will present.

DeWitt said the first order of business in the new operation was one of organization.

LIKES REGION PROPOSAL

He said that the program suggested by George Trautman, president of the National Association, to divide the nation into several regions for promotional operations sounded very interesting and he planned to confer with Trautman regarding his ideas.

"It will be my job after investigation to determine just who needs more help from the fund," DeWitt said. "More important than that, though, is to determine who deserves help. If the fellows involved aren't doing a conscientious job for baseball, and if they aren't trying to get people into the parks, then they won't get a very sympathetic audience with us."

DeWitt said he realized "it is a project that calls for a little ice water in your veins."

"You can't help a fellow just because he happens to be a friend or because you like him," he declared.

Another early project for the stabilizing committee will be to study the operations of successful clubs and leagues throughout the nation, DeWitt revealed.

"Year after year, there are fellows who operate profitably and you never hear them howling the blues or complaining about poor attendance," DeWitt observed. "And they are not all in the higher classification leagues, either." ...

LITTLE ADVANCE NOTICE

DeWitt said he was called into a meeting on Monday afternoon, December 3, and after a thorough discussion of what the job entailed, decided to accept.

The announcement of DeWitt's appointment was made shortly afterward jointly by George Weiss, Yankee general manager, and John Quinn, Braves' general manager, who also is head of the minors' stabilization fund.

"This is a very important job in baseball," Weiss said. "We are very sorry to lose Bill DeWitt from our organization, but we never have prevented anyone with our club from improving his position in baseball. We send Bill our very best wishes for a highly successful career as baseball co-ordinator."

DeWitt said he was "highly honored to be the man to be selected" and added:

"I am looking forward to the challenge of this newly created position in baseball."

The other members of the stabilization committee are Joe L. Brown of the Pirates, Weiss, Walter [Spike] Briggs of the Tigers, Grayle Howlett of Tulsa [Texas] and Claude Enberg, president of the Pioneer League.

43

O'Malley Buys Los Angeles Minor League Team and Ballpark (1957)

SOURCE: *Los Angeles Herald Express*, February 21, 1957

For nearly two years, Dodger fans had seen signs that their beloved Bums might be considering the unthinkable—moving out of Brooklyn. In August 1955, Dodgers owner Walter O'Malley announced that his club would play seven games in Jersey City the following season. At the conclusion of the 1956 season he stunned the borough by revealing that he had sold Ebbets Field to developer Marvin Kratter, who in turn would lease the park to the Dodgers. Throughout this period, starting in 1953, O'Malley repeatedly stated his desire to construct a new stadium in Brooklyn. However, he was unable to strike a deal with either New York City officials (especially parks commissioner Robert Moses) or the Brooklyn Sports Center Authority to obtain suitable land in Brooklyn.

Knowing this, Brooklyn fans had good reason to panic when they learned that O'Malley had gained title to the minor league park of the Los Angeles Angels, Wrigley Field, in a trade with Cubs owner Philip Wrigley. O'Malley denied in a February 22 New York Times article that the Dodgers were to be moved, but Dodger fans remained suspicious.

DODGERS BUY ANGELS IN MOVE TOWARD L.A.

Wrigley Field Is Sold in Big Deal

By John B. Old

The Brooklyn Dodgers today officially took their first step towards Los Angeles.

Purchase of the Los Angeles baseball club, the Coast League franchise right and Wrigley Field was announced this morning by Angel President Clarence "Pants" Rowland, for an undisclosed amount.

Rowland said 32 players currently on the Angel roster would remain with the Angels as farmhands of the Dodgers and that Manager Gene Handley would be retained.

As part of the deal the Chicago Cubs, former owners of the Angels, will take over the Fort Worth club of the Texas League, formerly operated by the Dodgers.

CUBS GET PORTLAND

Moreover the Cubs will assume the working agreement with Portland now held by Brooklyn.

While Rowland declined to comment on the possibility of Brooklyn moving to Los Angeles, it is known that the Dodgers' lease on Ebbets Field in Brooklyn expires at the close of the 1959 season.

However, as exclusively revealed by this reporter from New York last week, Dodger President Walter O'Malley served a six-month ultimatum on Manhattan officials who are proposing a new Brooklyn park.

O'Malley was in Los Angeles about a month ago with his board of directors, inspecting Wrigley Field and Chavez Ravine, proposed site of a new major league baseball park to be financed without cost to the taxpayers by the city and county.

Under baseball league regulations, purchase of Wrigley Field by the Dodgers is the first essential step toward transferring the major league club to a minor league territory.

WRIGLEY FIELD TOPS

Wrigley Field, currently valued at $1,500,000, was built in 1925.

It is regarded as the finest baseball park in the minor leagues.

Should the proposed Chavez Ravine Park plans fall through, the Dodgers could enlarge Wrigley Field if and when they come to Los Angeles.

Meanwhile, the Angels, as far as the 1957 season is concerned, will have first call on Brooklyn surplus players.

Likewise, the Portland Beavers will have first pick of surplus Chicago Cubs players.

While O'Malley was not immediately available, it is assumed Rowland will continue as head of the Angels until such time as the Dodgers send their own officials west.

President P. K. Wrigley of the Cubs, through Rowland expressed regret over the sale of the Angels.

Those close to the situation, however, believe Wrigley sold the club in an effort to speed the coming of major league baseball to Los Angeles.

44

Supreme Court Decision Casts Doubt on Baseball Antitrust Exemption (1957)

SOURCE: *Washington Evening Star,* February 26, 1957

Just four years after the Supreme Court affirmed baseball's historic exemption to anti-trust laws, it ruled that professional football—like all other businesses in the United States—was subject to them. Former pro football player William Radovich filed suit in 1949 after the National Football League had blackballed him for jumping to a rival league, claiming that he had been illegally denied employment opportunities. In its 6–3 decision the Court sent the case back to the appellate court, which had ruled against Radovich. Justice Tom C. Clark, who wrote the majority opinion, noted that the only reason for the baseball exemption was the 1922 Federal Baseball decision in which baseball received its exemption. Clark noted that without this precedent "we would have no doubts" about holding baseball to the same standard as football.

As a result of the confusion surrounding the apparent contradiction regarding the status of baseball versus football and other sports, Congress, led again by Representative Emanuel Celler, held additional hearings during the summer of 1957. These proceedings generated more than three thousand pages of testimony, attached documents, and the text of seven proposed amendments to antitrust legislation. Not surprisingly, baseball's exemption survived.

SURPRISE, CONFUSION FOLLOW FOOTBALL ANTI-TRUST RULING

Court's Decision Clashes With Its Baseball Stand

By George Huber

Reactions to yesterday's Supreme Court decision that holds professional football subject to anti-trust laws range from surprise to confusion.

One of the first questions raised was how much longer baseball is likely to remain immune.

It is likely that among other results of the decision, Congress will consider bills designed to bring baseball under the anti-trust laws. It's also likely that friends of pro football will introduce measures exempting it from anti-trust legislation.

The court itself acknowledged an apparent contradiction between its previous baseball decision and the one yesterday involving football. It suggested that the way to resolve any inconsistencies was by legislation, not by judicial decisions.

There were many similarities between the two cases that resulted in two different decisions.

6–3 DIVISION

The Court was split 6–3 on yesterday's decision on an appeal of William Radovich, a onetime University of Southern California player who played with Detroit of the National Football League. He later jumped to the Los Angeles Dons of the now defunct All America Conference. In a still later attempt to return to pro football, he found no one would hire him.

Radovich had sued the league and its clubs for $105,000 damages. Lower courts, basing their decisions on the baseball case, had held he had no basis for a suit under the antitrust laws.

The Supreme Court last considered baseball in 1953. It referred then to a decision in 1922 in which baseball was termed a sport and not a business and thus outside the scope of anti-trust laws, and noted that Congress had not acted on the subject in the years following 1922.

Justice Clark in writing the majority opinion delivered yesterday said, "were we considering the question of baseball for the first time upon a clean slate we would have no doubts."

Noting that the baseball decision has been cited in anti-trust cases involving other businesses, he added: "We now specifically limit the rule there established to . . . the business of organized professional baseball."

Yesterday's decision did not give Radovich the $105,000 he asked for. It merely sent his case back to a lower court, saying, "We think that Radovich is entitled to an opportunity to prove his charges.

"Of course, we express no opinion as to whether or not respondents have, in fact, violated the antitrust laws, leaving that determination to the trial court after all the facts are in," the decision added.

Justice Clark was joined in the majority opinion by Chief Justice Warren and Justices Black, Reed, Douglas and Burton.

Dissenting were Justices Harlan, Brennan and Frankfurter. The gist of their stands was that they could see no difference between baseball and football in respect to antitrust laws.

Justice Clark's comment said that the majority decision may sound "unrealistic, inconsistent or illogical," in view of the previous baseball decision. He added that "the orderly way to eliminate error or discrimination, if any there be, is by legislation and not by court decision."

CONFLICTING REACTION

There were conflicting reactions from sports, legal and legislative personalities regarding the decision.

Baseball Commissioner Ford Frick said he had no comment "because we were not involved."

On Capitol Hill, Representative Celler, Democrat of New York, chairman of the House Judiciary Committee, was surprised at the decision and said he would move for quick action on a bill now before his committee to bring baseball under the anti-trust laws.

Although no other member of Congress has yet come forward on behalf of baseball, that sport does have many friends in Congress, and such a bill probably would face tough going. There is also a chance that a bill exempting pro football from anti-trust laws will be introduced.

Boxing and basketball also could be involved again. Lower court decisions, which have not yet reached the Supreme Court, have held both subject to antitrust laws.

45

Montgomery, Alabama, Institutes Racial Segregation in Sport (1957)

SOURCE: *Race Relations Law Reporter* 2 (June 1957): 714

In January 1954 the Birmingham City Commission, hoping to persuade major league clubs to play preseason exhibition games in the city, overturned the ban on interracial sport. A number of exhibition games, including some in which African American players participated, were staged without controversy. However, after the Supreme Court ruled in Brown v. Board of Education *in mid-May 1954, the outraged citizenry responded by passing a resolution that mandated segregation in athletic competition. The resolution passed by nearly a three-to-one margin.*

Nearly three years later, officials in Montgomery joined a number of other southern cities in passing nearly identical laws. Montgomery Ordinance 15-57 was approved on March 19, 1957.

AN ORDINANCE NO. 15-57

Be it ordained by the Commissioners of the City of Montgomery, as follows

(a) It shall be unlawful for white and colored persons to play together or, in company with each other, in the City of Montgomery and within its police jurisdiction, in any game of cards, dice, dominoes, checkers, pool, billiards, softball, basketball, baseball, football, golf, track, and at swimming pools, beaches, lakes or ponds or any other game or games or athletic contest or contests, either indoors or outdoors.

(b) Any person, who, being the owner, proprietor, or keeper or superintendent of any tavern, inn, restaurant, park or other public house or public place, or the clerk, servant or employee of such owner, proprietor, keeper or superintendent, knowingly permits white persons and colored persons to play together or in company with each other in the City of Montgomery and within its police jurisdiction any game of cards, dice, dominoes, checkers, pool, billiards, softball, basketball, baseball, football, golf, track, and at swimming pools, beaches, lakes or ponds, or any other game or games or athletic contest or contests, in his house, or on his premises, or in a house or on premises under his charge, supervision or control, shall be guilty of a misdemeanor against the City of Montgomery.

(c) The words "colored person," as used herein, shall have the same meaning as "person of color" as defined in Section 2 of Title 1 of the 1940 Code of Alabama.

(d) Any person, firm or corporation, violating any of the provisions of this ordinance shall be guilty of a misdemeanor against the City of Montgomery.

(e) The provisions of this ordinance are severable and should any sentence, paragraph, section, or clause of this ordinance be declared unconstitutional by any Court of competent jurisdiction, then such action by said Court shall not affect the other provisions of this ordinance which are otherwise constitutional.

(f) This ordinance shall take effect as provided by law after passage, approval and publication.

Adopted March 19, 1957
Silas D. Cater, City Clerk

Approved March 19, 1957

W. A. Gayle
Frank W. Parks
Clyde C. Sellers
    Commissioners

46

Herb Score Seriously Injured by Line Drive (1957)

SOURCE: *Cleveland Plain Dealer*, May 8, 1957

On May 7, Herb Score joined the ranks of Mickey Cochrane, Dizzy Dean, Joe Medwick, and Pete Reiser—star players whose careers were severely curtailed by on-field injuries. Hailed as one of the best young pitchers to emerge in many years, Score was hit in the right eye by a Gil McDougald line drive and was never the same afterward. In his first two seasons Score led the majors in strikeouts each year and won thirty-six games, twenty in his second year. Although he remained in the majors until 1962, Score won only nineteen games during the rest of his career—not because of the aftereffects of the eye injury but because of an arm injury suffered shortly after his return in 1958. However, he enjoyed a lengthy career as an Indians broadcaster after his retirement.

The writer of the following column, Gordon Cobbledick, was the longtime sports editor of the Plain Dealer. The article reflects his experience and deep knowledge of baseball.

PLAIN DEALING

Score's Accident Jeopardizes Career of Baseball's Most Talented Youngster

By Gordon Cobbledick

This was only last Wednesday in the stadium press box, and Tris Speaker sat as enthralled as any teen-age hero worshipper while the lightning from Herb Score's left arm flashed and crackled in the bewildered faces of the Washington Senators.

"If nothing happens to him," said the old Gray Eagle, "this kid has got to be the greatest."

Last night something happened, and a shocked and sickened audience forgot the importance of the Cleveland Indians' first game of the season with the New York Yankees as the most talented young pitcher of our generation was carried off the field on a stretcher.

It may be days before the full extent of his injury will be known. It may be weeks or months before it can be told whether Herb Score will pitch again.

A vicious line drive from the bat of Gil McDougald, the second Yankee at bat in the first inning, struck him flush in the right eye, and as he fell blood gushed from his nose and mouth.

WERTZ STOPS SHORT OF FALLEN MATE

The ball caromed to Al Smith at third base, and the throw to Vic Wertz retired McDougald. As he made the catch Wertz dashed toward the pitcher's box, where Score lay inert, but when he came within 10 feet of the stricken boy he stopped abruptly and turned away, his shoulders sagging. The stunned and silent crowd knew then that this was bad.

One remembered then a day at the Indians' training camp in Fort Myers, Fla., in 1940 when Paul O'Dea, a promising young outfielder, carelessly poked his head from behind the batting cage and a foul from a teammate's bat caught him flush in the eye, even as McDougald's rifle shot caught Score last night.

O'Dea's eye was destroyed and a young career was blighted.

One remembered, too, a night in Philadelphia in 1950, when a blast from big

Ted Kluszewski's bat hit Bubba Church, a young pitcher for the Phillies, on the cheek bone just below the eye. Church never pitched effectively again.

Score didn't lose consciousness. In the club house he sat on the rubbing table, accepting the ministrations of Dr. Don Kelley while waiting for the ambulance to take him to Lakeside Hospital. Singly and in pairs the Indians came in, grave faced, from the dugout and shook their heads sadly and went back to the night's business.

TELLS ROCKY TO GET SOME HITS

Rocky Colavito, Score's roommate at Indianapolis and here with the Indians, was near tears as he peeked into the trainer's room.

"What are you doing in here?" Score demanded. "Get out there and get me a couple of hits."

The tension was lessened and a reporter cracked, "You look as if you'd just gone 10 fast rounds, Herbie."

"Yeah," the fallen warrior agreed. "Now I know how Fullmer felt."*

The ambulance backed up to the clubhouse door and took him away, and Mike Garcia said, "Don't count him out. He's got guts."

"He's got guts and he's got brains," Speaker added, "and if he comes out of this he still has to be what I said he'd be. The greatest."

And now the crowd had found its voice again. They were closing the ambulance doors when a roar went up and Score's good eye opened wider. This was his ball game and this was his team, and the sound meant that the Indians had done something good. You know he was rooting when the long car rolled away.

47

Frick Overturns All-Star Game Vote (1957)

SOURCE: *Cincinnati Enquirer*, June 29, 1957

Less than two weeks before the July 9 All-Star Game in St. Louis, Commissioner Ford Frick stepped in and invalidated a large bloc of votes submitted by Cincinnati fans. If he had allowed the votes to stand, every National League starter—save the pitcher, chosen by the manager, and Stan Musial—would have been a Reds player. Frick permitted five Reds to start the game and unilaterally installed Willie Mays and Hank Aaron in the lineup. The following season the All-Star Game vote was removed entirely from the fans, not to be returned until 1970, when the game was held in Cincinnati.

*Gene Fullmer was a boxer who lost the middleweight title in a fifth-round knockout to Sugar Ray Robinson on May 1—Ed.

CHANGE IS MADE IN ALL-STAR CAST

Frick Steps In, Names Three Starters, To Oust Reds

By Bill Ford

Enquirer Sports Reporter

Baseball Commissioner Ford Frick, reversing an agreement of 24 years standing, yesterday stepped into the mushrooming All-Star Game voting controversy and arbitrarily named three players to the National League team.

Frick, in an unprecedented move, said he had selected Stan Musial of the St. Louis Cardinals, first base; Hank Aaron of the Milwaukee Braves, right field, and Willie Mays of the New York Giants, centerfield, after it appeared that a late avalanche of votes by Cincinnati fans would place eight Redlegs in the starting lineup.

Frick "benched" George Crowe in favor of Musial, Wally Post for Aaron and [Gus] Bell for Mays. The commissioner agreed that five other Cincinnati players were likely winners at the respective positions, because they have been "either leading or in contention with the leader" in the nationwide balloting.

This means that Ed Bailey will be the catcher; Johnny Temple at second base; Roy McMillan at shortstop, Don Hoak at third base and Frank Robinson in left field.

Probability that eight Reds had won enough support of the fans to merit starting positions on the National League team for the midseason game against American League All-Stars July 9 at St. Louis became a fact when the Cincinnati agent of the commissioner forwarded more than a half million votes.

Simply, Frick ignored the voice of the fans by removing three Reds from probable selections. Because pitchers and other squad members are selected by the manager of the All-Star team, Crowe, Post and Bell still could be chosen.

Reds' General Manager Gabe Paul and Manager Birdie Tebbets, gratified by fan support for the eight players, urged Frick to reward Post, Bell and Crowe in some way.

"Whatever the commissioner and the league presidents decide is all right with me, and I am sure is all right with my players," Tebbets said. "I think, however, in all fairness to these boys, that they be named honorary members of the All-Star team."

Paul said, "Since the commissioner has seen fit to disregard the vote of the fans in three instances, it is my opinion the least that should be done for Wally, Gus and George is to include them on the All-Star squad."

Frick said he took the action in concurrence with Warren Giles, president of the National League, and Will Harridge, president of the American League, explaining that "an over-balance of Cincinnati ballots has resulted in selection of a team which would not be typical of the league and which would not meet with approval of fans of the country over who are interested in and support the All-Star Game."

It was pointed out that the more than half a million votes of Cincinnati fans were greater than the total cast by all other sections of the nation.

Thus, the enormity of Cincinnati area voting for the second year in a row has moved baseball officials to seek a change in the method of selection to both leagues' All-Star teams.

A suggestion from some quarters to remove the voting power from fans and give it to the eight managers in each league was made last year when five Red regulars were selected to start (Bailey, Temple, McMillan, Robinson and Bell) and three others, Ted Kluszewski, Joe Nuxhall and Brooks Lawrence, were named by Manager Walter Alston of Brooklyn, who again will guide the senior circuit club in the exhibition game.

Frick at that time defended the method of selection, declaring that "everybody had a chance to vote, so there should be no squawks. Nobody is on the National League team who doesn't belong on it. Besides, Cincinnati has a good team."

At yesterday's conference Frick indicated a change might be in order. He said, however, he "was not prepared" to say what measures would be taken about a future system of All-Star voting that would eliminate a monopoly by one team.

Currently regulations governing election to the star team legally permit stuffing of the ballot box, because any fan may vote as many times as he or she desires, simply by writing in names for the eight eligible positions and signing it.

It would appear, however, this method is on the way out. Exactly what system would be adopted has not been determined, since at the moment the league presidents are not in agreement.

Giles does not favor selection of the team by the managers, thus curtailing fan interest and enthusiasm. American League officials, led by Harridge, want a sensible, unbiased approach to naming the team and feel that the managers are the only qualified electors.

48

Feller Defuses Controversy over Congressional Testimony (1957)

SOURCE: House Antitrust Subcommittee, *Organized Professional Team Sports*, 85th Cong., 1st sess., 1957, 2489–90.

On June 25, Bob Feller, who, even though retired, was still head of the Major League Baseball Players' Association, testified at length before Representative Emanuel Celler's subcommittee. During his testimony (which appears on pages 1309–31), Feller remarked that "the owners basically do regard the players as pawns." Even after Celler (who, according to Feller, had expressed that opinion earlier) gave Feller an opportunity to retract his statement, Feller declined.

*In order to appear before Congress, Feller interrupted a nationwide tour of boys'
clubs sponsored by Motorola. The day following his testimony, Feller was informed by
Bill Heymans, general manager of the Los Angeles Angels, that his scheduled appearance
before a July 9 game at Wrigley Field was canceled. At least one congressman, spurred by
an article by* Los Angeles Examiner *reporter Melvin Durslag (reprinted on page 2490),
suggested publicly that baseball—in particular new Angels owner Walter O'Malley—was
punishing Feller for his audacity.*

*The controversy, defused by Feller in the following letter, was quickly forgotten, but it
is significant because it reveals the antipathy between owners and the young union. Even
though the* MLBPA *had little power at this time, the association symbolized insolence to
the owners and unity to the players. The existence of the union was evidence that
baseball was splitting into two factions.*

Cleveland, Ohio, July 16, 1957.

CONGRESSMAN EMANUEL CELLER, Chairman of Antitrust Committee, Old
House Office Building, Washington DC

DEAR CONGRESSMAN CELLER: In reply to your counsel's request for a chronology of circumstances which came to my attention surrounding the cancellation
of my scheduled appearance at Wrigley Field in Los Angeles on the evening of
July 9, the following is my outline of the events.

Arrangements for this particular appearance, as part of a 5-day tour of
western cities sponsored by Motorola, were handled by Motorola's Los Angeles
distributors with guidance from responsible people in the advertising and
public-relations departments at the Chicago headquarters. In this case, Hixson & Jorgesen, Inc., advertising agency was representing Kierulff & Co., the
Motorola distributor, in making the arrangements. Richard McFarland, who is
the account executive for the Kierulff account, made the contacts and set up the
schedule for my appearance.

It was mutually agreed during the week of June 17 that I was to conduct my
baseball clinic or a similar type of instruction program prior to the regularly
scheduled Los Angeles Angels night game on Tuesday, July 9. It was to be called
Bob Feller Night. Furthermore, I understood that a reduced ticket price for the
game that night was planned for the Little League players to encourage their
attendance.

On Thursday, June 25, the day of my testimony before the House subcommittee, the final arrangements were concluded between Mr. McFarland and Mr.
George Goodale, the public-relations director of the Angels.

The following day at 11 A.M., Mr. McFarland received a telephone call from
Mr. Goodale canceling Bob Feller Night. The reason was that his management
had advised him that a Jaycee Youth Night coming up and an impending
Emmet Kelly appearance combined into adequate children's activities for the
immediate future.

When I learned of the cancellation on July 2, I contacted Paul Zimmerman in the sports department of the Los Angeles *Times*. Mr. Zimmerman had heard of the incident and had talked with Mr. Goodale who confirmed the cancellation for the above-mentioned reasons.

In the meantime, Hixson and Jorgesen had made substitute arrangements for me to visit six boys' clubs in the Los Angeles area.

The cancellation again came to my attention in Los Angeles on July 7 when I saw the enclosed two conflicting articles that appeared in the Los Angeles newspapers. I also learned at that time that Mr. Goodale had contacted Mr. McFarland on July 5 to see if he would like to reschedule Bob Feller Night for the latter part of August or early in September.

At a meeting on July 8, several reporters mentioned the Los Angeles cancellation.

I have no personal feelings about the matter one way or another except that the extremely poor timing of the cancellation gave a great many people the impression that there was a connection with my testimony. As far as I'm concerned, if the Los Angeles Angels' management wanted to change their minds about having Bob Feller Night, for whatever reason, it was their option to do so.

On Wednesday, July 10, I was in Seattle, Wash., to conduct a baseball clinic which, this time, was cosponsored by the Motorola distributor and the *Press Intelligencer*. Reporters asked about the Los Angeles clinic cancellation.

Later, in Seattle, I learned that Representative Hillings had suggested that the subcommittee investigate the circumstances surrounding the cancellation. Meantime, a Motorola spokesman, reading conflicting reports, told a United Press reporter that the company had no facts, but had an "impression" there had been a connection between the cancellation and the testimony. Still later, an Associated Press story reported Representative Celler as having said that the situation was "not important enough" to require investigation.

On July 15, Mr. O'Malley, of the Brooklyn Dodger organization which owns the Los Angeles club, telephoned Mr. Galvin, president of Motorola, Inc. He assured Mr. Galvin that it was, in fact, a conflict of scheduled events which occasioned the cancellation. Mr. Galvin expressed complete satisfaction with the reassurance, indicating that his firm had no convictions concerning any views expressed in the subcommittee hearings, but was glad to know that personal views did not enter into the availability of baseball club facilities for youth clinics.

Perhaps the incident has been magnified out of proportion. However, as far as I and my associates at Motorola are concerned, it is closed.

Very truly yours,

BOB FELLER.

49

Giants Agree to Move to San Francisco (1957)

SOURCE: *New York Herald Tribune*, August 20, 1957

At last the horrible rumors were confirmed: the New York Giants board of directors voted eight to one to transfer the storied franchise to San Francisco for the 1958 season. San Francisco's offer included a 45,000-seat stadium, all concession income, and parking for up to 12,000 cars—features which, the club hoped, would lead to larger crowds and increased revenues. Walter O'Malley, whose Dodgers would not officially announce their move to Los Angeles until October 8, refused to comment on the Giants' move.

The only Giants director to dissent was M. Donald Grant, who within a few years would become part of the ownership of the New York Mets.

GIANTS ACCEPT SAN FRANCISCO OFFER, MOVE IN 1958 AFTER 74 YEARS HERE

Directors 8 to 1; Stoneham Says Crowds Fell Off
By Sid Gray

The New York Giants decided yesterday to become the San Francisco Giants—or maybe the Seals—next year.

The franchise switch, which will end the club's seventy-four-year tenure in New York and start major league ball rolling on the Coast, was voted, 8 to 1, by the Giants board of directors. It is contingent on the fulfillment of conditions set forth by Mayor George Christopher, of San Francisco, in a letter sent Aug. 6 to Horace C. Stoneham, Giant president. Therein the mayor stated that when the Giants' board of directors accepted his terms, he immediately would confer with the heads of city departments to draft official documents in accordance with the city's charter and general laws.

SMALL CROWDS BLAMED

"Lack of attendance was the real reason for moving," Mr. Stoneham said. "Baseball is a sport, but you need money to operate."

The San Francisco offer included (1) an $8,000,000 Municipal Stadium, under a thirty-five-year lease, with a 40,000–45,000 seating capacity, so constructed as to permit expansion, (2) all income from concessions will go to the Giants, (3) a parking area for 10,000–12,000 cars, with the city receiving that revenue, (4) stadium rental will be 5 per cent of the gross receipts after deducting taxes, visiting club's share and league's share.

Also, (5) no rent for World Series, all-star or charity games, (6) the Giants will guarantee to pay $125,000 rental a year against the 5 per cent rental, (7) if the new stadium won't be ready by '58, the city will contract to lease the present Seal stadium—seating 22,500—from owner Paul Fagan. The Giants, in turn, will lease it from the city under the same stipulations as for the new field.

Charles Harney, contractor, says he might finish the job by next year. The site is in the Bayview Park section, about two or three miles from midtown San Francisco. It is near the Bay Shore Freeway that connects with Bay Bridge, link with Oakland. San Francisco's population is 800,000 but the potential draw in the area is 2,000,000.

A few years ago the voters approved a $5,000,000 bond issue towards erection of a major league stadium. City officials are certain that the approximate $3,000,000 additional financing will be forthcoming. The mayor, incidentally, intends to appoint a Northern California Citizens' Committee to boost the sale of tickets.

Walter F. O'Malley, Brooklyn Dodgers president, was hardly surprised by Mr. Stoneham's announcement. "He has completed preparatory arrangements," said Mr. O'Malley. "However, I don't think it is in order for us to offer any comment."

Mayor Wagner was out of town, a City Hall spokesman said, and unavailable for comment on the official loss of one of the city's two National League clubs.

John Cashmore, Brooklyn Borough President, had no statement when told of the Giants' action. He didn't know if it would have any bearing on the Flatbush situation.

ONE DIRECTOR DISSENTS

Mr. Stoneham would not reveal the name of the lone dissenter in the vote but later it was learned M. Donald Grant was the man. . . .

Among the questions put to Mr. Stoneham and his answers:

Main reason for leaving? Lack of attendance. We had to move immediately or we wouldn't be able to move to a city under such good conditions. Next to New York, San Francisco is the only city in the world.

How about the possibility of another National League club switching to New York? That I can't answer but I'm convinced many changes will take place on the baseball map such as the expansion of both major leagues and a soon-to-be third major league. I don't see why a club would want to move into New York. I don't think this city can support two major league teams, let alone three. I've said it before. The suburban influx has hurt attendance here. People don't want to be bothered travelling to inaccessible ballparks with little parking space.

Do you regard baseball as a sport or business? (Hesitating) Depends on how you look at it.

PAN [SIC] TV IN PICTURE

Will there be immediate pay TV when the Giants play in San Francisco? Yes.

Midst the barrage of questions, Mr. Stoneham parried all that concerned his views on the Dodgers–Los Angeles negotiations.

Mr. Stoneham, whose family owns 60 per cent of the stock, said he could have made the move strictly on the family vote, "but I didn't want to take advantage and try to force the transfer without the approval of the others." . . .

What first gave Mr. Stoneham the idea to move was "the barely over a million attendance" when the Giants won the 1954 pennant and swept the Cleveland Indians in four games in the World Series. "I figured then that if we couldn't draw with Willie Mays and such a team, it was time to look elsewhere."

The Giants' lease on the Polo Grounds expires in April, 1962. Mr. Stoneham thought the property would be sold and converted for low-rental housing. The Giants' rental was $55,000 a year, including taxes and parking lot rental.

Although Mr. Stoneham denied that closed circuit TV was necessarily the big factor in the Giants' charges, there has been no denying that contract propositions along those lines entailed a minimum guaranty of $1,000,000 a year. Mr. Stoneham reportedly told his stockholders last week that the move to the coast could almost guarantee a net profit of $200,000 to $300,000 a year, exclusive of TV and radio.

According to one source, the Giants' profit last year was only $26,000 when they drew only 630,000 fans as compared to 1,400,000 a few years back.

On May 27 Warren Giles, president of the National League, granted permission for the Giants to move to San Francisco and the Dodgers to Los Angeles. It was thought at the time that such approval depended on both teams moving. That isn't so. Upon formal application now by the Giants, Mr. Giles can sanction the switch even if the Dodgers decide not to move.

50

Burdette, Braves Interrupt "Normalcy" by Beating Yankees in World Series (1957)

SOURCE: *New York World-Telegram and Sun,* October 11, 1957

From 1923 through 1956 the New York Yankees won half of the thirty-four World Series played while losing only three times. During this period they enjoyed streaks of four straight (1936–39) and five straight (1949–53) Series wins, and twice they swept consecutive Series without losing a game (1927–28 and 1938–39)—a feat the Yankees repeated in 1998–99. For Yankee fans, winning the World Series was almost a birthright. When the Yankees faced a seventh and final game in the 1957 Series at home against the upstart Milwaukee Braves, with Don Larsen—who the previous year had thrown a perfect game in the Series—on the mound, their fans expected a victory.

The result was quite different. Braves pitcher Lew Burdette, with just two days' rest, threw his second straight shutout and benefited from some uncharacteristically poor Yankee fielding to lead his club to a 5–0 win, his third of the Series. Veteran sportswriter Joe Williams attempts to capture the sense of surprise and disappointment he and other non-Braves baseball fans experienced.

Williams's son Peter collected some of Joe's baseball articles in The Joe Williams

Reader: The Glorious Game from Ty Cobb and Babe Ruth to the Amazing Mets: Fifty Years of Baseball Writing by the Celebrated Newspaper Columnist *(Chapel Hill: Algonquin Books, 1989).*

JOE WILLIAMS' COLUMN

Burdette Tops All Others in Series Heroics

Right up to the last out practically everybody in the Stadium felt that, come what may, the Yankees would, in the end, break through the Braves defense, get to Lew Burdette and restore normalcy to the World Series pattern.

They had done it so often in the past that Yankee fans had every reason to feel they could do it again . . . and for precisely the same reason the Milwaukee fans entertained a clammy fear that they would.

Besides, Burdette couldn't keep on pitching one scoreless inning after another, game in and game out. Anyway, with only two days' rest, he'd fall over on his face before it was over.

This situation had begun to get a little preposterous at that. Burdette came into the game with two wins and a string of 15 consecutive runless innings against the AL champions. They didn't score off him in the last six innings of the second game, a 4–2 defeat, and they didn't score at all in the fifth game, a 1–0 result.

The only reason Burdette was asked to make like an iron man in the finale was because the veteran Warren Spahn, who was 1–1 in the series; got himself fanged by an Asian flu bug, with enfeebling consequences. Burdette had proved he could handle the Yankees. The question now was whether he could handle 'em between naps, or nips, so to speak.

The Braves quickly game him a comfortable cushion when more gaping flaws popped up in the once matchless Yankee defense.

EVERYBODY'S HERO

Normally, a very modest lead would have been considered reasonably secure for the master of the dry spitter, in the light of his previous successes. But the two earlier games had seen a strong, well-rested Burdette. This was a much different situation, and Burdette himself didn't know whether he was physically equal to the stern challenge.

Naturally, he'd try. The tall 30-year-old right-hander, originally out of the West Virginia hills, is a good worker and a good competitor. As you may have noted on your home screen he practically leaps out of the dugout when it's time to pitch. Also when it's time to bat. Since he's a .148 hitter this may be due less to zeal than a desire to get the act over with as speedily as possible.

Burdette pitched one-hit, runless ball for four innings. This wasn't too surprising. The strain would begin to show in the middle and later stages. When Gerry [*sic*] Coleman singled to center with one out in the fifth and the massive Bill Skowron came into the game to pinch hit, Braves fans stirred uneasily . . . "Was this it?" It wasn't.

And for agonizing moments in the ninth it looked as though the young man wasn't going to make it, after all. He had begun to show the effects of the ordeal. The Yankees filled the bases. If Skowron got hold of one, the Yanks would need only one more run to tie it.

It was at this point that the baseball gods and Eddie Mathews' fielding brilliance . . . a remarkable one-hand stop of Skowron's scorcher down the third-base alley for the closing out . . . combined to see that justice was properly and happily served.

A SPITTING IMAGE

Burdette is the first legitimate full-length three-game winner the Series has produced since Stanley Coveleskie of the Indians racked up a triple against the Dodgers in 1920. As we had seen that one, too, we got an extra bang out of Burdette's magnificent performance.

There are some interesting similarities. Like Burdette, the Cleveland star allowed only two runs in the three games, but the only shutout he scored was in the 3–0 wrapup against Burley [sic] Grimes. And Coveleskie also got his shutout with only two days' rest.

Burdette has a time of it trying to convince people he does not throw the illegal spitter. (If he threw any against the Yankees no official detection was recorded.) The spitter was Coveleskie's meat and potato pitch. It made him a frequent 20-game winner. And in those days it wasn't agin' the law, either.

4

Continental Divides

After making a political decision not to fund or subsidize new stadiums for the Brooklyn Dodgers and the New York Giants—and losing the franchises as a result—New York City mayor Robert Wagner, faced with an outraged populace, reacted with another political decision. His decision led indirectly to the transformation of the major leagues and a dramatic shift in the relationship between cities and their professional sports teams. The chairman of the Mayor's Baseball Committee of the City of New York, William Shea, adopted a strategy of forming a third major league, hoping to attract major cities and wealthy investors willing to spend millions of dollars to earn the prestige of being associated with a professional sports team—a plan also followed by creators of the American Football League. Not only did many of the cities involved in the Continental League end up with major league franchises, but existing teams learned that they could use the threat of moving to another city to persuade their city and state legislatures to build them new stadiums. Voters often resisted such largesse, but politicians and the media were frequently successful in achieving their objectives, as they were in Los Angeles in 1958. Their efforts were appreciated by fans in the new cities—between 1957 and 1966 seven World Series featured at least one team that had moved during the period.

The divide between the past and the present in baseball was also expressed in other forms. Although the new players' union, the Major League Baseball Players' Association (MLBPA), had little bargaining power (as reflected by their low salaries), they did manage to persuade management to stage a second All-Star Game to further benefit their pension fund. The racial divide continued to close at a glacial pace, but this progress was not evident in Birmingham, Alabama, when local officials refused to permit black minor leaguers to appear in a playoff series. Nor was it appreciated by fans and officials of the Negro American League, who could see the death of that organization in the near future. Yet in the aftermath of "the era," the on-field exploits of men like Harvey Haddix and Bill Mazeroski helped fans believe that baseball, despite the turbulence of the world around it, continued to live up to its past standards of excellence.

51

Mayor's Baseball Committee of the City of New York Established (1957)

SOURCE: *New York Journal-American*, December 1, 1957

Under immense political pressure, New York City mayor Robert Wagner fulfilled a promise of a month earlier and named four prominent men to the Mayor's Baseball Committee of the City of New York. The purpose of this committee was to obtain a second major league franchise for the city. William Shea, a lawyer later named chairman of the committee, would soon develop an unexpected strategy to accomplish its goal.

Columnist Bill Corum noted that in order to attract a National League or "a third big league" team, the city would have to construct a new ballpark. His readers knew that a primary reason for the departure of the Dodgers and the Giants was the failure of city leaders to cooperate with (or kneel under to) team officials in their efforts to obtain new stadiums. With this in mind, Corum was pessimistic that the committee could achieve its objective.

SPORTS TODAY BY BILL CORUM

What Will N.Y. Offer?

PHILADELPHIA, Nov. 30.—That's a first rate committee that Mayor Bob Wagner appointed to start the baseball rolling toward another major league club for N.Y.C.

Whether the four men, Messrs. James A. Farley, Bernard Gimbel, Clinton W. Blume and William A. Shea, will agree to serve on such a committee is not known.

Not over here at the site of the Army-Navy [football game], as this is written, at any rate. But all good N.Y. baseball fans must hope so.

This includes Yankee fans of which Mister Jim is a staunch example. I do not believe that the Yankees would stand in the way of another major league team in Greater New York.

Indeed, Dan Topping told me as much one night last Summer in the Stadium. The Yankees take care of themselves, both on the field and off, and can be counted on to continue to do so.

But I don't think they are the sort of people who would intentionally do anything to hurt baseball in its broader aspects.

What they might think would be helpful, even generous on their part, might not be what many New Yorkers would want, however. Specifically, a National League team.

The Yankees might say, and with considerable logic: All right, the National League has chosen to make the Pacific Coast its territory, why shouldn't the American League do likewise on the Eastern Seaboard?

Plainly it would be the Yankees' advantage to have another A.L. team in Queens—possibly the only place a stadium could be built—to establish a rivalry such as existed between the Giants and Dodgers for so many years.

But would that help baseball and strengthen it over-all. I'm sure I don't know. It would obviously shutout here many thousands of National League fans in N.Y. as of now.

In another and new generation, it might not matter. Yet there's a point to be considered. With the outstanding stars of the game, such as of now, Mantle, Williams, Musial, Mays, Aaron, Snider, et. al., the fans of both coasts would be denied the opportunity to see them, save possibly in an All-Star Game or World's Series.

The teams that play in a World's Series aren't decided by geography, as all the interborough series we have seen through the years in N.Y. amply prove.

FIRST, THE HORSE

That part of the problem is baseball's own. Certain angles of it are virtually sure to come up for the discussion at the joint-meetings of the two leagues that start tomorrow in Colorado Springs.

It may be that they will prove explosive. In any case, no committee, even one as good as this, can be appointed by Mayor Wagner, or any mayor anywhere, that will have anything to say about that.

But there is one basic thing that nobody who knows the difference between the bat and the ball can escape.

Nothing, but nothing, Mr. Gimbel, can be done about baseball in N.Y.C. until the horse is put ahead of the cart. Which means that a stadium in which any N.Y. team, either present big league or a third big league, can play.

Minneapolis has one and is fighting for a big league franchise. Next door to it, St. Paul has a stadium. Toronto has one.

Two Texas cities, with big growth patterns in population, are ready to build one—or two—at the drop of a big white hat.

Miami has a dandy, capable of quick enlargement. The Florida metropolis has yet to prove itself a good ball city. Most of the others have. In the nature of its size and name, Texas always has been big for baseball.

BUT THE BIG POINT IS THAT ALL THESE PLACES HAVE THE PLACE FOR A TEAM TO PLAY.

Until N.Y. has the guarantee of such a stadium, it hasn't made a start. . . .

Gentlemen, this column wishes you well and, in its small way, is on your team. N.Y.C. needs two big league teams. One in the N.L., its guess would be. Not three.

You will have rendered a great civic service if you can help our city to work this out.

52

Richard Nixon Advocates True "World" Series (1958)

SOURCE: *New York Herald Tribune*, January 29, 1958

Richard Nixon compensated for his poor athletic skills by studying and passionately following sports, especially baseball and football. As president he became famous for occasionally recommending plays for the Washington Redskins, and in late June 1972 he and his son-in-law, David Eisenhower, selected an all-time baseball all-star team. (For more information see Nicholas Evan Sarantakes, "Richard Nixon, Sportswriter: The President, His Historical All-Star Baseball Team, and the Election of 1972," Journal of Sport History 24 [Summer 1997]: 192–202.) Early in 1958 he appeared on NBC's Today program to discuss his love of sport. As the following article notes, Nixon believed it was time for major league baseball to expand internationally in order to justify staging a "World" Series. He expanded on these statements at a press conference in Wichita, Kansas, on October 31. Nixon's area of expertise as both vice-president and president was foreign relations, and it is possible that his comments were intended to be interpreted as a gesture of goodwill, especially by countries like Mexico and Cuba, where Nixon and the Eisenhower administration were unpopular.

WORLD SERIES SHOULD BE INTERNATIONAL—NIXON

Vice-President Nixon suggested yesterday that the baseball World Series should be an international, rather than a national, competition and asked how the games could be called "World Series" when they are limited to United States teams.

In an interview devoted to sports on the television show "Today," the Vice-President said Mexico City, Havana and Montreal could support major league teams and raised the question why the World Series games should not be international in character.

WOULD ADD TO LEAGUES

Mr. Nixon also suggested that the size of the two major leagues be increased, rather than having a third league.

Declaring that he gets "more of a kick" out of reading sports news than detective stories, the Vice-President said this was perhaps because "they wouldn't even give me a mitt in baseball."

He said he was a great believer in Little League baseball and thought this type of activity should be expanded, with the major leagues giving it greater support and perhaps subsidizing it.

Mr. Nixon was questioned about the Celler Congressional Committee's investigation of baseball, and what results could be expected from it. He said such committees often bring into the open "helpful facts" and thus proved beneficial, although he did not expect baseball to be put under anti-trust legislation as a result of the inquiry.

"Everything good in baseball has nothing to fear" from the investigation, he declared.

Mr. Nixon said he considered the move by the Dodgers and Giants to California a good thing and expected large crowds to attend ball games in Los Angeles and San Francisco, with the former city obtaining baseball's first attendance of 100,000.

Because of its team's "not too high standing," Washington now draws the fewest fans, the Vice-President said, but he held the city has a large number of fans and said it will "pack them in" when it gets a new stadium.

Legislation for a stadium has been held up for several reasons, but it will come, Mr. Nixon said. He claimed that the south has a greater interest in baseball than the north.

After his TV appearance Mr. and Mrs. Nixon departed for Washington aboard a Military Air Transport Service plane.

53

Roy Campanella Paralyzed in Car Accident (1958)

SOURCE: *New York Herald Tribune*, January 30, 1958

As if the pain caused by the departure of the Dodgers were not bad enough, fans of the club suffered a more intense blow with the stunning news that beloved catcher Roy Campanella had been paralyzed in a predawn automobile accident on Long Island. It did not matter that the career of the thirty-six-year-old Campanella was nearly over. It was another reminder of a ballplayer's mortality. Campanella's accident happened less than two years after Herb Score's near-blinding and only two and a half years after the tragic death of Harry Agganis, a superb young athlete. No doubt the hearts of Dodger fans fluttered when, in the next three months, two other Dodgers were involved in car crashes. They never wavered when it came to remembering Campanella, who was described as intelligent, kind, and giving—the same terms used to characterize him while he was a feared and respected player. Those qualities made it that much easier to root for his recovery, and that much harder to accept the truth of his paralysis. At the time this article was written, that truth was just starting to set in.

PARALYZED CAMPANELLA TO RECOVER

But He May Not Play Ball Again

GLEN COVE, L.I., Jan. 28—Roy Campanella—one of baseball's great catchers with the Brooklyn (now Los Angeles) Dodgers—underwent a long emergency operation today in Community Hospital on a broken neck suffered in an early morning auto accident.

Tonight, while doctors pronounced the operation a "success" and forecast "complete recovery" from a partial paralysis still afflicting the thirty-six-year-old catcher, there was no assurance that he would resume an active playing career with the Dodgers.

Mr. Campanella would be in the hospital for at least six weeks, physicians said, and it would be "several days" before they could suggest whether the period might run longer.

Dr. Robert W. Sengstaken, thirty-five-year-old neurological surgeon, head of the team of physicians who worked over Mr. Campanella during a four-hour-and-twenty-minute operation, said:

"Assuming a complete recovery, he could not play ball before a year."

Inasmuch as Mr. Campanella's catching and hitting performances have fallen off in the last two years from his previous brilliant form, and considering that he suffers from weakened hands after several operations, it seemed possible that today's accident a mile south of his home here wrote an end to his playing career.

At the Campanella home, Mrs. Campanella said tonight she had received "thousands of telegrams," including one from President Eisenhower and another from Vice-President Richard M. Nixon, wishing her husband well.

"Every one has been so kind," she said.

ALSTON STATEMENT

Out in Darrtown, Ohio, the Dodgers' manager, Walter Alston, said today:

"I'm very sorry to hear about the accident, but, knowing him as I do, he'll be back as soon as he can, if at all possible. He's a very rugged-type individual."

The fact that he was a "very rugged type" almost certainly saved Mr. Campanella's life today. The crash, in which his car struck a telephone pole and overturned, fractured and dislocated the fifth and sixth cervical vertebrae and pinched the spinal cord.

Physicians said that this damage was limited by the fact that Mr. Campanella's neck was "very heavily muscled." National League base runners who found the burly catcher often blocking their access to home plate could have told the doctors that the 200-pound Mr. Campanella was very heavily muscled indeed.

Mr. Campanella, third Negro in organized baseball when he signed with the Dodgers in 1945, went on to be thrice the National League's Most Valuable Player and set slugging and endurance records for catchers.

Married and father of six children, he bought a spacious fieldstone ranch-house on Landing Drive on East Island three years ago and became a popular figure in this community. He taught baseball to neighborhood kids, sent children to local schools, and cruised and fished in the Sound in his forty-one-foot boat, The Princess.

After dinner last night Mr. Campanella drove to Manhattan in a 1957 Chevrolet sport sedan he had rented from an uptown concern that was giving a routine check to his own Chevrolet. He also owns a Cadillac.

Associates said that Mr. Campanella planned to make a television appearance with Harry Wismer on Channel 5 of the DuMont Broadcasting Corp., at 10:45 P.M. However, they said, Mr. Wismer asked Mr. Campanella to delay his appearance for a week so that it could be advertised in the interval.

COMES TO S-CURVE

Mr. Campanella agreed to this. Some time later he headed for home in the rented Chevrolet. At 3:34 A.M. he was headed north in Glen Cove on Dosoris Lane. Near Apple Tree Lane the narrow blacktop road makes an S-curve, first to the right, then to the left.

Mr. Campanella's car—its speed was not known—simply went straight instead of to the right. It struck Pole No. 25 of the New York Telephone Co., whirled about, edged up a slight embankment and turned over on its right side.

Dr. W. Spencer Gurnee, gynecologist living at 79 Dosoris Lane, heard the crash. While some one in his household called police, he put on a coat and ran out to the car.

He found Mr. Campanella, though he didn't know who he was, crumpled in the front of the car and crying out:

"Somebody help me. Somebody help me. Get me out of here."

Glen Cove Patrolman Joseph Brino was the first policeman on the scene. He crawled into the car, gave Mr. Campanella sedation pills handed him by Dr. Gurnee and he braced himself against the injured man to prevent too sudden movement a half hour later when a wrecker car righted the Chevrolet to facilitate moving Mr. Campanella.

"It's Campy"

By this time a small crowd had gathered and the catcher was recognized.

"It's Campy," some one called out.

One witness said that Mr. Campanella was "curled up like a pretzel" and complaining that he couldn't move his legs. No effort was made to straighten him out. He did not lose consciousness. A police ambulance took Mr. Campanella to the hospital here and X-rays were taken.

Dr. Sengstaken, in consultation with other physicians, told Mr. Campanella of the fractures, dislocations and compression of the spinal cord. They advised him that an operation must be undertaken to correct the damage to the vertebrae and to remove the pressure on the spinal cord which was causing the paralysis.

"Do whatever you have to do," Mr. Campanella was quoted as telling them.

Mr. Campanella was taken into the operating room shortly before 8:30 A.M. and was not brought out until 12:45 P.M. He was conscious soon after, and asked for his wife, Ruthe. She visited him soon after and again in the evening.

Dr. Sengstaken, who has offices in Garden City, said:

"The operation was a success. Mr. Campanella's condition is satisfactory and we expect complete recovery."

The patient was, however, kept on the critical list, considering the major and delicate nature of the operation. The paralysis which affected him from the lower shoulders downward, except for certain arm movements, was expected to diminish slowly.

Walter O'Malley, president of the Dodgers, came to the hospital this afternoon from New York and was asked about Mr. Campanella's playing future. Mr. O'Malley said:

"We're not even thinking of Roy's future in baseball. All we're thinking of is his health and restoring him to a normal life."

Mr. Campanella, whose 1956 salary of $42,500 made him the highest paid player in Dodger history, owns a prosperous liquor store in Harlem. Two of his children, Joyce, eighteen, and Beverly, seventeen, are in a private school in Philadelphia. David, fourteen, attends a school in Queens. Roy jr., nine, and Tony, seven, attend Glen Cove school. Ruthe, the youngest, is four.

54

L.A. Voters Narrowly Approve Stadium in Chavez Ravine (1958)

SOURCE: *Los Angeles Herald Express,* June 5, 1958

Two months after the Dodgers started playing in Los Angeles, and nearly a decade after the local controversy over the fate of Chavez Ravine first made headlines, voters approved a referendum to permit the construction of a baseball stadium on the site. The land was purchased by the city with the intention of erecting public housing, but critics, led by mayor-to-be Norris Poulson, succeeded in persuading the City Council to break its contract with the City Housing Authority, a vote later supported by a referendum. Both these actions were invalidated by the courts, forcing Mayor Poulson to strike a deal with the federal government to use Chavez Ravine for a public purpose other than housing. The June 1958 referendum rested on the question of whether the subsidization of professional sport was a legitimate function of government. The campaign for and against Proposition B was fierce, and the second article makes clear that future legal action was anticipated.

Several outstanding accounts of the battle have been written, but the best source remains Neil J. Sullivan, The Dodgers Move West *(New York: Oxford University Press, 1987). In addition, there is considerable material on the Dodgers' move in* Organized Professional Team Sports *(1958).*

"YES" VOTE SWELLS

Chavez Victors Jubilant

Supporters of the city's contract to let the Los Angeles Dodgers build a mammoth stadium in Chavez Ravine today claimed victory as a swelling tide of votes continued to add to the majority, which may exceed 30,000 "for baseball."

Mayor Norris Poulson, Chairman Joe E. Brown of the Committee for Yes on Baseball, and other supporters of Proposition B were jubilant as the "yes" votes continued to pile up.

With ballots counted from 4250 of the city's 4519 precincts, the proposition had a lead of 23,988. The vote:

Yes: 324,799; No: 300,811.

LEADS FROM START

The Proposition had led from the time the counting of votes was started Tuesday night after the polls closed continued to show a consistent percentage lead of about 52 per cent, and passed that figure as the vote count continued.

Several opponents of the Dodger contract also conceded that the measure had passed.

One Councilman, Earle D. Baker, who had voted against the Dodger contract, said:

"The vote appears to be conclusive. I'll consider it a mandate of the people, and no longer oppose the Chavez Ravine project."

POULSON JUBILANT

Mayor Poulson's "victory statement" follows:

"The voters apparently have approved Proposition B, and I wholeheartedly agree with their decision. The voters have upheld the city's integrity. Now that this progressive step has been taken we must close ranks and work together to find solutions for the mutual community problems which face us as citizens of this great city."

Brown said in part that "it has been a long hard fight, but it was worth it. Now we can look forward to a new era of growth; to greater employment and greater tax revenues; to the location here of the baseball showplace of the world."

Councilwoman Rosalind Wyman, chairman of the Recreation and Parks Committee, a solid fighter for the Dodgers, said:

"The people of Los Angeles are to be congratulated for the vote that keeps the Dodgers in our city.

"I sincerely hope that the City Council now will pull together and aid the

Dodgers in the plan to build the finest baseball stadium in the nation as soon as possible."

STADIUM DELAY SEEN

Legal Obstacles in Way of Quick Start

By Bud Furillo

The Dodgers may have scored with the voters, but it was the opinion of City Attorney Roger Arnebergh today that they must compile a whopping total of legal and technical "base hits" before thinking of setting up housekeeping in Chavez Ravine.

Walter O'Malley, president of the Dodgers, expressed the hope that work could be launched on the new $12,000,000 stadium "by July 5 or 6" after Proposition B won favor with the voters Tuesday.

But Arnebergh anticipates considerable delay before a spade of earth is turned in the Ravine.

"I can't see how it could get underway in July," Arnebergh observed. Reasons for Arnebergh's pessimism, follow:

THREE SUITS PENDING

1. There are three suits pending, testing the validity of the contract, and seeking to enjoin the Housing Authority from modifying the present deed restrictions so as to permit the use, contemplated by the ball club. Councilman John Holland, who led the fight against the contract, predicts that many more suits will be filed.

2. The actual contract must be prepared by the Mayor and the proper officials of the Dodgers Corporation.

3. The Dodgers must present a precise plan of development, which in turn must be submitted to the Planning Commission with an applied-for change of zoning. Public hearings will follow along with a recommendation by the Planning Commission for appropriate zoning.

In connection with this, a re-subdivision of the property will be required, which will vacate some existing streets, and provide for new streets within the area to be conveyed to the Dodgers.

4. These matters must be submitted to the City Council for approval. In addition, the exact layout of the access roads must be determined so that streets within the boundaries will conform to the access roads.

5. The city must continue with its efforts to acquire the property not yet owned by it.

6. No property can be deeded to the Dodgers until the $500,000 recreational facilities promised by the Dodgers can be agreed upon.

Representative Emanuel Celler (D-NY), a native of Brooklyn, in his study during the first of many congressional investigations of baseball, June 1951. Reproduced from the collections of the Library of Congress.

THE $64 QUESTION—

WHY DOES THE N.Y. YANKEE MANAGEMENT REFUSE TO PLACE A NEGRO PLAYER ON ITS MAJOR TEAM?

WHAT EXCUSE WILL MR. GEORGE WEISS, GENERAL MANAGER OF THE N.Y. YANKEES GIVE THIS YEAR?

BASEBALL FANS DEMAND AN END TO DISCRIMINATION IN SPORTS!

WRITE OR PHONE MR. GEORGE WEISS —

Urge him to make the N.Y. Yankees a real all American team truly representative of our great city in the interest of democracy and fair play.

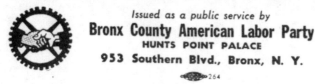

Issued as a public service by
Bronx County American Labor Party
HUNTS POINT PALACE
953 Southern Blvd., Bronx, N. Y.
264

One of several flyers distributed at Yankee Stadium prior to opening day in 1953 (see document 28). Both flyers were produced by groups later identified as being affiliated with the American Communist Party, a longtime advocate of intregration in baseball. Courtesy of the National Baseball Hall of Fame Library, Cooperstown, New York.

Brooklyn Dodgers president Walter O'Malley (*left*) and television executive Arthur Levey watching an experimental pay television broadcast by WOR in the Ebbets Field press box, June 1953. O'Malley pursued this dream for more than a decade in Brooklyn and Los Angeles. Reproduced from the collections of the Library of Congress.

Brooklyn Dodgers statistician Allan Roth busy at his desk in the midst of the 1954 season. Reproduced from the collections of the Library of Congress.

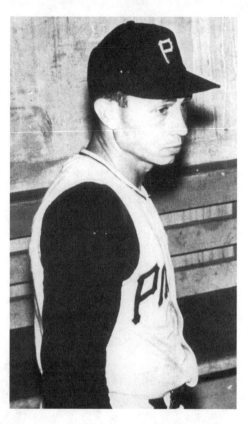

(*Top left*) Cleveland Indians pitcher Herb Score immediately after being struck in the eye with a line drive hit by New York Yankees second baseman Gil McDougald, May 1957. Courtesy Associated Press.

(*Bottom left, left to right*) Walter O'Malley, New York City mayor Robert Wagner, New York Giants owner Horace Stoneham, and Brooklyn Borough president John Cashmore at the press conference at which both owners assured Wagner that they had no commitments to move to the West Coast, June 1957. Courtesy Associated Press.

(*Right*) Pittsburgh Pirates pitcher Harvey Haddix, in a daze, looks at the scoreboard after losing to the Milwaukee Braves despite pitching twelve perfect innings, May 1959. Courtesy Corbis Photos.

(*Top left*) New York lawyer William Shea announcing the formation of the Continental League, July 1959. Reproduced from the collections of the Library of Congress.

(*Bottom left*) Sportswriter Charles Einstein and his favorite player, Willie Mays, during the filming of a television documentary written and hosted by Einstein, "A Man Named Mays," September 1963. Courtesy NBC Television Network.

(*Top*) A publicity photograph of the Houston Astrodome featuring a glass-paneled roof, which would cause significant problems for fielders, and a grass field made possible by the panels, 1965. Neither the glass panels nor the grass would survive. Courtesy of the National Baseball Hall of Fame Library, Cooperstown, New York.

(*Top left*) New York Yankees announcer Red Barber before the WPIX cameras, ca. 1965. Courtesy of the National Baseball Hall of Fame Library, Cooperstown, New York.

(*Bottom left*) Newly elected baseball commissioner General William "Spike" Eckert (*left*) being defended by the outgoing commissioner, Ford Frick, at his initial press conference after being asked a question about the antitrust lawsuit filed against the Milwaukee Braves by the state of Wisconsin, November 1965. Eckert's reputation for ignorance about baseball matters never improved. UPI photo courtesy Corbis Photos.

(*Above*) Colorful umpire Emmett Ashford making a call at Yankee Stadium, ca. 1966. The first African American umpire in the major leagues, Ashford was noted primarily for his flamboyance during his brief five-year career, but he was awarded with a World Series assignment in his final season, 1970. Courtesy of the National Baseball Hall of Fame Library, Cooperstown, New York.

A publicity photo of St. Louis Cardinals outfielder Curtis Flood during happier times, ca. 1968. Courtesy of the National Baseball Hall of Fame Library, Cooperstown, New York.

Newly elected baseball commissioner Bowie Kuhn at the door of his office, ca. 1970. Photo by Bob Olen.

Houston Astros pitcher Jim Bouton leaving Commissioner Kuhn's office after being summoned to discuss his controversial new book *Ball Four*, June 1970. Courtesy Corbis Photos.

The members of the Committee on the Negro Leagues, formed after years of pressure to elect Negro Leaguers to a special wing of the Hall of Fame, February 1971. The committee's first selection, Satchel Paige, was quickly approved for admission to the Hall of Fame as a full-fledged member following intense criticism of the Hall's initial plan. Photo courtesy *New York Daily News.*

55

Frick on the State of Baseball (1958)

SOURCE: Senate Subcommittee on Antitrust and Monopoly, *Organized Professional Team Sports*, 85th Cong., 2nd sess., 1958, 193–204

In the spring of 1958 both the Senate and the House of Representatives considered bills (S. 4070 and H.R. 10378) intended "to limit the applicability of the antitrust laws so as to exempt certain aspects of designated professional team sports, and for other purposes." The bills would, among other things, permit major league baseball to keep the reserve clause, control franchise relocation, enact restrictive rules regarding the broadcast and telecast of baseball games into the defined territories of other teams (especially minor league teams), and protect baseball from further antitrust-related lawsuits and continued congressional investigations. Commissioner Frick supported the legislation, and in his statement, given on July 16, he details the reasons for his position and the likely positive effect of the legislation on baseball. In spite of his support and the support of the leaders of professional basketball, football, and hockey, the bills never left their respective committees and were not enacted. The following excerpt from Frick's statement, taken from pages 195–96, describes the structure of baseball and recent changes in the powers of the commissioner.

STATEMENT OF FORD C. FRICK, COMMISSIONER OF BASEBALL

WHAT IS ORGANIZED BASEBALL?

At the outset, I believe it would be in order and helpful for me to describe briefly the scope of organized baseball and the functions of my office of commissioner of baseball. Organized baseball today is composed of 26 leagues arranged in a pyramid structure with the 2 major leagues at the top, ranging down through 3-AAA, 3-AA, 3-A, 3-B, 4-C, and 8-D classifications. These 26 leagues comprise 191 clubs operating in 38 States and 3 foreign countries.

The 16 major league clubs are located in 15 of the larger cities of the country. They and their 2 major league organizations, the National League of Professional Baseball Clubs and the American League of Professional Baseball Clubs, are joined in a major league agreement dating from 1921, which creates the office of commissioner of baseball and provides for the machinery for adopting major league rules. Those rules, among other things, provide for the playing of the world series between the champions of the National League and the American League as the annual culmination of professional baseball competition. The major league agreement also provides for the major league executive council, which is authorized to exercise all of the powers of the commissioner in the event of a vacancy in that office. In addition, the executive council has jurisdiction to survey, investigate, and submit recommendations for changes in rules and other matters and has power to act for the major leagues in the interim between their joint meetings. A player representative of each major league attends and votes at all meetings of the executive council at which matters concerning the standard form of player's contract or its provisions or regulations or the players' pension plan are acted upon.

All of the other leagues, generally referred to as minor leagues, are members of the National Association of Professional Baseball Leagues under a national association agreement. The national association is administered by a president and an executive committee. The president for more than 10 years has been George M. Trautman. The national association and the major leagues have joined in the professional baseball agreement, under which the major and national association leagues agree to be bound by the decisions of the commissioner rendered in accordance with the provisions of the agreement. The professional baseball agreement prescribes the procedure for adoption of the professional baseball rules which govern the major-minor leagues' relations.

The fundamental function and power of the commissioner is to deal with conduct detrimental to baseball. He is given authority to investigate any act, transaction, or practice charged or suspected to be detrimental to the best interests of baseball, and to determine after his investigation what preventative, remedial, or punitive action is appropriate and to take such action against leagues, clubs, or individuals in organized baseball. This authority has proved an effective means of keeping baseball's skirts clear of crookedness, game throwing, gambling, and unsportsmanlike conduct of every kind. Without this right and authority within baseball's own organization, public confidence and public faith in the integrity of the game could not, in my opinion, be maintained.

Another function of the commissioner is to hear and determine disputes between leagues, between clubs, and between players and their clubs. In this capacity, the commissioner is an arbitrator who interprets and enforces the many rules of the game which have grown up over the years. Following the precedent set by the first commissioner, Kenesaw Mountain Landis, I deem it the special concern of the commissioner to safeguard the rights of the players.

The commissioner is also empowered to propose changes in the rules, to compel a reconsideration of a rule after its adoption and to cast the controlling vote for adoption or rejection of a major league rule if the two major leagues disagree.

I would like to set the record straight as to what changes were made in the provisions of the major league agreement concerning the commissioner after Judge Landis' death and before the election of his successor, Mr. Chandler. There have been no changes made regarding the commissioner's authority since the election of Mr. Chandler.

On December 12, 1944, the major leagues amended the major league agreement in three respects involving the commissioner: (1) section 3 of article I was amended to provide that no major league rule or joint action of the major leagues should be considered detrimental to baseball but the commissioner should have power to propose changes and reconsideration of rules or action which he deemed disadvantageous to baseball; (2) section 6 of article I concerning the election of the commissioner was amended to provide for election by a vote of 12 of the 16 clubs instead of by a majority vote. Provision was also made for exercise of the commissioner's powers by the Major League Advisory Council during a vacancy in his office and the provision for designation of a commissioner by the President of the

United States after a vacancy of 3 months was eliminated; (3) section 1 of article VII was amended by eliminating a provision that the major leagues and their club waived the right of recourse to the courts. This change was made upon advice of counsel that the provision was not valid. However, section 1 of article VII continued to contain and today contains the following language:

"The major leagues and their constituent clubs severally agree to be bound by the decisions of the commissioner and the discipline imposed by him under the provisions of this agreement."

If the chairman wishes, I will provide copies of the major league agreement as it existed in the year 1944, the last year of Judge Landis' administration, and as it was amended December 12, 1944, for purposes of such comparison as your committee may wish to make. There has been no change in the commissioner's powers since December 12, 1944.

The organization of professional baseball, which I have described, has evolved by trial and error over a period that is longer than the existence of the antitrust laws. It has brought the game into high public favor and established a noble reputation for integrity without regulation by the antitrust laws.

56

MLBPA **Report on Salaries** (1958)

SOURCE: Senate Subcommittee on Antitrust and Monopoly, *Organized Professional Team Sports*, 85th Cong., 2nd sess., 1958, 793–810

The few writings about the early history of the Major League Baseball Players' Association—that is, prior to the hiring of Marvin Miller as executive director in 1966—indicate that it was an impotent organization which did not provide its members with adequate information about their relationship with their owners. The following document, "Salary Report for Major League Baseball Players," offers evidence that the union made a concerted effort to inform its members of their financial status as compared with that of owners. The report's conclusion—that players were underpaid—could not have surprised the players, but the detail supplied within gave them information that added to their resentment and, in time, led them to seek and hire a leader who could empower them.

SALARY REPORT FOR MAJOR LEAGUE BASEBALL PLAYERS

Prepared Pursuant to Resolution of Player Representatives
Lewis, Durante & Bartel
Attorneys for Major League Baseball Players
September, 1958

At the Player Representatives' meeting in Key West, Florida, in February, 1958, a resolution was unanimously adopted directing counsel to gather together available statistical data for the purpose of providing Major League players with pertinent information to be contained in a Salary Report.

In 1946, the Major Leagues were faced with two important and pressing problems. One was the efforts of the Pasquel brothers of Mexico to induce Major League players to jump to the Mexican League. The other was the effort of one Murphy* to unionize Major League baseball players. The pressure of these problems mounted as several prominent players signed with the Pasquels, and at least one Major League club† notified its owners that it intended to become unionized and a member of a national labor union.

Most players refused to jump to the Mexican League and Bob Feller rejected an offer of $500,000. Nevertheless the situation was so serious that after many meetings, and discussions and appointments of committees, the Major League owners felt compelled to take affirmative action to improve the situation of the players. The most significant actions were the setting of a $5,000 minimum salary; the establishment of a pension plan which the owners could cancel at any time on 60 days notice; and a loose Player Representative system.

Through the efforts of the Major League Baseball Player Representatives, in 1954, the minimum salary was increased to $6,000 and in 1958 to $7,000. In April, 1946, the cost of living as established by the United States Department of Labor on all items in the United States was 78.5. In July, 1958, the same cost of living was 123.9 or a 45.4 increase. Therefore, in July, 1958, a ballplayer required approximately $7,850 in order to purchase the same items that could be bought for $5,000 in 1946 when the $5,000 minimum was established. Similarly, a player who received $10,000 in 1946 needed about $15,700 in 1958 to buy the same articles he was able to purchase in 1946; and the 1946 man of $20,000 a year needed about $31,400 a year in 1958. In addition, the player of today has a much heavier tax burden than the player of 1946. . . .

Following the hearings in 1951 the Committee prepared a report which, in part, stated:

> They (Major League baseball players' salaries) have not, however, kept pace with the increased receipts of the game. By 1929, however, team salaries accounted for only 35.3 per cent of Major League expenses. This share has continued to drop, reaching 32.4 per cent in 1939, 28.9 per cent in 1943, 24.8 per cent in 1946 and 22.1 per cent in 1950.

The foregoing tables show that although in the year 1956 the club owners took in $10,800,846 more than they received in 1950, the players received in 1956 only $229,665 more than they received in 1950. This means that the owners retained for themselves or used for other purposes than players' salaries, $10,571,181 of the $10,800,846 increased income which they made in 1956 over 1950.

*Robert Murphy founded the American Baseball Guild in 1946—Ed.
†The club was the Pittsburgh Pirates—Ed.

In 1950, the amount actually paid for players' salaries alone (not including managers, coaches, trainers, and clubhouse personnel) was 16.5% of the clubs' income. But in 1956 the percentage had dropped to only 12.9% for players' salaries.

In fact, in the American League the total amount paid for players' salaries in 1956 was actually less than was paid in that league in 1950. And this was after a tremendous increase in income received by the clubs. . . .

As every Major Leaguer today knows, the proceeds from the televising and radio broadcasting of the World Series and All Star games are distributed in another manner.

As a result of the actions taken by the Player Representatives in 1953–1954 an agreement was executed with the owners whereby 60% of the proceeds from radio and television rights to the World Series and All Star games, as well as 60% of the gate receipts from the All Star game, are allocated to the Major League Baseball Players' Pension Plan. These payments are guaranteed up to and including the 1961 season. The agreement further provides:

"It is the intention of the Club Owners and the Players that a Pension Plan will be continued after 1961."

The radio and television rights to the World Series and All Star games have been sold for the five year period, from 1957 to 1961, inclusive, for $3,250,000 a year. This means that $1,950,000 every year is allocated to the Pension Plan, in addition to the 60% of the gate receipts from the All Star game, which usually is in excess of $50,000. Therefore, the Players' Pension Plan is assured of receiving approximately $2,000,000 every year up to and including 1961, plus the additional contributions from the players. As a result, the Pension Plan today provides for a minimum payment of $88 a month for life for players of five years' experience at 50 years of age, to a maximum of $550 a month for life for players of 20 years' experience at 65 years of age.

In addition, the Pension provides for satisfactory payments covering family hospitalization, disability benefits and life insurance. Finally, the Pension Plan is administered by a committee of four, of which two are players elected by the Player Representatives.

Although the players have fought for and achieved a substantially better pension arrangement than before, it must be remembered that the payment for the improved pension is not being paid directly out of the owners' pockets. On the contrary, up to 1956, the World Series and All Star Game radio and television income totalled $1,075,000 per year. And a large percentage of this amount was applied for the old pension.

Now that the receipts for these rights until 1961 are $3,250,000 per year, the application of approximately $2,000,000 of this amount for the improved pension still leaves the owners with approximately $1,250,000 free and clear for their own uses, and which they need not, and do not, apply for the players' pensions. So, it is clear that the improved pension has been achieved without any additional payments from the owners, and in fact the 60%–40% arrangement on the distribution of the World Series' TV and radio receipts has resulted in an increased income of $1,250,000 for the owners. . . .

CONCLUSIONS

The statistics set forth in this report are even more underlined by the available 1957 figures and by the indicated figures for 1958. From the over-all picture, certain irrefutable conclusions seem warranted:

1—The total gross incomes of the 16 Major League baseball clubs have increased substantially during the last 12 years.

2—The percentage of their gross income paid out by the clubs for players' salaries has progressively decreased.

3—The average salary of a Major League baseball player has not kept pace percentage-wise with the increases in salaries of other American businesses, or even with other recreation businesses.

4—The value of the 16 Major League club franchises has risen astronomically, but no share of this increment has gone for players' salaries.

5—No adequate compensation has been given to players to make up for increases in the cost of living or in taxes.

6—Although the income of Major League clubs from radio and TV (exclusive of the World Series and All Star Game) increased from $3,365,000 in 1950, to $7,306,259 in 1956, the players have never received any share of these funds. In fact, the 16 clubs now receive for radio and TV of championship games a sum equal to more than 1½ times the total salaries of all Major League baseball players.

7—Major League players do not seem to have received an adequate share of the vastly increased revenues received by the owners. Suggestions for correcting this situation are under discussion and advisement, and it is likely that specific recommendations in this regard will be proposed.

57

Dixie Series Threatened by Birmingham Racial Laws (1958)

SOURCE: September 24, 1958, letter (Bulletin No. 1220), "Minor Leagues" file, National Baseball Hall of Fame Library

Thirteen years after the twentieth-century integration of professional baseball, the battle was still being waged, and in some cases the eventual victors surrendered. One example is with the 1958 Dixie Series, a postseason series between the winners of the Southern Association and the Texas League. Several Texas League clubs had black players, but the Southern Association (which folded in 1961) never integrated, save for a two-game appearance by Nat Peeples for the Atlanta Crackers in 1954. Moreover, the city of

Birmingham, which five years earlier had prevented Jackie Robinson's integrated barn-storming team from playing, had since passed a new ordinance banning blacks and whites from playing sports with or against each other. National Association of Professional Baseball Leagues president George Trautman, after confirming the existence of the ordinance, stated that he would not capitulate to the Birmingham law, but in fact the Texas League representative, the Corpus Christi Giants, willingly replaced its three African American players—including Texas League MVP Mike Lutz—on its postseason roster, as they and other Texas League clubs with black players had done during the regular season. The Birmingham Barons won the series, four games to two.

Subject: DIXIE SERIES

To all National Association Clubs and Leagues

For many years the play-off winners in the Southern Association and the Texas League have engaged in a post-season series known as the Dixie Series. The rules provide that this series is to be conducted under a Board of Control consisting of the Presidents of the two leagues and the President of the National Association, or his designee. The rules also provide that any inter-league series must have the approval of the President of the National Association. Notice was given this office some time ago that the Southern Association and the Texas League wished to conduct a Dixie Series in 1958, the proposed series was routinely approved and Chauncey DeVault, President of the Appalachian League, was appointed to represent the President of the National Association on the Board of Control. The Birmingham Club won the play-offs in the Southern Association and has been standing by awaiting the outcome of the final play-off series in the Texas League. At this writing the Austin and Corpus Christi clubs, of that league, are contending in a best-out-of-seven series for the right to represent the Texas League in the Dixie Series, each team having won three games.

Following approval of the Dixie Series, this office was informed that the City of Birmingham has an ordinance under which white players cannot participate in baseball games in which Negro players appear. To ascertain whether such an ordinance actually exists and, if so, whether it could be repealed, or suspended to enable playing of the Dixie Series games scheduled for Birmingham, I telegraphed Honorable J. W. Morgan, Mayor of Birmingham, on September 22 as follows:

Reported here City of Birmingham has ordinance under which Negro players cannot participate in baseball games with white players. Please wire collect whether this is correct and it if is correct, whether ordinance could be repealed or suspended to enable playing of Dixie Series baseball games in Birmingham. Query occasioned by fact that Austin and Corpus Christi baseball clubs, now contending to represent Texas League for right to meet Birmingham Club, champion of the Southern Association, for the Dixie Series championship, both have Negro players.

Mayor Morgan replied:

There is an ordinance prohibiting playing of games between the races here in Birmingham. It was voted three one June first, 1954. Shortly after the Supreme Court decision.* Therefore, we cannot repeal or suspend it.

The Dixie Series in 1958 was proposed as a best-out-of-seven series, the first two games to be played in Birmingham, the next three in the city of the Texas League play-off winner and the final two, if necessary, in Birmingham. My information is that 4 of the eligible players on the Austin team are Negroes as are 3 on the Corpus Christi team. To ascertain whether the Austin or Corpus Christi clubs would play in Birmingham in view of this ordinance, an inquiry was dispatched to those clubs. Austin has informed me that it will not play any games in Birmingham so long as the ordinance exists but that it would be willing to play the entire series in Austin, or in a neutral city, if a transfer of the Birmingham games could be arranged. Corpus Christi has stated that it has agreed with Birmingham to play the Birmingham games by substituting 3 white players, not now on its roster of eligible players, for its 3 Negro players, such white players to appear only in the Birmingham games.

The Birmingham Club was contacted to ascertain whether Birmingham would be willing to play all seven games in Austin, or in a neutral city, in the event Austin wins the Texas League play-offs. Birmingham has stated that it cannot see its way clear to do so. Therefore, the Dixie Series will not be played if Austin wins the Texas League play-offs.

As to the Corpus Christi–Birmingham agreement for the substitution of players, no provision of any professional baseball rule bars a man from appearing in a game because of his race, color or creed. There is, therefore, no reason, under baseball rules, why the Negro players could not participate in the games at Birmingham. Because of this, I will not approve any agreement for substitution solely to enable the playing of a white player for a Negro. Such approval would, in my opinion, constitute a yielding, in the interest of expediency, to the Birmingham ordinance, which ordinance, as indicated, conflicts with the traditional attitude of professional baseball on this question. Therefore, the request that Corpus Christi be permitted to expand its eligible player list must be denied, and if Corpus Christi elects to play the games in Birmingham, it may play only such players as it has already certified as being eligible for the Dixie Series. Should Corpus Christi feel

*The Supreme Court decision in question is *Brown v. Board of Education,* announced on May 17, 1954. On June 1 the voters of Birmingham approved, by a three-to-one margin, the ordinance banning interracial athletic competition, which overturned a January 1954 ordinance passed in order to attract major league exhibition games.—Ed.

that it cannot participate under these circumstances, the approval given the Dixie Series by this office will be withdrawn.

Should the Dixie Series not be played, substantial losses will be suffered by the players who were to participate and by the competing clubs and their leagues. It also would cause the loss to baseball for 1958 of a series which has earned, over the years, an enviable place in the affections of the fans of its area. Regrettable though it is, it must be preferred over the far greater loss that would come from a surrender by professional baseball of the principle that no man shall be barred from participation in a game solely because of his race, color or creed.

Very truly yours,

George M. Trautman

President

58

Second All-Star Game Approved (1959)

SOURCE: *New York Herald Tribune*, May 2, 1959

In an effort to bolster the players' pension fund, the MLBPA endorsed a proposal from NL representative Robin Roberts to play two All-Star Games annually. The suggestion was quickly approved by the owners. The second game for the 1959 season was awarded to Los Angeles, where the American League avenged its loss in the first game by winning 5–3. Two All-Star Games were played in each of the next three seasons, but on August 8, 1961, Commissioner Frick decided to eliminate the second game.

TWO ALL-STAR CONTESTS PROPOSED EACH SEASON

Two major league All-Star baseball games may be played this year and there is a strong probability two such games will be played each year in the future.

Robin Roberts, Phillies pitcher and National League player representative, presented the proposal to the major league executive council yesterday and it was favorably received by that group.

"The council liked it immediately," commissioner Ford Frick, who is chairman of the council, said today.

"Now it is up to a vote of the players, and I understand Frank Scott, the representative of the new players' central office, already has started the poll.

"If the suggestion is approved by the players it will be submitted to the club owners for their approval.

"It is impossible to say what the chances are of playing two all-star games this year, but I imagine the players can act very fast, and I know the council and club owners can act fast if necessary."

Roberts' proposal, which has the approval of Eddie Yost, the American League representative on the pension committee, would have the two games played in different sections of the country, with the proceeds from the additional games used for the promotion of amateur baseball, the Old Timers Association pension, and other purposes to be decided upon later.

Frick said that if the players vote for the two games and the club owners follow the recommendation of the council, the two contests might yet be played this year if a second break in the schedule could be arranged.

In future years, if the resolution is adopted, the two games would be played during one break [if] the schedule could be arranged.

SAME TEAMS

"With plane travel as it is today it would create no problem," Frick said. "The same teams would compete in both games." The teams now are chosen by the players, managers and coaches, with the managers naming the pitchers. The game this year is scheduled for July 7 at Pittsburgh.

Only one member of the council—Chuck Comiskey, of the Chicago White Sox—was absent when Roberts' suggestion was received and approved.

The members are National League president Warren Giles, American League president Joe Cronin, Walter O'Malley, of the Los Angeles Dodgers and Bob Carpenter, of the Phillies, representing the National League, and George Weiss, of the New York Yankees and Comiskey, representing the American League.

Although saying it was impossible to forecast the result of the players' poll, Frick hinted the club owners would go for the idea. "We had three of them here giving their approval," he remarked.

59

Haddix Pitches Twelve Perfect Innings and Loses (1959)

SOURCE: *Pittsburgh Press*, May 27, 1959

Harvey Haddix enjoyed more than a one-game career. He won twenty games for the St. Louis Cardinals in 1953, when he was named to the All-Star Game for the first of three consecutive seasons. The diminutive lefthander had nine seasons with ten or more victories, finishing his fourteen-year career with a respectable 136-113 record. Yet, like Bill Mazeroski and Bobby Thomson, Haddix was a veteran player destined to be forever remembered for one historic performance.

Haddix, pitching against the two-time defending National League champion Milwaukee Braves in their ballpark, retired the first thirty-six batters he faced, a feat never matched in a single game. Only the ineptitude of his teammates, who were unable to score off Lew Burdette despite getting twelve hits, prevented Haddix from winning the game in regulation. In the thirteenth inning the Braves converted an error, a walk, and a

Joe Adcock blast over the fence into only one run, but that was all Burdette needed. Although Haddix lost the game, for thirty-two years he would hold the honor of pitching a perfect game—until the official definition of a no-hitter was changed in 1991. Nevertheless, his achievement will be remembered as one of the greatest in baseball history.

HADDIX LOSES "GREATEST GAME"

Pirate Lefty Hurls 12 Perfect Innings Before Bowing, 1–0

By Lester J. Biederman, Press Staff Writer

MILWAUKEE, May 27—Harvey Haddix, a slightly built 33-year-old Pirate lefthander, lost the greatest game ever pitched in the long history of baseball here last night but he took the 1–0 defeat like the man he is.

Haddix regretted the loss of the one-hit game more than he appreciated the glory of pitching 12 perfect innings before the Braves won the bitterly-contested battle in the 13th inning on an error, an intentional walk and a "double."

"I knew I had a no-hitter because the scoreboard is in plain view but I wasn't so certain about it being a perfect game," Haddix calmly related the details of baseball's finest pitching spectacle.

"I thought perhaps I might have walked somebody in the early innings but going down the stretch, my main idea was to win. We needed this one badly to keep going."

The Braves went up and down in one-two-three order for the first 12 innings as the 19,194 fans realized they were witnessing one of the epics of baseball. Many of the fans cheered each Brave putout but when the Milwaukeeans finally broke through in the 13th inning, the local fans began yelling for the victory.

ERROR GIVES BRAVES BREAKTHROUGH

Felix Mantilla hit an ordinary grounder to Don Hoak in the Braves' 13th inning and in Hoak's haste to keep Haddix's streak going, he threw low into the dirt and the ball skipped off Rocky Nelson's left foot for an error.

Ed Mathews sacrificed Mantilla to second and Haddix gave up his only walk of the night, an intentional pass to the major leagues' leading batter, dangerous Hank Aaron.

Joe Adcock, who had fanned twice and grounded out the other two times, picked on Haddix's second pitch—a high slider—and sent it into right-center.

Bill Virdon and Joe Christopher raced to the spot and Virdon made a frantic leap but the ball barely cleared the fence about 375 feet away. The fans roared as Haddix and his Pirate teammates walked off the field heartbroken at the sudden turn of events.

But the excitement still wasn't ended. Mantilla, who was on second base, scored easily but Aaron rounded second base then cut across the pitcher's mound for the Braves' dugout.

Adcock, seeing the umpire's signal for a home run, simply kept on running and passed Aaron between second and third base. The umpires stood on the field as Fred Haney and his coaches tried to regroup their runners.

Finally, Aaron and Adcock began retracing their steps from third to second but actually, Adcock was out when he passed Aaron. Adcock thus received credit for a double and a run batted in.

BUCS' 12 HITS TO NO AVAIL

The run was unearned. Thus Haddix lost, 1–0, on one hit, although his teammates nicked Lew Burdette for 12 safeties but just couldn't score.

{The score last night was announced as 2–0, but Warren Giles, president of the National League, today ruled that the official score was 1–0. Giles ruled that Joe Adcock, who hit a three-run "homer," would be credited with a two-base hit because he didn't touch all the bases and the Braves given one run since this was all they needed to win.}

The Pirates could have won the game in the third inning when they bunched three singles. But Roman Mejias tried to go from first to third on Haddix's sharp rap off Burdette's leg.

The ball rolled a few feet toward second base but Johnny Logan grabbed it and made a fine throw to third to nail Mejias. Dick Schofield, who singled three times off Burdette, came through with a single but Bill Virdon flied out.

Nelson had singled in the second inning and was rubbed out on Bob Skinner's double-play ball. Mejias singled in the fifth and this time, Haddix rolled into a double play.

Burdette peeled off the next 10 batters before the Pirates made a bold bid for victory in the ninth inning. Virdon singled to center with one out, held first as Smoky Burgess flied out but rolled to third on Nelson's single to right. But Skinner grounded out to Adcock.

Haddix took the mound to meet the test of nine perfect innings as he faced the Braves in their half and he did. It was very easy as he fanned two of the three batters.

Hoak singled with one out in the 10th but didn't move. Schofield scratched a single off Burdette's bare hand to open the 11th but Virdon, after trying to bunt, forced him. Then Burgess hit into a double play.

Bill Mazeroski singled with two gone in the 12th but Hoak forced him and Schofield turned up with his third hit after two were out in the 13th, but Virdon grounded out.

Haddix struck out eight, all in the first nine innings and the only walk issued by either pitcher in the 13 innings was the intentional pass Haddix yielded to Aaron in the final frame.

If both teams can come down to earth tonight, Warren Spahn will pitch against Vern Law.

60

Formation of Continental League Announced (1959)

SOURCE: Senate Subcommittee on Antitrust and Monopoly, *Organized Professional Team Sports*, 86th Cong., 1st sess., 1959, 76, 212–14.

William Shea, chairman of the Mayor's Baseball Committee of the City of New York, was a fast worker. Less than two years after being charged with the responsibility of obtaining a major league team for New York, he and Branch Rickey led an effort that gave hope to many other large cities with similar aspirations. The creation of the Continental League (CL) was announced on July 27, but it had been an open secret almost from the beginning. Although Commissioner Frick promised cooperation, he and the baseball owners hoped to subvert the movement before it started. On May 21 they met in Columbus, Ohio, and agreed on a resolution which listed the conditions that must be met for a rival league to gain their endorsement as a legitimate major league.

Shea's press release is reprinted on pages 212–14. The Columbus resolution, along with Frick's notes on the session, appears on page 76. Frick and Shea both testified at this session, and they were joined by new CL president Branch Rickey (who accepted the position on August 18) in hearings the following year published as Organized Professional Team Sports—1960.

PRESS RELEASE ISSUED BY WILLIAM A. SHEA, JULY 27, 1959

Formal organization of a third major league to be called "The Continental League of Professional Baseball Clubs," was announced today by the five founding cities—New York, Houston, Toronto, Minneapolis/St. Paul, and Denver.

William A. Shea, New York attorney who is chairman of Mayor Robert F. Wagner's baseball committee, was selected chairman of the founders' group of the new league.

The new league contemplates playing its first major league season of 154 games in 1961 with a minimum of 8 clubs. The league's founders indicated that the active interest and demands of other cities in obtaining franchises in the new baseball organization could conceivably result in a larger circuit. Among the other cities who have evidenced interest in obtaining franchises in the Continental League are Buffalo, Montreal, Atlanta, New Orleans, Miami, Indianapolis, Dallas/Fort Worth, Seattle, Portland, San Diego, and San Juan, P.R.

Each of the five founders has deposited the sum of $50,000 in the Continental League treasury for organizational purposes and franchises have been awarded to—

New York, Mrs. Joan W. Payson, Mrs. Dorothy J. Killam, Dwight F. Davis, Jr.,
    G. Herbert Walker, Jr., William Simpson, and Donald M. Grant. [*sic*]
Houston, Houston Sports Association, Craig F. Cullinan, Jr., chairman.

Toronto, Jack Kent Cooke.

Minneapolis/St. Paul, Wheelock Whitney, Jr., et al.

Denver, Robert L. Howsam.

During meetings over the past 3 days in New York, the founders' group, which has been working on formation of the new league since last March, adopted a constitution; set up procedures for screening and qualifying other cities for membership; made plans to comply with Senator Kefauver's request to appear before his antitrust subcommittee in Washington, July 31, and prepared to confer in joint session with the two major leagues in New York August 18.

"The Continental League is the result of the increasing demand from cities in this country and Canada for major league baseball," said Mr. Shea. "Not only New York, since losing the Giants and Dodgers, but many other cities have done everything within their power to obtain franchises in the two existing major leagues without success. By trial and error it developed that the only way to provide major league baseball for an increasing number of communities on this continent was to form a new major league. There was no other way.

"The Continental League will offer baseball of the highest quality. Its stadiums and its talent will be second to none. This will require a substantial capital investment by every member of the league, a minimum of $2,500,000, exclusive of the cost of providing a stadium and other facilities."

The new league set a minimum seating capacity for its parks at 35,000. Minneapolis/St. Paul already has a $5 million stadium, built in 1955, which can easily be enlarged to meet the minimum requirement. Two other cities, New York and Houston, have plans to build new stadiums. Denver is presently working on plans for expansion of its stadium and increased parking. Toronto is negotiating with city officials for a major league stadium.

Mr. Shea said he looked forward to the fullest cooperation of the National and American Leagues, and expects that a program will be initiated at the joint meeting August 18 to bring the Continental League into the structure of major league baseball.

"We are, therefore, proceeding on the basis of complete and unqualified cooperation of the two existing major league," said Mr. Shea, "and have been encouraged by them in our efforts to proceed along that line. The Columbus declaration (May 22, 1959) [sic] of the two major leagues and their subsequent invitation to confer with them clearly establish that the National and American Leagues are ready to help the new league in a friendly and cooperative climate in return for the tremendous contribution being made by the new league to the national pastime."

Committees and individuals have been appointed to undertake the organizational work required in bringing the new league into fruition, said Mr. Shea. Among the important topics under consideration are: Selection and qualification of the additional cities; selection of a president and other officials; location of the league's offices; a study of pertinent baseball problems, including television, pensions, bonus payments, and major league-minor league relation. . . .

ATTACHMENT NO. 2

On May 22, 1959, in Columbus, Ohio, the press associations carried the formal announcement that the National and American Leagues agreed unanimously "to favorably consider" applications for major league status by "an acceptable group of eight clubs which could qualify."

Commissioner Fred [sic] Frick was quoted as saying, "There is no existing plan to expand the present major leagues."

"The best approach is to a third major league," Commissioner Frick was quoted by the press associations.

The commissioner stated that the principal purpose of the meeting was to discuss the policy of the major leagues regarding expansion of major league baseball. He reported that to his knowledge groups in various cities were actively engaged in seeking to organize a third major league and that he was aware that members of the two major leagues had been considering the possibility of expanding the present leagues to 10 or 12 clubs.

He stated that there was unquestionably great public interest and pressure for major league expansion and that it was important from the overall baseball standpoint to approach the problem in a constructive way. The commissioner recommended that baseball make a declaration of policy on the question of expansion for the guidance of all interested parties. It was pointed out that major league rule 1 (d) now provides certain requirements for an advance of an existing league to major league status.

After extended discussion of the matter, upon motion duly made and seconded, the following declaration of policy was adopted:

The major leagues recognize the desire of certain groups to attain major league franchises and since there is no existing path to expand the present major leagues, the two major leagues hereby declare they will favorably consider an application for major league status within the present baseball structure by an acceptable group of eight clubs which would qualify under the following:

(1) It is understood that the eight clubs making such application, themselves will be responsible for all territorial provisions and for all financial obligations necessary in setting up their organization and making their application.

(2) The clubs shall present with their application full and complete data establishing their abilities to meet the requirements for status including a full statement as to stock ownership, financial ability, and character, both of the group and the individual members.

(3) The population of each city of the proposed league shall be not less than the population of the smallest city in the present major leagues.

(4) Each club shall have available, or a commitment for, a park with a minimum of 25,000 capacity.

(5) They shall provide a balanced schedule of at least 154 games.

(6) They will adopt the major league minimum salary agreement with no maximum salary limitations.

(7) They will become parties to the major league agreement and the professional baseball agreement.

(8) They will accept the uniform major league baseball player's contract and agreement with all provisions therein.

(9) They will join in the players' pension plan or adopt a comparable plan, whichever may be acceptable at the time to the major league executive council.

(10) They shall file application for major league status at least 6 months prior to the meeting at which the application for major league status must be considered and at least 10 months before the opening of the season in which they hope to participate under major league status.

61

Negro American League Nearing the End (1959)

SOURCE: *Chicago Defender*, August 22, 1959

Amid the excitement generated by the prospect of eight new major league teams was the disappointment accompanying the collapse of the Negro American League (NAL). Following the death of the Negro National League after the 1948 season, the NAL's president, Dr. J. B. Martin, had managed to keep his organization alive. However, the very success of the Negro Leagues in finding and fostering African American players and fans led to their abandonment of the mother circuit for the major leagues, which all too often took the best talent without adequate compensation (if any was offered at all). Chicago Defender columnist Lee D. Jenkins makes clear that the promise of integration severely damaged the Negro Leagues, but he and Martin express their belief that the NAL can still be saved—if the black community acts quickly. That help—which some thought would come from Continental League president and former Dodger president Branch Rickey—would not arrive. The final NAL All-Star Game, traditionally the most important source of income for the league, was held in New York in 1961. The NAL officially folded after the 1963 season.

Lee D. Jenkins

NEGRO BASEBALL SHAKY; CONSIDER CLOSING SHOP

Opportunity is knocking loudly for a bright boy with workable ideas that will save the Negro American League from obscurity. Dr. J. B. Martin, league president, has sounded the death knell of the nation's last Negro professional baseball league. On the receipts of this year's play, the loop is on the threshold of becoming a fond memory.

Dr. Martin, league's president for the past 20 years, sees little hope that the NAL will be able to operate in 1960. Dr. Martin outlines the present season as a total failure.

"Everyone of the remaining five ball clubs is deep in the red," the Negro baseball veteran says. "The attendance has just been terrible. I've been doing everything I can to keep them playing but it looks hopeless."

The East-West classic performed for the 27th time in Comiskey Park was the last hope to bring the teams to a reasonable financial status. Only a few over 7,000 paid fans showed up for the game. The net amounted to $5,006.

This amount was divided equally between the Kansas City Monarchs, Detroit Stars, Raleigh Tigers, Birmingham Black Barons and the Memphis Red Sox. Needless to say, the take was far from enough to smooth out the money chaos.

"I have made money in Negro baseball," said Dr. Martin, "but for the past five or six years there has been no money made in Negro baseball."

The inroads of racial progress put the skids under the Negro league. The combination of Jackie Robinson and Branch Rickey brought forth the first painful symptoms. It has steadily dropped Negro baseball from a successful enterprise to a liability operating from the purse strings of Dr. Martin and a few other sincere supporters. These purse strings have worn thin and the purse itself has reached the inevitable emptiness.

Dr. B. B. Martin of the Memphis Red Sox has definitely thrown up his hands. Five thousand dollars in the hole from this season's play, he will not operate the Red Sox next season.

Ted Rasberry [sic] of the Detroit Stars is on the fence. His indecision may be shortlived though. Mrs. Rasberry may make his decision loud and clear.

"I've sunk a great deal of money into this year's play," Ted says, "and I don't think my wife is going to stand for this much longer. When I get home she may have everything locked up so I can't spend anymore."

Rasberry also manages the Harlem Satellites, one of the few remaining Negro owned touring basketball teams. Headed by Rookie Brown, the Satellites have been gaining friends and paying customers for the past two years during their circuits of the nation.

While his baseball interests have hit bottom, Rasberry has hopes of recouping his losses when the Satellites hit the road. On an optimistic note, he says: "The first two years you spend gaining friends. I think that we have done this. Everywhere we went, we can go back. We have a good team and we put on a good show. This should be the year for us to hit it big."

For Dr. Martin, the justice of the situation is not poetic. He was one of the staunchest boosters for the inclusion of Negro players in the major leagues. It seems a bit incongruous that this progressive interest should backfire to kill the thing that he loves most.

The major leagues can thank the NAL and the almost Negro National league for a multitude of colored big leaguers dating back to Jackie and going through the Milwaukee Braves bellwether Hank Aaron. It may be that the moguls will see fit to keep alive what has proved to be a sound training board for major league talent.

Certain overtures have come from the majors to Dr. Martin but the deals have been much too slight for serious consideration. A thin hope still remains that the majors will subsidize the NAL.

But at moment, the red ink is blinding NAL owners to any possibility of continuation. Just about everybody is positive in their conviction that there is a place for Negro baseball. A number are most optimistic concerning inclusion in the much-talked about third league.

The NAL needs little sympathy at [the] moment and even less non-constructive discussion. Negro baseball needs a shot in the arm but good. A shot consisting of money and solid ideas for survival is the prescription.

The shot better come quick or you can make ready to bury a most illustrious corpse suffering a most untimely death.

62

Los Angeles Wins Playoff, Goes to Series (1959)

SOURCE: *Los Angeles Herald Express,* September 30, 1959

After losing in the only two previous playoff series in major league baseball history, the Los Angeles Dodgers rewarded their new fans with its first World Series berth in California by completing a two-game sweep of the Milwaukee Braves with a dramatic twelve-inning 6–5 victory. In a reversal of the final 1951 playoff game, the Dodgers scored three runs in the bottom of the ninth to tie the score, then tallied the winning run on a two-out error by Felix Mantilla, who had moved from second base to shortstop in the seventh inning after an injury to Johnny Logan. In each case the run-producing batter was Carl Furillo, who fully redeemed himself for a subpar regular season. Los Angeles proceeded to win the World Series in six games over the Chicago White Sox, although Furillo—who went only 1-4 in the Series—ceded the hero roles to second baseman Charlie Neal and pitcher Larry Sherry.

The following article offers a preview of the upcoming World Series matchup with the White Sox prior to its analysis of the pivotal playoff game. The reporter notes that the Dodgers were an underdog to the upstart White Sox, to the amazement and amusement of Dodgers players and officials. Their confidence remained intact, even after being shellacked 11–0 in the opening game of the Series.

The incomplete Herald Express *box score has been supplemented with information from Jerry Lansche,* The Forgotten Championships: Postseason Baseball, 1882–1981 *(Jefferson* NC: *McFarland, 1989), p. 330.*

VICTORY VOWED BY "UNDERDOG" DODGERS

L.A. Club Laughs Off 11–10 Odds
By John B. Old

CHICAGO, Sept. 30—The Los Angeles Dodgers, fired up over their sensational victory in the National League playoff with the Milwaukee Braves, roared into Chicago today for the start of the World Series with the Chicago White Sox, opening tomorrow.

The Dodgers arrived to find themselves installed the underdogs at 11 to 10 odds in the series, 6–5 underdogs in the first game. This brought a derisive laugh from players and Mgr. Walt Alston.

The Dodgers have laughed at odds all season long, coming back to win "the hard way" in many of their crucial encounters. So the conflict with the White Sox, who swept the American League, scares them not a bit.

CRISP WEATHER

Partly cloudy skies are predicted for the opener, with crisp autumn weather. The outlook for Friday, the second day of the series, is the same.

Roger Craig is Manager Alston's opening nomination to hurl, and his opponent will be Early Wynn. Craig has a record of 11 wins, 5 losses; Wynn has 22 wins, 10 losses.

Alston, a usually reserved man who shows little emotion, was still "high" over his club's victory in that startling 6 to 5 victory in the second playoff game with Milwaukee.

PRAISE DODGER FANS

He was profuse in his praise of the Dodger fans who did so much to inspire the club to victory.

"There's no way to measure how much how wonderful fans helped the Dodgers win the National League pennant.

"But, all of us know—and sincerely appreciate—the big part you fans played. Every Dodger will do his level best to win the World Series."

That was the deep-rooted greatfulness [sic] expressed today by the Dodgers before plunging into preparation for tomorrow's opener—a 2 o'clock meeting to study reports on the White Sox hitters and a probable light workout at Comiskey Park.

BIGGEST WINDFALL

For the Cinderella Dodgers, case-hardened to uphill climbing, yesterday's 12-inning 6–5 Coliseum victory over the Braves set the stage for the richest player pool in World Series history—an estimated $10,000-$12,000 for losers, $15,000-$16,000 for winners.

"Being underdogs doesn't worry us. We've been playing that role all season," assured Alston.

After the first two games in spacious Comiskey Park (43,600) Thursday and Friday, the rivals will fly to Los Angeles where the third, fourth and fifth games, if necessary of the best four of seven series, will be played Sunday, Monday and Tuesday.

EDGE IN EXPERIENCE

Should sixth and seventh games be required, play will be resumed in Chicago the following Thursday and Friday.

Felix Mantilla's lack of experience at shortstop catapulted Los Angeles into its first major-league pennant. . . .

Two were out when Gil Hodges worked loser Bob Rush, last of the Braves' pitchers, for a walk, then catcher Joe Pignatano singled to left, advancing him to second.

Carl Furillo, responding to the screaming pleas of the 36,528 faithful, exploded a grounder slightly to the right of second base as Hodges sped to third.

Mantilla, moved over from second to short when Johnny Logan was sidelined in the seventh when hit by Norm Larker attempting to break up a double play, raced over to retrieve the ball and fired while off balance.

The ball bounded beyond the reach of first baseman Frank Torre as Hodges hied home with the biggest run in Los Angeles major league history.

Victory for the Dodgers seemed almost beyond reach as they came to bat in the ninth trailing 5–2, and Lew Burdette seemingly still in stout command.

Then the unbelievable happened. Wally Moon opened with a single through the box, his third hit of the game.

Snider, hitless in three times at bat, singled to center, and Hodges poled a line drive to left, filling the bases.

With Larker coming to bat Manager Fred Haney desperately rushed in Don McMahon in relief of Burdette.

Larker, though, wasn't to be denied, belting a single to left, scoring Moon and Snider and advancing Hodges to third.

Now Warren Spahn attempted to quell the uprising.

CLUTCH SACRIFICE

Furillo, a clutch player with the blue chips beckoning, promptly brought Hodges plateward with the tying run via a sacrifice fly to deep right.

Strangely, Pignatano didn't tag up and take second after the catch—a move that might have won the game in regulation distance, as Maury Wills followed with a single to center.

Leastwise, it would have advanced Pignatano to third from where he would have had a second chance as Ron Fairly forced Wills.

Pignatano's lapse loomed even larger as the Braves filled the bases in the eleventh. But Williams proved equal to the occasion, causing big Joe Adcock to ground into an inning-ending force play.

Taking a cue from the Braves, the Dodgers jammed the bases in the home half only to have Neal, who packed the big Dodger stick with a homer and a triple, ground out to end the threat.

Here Come Dodgers

	AB	R	H	BI	AVG.		AB	R	H	BI	AVG.
Bruton, CF	6	0	0	0	.289	Gilliam, 3B	5	0	1	0	.282
Mathews, 3B	4	2	2	1	.306	Neal, 2B	6	2	2	1	.287

	AB	R	H	BI	AVG.
Aaron, RF	4	1	2	0	.355
Torre, 1B	3	0	1	2	.228
Maye, LF	2	0	0	0	.307
Pafko, PH-LF	1	0	0	0	.218
Slaughter, LF	1	0	0	0	.167
DeMerit, LF	0	0	0	0	.200
Spangler, PH-LF ...	0	0	0	0	.417
Logan, SS	3	1	2	0	.291
Schoendienst, 2B ..	1	0	0	0	.000
Vernon, PH	1	0	0	0	.220
Cottier, 2B	0	0	0	0	.125
Adcock, PH	1	0	0	0	.292
Crandall, C	6	1	1	0	.257
Mantilla, 2B-SS	5	0	1	1	.215
Burdette, P	4	0	1	0	(21-15)
McMahon, P	0	0	0	0	(3-3)
Spahn, P	0	0	0	0	(21-15)
Jay, P	1	0	0	0	(6-11)
Rush, P	1	0	0	0	(5-6)
Totals	44	5	10	4	

	AB	R	H	BI	AVG.
Moon, RF-LF	6	1	3	1	.302
Snider, CF	4	0	1	0	.308
Lillis, PR	0	1	0	0	.229
Williams, P	2	0	0	0	(5-5)
Hodges, 1B	5	2	2	0	.276
Larker, RF	4	0	2	2	.289
Pignatano, PR-C ..	1	0	1	0	.237
Roseboro, C	3	0	0	0	.232
Furillo, RF	2	0	2	1	.290
Wills, SS	5	0	1	0	.260
Drysdale, P	1	0	0	0	(17-13)
Podres, P	1	0	0	0	(14-9)
Churn, P	0	0	0	0	(3-2)
Demeter, PH	1	0	0	0	.256
Koufax, P	0	0	0	0	(8-6)
Labine, P	0	0	0	0	(5-10)
Essegian, PH	0	0	0	0	.247
Fairly, CF	2	0	0	0	.238
Totals	48	6	15	5	

Milwaukee	2	1	0	0	1	0	0	1	0	0 0 0—5
Los Angeles	1	0	0	1	0	0	0	0	3	0 0 1—6

E—Snider, Neal, Mantilla 2. PO-A—Milwaukee, 35-13 (2 out when winning run scored); Los Angeles, 36-15. DP—Wills, Neal and Hodge Torre, Logan, and Torre. LOB—Milwaukee, 13; Los Angeles, 11.

2B—Aaron. 3B—Neal, Crandall. HR—Neal, Mathews. SF—Mantilla, Furillo.

Pitchers	IP	H	R	ER	BB	SO
Burdette	8+	10	5	5	0	4
McMahon	0	1	0	0	0	0
Spahn	⅓	1	0	0	0	0
Jay	2⅓	1	0	0	1	1
Rush (L, 5-6)	1	2	1	0	1	0
Drysdale	4⅓	6	4	3	2	3
Podres	2⅓	3	0	0	1	0
Churn	1⅓	1	1	1	0	0
Koufax	⅔	0	0	0	3	1
Labine	⅓	0	0	0	0	1
Williams (W, 5-5) ..	3	0	0	0	3	0

Burdette pitched to 3 batters in 9th; McMahon pitched to 1 batter in 9th.

HBP—Jay (Pignatano). WP—Podres. PB—Pignatano. U—Barlick, Plate; Boggess, 1B; Donatelli, 2B; Conlan, 3B; Jackowski, LF; Gorman RF. T—4:06. A—36,528.

63

Review of *Baseball: The Early Years* (1960)

SOURCE: *American Historical Review* 66 (October 1960): 239

Harold Seymour is rightly remembered as a pioneer in the field of sport history. Yet, as Seymour admitted in the preface to his 1956 dissertation (which was the basis for The Early Years*), he was not the first to attempt a scholarly examination of baseball history. A list of unpublished theses in the September 1936 edition of* Journalism Quarterly *(p. 353) mentioned six theses on sports journalism, several of which appear to take a historical perspective. Richard Armstrong (1947) and Peter Craig (1950), both cited by Seymour, wrote detailed analyses of the economic aspects of baseball through history, and graduate students like Robert Smith (1947) also addressed baseball history. In that same year, Robert Henderson published* Ball, Bat, and Bishop: Five Thousand Years of Sport *(New York: Rockport Press, 1947), which today remains an important resource after more than half a century. Moreover, the surge in antitrust lawsuits against baseball in the decade following World War II spurred many law students (including Craig, who was on the editorial board at the* Yale Law Review*) and legal scholars to publish law review articles on baseball, past and present. The massive 1951 congressional investigation of baseball, published the following year as* Organized Baseball, *compiled copious data on baseball for the first time. Although Seymour's contribution to baseball historiography was enormous, and his books, along with those of David Quentin Voigt, are still the authoritative sources on the subject, he was not the trailblazer he portrayed himself as.*

Nevertheless, Baseball: The Early Years *was the first scholarly book on baseball history, and it received strong reviews in the major historical journals, including the* Mississippi Journal Historical Review *(47 [December 1960]: 526–27) and the* American Historical Review. *The author of the latter review not only praised the book, but recommended that the entrepreneurs in charge of the Continental League and the American Football League read it in order to improve their chances of success.*

BASEBALL: THE EARLY YEARS. By *Harold Seymour.* (New York: Oxford University Press. 1960. Pp. x, 373. $7.50.) As the description on the jacket of this book states, it is not another history of players' exploits and batting averages but a serious study of the game both in the business offices and on the field. The titles of the four parts of the book give a good indication of the ground covered; "The Amateur Era," "Baseball Becomes a Business," "Organized Baseball," and "Monopoly at Its Apex." The first part deals with the origins and development of the game and the activities of the National Association of Professional Baseball Players through the year 1875. The second part treats the founding of the National League in 1876 and the financial problems that grew out of making the professional game pay as a business. Among these were salaries, discipline, and the reserve clause. The third part concerns rival organizations that attempted to compete with the National League and with bitter owner-player clashes. The fourth part describes vividly the highhanded actions of the National League owners during their years of monopoly under the twelve team league of 1892 to 1899 and with the successful fight made by the American League from 1901 to 1903 to become a permanent and equal rival of the older league. Sections of the book vary in appeal to different types of readers. Both historians and ordinary baseball fans will enjoy the chapters on the amateur era. Adherents of the American League will be delighted with the tribute in Part IV paid to its real founder and first president, Ban Johnson, and with the account of his achievements in raising the standards of the game above the sordid level that the National League permitted during the 1890s. For those today who are planning to invest in a new major league or in a new professional football league, Parts II and III should be compulsory reading. On the whole Parts I and IV are superior to II and III. The contention stated on the jacket that baseball "has always mirrored the economic and social growth of America" does not receive sufficient attention in the second and third parts, except for the chapter on the reserve clause. If a brief description at the beginning of several of the chapters had been given of typical practices in other businesses during the age of the robber barons, many of those in baseball would be seen in the proper setting. Short summaries at the end of Parts II and III of the features that were common to most businesses and those unique in baseball would have made a good book even better.

Donald Grove Barnes
Western Reserve University

64

Mazeroski Home Run Lifts Pirates to Stunning Series Win over Yankees (1960)

SOURCE: *Pittsburgh Press*, October 14, 1960

It could be argued that Bill Mazeroski's dramatic, Series-winning home run—at that time the only such blow in World Series history—delayed his selection to the National Baseball Hall of Fame. In his seventeen-year career Mazeroski was elected to seven All-Star Games, helped the Pittsburgh Pirates win two World Series, and is widely acclaimed as the greatest defensive second baseman in baseball history. However, he is remembered today mostly for one hit, which critics can dismiss as a lucky blow, or as an example of being in the right place at the right time.

Both arguments are refuted in the following article. Reporter Lester J. Biederman notes that the Pirates' only home run prior to the seventh game was also hit by Mazeroski. Moreover, Mazeroski contributed to the offense in other ways, as his .320 average demonstrates. He was the only Pirate to score more than one run in the final game, an illustration of the balance that enabled Pittsburgh to overcome the astonishing offensive performance of the New York Yankees and win their first world championship since 1925.

PIRATE CHAMPS "TEAM OF DESTINY"

Maz, Smith Homers Kill Yankee Hopes
Nelson Also Bombs As Haddix Gains Win in 10–9 Finale

By Lester J. Biederman

CLOUD NINE, Pa., Oct. 14—Team of destiny? Well, can you think of a better word to describe the brand new World Champion Pirates?

This surely was a team of destiny with tremendous spirit and unmatched desire. They bolted through the National League like true champions, then carried the power-packed Yankees to seven games before beating them yesterday at Forbes Field, 10–9, with their very own weapon—the deadly home run.

And with it, they won the greatest prize baseball has to offer—the world championship in their first opportunity since 1927, when the same Yankee organization humiliated them in four straight games.

Mark it: Dept repaid in full.

Until yesterday, the Pirates had only hit one home run (Bill Mazeroski in the opener) to eight for the Yankees in the first six games. Then after the American Leaguers blasted a pair in this vital seventh game, the Pirates saved their best two shots until they needed 'em.

Hal Smith came through with a dramatic three-run blast over the left-field wall with two outs and the Pirates trailing, 6–7, in the eighth inning that rocked old Forbes Field and brought the 36,683 fans up screaming.

The Yankees tied it in the top of the ninth but this was only temporary.

Then when Bill Mazeroski drilled Ralph Terry's second pitch over the left-field wall leading off the ninth inning to crack the 9–9 tie and bring Pittsburgh its first world championship since 1925 with a 10–9 victory, there was a thunderous ovation awaiting Maz and his teammates when he finally touched home plate.

There have been similar scenes at Forbes Field all season long but none that meant as much as this one.

The whirlwind finish was as dramatic as any World Series game in many years. Yet it seemed the Mazeroski game-winning homer was a little anticlimactic after Smith's two-out three-run homer that came with such swiftness it almost numbed the fans before they really cut loose.

The Pirates and their fans figured the game was over then and there but the Yankees tied it in the ninth only to allow Maz to become the hero with his home run that sailed majestically over the left-field wall and sent the crowd into a frenzy never matched in this city.

This blow touched off a celebration in Pittsburgh that lasted far into the night and was heard around the world.

The Pirates simply had one more last-inning rally left in their systems and they gave the Yankees a dose of it. They won 23 games during the year in their final turn at bat and this time they proved that lightning can and does strike more than once.

By the time Maz circled the bases and was escorted to the dugout, the fans had started swarming on the field, making it difficult for the Yankees to trudge silently and solemnly to their clubhouse.

The game started out as a duel between Vern Law, trying for his third victory despite a lame right ankle, and Bob Turley, who won the second game here.

Rocky Nelson gave Law a fast 2–0 lead when he homered in the first inning after Bob Skinner walked and in the second inning, the Pirates chased Turley when Smokey Burgess led off with a single.

They filled the bases on Bill Stafford with a walk and Maz's safe bunt but when Stafford took Law's bouncer and started a double play, it appeared he was home safe. However, Bill Virdon cracked a two-run single and now Law enjoyed a 4–0 lead.

Bill Skowron spoiled the shutout with a right-field homer in the fifth but when Bobby Richardson singled and Tony Kubek walked to open the sixth, Danny Murtaugh felt Law's ankle was acting up and he called in Roy Face.

Face retired Roger Maris but Mickey Mantle singled for one run and Yogi Berra drilled a three-run homer into right field and now the Yankees had a 5–4 lead.

Bobby Shantz protected this margin expertly and then Face yielded two more runs in the top of the eighth on a walk, Skowron's scratch single, John Blanchard's looping single to center and Cletis Boyer's double to left.

But in their half of the eighth, the Pirates got a break, a big break. Gino Cimoli dropped a pinch-single into right, and Kubek waited for Virdon's grounder but it took a bad hop and hit him in the throat.

Instead of one out or a double play, the Pirates now had runners on first and second, and the fans were screaming. Dick Groat singled for a run and Jim Coates relieved Shantz. Skinner sacrificed but Nelson flied out and fans moaned.

Then came another real break. Roberto Clemente grounded to Skowron but Coates didn't cover first base and Clemente beat it for a hit, Virdon scoring.

This seemed to breathe new life into the Pirates and they took advantage of it as they've done so often during the season.

Coates had two strikes on Smith and even had him swing and miss strike two but the husky catcher took dead aim on a 2-2 low fast ball and the moment he connected everybody knew the destination—Schenley Park.

When Smith touched home plate with the run that gave the Pirates a 9–7 edge, the customers were limp from excitement.

But the Yankees still had some fight left. Bob Friend came in to pitch the ninth and Richardson singled and so did pinch-hitter Dale Long. Exit Friend, enter Harvey Haddix. Maris fouled out but Mantle singled for a run.

Berra hit a sharp grounder down the first base line but Nelson grabbed it, stepped on first and tried to tag Mantle but Mickey slid back safely as the tying run crossed the plate.

Maz didn't keep the fans waiting long in the Pirate ninth. He took the first pitch for a ball, then met a high fast ball and sent it sailing over the left-field wall and the Pirates became the champions of all baseball.

No game today!

5

Legislating Baseball

During the early 1960s the commissioner and baseball owners, governmental agencies, and the judiciary took steps to manage the future (and protect the past) of the sport. Congress continued to stage occasional investigations of the major leagues, although after 1965 it waited a decade for its next baseball hearing. The result of these efforts was negligible, except in the record books, where Commissioner Ford Frick's "distinctive mark" branded Roger Maris's new home run record as an outsider to baseball tradition. After a tumultuous decade of legal and legislative challenges to baseball's reserve clause and a variety of other disruptions, baseball officials needed to reestablish control over their game, or someone else would.

This process started with the agreement with Continental League officials to place expansion teams in four of their cities in 1961 and 1962—a promise broken by the American League. Shortly afterward the owners slowed the hemorrhaging of the minor leagues by placing them totally under the control of the majors. Two years later, during the winter meetings in late 1964, the retiring Frick convinced owners that the powers of the commissioner's office, reduced twenty years earlier, had to be restored for the good of the game.

New York's Yankees dominated the game on the field, winning five consecutive AL pennants, but Kansas City was arguably the focal point of the game during this era. A Kansas City native, Casey Stengel, survived his controversial firing by the Yankees to resurface with the expansion New York Mets in 1962. In 1961 local fans endured the debut of volatile Athletics owner Charles O. Finley, mourned the retirement (almost) of Monarch legend

Satchel Paige, and cursed the trade that sent Maris to the Yankees in 1959. No doubt they wished someone had reestablished control over the game earlier.

65

NL Upholds Promise, Awards Franchises to Two CL Teams; AL Reneges (1960)

SOURCE: October 21, 1960, letter to M. Donald Grant, Branch Rickey Papers, Box 40, Folder 3, Manuscript Division, Library of Congress; November 1, 1960, Press Release, Branch Rickey Papers, Box 40, Folder 8, Manuscript Division, Library of Congress

The Continental League died on August 2, 1960, and William Shea was pleased—but not completely satisfied. On that date representatives of the NL and AL promised Shea that each league would accept two of the CL franchises. The NL upheld its promise by granting Houston and New York expansion teams for the 1962 season, and Shea received his reward by having the Mets' new stadium named for him. However, the AL reneged by ignoring other CL investors and instead voted Los Angeles and Washington (to replace the original Senators, who fled to Minneapolis, a CL city) into the league for the 1961 season.

The following documents reveal that CL president Branch Rickey suspected that the AL might not fulfill the August agreement on the prescribed timetable, but that he would proceed on the assumption that the AL would eventually comply. When the AL's expansion plans were announced, Rickey was outraged, but not defeated. He held out the hope that baseball officials, perhaps encouraged by the support of Congress, would stop interfering with efforts to create a third major league. His wish was never fulfilled, but the majority of CL cities eventually obtained major league franchises.

October 21, 1960
Mr. M. Donald Grant
Fahnestock & Co.
65 Broadway
New York City
Dear Don:
The National League has selected New York and Houston as the two additional clubs.

The American League is meeting in New York this coming Wednesday, October 26th, for the avowed purpose of selecting two additional clubs.

If, at this meeting, the American League names the two additional clubs, then in accordance with our previous understanding the four clubs so selected by the two majors should meet immediately.

Therefore, I am now requesting that the four clubs meet in New York not later than Friday, October 28th, at 10 A.M. at the League office, 680 Fifth Avenue.

The American League at its meeting may not make a selection, but may issue a public statement to the effect that it must take further investigation and possibly name a later date for the decisive meeting. In that case it seems to me that it is equally important for an immediate meeting of the prospective American League clubs to meet with the two clubs now selected by the National League to discuss the effects of this surprising delay. Obviously, involved as one of several items, is the December draft of players.

Therefore, in case of indecision by the American League next Wednesday, it seems necessary that all Continental League clubs meet at the earliest convenient date, certainly not later than Monday, October 31st, at the League office.

You will recall, I am sure, the four points discussed at some length by your President on the occasion of our last meeting. I mention them again as follows:

1. Availability of players on major league rosters.
2. Priority on waiver players.
3. Priority on draft.
4. *And, extremely important*—Organized production of players from the free agency field.

I think that any one of these four items is of sufficient importance to justify the meeting. But particularly the fourth one challenges without delay your consideration of ways and means of implementing that program.

The above letter has been sent to all eight clubs in the Continental League.
Very truly yours,
Branch Rickey
President

RELEASE 12 NOON—TUESDAY, NOVEMBER 1, 1960, AND THEREAFTER STATEMENT BY MR. BRANCH RICKEY

The action of the American League at its recent meeting was a very great disappointment. I believed for two years that the American League actually favored expansion of baseball, i.e. internal expansion. They were constantly opposed to the organization of a third major league, but favored expansion of their own league to include other cities. Eight Continental League cities did apply for admission to major league status and the American League committee in Chicago on August 2nd unanimously agreed to accept four of these Continental League cities, two immediately and two later.

About two weeks later under date of August 17th, the New York Journal-American reported as follows:

"Commenting on Topping's insistence that the American League move into Los Angeles, Webb declared: "We don't care what happens in Los Angeles too much, either. The Continental cities will get the first four franchises. There's no question about that . . ."

On August 18th, Mr. John Drebinger of the New York Times, reported in his column as follows:

"A prominent member of that major league committee that sat with the Continentals in Chicago is understood to be most determined the major leagues stick to the agreement they made that day.

"We gave our word to these people (meaning the Continental League) that we would accept four of their cities in our ten-club expansion plans, this committeeman is quoted as saying, "and, for one, I intend to see that agreement is kept."

No one will deny that the American League committee in Chicago on August 2nd agreed unanimously to accept the personnel of the Continental League in the expansion program. There was a conversational understanding that there would be action within 30 days. It was 85 days before the American League took any action whatever on their committee's recommendation. During that period the Continental League cities applying for major league admission were admonished time and again by one or another of the American League members to develop its qualifications—here as to personnel—there as to park construction—or financial status. The Continental League group were ardent locally on the subject of indemnities, hiring personnel and particularly dealing with the city authorities on park construction.

About the middle of September, the American League held an all-day and evening meeting and at the close of the evening session a leading member said: "You have been in session all day long and you have not done a G--D--- thing." From August 2nd until October 26, the Continental League group was consistently led to believe that two of their clubs would be chosen by the American League.

The prominence of the American League committee indicates beyond doubt that in appointing those four members for the purpose of coming to an expansion agreement with the Continental League, there would be no dissenting vote to the recommendations of its committee. What happened on October 26th in New York at the meeting of the American League must have been shocking to certain members of that committee and indicates a designing insincerity on the part of some members of the American League to defeat any possibility of the organization of the Continental League. Their action on October 26th was not only unfair to the Continental League and the National League, but it was unfair to the American public in defeating any proper concept of major league expansion into a number of great cities throughout our country.

Every member of the American League committee should know that they have thrown down its committee recommendations and no dissimilation of language can change the unwelcome facts. It was not a philologist who said the other day that the dictionary definition of perfidy was now confirmed.

The American League did not choose a single one of the Continental League group and they did not expand except to move the Washington club into one city that had not previously been in either major league. That is not expansion. That is simply extension. It is difficult to understand how reputable gentlemen will explain this breach of good faith.

The Continental League effort has resulted in inclusion by the National League of two cities, namely Houston and New York. The National League "kept its word" and, I am sure, will continue to "keep its word," by selecting two additional teams from the Continental group. Surely, the American League must do likewise.

What is the Continental League going to do about it? Neither that group nor any other future group can further expand, if now the American League can validate the reserve clause. In that case, 20 great cities, having in mind the recreational advantages of 180,000,000 people, will have to go, hat in hand, to the American League for procedural instruction if a third major league is ever to be organized. The high minor leagues are doomed and the expansion of baseball, major-league wise, becomes otherwise impossible.

It is now squarely up to the Congress of the United States to protect major league expansion in this country.

66

The Major League Perspective on
Congressional Investigations (1961)

SOURCE: Paul A. Porter, *Organized Baseball and the Congress: A Review and Chronological Summary of the Past Ten Years*, Box 9, Philadelphia National League Club Records, Hagley Museum and Library.

After surviving three-quarters of a century without interference or inquiry from the U.S. Congress, major league baseball officials testified at a half-dozen congressional hearings over the next decade. The hearings dealt with baseball's antitrust exemption as it applied to franchise relocation, expansion, player transactions, and television regulations, among other subjects. Although the major leagues received much criticism from senators and congressmen during these hearings, baseball's exemption remained intact. Baseball officials prepared for congressional hearings as carefully as they did for the numerous court cases they faced during the same period. Paul Porter, lead attorney for organized baseball, attributed baseball's success in the judicial and legislative arenas to the inherent wisdom of the original decision to grant the exemption, but he took care to aggressively publicize, and lobby for, baseball's legal position.

Organized Baseball and the Congress was prepared on the request of Commissioner Frick for the benefit of baseball owners. Porter delivered the draft on February 25, 1961, after the bruising battle with the founders of the Continental League had been concluded. Excerpted below are the introduction and summary of the 1960 hearing at which issues raised by CL *supporters were heard. The excerpts are taken from pages 5–7 and 33–41.*

On January 30, 1970, Porter updated and adapted this document. Organized Baseball and the Antitrust Laws *is reprinted in House Select Committee on Professional Sports,* Inquiry into Professional Sports, *94th Cong., 2nd sess., 1976, 426–39.*

I. INTRODUCTION

By express authority of the Supreme Court, Organized Baseball—the National Pastime—has long been exempt from the antitrust laws. This immunity was first recognized by the High Court's 1922 decision in *Federal Baseball Club v. National League,* 259 U.S. 200, that baseball was not "trade or commerce" within the meaning of the Sherman Act. That decision was reaffirmed in *Toolson v. New York Yankees, Inc.,* 346 U.S. 356, decided in 1953.

Nevertheless, during the past ten years, Organized Baseball has been the subject of repeated congressional inquiries—including six formal committee hearings—concerning its status under the Federal antitrust laws. During that period, no less than 37 separate bills dealing with this subject have been introduced in the Congress. These have varied widely in their provisions—ranging from proposals that Organized Baseball be subjected to the full sweep of the antitrust laws, on the one hand, to measures which would legislatively endorse the current complete judicial exemption, on the other hand. Intermediate positions would have authorized limited immunity for some aspects of Organized Baseball, such as player-club relations, recognition of exclusive territorial rights, and rules of the game.

Congress enacted none of these bills, although most of them were the subject of intensive hearings on both sides of the Congress, and two, one in the House and one in the Senate, reached the floor.

The antitrust status of Organized Baseball has been and remains the subject of sustained legislative concern in part because of high public interest in the national game and, more recently, because of the Supreme Court decision, in *Radovich v. National Football League,* 352 U.S. 445 (1957), denying antitrust exemption to another organized team sport, Professional Football.

Representatives of Organized Baseball have played an active role throughout the various congressional proceedings dealing with its antitrust status. They have presented witnesses at every hearing. Baseball's views have been circulated in writing to every member of the Congress at those sessions in which legislation reached the floor. The position of Organized Baseball, including both the Major and Minor Leagues, has been, and continues to be, that any legislation adopted should preserve and reinforce its immunity from the antitrust laws. Baseball endorses similar immunity for other team sports.

Organized Baseball is gratified that its position has been vindicated by the action of the Congress on both of the occasions when legislation reached the floor. In the first instance, during 1958, the House enacted legislation continuing Baseball's unambiguous exemption from the antitrust laws and extending the same exemption to the other leading organized team sports—football, basketball and hockey. In the second instance, during 1960, a regulatory bill, limiting Baseball's exemption, was defeated on the Senate floor and remitted to committee.

The purposes of this memorandum are to summarize in chronological order the numerous antitrust proposals and hearings, including related judicial decisions, in which Baseball has been involved in the past ten years and briefly to analyze the bills that are pending in the current session of Congress. There is appended hereto a chronology of the key developments since the first congressional inquiry into Baseball's operations in 1951. . . .

VII. THE THIRD KEFAUVER HEARING

Early in 1960, the sports pages were filled with reports of the proposed formation of a third Major League, the Continental League. Promoters of this new league persuaded Senator [Estes] Kefauver to include a provision in his 1960 "Sports Bill" designed to assist in the formation and development of the new league.

On May 5, 1960, Senator Kefauver accordingly introduced S. 3483 (86th Cong., 2d Sess.). This bill was divided into two sections. The first section provided basically the same anti-trust exemptions for football, basketball and hockey as were contained in Senator Kefauver's 1959 bill, S. 2545, which had excluded Baseball from its scope. The second part of the bill was directed at Baseball alone, and proposed the following:

1. Application of the Sherman, Clayton and Federal Trade Commission Acts to Baseball, except as the bill (S. 3483) otherwise provided.

2. Antitrust exemption for contracts, rules, etc., relating to:

(a) equalization of playing strength;

(b) acquisition by a Major League club of absolute control over 40 players (plus 60 other players in their first 4 years of organized baseball), thus subjecting all other players to unrestricted draft;

(c) territorial rights; and

(d) the preservation of public confidence in the honesty of sports contests.

3. Condemnation, as an antitrust violation, of any contract, rule, etc., preventing, hindering, obstructing or adversely affecting the formation and operation of a new major league.

4. A 75-mile limitation on Baseball's regulation of television and other broadcasting.

On May 19–20, 1960, hearings were held before the Kefauver Antitrust Subcommittee of the Senate Judiciary Committee pursuant to Senate Resolution 238 (approved on February 8, 1960). There were only five witnesses: Commissioner Frick and George Trautman appeared in behalf of Organized Baseball; Branch Rickey, William Shea, and former Senator Edwin Johnson appeared in behalf of the Continental League. . . .

During the hearings, Commissioner Frick emphasized, among other points, the financial support given to the Minor League structure from Major League sources. He pointed out that, in the years 1957, 1958 and 1959, the Major Leagues paid to the Minor Leagues through working agreements, defrayal of farm club losses, and direct subsidies for special funds, a total of $16,443,711. All of these figures were exclusive of bonuses paid as an inducement for free agents to sign baseball contracts. Commissioner Frick emphasized particularly the fact that any efforts to legislate "player control" would remove the incentive for the substantial amount of financial assistance provided to the Minor Leagues. At the least, he said this would accentuate their difficulties and it could conceivably force their ultimate liquidation. Commissioner Frick, in support of his position, quoted Branch Rickey's statement before the same committee that ". . . there are no minor leagues if you withdraw ownership and working agreements." . . .

Before the Senate began its debate on S. 3483, Organized Baseball prepared a statement of its position and circulated it to the members of the Senate. This document, entitled "Statement of Organized Baseball on S. 3483—Professional Sports Antitrust Act of 1960," was signed by Commissioner Frick, George Trautman (President of the National Association of Professional Baseball Leagues), Warren Giles (President of the National League of Professional Baseball Clubs), and Joseph Cronin (President of the American League of Professional Baseball Clubs). Baseball's *Statement* made the following points:

1. Baseball's antitrust status should be equal to that of football, basketball and hockey.

2. The unrestricted draft would wreck the Minor Leagues by removing all incentive for Major League support of Minor League clubs.

3. An unrestricted draft was not needed to enable a new Major League to recruit an ample supply of players.

4. Title II of S. 3483 would enable a new Major League, which had made no contribution to the procurement and development of Minor League players, to confiscate the very large investment of the present Major Leagues in Minor League player development and contracts.

5. Title II of S. 3483 was so ambiguous that it was bound to provoke damaging litigation.

Organized Baseball stated that S. 3483 would be acceptable if Title II were stricken and "baseball" were added to Title I's antitrust exemption for professional team sports. To effect this change, Organized Baseball supported the introduction of an appropriate amendment on the floor of the Senate. On June 28, 1960, the Senate debated S. 3483. Senator Wiley introduced the amendment favored by Baseball. It was passed by a 45–41 roll-call vote (Cong. Rec., 13686–87). After the passage of this amendment, Senator Carroll moved to have S. 3483, as amended, recommitted to the Senate Judiciary Committee. This motion was agreed to by a 73–12 roll-call vote (Cong. Rec., 13687–88). The session of Congress ended with the bill still before the committee. . . .

Commissioner Frick has made it clear that Baseball is not demanding or requesting legislation. The system can continue to function effectively under the judicial exemption granted in *Toolson*. However, it has been emphasized that in the event Congress enacts legislation which would grant exemption from the antitrust laws to other organized team sports, Baseball would seek to be accorded the same treatment as others. In brief, it has consistently been the Commissioner's position that there should be no legislative enactment which could be interpreted as in any way modifying or diluting the present status which Baseball now enjoys under judicial decisions.

As long as other sports are not accorded similar treatment, however, Baseball will be faced with the continuing need of seeking to protect its existing status under the antitrust laws. This it has successfully done over the past ten years. Other team sports will of necessity continue to petition Congress for the kind of legislative exemption which Baseball has obtained in judicial decisions.

Until the Congress enacts suitable exemption legislation for these other team sports, Baseball's dilemma of the past decade persists. It neither seeks nor sponsors remedial legislation which it does not need but which the other sports require. Baseball has made it clear that it will join with these other sports in supporting a clearcut exemption statute for all. Baseball will renew these efforts at the current session of the 87th Congress.

67

Frick Places "Distinctive Mark" on
162-Game Home Run Record (1961)

SOURCE: *New York Herald Tribune*, July 18, 1961

Commissioner Ford Frick never ordered that an asterisk be placed next to the name of the person who broke Babe Ruth's home run record in more than 154 games. Frick, in his official statement (inspired by a Dick Young column in the New York Daily News*), declared that "some distinctive mark" would distinguish records set in a 154-game season from those established by those who played in more than 154 games. Although a majority of sportswriters polled by the* Sporting News *agreed with Frick's decision, many felt that Frick acted as he did because of his friendship with Ruth when Frick was a sportswriter. Major League Baseball officially removed the "distinctive mark" on September 4, 1991.*

RUTH RECORD SAFE AFTER 154 GAMES—FRICK

Babe Ruth's home run record is under such heavy fire from the Yankees' Roger Maris and Mickey Mantle that baseball commissioner Ford Frick yesterday felt impelled to rule that any player who hits more than 60 homers in his club's first 154 games shall be recognized as having broken the record Ruth set in 1927. If he hits 60 in the first 154 games, he shall be said to have tied the record.

However, any player who shall hit more than 60 after the 154th game would be given a distinctive mark in the record books to call attention to the fact that it was compiled under a 162-game schedule.

The American League, of course, is playing a 162-game schedule this year with its 10 teams. The National League will play 162 games next year when it adds Houston and New York. In fact, the leagues may never again play 154-game schedules.

Maris is winging along ways head [*sic*] of Ruth's pace. Mantle also has a comfortable lead on Babe's 1927 performance. Going into last night's twi-night doubleheader at Baltimore, Maris had 35 homers and Mantle 32. Maris was 19 games ahead of Ruth who did not hit his 35th until game No. 106 and Mantle was eight games ahead of Ruth who hit No. 32 in game No. 95. Counting one tie game, the Yanks had played 87 games through Sunday.

It had been assumed all along that Frick would require some distinctive mark if the record was set in more than 154 games but he decided to make a formal ruling because of the unusual interest in the case. He did not go into other records that might fall under the longer schedule.

Frick's ruling:

"Any player who may hit more than 60 home runs during his club's first 154 games would be recognized as having established a new record. However, if the player does not hit more than 60 until after his club has played 154 games, there would have to be some distinctive mark in the record books to show that Babe Ruth's record was set under a 154-game schedule and the total [of] more than 60 was compiled while a 162-game schedule was in effect.

"We also would apply the same reasoning if a player should equal Ruth's total of 60 in the first 154 games, he would be recognized as tying Ruth's record. If in more than 154 games, there would be a distinction in the record book."

68

Satchel Paige MVP in Last East-West Negro All-Star Game (1961)

SOURCE: *New York Herald Tribune, August 21, 1961*

In a 1959 interview, Negro American League president Dr. J. B. Martin noted that the poor attendance at that year's East-West All-Star Game, traditionally the most profitable event of the season, signaled the impending death of the Negro Leagues. The final game in the series was held in Yankee Stadium in 1961. Even with the added attraction of the legendary Satchel Paige, only 7,245 people bothered to attend. The author of the following article, who describes the event in a condescending, bemused tone, waited until the final sentence to mention that Paige's West squad won the game 7–1.

SATCHEL PAIGE BACK AT STADIUM, STEALS SHOW AT NEGRO GAME
By Ed Sinclair

Ageless Leroy (Satchel) Paige returned to Yankee Stadium yesterday after eight years of his second administration as the top attraction in the Negro American League. A couple of thousand fans on hand for the 29th annual East-West Negro All-Star game greeted him as if he were Mantle and Maris all rolled into one.

One of the few legends in baseball still living, Ole Satch came back not as the major leaguer he was early in the last decade with the now-extinct St. Louis Browns and the slowly expiring Cleveland Indians. He appeared as a representative of the Kansas City Monarchs, a team he played with a quarter of a century ago, and as the starting pitcher for the West team.

The lanky, loose-limbed character played everything as cool as he always has: He addressed "long time no see" friends by their first names. He moved as though unconcerned amid the adulation heaped upon him in the clubhouse, the dugout and on the field.

"I feel great," he said with a straight face, banging his fist into his glove. "They can make me 65 or 70, I don't care." With the possible exception of himself, no person alive has been found able to give a correct reading on his age.

The inevitable question of the Maris-Mantle home run act came up. "Well, I can't say," Paige answered, still with a straight face, "because I'm not around. If I were around that would be different. But I can say this. I fault the league for pitching to their power.

"You keep that ball low and away from those guys and they ain't gonna pull it. Did you ever see Ted (Williams) pull the ball on me? You did not. If you think you did and can prove it, I'll leave a new car for you right here. You ask Doby over there. He'll tell you."

Larry Doby, former star centerfielder for the Indians, was one of the many visitors in the room. Henry (Hank) Thompson, former New York Giant infielder-outfielder, was another. When the latter declared with a big grin, "he (Paige) would never get me out," Paige snorted, "you wouldn't get a hit off me in 20 years."

CAMPY PRESENT

Outside in the stands Roy Campanella was a part of the crowd that was celebrating Elks Day in honor of the Negro Elks convening here. So were Doris Chambers, Miss Beaux Arts of 1961; and Althea Gibson, the tennis star who was called upon to present the awards to the two fastest runners around the bases.

They were Herb Paymond, of the Birmingham Barons, and Johnny Miller, of the Raleigh Tigers. Paymond also won the egg-and-spoon contest, while Price West and Larry Lagrande, of Kansas City, prevailed in the three-legged race. When it came to throwing balls into a barrel Raleigh's Bob Fowler was the best.

By the time the game started there were an announced 7,245 witnesses present, many of them Elks with brilliant-colored fezes on their heads and long gold chains hanging around their necks. Hobson Reynolds, the Grand Exalted Ruler from Philadelphia, was there to introduce Governor Rockefeller.

From under his fez the Grand Exalted Ruler of New York State made a big pitch for the Republican slate in the coming city elections. After a concert of boos had overpowered mild applause, the Governor went through with the ceremony of tossing out the first ball. One inning later a brief shower prompted his departure.

HESITATION PITCH

Ole Satch didn't mind a few li'l ole raindrops. He pitched three innings of scoreless ball, allowed one infield single of the scratch variety. He threw his famous hesitation pitch twice, missing the first time and then the following inning getting it over for a perfect third strike. When the East tried to bunt against him in the third, he fielded the ball without appearing to move, although he had to, and threw the runner out by a stride.

While the old guy was in there he was great. After he departed, his teammates went through the exercises necessary for a 7–1 victory.

69

Roger Maris Establishes Record with Sixty-First Home Run (1961)

SOURCE: *New York Herald Tribune*, October 2, 1961

In the Yankees' final game of the 1961 season, Roger Maris placed his "distinctive mark" in the record books with a fourth-inning blow against Red Sox pitcher Tracy Stallard, a rookie righthander. Although Maris's race for Babe Ruth's home run record had been the subject of controversy throughout the season, Yankee Stadium was less than half full for his final opportunity at the record, and the nineteen-year-old man who caught the ball (and sold it for $5,000) had the freedom to decide to attend at the last minute. Maris's blast was a record setter in another way: it was the 240th home run by the club in 1961, decisively beating the previous standard of 221. It was also the only run scored in the game, a 1–0 win for the Yankees.

MARIS WALLOPS NO. 61—INTO THE RECORD BOOK

Roger Eclipses Ruth's Season Mark

By Tommy Holmes

The final countdown approached for Roger Maris, most successful challenger of Babe Ruth's ghost yet produced in modern baseball. Coming to bat in the fourth inning of yesterday's final ball game, the sharp-chinned blond bomber of the Yankees could count on only two more swings, maybe only one, for his 61st home run of the long season.

Twenty-four-year-old Tracy Stallard, pitching for the Red Sox, is right-handed, tall, fast, and sometimes wild. He tried the same pattern used with great success by Boston pitchers last week end and this one.

He threw high and away for ball one, low and inside for ball two. The idea was to make the next pitch a little better but not good enough for the long ball. Maris, in desperate urgency, could almost be guaranteed to swing. Something went wrong—the pitch was too fat!

The crack of the bat was solid and sharp. The crowd—23,154 paid—arose and roared. There were a couple of moments of uncertainty as Lu Clinton, the young Boston outfielder, back up to the fence in rightfield.

The high fly into the wind dropped out of Clinton's reach, about six rows back, halfway between the 344-foot mark and the entrance to the Yankee bullpen.

As others in the ball park screamed there was a frantic scramble for the valuable trophy. A young man who is a ringer for Billy Martin, the ex-Yankee second baseman, got it and bounded triumphantly to his feet.

Maris loped through the necessary ritual of rounding the bases. As he passed third, Frankie Crosetti shook his hand and sped him on his way with a clap on the shoulders. A beaming Yogi Berra and the bat boy met him at home plate. A young man in a plaid windbreaker got out of the stands and into the act before Roger could reach the bench and be mobbed by his team mates.

The crowd kept yelling. It wouldn't stop until Maris—not once, but twice—climbed the steps of the dugout, bared his crewcut and waved a smiling acknowledgment. He looked a bit like Kirk Douglas at a moment of triumph in Spartacus.

Certainly, this was a moment of triumph for Maris. Roger's 59th home run came Sept. 20 in Baltimore in the 154th Yankee game of the year. He needed all eight of the contests added through the 1961 expansion for the two that gave him the distinction of having hit more homers in one major league campaign than any slugger who ever lived.

It turned out to be 61 in '61 for Maris and that's one more than Ruth hit in 1927, his best season. A record? There are some who say so, but Ford Frick, baseball's commissioner, rules that the Ruth mark must be exceeded within 154 games to be broken.

What is certain is that Maris is a man on his way to relative riches as the result of his performance on the baseball field in the 27th summer of his life.

For the time being, Maris indicated he would settle for what he accomplished. He called his 61st homer the "great thrill of his life," but he had said much the same thing about his 60th off Jack Fisher last Wednesday and his 59th off Milt Pappas.

"Stallard threw me a fastball," he said. "I guess he didn't get it just where he intended to. At any rate, it was my pitch. Sometimes you're lucky. Bill Monbouquette gave me my pitch Saturday, but I didn't hit it right."

It turned out that Maris came to bat four times in his final effort. In the first inning, he hit the ball hard but met a fast ball tailing away from him for a long fly to left field. In the fourth inning came the big one. He didn't care too much when he fanned in the sixth or popped up in the eighth.

The homer was the whole ball game, for the Yankees won, 1–0. Billy Stafford, Hal Reniff and Luis Arroyo combined for a four-hit shutout. Stallard, of course, lost but the tall young Virginian won the applause of the crowd. The fans like everything about the way he pitched.

The Yankees wound up with a home attendance of 1,747,726, the largest in the Bronx for ten years. They played to 1,946,292 on the road, which is a record. So is the grand total of 3,694,081 who watched them in the flesh.

70

Major Leagues Vote Down Return of Spitball (1961)

SOURCE: *Sporting News,* December 6, 1961

More than forty years after the major leagues banned the spitball (save for seventeen designated pitchers whose careers depended on the pitch), Commissioner Ford Frick suggested that the prohibition be rescinded. The proposed change was discussed during a meeting of the Official Playing Rules Committee on November 26, but was voted down by a 8–1 margin, supported only by American League umpire supervisor Cal Hubbard.

Frick did not discuss this issue in his autobiography, but it would be fair to speculate that his support for the spitball, and for a different proposal to widen home plate by two inches, was in part inspired by the assault on Babe Ruth's home run record in the 1961 season. In any case, his arguments were not accepted by the members of the committee, who noted that pitchers already seemed to be dominating batters. However, their views apparently changed soon thereafter, because prior to the 1963 season the strike zone was effectively widened, in accordance with Frick's wishes. As a result the dominance of pitchers increased dramatically, and offensive output plunged to a historic low.

RULES MAKERS TAKE TOEHOLD ON SPITTER, BEAT IT DOWN, 8–1

Hubbard, A.L. Umpire Chief, Casts Only "Yes" Vote; "Hurlers Don't Need Help," Committee Members Agree
By Clifford Kachline

TAMPA, Fla.—The much-discussed spitball, last legally used in Organized Ball almost three decades ago, will remain officially outlawed for at least another year.

Despite favorable support from Commissioner Ford Frick and American League President Joe Cronin, pleas to restore the damp delivery to legal respectability were solidly vetoed by the game's Official Playing Rules Committee. The action came during the first day of a two-day meeting of the code group here, November 26–27.

In announcing the committee's decision, Chairman Jim Gallagher declared: "After considerable discussion, it was decided to leave the rule (barring the spit-ball) as it is. There was very little sentiment for any change."

The vote on the proposal to okay use of the spitball was eight against to one in favor, he revealed. The only "yes" vote was cast by Cal Hubbard, American League umpire supervisor. Gallagher himself casts a ballot in case of a tie. While the campaign to restore the spitter for 1962 is now dead, Gallagher indicated the committee's stand did not bar further consideration of the matter in the future.

Return of the spitball had been officially proposed late in October by Ed Short, new general manager of the White Sox. In a letter to Gallagher, Short petitioned the rules-makers to legalize the delivery or take other, appropriate action to "eliminate the accusation and suspicion leveled on a number of pitchers in the last few years." His counter-proposal was to prohibit hurlers from going to their mouth or otherwise moistening their fingers before delivering a pitch.

Both Frick and Cronin came out in support of the long-prohibited delivery. However, President Warren Giles of the National League expressed his opposition to its return.

SPITTER BANNED IN 1920

The spitter was officially banned in 1920, but special provision was made to allow any major league hurler then employing the wet pitch to continue to use it for the remainder of his career. Seventeen hurlers were certified as spitballers at the time. The last of the group to practice its use was Burleigh Grimes with the Yankees in 1934.

In rejecting restoration of the outlawed toss, the Rules Committee vetoed the idea that today's curvers need help.

"The way the pitchers are dominating the batters, the committee agreed there didn't seem to be any great need to give the pitchers an extra weapon," declared Gallagher. "The return of the spitter might swing the balance to the defense."

He pointed out that while home run production may be on the rise, batting averages keep going down. "And there is no evidence that a player can't hit a homer off a spitter as easily as off any other pitch," he added.

MIGHT "FOUL UP" YOUNG HURLERS

Another factor which the committee considered, Gallagher said, was that legalizing the damp pitch might get some hurlers, especially good young pitchers, "all fouled up." Experimentation with the spitball, it was agreed, could spoil some chuckers.

"Cheating (by throwing on occasional spitter) isn't as great a problem as many think," Gallagher commented. "The umpires report they get complaints on only about two pitchers in each league."

While he declined to mention names, several pitchers have frequently been accused of employing it occasionally. The prime suspect of controversy has been Lew Burdette, the Braves' fidgety righthander.

Others who have been charged with loading 'em include Jim Brosnan and Bob Purkey of the Reds, Early Wynn of the White Sox, Pedro Ramos of the Twins and

Whitey Ford of the Yankees. However, Ford, for one, has said he doesn't even know how to throw the wet one.

While Hubbard was soundly outvoted, the veteran former umpire still feels the hurlers need the extra pitch.

"Records may not bear me out, but I believe the pitchers could use some help," commented Cal. "At any rate, they've been complaining that all legislation in recent years has benefitted the batters.

"I don't know if the spitter would aid the pitchers much physically, but they'd have the advantage of a psychological weapon."

71

Giants Rally in Ninth to Beat Dodgers in Playoff (Again) (1962)

SOURCE: *San Francisco Chronicle*, October 4, 1962

For the second time in eleven years the hearts of Dodger fans were shattered in the final inning of a playoff series to their greatest rivals, the Giants. To add to the painful irony, the winning pitcher for San Francisco was Don Larsen—who threw a perfect World Series game against the Dodgers six years earlier—in relief of starter Juan Marichal. The collapse took place in front of Dodger fans in Los Angeles, who were unable to rouse their club to stage a counter-rally in the bottom of the inning. As in 1951, the team that had led the National League for the majority of the season, and held a four-game advantage over the Giants with one week remaining in the season, failed to win the pennant it seemed to have clinched.

S.F. WINS PENNANT ON WILD FOUR-RUN RALLY IN 9TH, 6–4

World Series Opens at Candlestick
Ford vs. Sanford Today
By Bob Stevens

Los Angeles—The dream that was inconceivable six years ago, implausible six days ago and improbable after the sixth inning Tuesday became a roaring reality yesterday in the hush and gloom of Chavez Ravine.

The Giants, celebrated in the past as June Swooners, wrapped up San Francisco's first National League pennant by scoring four times in an unbearably tense ninth inning to defeat the Los Angeles Dodgers, 6–4.

So the team that "collapsed" three months ago, was five and one-half games off the pace as recently as August 9, and four back with only seven to go struts into Candlestick Park today at noon to open the World Series against the New York Yankees.

The gap between New York and San Francisco, America's two "big" cities, has finally been bridged. San Francisco will host the first two games of the 59th renewal of October madness, with the Yankees scheduled to start Whitey Ford, 34-year-old southpaw with a 17-8 record and 32 consecutive scoreless World Series innings going for him, in today's opener.

JACK SANFORD WILL PROBABLY PITCH

The Giants will go with their ace, Jack Sanford (24-7), or possibly Billy O'Dell (19-14).

The build-up to the crashing climax of yesterday's third and conclusive playoff game was a case of agony before ecstasy.

The Giants leaped out in front of Johnny Podres, a weary warrior, with two runs in the third inning, then went into the deep freeze until the ninth, the most unforgettable inning in San Francisco's baseball past.

The Dodgers, grim-lipped and battling, pushed a run over in the fourth against Juan Marichal, who pitched well and bravely. They went ahead to the sound of thunder in the sixth, when Tommy Davis smashed a two-run homer, his 27th. It seemed to be all over.

Agony moved in with despair, and set up housekeeping through the next drawn-out, seemingly unnecessary innings. Ed Roebuck was working smoothly in relief for Podres going into the final three outs, and the call was placed for the coroner.

But Matty Alou, swinging for winning pitcher Don Larsen, singled sharply into right field, and the afternoon somehow seemed to suddenly light up. A little of that brightness was wiped away when Harvey Kuenn forced Matty at second, and even manager Alvin Dark slumped slightly on the dugout steps as he glowered down at the tobacco juice-strewn floor.

But Willie McCovey, hitting for Chuck Hiller, walked on four pitches as Roebuck measured the big man's strike area too finely. Ernie Bowman went to first to become McCovey's legs, and Roebuck continued, with glaze in his eyes.

The great Dodger fireman, 10-1 by the books in 64 relief appearances, walked Felipe Alou, and the bases were loaded. The Dodgers were on their way out, their 4–2 lead in jeopardy, their dugout in a state of stunned and silent disbelief.

Willie Mays was next, and he crashed a horrendous blow back at Roebuck that Ed knocked down but could not retrieve in time to make a play. Kuenn scored. It was 4–3. Ecstasy began to sneak up on agony.

Stan Williams replaced the stricken Roebuck on the mound.

BOWMAN SCORES TYING RUN

Orlando Cepeda, who had contributed the early agony by leaving base-runners stranded all over the Southland, crashed a line drive deep into right field, and Bowman danced home after the catch. It was 4–4, and the Giants in the dugout were going out of their cotton-pickin' minds.

While pitching to Ed Bailey, Williams unleashed a wild pitch, and Felipe Alou and Mays moved up a base, leaving first base open. Dodger manager Walt Alston closed it by ordering Bailey purposely passed, loading the bases again.

Then, in their final moments of humiliation, the club that spent almost half the season looking back at the pursuing Giants, collapsed. Williams walked Jimmy Davenport on the three-and-two, forcing Felipe home with the run that took 165 games and six months to arrive.

It was 5–4.

But the inning wasn't over. The Dodgers had one more dignity-robbing move to make, and second-baseman Larry Burright made it. With Ron Perranoski now on the mound, Jose Pagan grounded to Burright, and Larry kicked the life out of it for an error. Mays exploded home with the insurance run, making Los Angeles' impending ninth a little more bearable.

IT'S UP TO BILLY PIERCE

It was up to 35-year-old Billy Pierce, 8–0 conqueror of the Dodgers in the playoff opener at Candlestick to clamp the lid on San Francisco's first flag.

He got dangerous Maury Wills, Davenport to the stretching grasping Cepeda.

He got Jim Gilliam to fly out to Mays.

He got pinch-hitter Lee Walls to fly to center field, and the next timeless moment was but a blur of white as the ball ate its way high into the blue and down again—into Mays' outstretched glove.

Willie squeezed it, went into a wild dance, threw the ball toward the right field stands, and the next moments were delirious. Giants cried, tugged, hauled, grabbed for Pierce, for Dark, for each other, in a wild melee in front of the dugout. It was pandemonium. It was majestic.

The pennant belonged to the Giants the club some people said was prone to choke, too immature to win.

The next distinct noise heard was the popping of champagne bottles in a clubhouse that writhed with excitement and triumph.

The Giants had won their 16th pennant, their first since another memorable ninth inning of a third playoff with the Dodgers when Bobby Thomson closed out the 1951 pennant by hitting a three-run homer.[*]

The odds are 8 to 5 on the Yankees winning the Series but nobody really cares. After this stretch drive, this unbelievable finish, the World Series will be anticlimactic.

The first break-through in this one came in the third inning when the Giants scored twice. Pagan singled, and Marichal bunted back to the mound. Podres threw the thing into center field, Pagan fleeing to third. Harvey Kuenn singled to left, scoring Pagan, then became involved in a rundown between first and second.

---

*Incorrect—the New York Giants won the pennant in 1954—Ed.

Gilliam's throw back to first after the outfield throw-in crashed against Harvey's back, and Marichal stomped home.

The Giants eventually loaded the bases, but Cepeda grounded into a double play to wipe out the rally.

Two Giant singles were wasted in the fourth, and believe it or not, so were three consecutive singles in the sixth.

Cepeda lined safely into right in the latter inning, Bailey singled infield, and Davenport bunted successfully down the third-base line, so successfully that no play ever was made.

Bases loaded, none out, Podres out, Roebuck in. Pagan grounded to Wills, who threw home to force Cepeda, and Marichal tapped into a Wills-to-first-baseman Wally Moon double play.

Marichal had swept through the first three innings easily, having only one minute of torment when Wills, who collected four of the Dodgers' eight hits, singled and stole his 102nd base. But Maury died on second when Gilliam lined to Felipe Alou in right.

Then the Dodgers broke through the laboring Dominican Dandy.

DUKE SNIDER HITS A DOUBLE

Duke Snider introduced the fourth with a double to right, the ball bouncing off Dodger Stadium's hard-packed airport and away from the clutching Alou to the wall. Tommy Davis singled the limping Snider to third, and after Moon went out to Alou, Frank Howard grounded into a force-out that scored the Duke.

The Dodgers, who fought from 0–5 behind Tuesday, overtook the Giants—again in the sixth. Snider singled to left, and Tommy Davis leaped out at a high Marichal fast-ball and drove it into the left-centerfield seats 300 feet away and 20 feet above the searching eyes of Willie Mays, who went to the wall, looked, and turned slowly around and away from the flight of the ball.

It was 4–2, and Chavez Ravine rumbled with the animal cries of the local natives, some of whom climbed atop the dugouts and danced with unrestrained joy.

There were, besides the frenetic ninth inning, two other rounds in which managerial gambles paid off for both Alston and Dark.

In the seventh and with two down, Hiller doubled, and Mays, the potential go-ahead run, was purposely walked—a rather insolent thing to do inasmuch as the home run and runs-batted-in champion of 1961, Cepeda, was next up. Orlando tapped weakly to second base.

In the eighth, with Larsen on the mound, Tommy Davis walked, and Ron Fairly sacrificed him to second. While Larsen was striking out the massive Howard, Davis stole third.

Dark met this evil maneuver by purposely walking Johnny Roseboro and Willie Davis, bringing Roebuck to the plate. He grounded to Davenport, who flamed the ball across the diamond to Cepeda.

In the next inning—ecstacy and the Pennant.

SAN FRANCISCO

	AB	R	H	RBI
Kuenn, LF	5	1	2	1
Hiller, 2B	3	0	1	0
McCovey	0	0	0	0
Bowman, 2B	0	1	0	0
F. Alou, RF	4	1	1	0
Mays, CF	3	1	1	1
Cepeda, 1B	4	0	1	1
Bailey, C	4	0	2	0
Davenport, 3B	4	0	1	1
Larsen, P	0	0	0	0
Marichal, P	2	1	1	0
Pagan, SS	5	1	2	0
M. Alou	1	0	1	0
Nieman	1	0	0	0
Pierce, P	0	0	0	0
Totals	36	6	13	4

LOS ANGELES

	AB	R	H	RBI
Wills, SS	5	1	4	0
Gilliam, 2B-3B	5	0	0	0
Snider, LF	3	2	2	0
Burright, 2B	1	0	0	0
Walls	1	0	0	0
T. Davis, 3B-LF	3	1	2	2
Moon, 1B	3	0	0	0
Fairly, 1B-RF	0	0	0	0
Howard, RF	4	0	0	1
Harkness, 1B	0	0	0	0
Roseboro, C	3	0	0	0
W. Davis, CF	3	0	0	0
Podres, P	2	0	0	0
Roebuck, P	2	0	0	0
Williams, P	0	0	0	0
Perranoski, P	0	0	0	0
Totals	35	4	8	3

M. Alou singled for Larsen in 9th; McCovey walked for Hiller in 9th; Bowman ran for McCovey in 9th; Nieman struck out for M. Alou in 9th; Walls flied out for Burright in 9th.

San Francisco .... 0 0 2   0 0 0   0 0 4—6

Los Angeles .... 0 0 0   1 0 2   1 0 0—4

E—Marichal, Podres, Roseboro, Gilliam, Pagan, Bailey, Burright. PO-A—San Francisco 27-7, Los Angeles 27-13. DP—Gilliam, Wills, and Moon; Wills, Gilliam, and Moon; Wills, Burright, and Fairly. LOB—San Francisco 12, Los Angeles 8.

2B—Snider, Hiller. HR—T. Davis. SB—Wills 3, T. Davis. S—Hiller, Marichal, Fairly. SF—Cepeda.

	IP	H	R	ER	BB	SO
Marichal	7	8	4	3	1	2
Larsen (W, 5-4)	1	0	0	0	2	0
Podres	5	9	2	2	1	0
Roebuck (L, 10-2)	3⅓	4	4	3	3	0
Williams	⅓	0	0	0	2	0
Perranoski	⅓	0	0	0	0	1

(Podres pitched to three batters in 6th; Marichal pitched to one batter in 8th).

WP—Williams. U—Boggess, plate; Donatelli, 1B; Conlan, 2B; Barlick, 3B. T—3:00. A—45,693.

72

American Association Latest Minor League to Be Dismantled (1962)

SOURCE: *Sporting News,* December 8, 1962

The major leagues initiated the reorganization of the minor leagues on May 18, 1962, when they agreed to reclassify all B-, C-, and D-class minor leagues as A-class leagues. The Eastern League and the South Atlantic League, formerly A-class leagues, joined the Mexican League and the Texas League as AA-class leagues. The final step was taken at the National Association meeting in Rochester, New York, November 26–29, 1962. The American Association, once the preeminent minor league, was terminated when five of its six clubs were reassigned to the Pacific Coast League (PCL) and the International League, the remaining AAA-class leagues. The surviving minor league teams were now subject to the Player Development Plan, in which the major leagues agreed to maintain twenty AAA clubs (the number left after the reorganization) and a minimum of one hundred minor league teams in all. The pact ensured the survival of the minors, but at the cost of their independence. The following article describes the events of the Rochester meeting and forecasts the steps necessary to complete the survival of the minor leagues.

22 CLUBS, ONLY 20 TIEUPS, ADD UP TO HEADACHE

Something Had to Give—But Triple-A Moguls Battled 4 Days to Break Impasse

By Oscar Kahan

ROCHESTER, N.Y.—Any schoolboy knows that eight plus six plus six equals 20 and that ten plus ten equals 20, but eight plus eight plus six equals 22. Yet inability to come to grips with this simple arithmetic created a chaotic condition without compare at the National Association convention here, November 26–29.

It took the entire four days of the confab and the combined efforts of major and minor league officials to figure out finally what takes what to make twenty.

The answer was the dismemberment of the American Association and the expansion of the International League and Pacific Coast Leagues so that each wound up with ten clubs.

The principal problem this year was so simple that it became complex.

Under the new player development plan, the major league clubs had decided to extend working agreements to only 20 Triple-A entries for next season. Unfortunately, there were 22 clubs in the three top circuits—eight in the International, eight in the Coast and six in the Association.

PACT FOR EACH INT CLUB

All eight in the International were given major league pacts, but the PCL had only seven and the Association only five. Eight plus seven plus five equals 20, but no league can operate successfully at the Triple-A level with seven clubs or, even worse, with five.

Several weeks before the convention here, work started on a plan to solve the problem. As step No. 1 in the proposal, the PCL would drop Vancouver, which had no working agreement, and take on Denver from the American Association. Denver is affiliated with the Braves.

As step No. 2, the American Association would drop Omaha, which had no major league connection, and merge its four other members with the eight in the International League to form a 12-club circuit, with two six-team divisions.

That would make eight in the PCL and 12 in the merged International-Association, which equals the magic number of 20.

Perhaps the plan was too simple. Leagues can be juggled around on paper much easier than they can in reality.

Starting the day before the convention officially opened, interminable meetings lasting through all hours of the night failed to produce an agreement.

The solvent International League, feeling that it had nothing to gain and everything to lose, voted against the merger with the A.A.

The idea men then switched the original package around, suggesting that the International continue with its eight clubs and that the Association merge with the PCL as a 12-club league with two six-team divisions.

This also was turned down. That left only one solution—the creation of two ten-club leagues—and, after much anguish, the proposal was accepted, although some of the club officials feared they were fathering a pair of "monstrosities."

The International League took in Indianapolis and Little Rock to make its ten, while Denver, Dallas–Fort Worth and Oklahoma City were assigned to the Pacific Coast League, which dropped Vancouver. Both circuits will receive a travel subsidy from the major leagues.

The Association was sacrificed, despite almost superhuman efforts by Jim Burris, its youthful president. Unable to keep his historic circuit alive, Burris labored to save as many of his clubs as possible for O.B.

The confusion at the Triple-A level was scarcely any greater than in Classes AA and A. Under the new player development plan, all of last season's AA and A leagues have been given the AA label and all the B, C and D leagues now are Class A.

The development plan provided for a minimum of 100 working agreements. With 20 for Triple-A, that left 80 for Class AA and A. When the farm directors began ladling out the pacts, there was one league casualty. The Alabama-Florida died.

Bill Moore, president of the 25-year-old circuit, said his league was the victim of its segregation policy. Major league organizations, unable to send Negro players to the Alabama-Florida, decided to pull out.

73

Marichal Bests Spahn in Sixteen-Inning Pitching Duel (1963)

SOURCE: *San Francisco Examiner,* July 3, 1963

During the first half of the century it was not uncommon for starting pitchers to complete extra-inning games. However, the emergence of relief specialists allowed managers to replace starters more often, even when the starter was pitching well but the game situation, or the number of pitches thrown, suggested that a change might be advantageous. Given this evolution of baseball strategy, starters who lasted well into extra innings often received extra attention in the media. When such a starter, even an established star like Warren Spahn, accomplished this feat at the age of forty-two, it made headlines.

In the game reported below, Spahn was defeated by young Giants star Juan Marichal, who was on his way to the first of his six twenty-win seasons. Marichal owed his victory not only to his own superb performance, but to the efforts of Willie Mays, whose sixteenth-inning solo home run saddled the Braves with a hard-luck 1–0 defeat.

JUAN, SPAHN 16 INNING DUEL; MAYS HR WINS IT

Marichal Notches 13th Win
By Harry Jupiter

Willie Mays walloped a home run in the 16th inning early this morning, ending a fantastic pitching duel between Juan Marichal and Warren Spahn, 1–0.

The 4 hour, 10 minute game came on the 30th anniversary of another Giant pitching classic, Carl Hubbell's 18-inning, 1–0 victory over the Cardinals.

Marichal, notching his ninth straight decision, gave up eight hits. Spahn, the greatest southpaw in history, allowed the same number before Mays lined his 15th homer.

Spahn had the Braves' only extra-base hit, a double in the seventh inning.

Mays had ended the Milwaukee fourth inning by throwing out Norm Larker out at the plate on Del Crandell's [sic] single to center. That was the closest anybody came to scoring until Willie sent the last of 15,291 fans home.

Marichal and Spahn both were committed for the duration. Juan ran to the plate whenever it was his turn to hit and ran to the mound when it was time to pitch. Spahn, a conservative 42 years of age, walked but with never a doubt he meant to stick around.

Marichal now owns a 13-3 record and is unbeaten since Sandy Koufax no-hit him and the Giants May 11. Spahn, the ace of the Milwaukee staff for lo these many years is now 11-4.

The defense was sensational. But the biggest thrill before Mays ended the game was a long, long foul by Willie McCovey in the ninth.

ROW WITH UMP

McCovey, Alvin Dark and Larry Jansen surrounded Chris Pelekoudas, claiming the ball left Candlestick fair. Pelekoudas stuck to his foul call, which took courage.

Although each club left 11 on base, there weren't many big opportunities to score. A boot at third base by Dennis [sic] Menke, the Braves' lone error, loaded the bases with Giants in the bottom of the 14th, but Spahn nailed Ed Bailey on a fly to center.

After Mays' throw got Larker in the fourth, the Braves never got two men on base at the same time again.

Marichal struck out 10, walked four. Spahn struck out only two, and walked just one. That lone walk off Warren was an intentional pass to Mays in the 14th, the first walk issued by Spahn in 31 ⅔ innings.

Harvey Kuenn opened that 14th with a bloop double that fell among Don Dillard, Lee Maye and Roy McMillan. The hit extended Harv's hitting streak to 13 games, longest the Giants have had this year.

The 16-inning game matched the longest the Giants have played since coming west in '58. It took 'em 16 innings to beat the Dodgers, 6–5, on Sept. 1, 1958.

Last night's wasn't the most time-consuming for the Giants. The second playoff game with the Dodgers last Oct. 2, took 4 hours, 17 minutes, even though it went only nine innings.

GREAT DEFENSE

Little Ernie Bowman, Kuenn, Orlando Cepeda and Marichal all provided brilliant defense plays. Bowman, who didn't get into the game until the eighth, got two hits in addition to making two great fielding plays.

Marichal now has gone 24 innings without allowing an earned run. Spahn had pitched 27 scoreless frames before throwing the game-ending pitch to Mays.

Ken Burkhart was the plate umpire and he did a whale of a job. Hardly a peep to him through all those tense, thrilling innings.

Jack Sanford (9-7) pitches today against Milwaukee righthander Tony Cloninger (4-4). Marichal and Spahn get to sleep late.

74

Preview of TV Special "A Man Named Mays" (1963)

SOURCE: *San Francisco Examiner*, October 3, 1963

Willie Mays was not the first baseball player to be the subject of a television show. As early as June 1949, the Cleveland NBC affiliate aired a program named "The Ballad of Satchel Paige," later replayed as "Destination Freedom." Numerous players were interviewed by television personalities like Laraine Day and Edward R. Murrow. Mays, however, may have been the first to merit a full hour-long documentary.

*The show, "A Man Named Mays," was written and narrated by Charles Einstein, a veteran sportswriter who had written two biographies of Mays—*Born to Play Ball *(1955) and* Willie Mays: Coast to Coast Giant *(1963)—and a third book on the Giants' 1961 season. Einstein would write two more books on Mays, including the superb* Willie's Time: A Memoir *(New York: Lippincott, 1979), which was a finalist for the Pulitzer Prize in biography. Obviously Einstein was close to his subject, a fact known to columnist Dwight Newton, who argues in the following article that the documentary is not a hagiography, but an expression of admiration well worth watching.*

Dwight Newton

WITH WILLIE AT THE BAT

Speaking of baseball on television (who isn't?), I want to remind you here that the Giants haven't got in their last licks yet. No, siree, Willie!

Come Sunday night at 10, they'll be swarming all over the NBC dial, channels 4–3-4R-24, in an extraordinarily fascinating hour called "A Man Named Mays."

At precisely the same time when Elizabeth Taylor on CBS is taking viewers on a tour around London, former Examiner columnist Charles Einstein will be taking viewers on a tour around Willie Mays.

I can't vouch for the London cruise, but I can for Willie's. I've seen a big hunk of it at a special preview with Willie. It is revolutionarily different from those standard brand TV biographies we've seen of Gary Cooper, Will Rogers and Humphrey Bogart.

BASEBALL PAGEANT

It is invested with ingenious imagination by local producer Lee Mendelson whose skillful knowhow won KPIX the Peabody Award for its "San Francisco Pageant." In this show, Lee has created a San Francisco baseball pageant to remember.

It is jammed with sensational action, charged with tense drama and peppered with good and dry humor by Einstein, the narrator. Charlie Einstein knows Willie better than anybody. He has been reporting Willie's diamond deeds for 12 years, he has written two books about him.

Charlie has never narrated a network show before, thank goodness. Nor has Mendelson produced a network program, nor has Willie Mays starred in one. Consequently they are as free as the birds from the ponderous, heavy-handed techniques so dearly beloved by the professional documentarians.

Nobody told them they were supposed to be solemn for an hour. They just went out and spent six months building and filming the sort of show they would like to see. The result is more than just a biographical hour. It is an entertainment hour.

Charlie's narration is brisk, pithy, pungent and totally devoid of the false hero worship that has drowned the life out of so many documentaries. Rather, it is like hearing a man fling bouquets, and barbs, too, at a buddy.

The show sings the saga of Willie from 1951 when he walked onto the Giants' center field as Joe DiMaggio was leaving the Yankees' center field. The end of one era, the beginning of another. You'll see his phenomenal back-to-the-ball catch in the World Series of 1954. You'll see him hit four home runs in a single game, bag his 2,000th hit and wham his 400th home run.

The show takes Willie down to the wire of the last game of this last season. It is a whale of an appropriate nighttime program for this week when baseball is King of the daytime Kilocycles.

WHAT WILL WILLIE WATCH?

What baseball bug will watch Liz when this show is on? Willie will, he says. He has seen his own show and he is curious about what Elizabeth Taylor will do to London. But Sunday night when the chips are down and his friends are around, I imagine they will insist that he watch with them "A Man Named Mays."

But then Willie has more TV sets than San Francisco has channels. He can catch fragments of all shows by remote control without turning a dial if he wants to, and he often does. If a rating service called Willie some night he might truthfully say that he had all stations tuned in. (Unless they demanded to know on which channel the sound was turned up.)

Willie, by the way, is my new dietitian. He is in great shape and he confided suggestions on how to mold my own frame into passably presentable shape which would make another column if anybody's interested.

75

NL **Wins Only Latin All-Star Game** (1963)

SOURCE: *New York Daily News,* October 13, 1963

Just two years after the final East-West Negro All-Star Game was played, the only All-Star Game reserved for Hispanic players was played in New York. The Negro Leagues died after its star players—and their fans—were integrated into the major leagues. Although there was never a similar league for Latin players in the United States, these players attracted Hispanic spectators to major league ballparks, and more importantly, they demonstrated the depth of talent in the Caribbean and throughout Latin America. Hispanic players, starting with Esteban Bellan in the 1860s, had long been present in American baseball, but as a group they were not widely recognized until the 1950s, when players like Minnie Minoso, Luis Aparicio, and Roberto Clemente emerged. By the 1960s the popularity of young stars like Juan Marichal, Tony Oliva, and Tony Perez ensured that white and black fans alike would accept that Hispanic players constituted a third pool of players which would enrich baseball for years to come.

The game's proceeds were donated to an unnamed charity. The contest was the final baseball game played at the ancient Polo Grounds, which was destroyed soon afterward.

The best history of Hispanic baseball players in the United States is Samuel Regalado, Viva Baseball! Latin Major Leaguers and Their Special Hunger *(Urbana: University of Illinois Press, 1998).*

NL **LATIN STARS PIN 5–2 LOSS ON** AL **ACES**
By Chris Kieran

The National League continued its dominance over the AL at the Polo Grounds yesterday, where the senior circuit's Latin All-Stars whipped their American League counterparts, 5–2, in a charity affair that was billed as absolutely the last game at the old ballpark. That made it three straight for the NL, including the All-Star game at Cleveland and the recent World Series.

Juan Marichal, the Giants' 25-game winner, and Buc reliever Al McBean combined for a shutout for eight innings before the Mets' (wouldn't you know it?) Ed Bauta blew it in the ninth when he gave up two hits, a walk and a wild pitch. Marichal threw four scoreless innings, allowing two hits and fanning six, while McBean was touched for three safeties and whiffed four. Pedro Ramos, Twins' righty, was the loser.

An announced crowd of 14,235 saw the Nationals jump out in front in the first inning when Felipe Alou singled home Tony Taylor and then wrap it up in the fourth with three more. Singles by Orlando Cepeda and Tony Gonzalez preceded Julian Javier's run-scoring bingle [single], with pinch-hitter Manny Mota clubbing home the other pair with the fourth safety off Ramos.

Biggest blow of the game was delivered by winning pitcher McBean in the sixth. After Tony Gonzalez opened with a single, the lanky Pirate chucker blasted one to deep left on which Minnie Minoso got a late jump. McBean had three bases easily, but when he tried to go all the way he was cut down on a Minoso-Aparicio-Azcue relay, five feet in front of the plate.

76

Charlie Finley Suggests Playing Night Games during World Series (1963)

SOURCE: November 7, 1963, letter to Ford Frick, Charles O. Finley file, National Baseball Hall of Fame Library

Although four groups of investors earned the right to become owners of expansion teams in 1960, the most notable—some would say notorious—new major league team owner of the year was insurance executive Charles O. Finley, who in late December 1960 purchased a majority share of the Kansas City Athletics from the estate of Arnold Johnson. Almost immediately after his first season as owner started, Finley created controversy by firing manager Joe Gordon and threatening to move the club to Louisville. Finley instantaneously earned a reputation as a maverick, which he would proudly maintain until he sold the Athletics in August 1980.

Some of the ideas for which Finley was widely attacked, however, have since been adopted or recognized as innovative. During the early stages of free agency in the mid-1970s Finley suggested that all players be granted free agency after each season, realizing that the result would be a flooded market that would keep salaries low, but owners (and an alert Marvin Miller) rejected the notion. Even his penchant for wildly colorful uniforms was in a sense adopted by several teams in the 1970s and by many teams in the late 1990s that wore a dizzying array of different uniforms calculated to increase souvenir sales.

One of Finley's best suggestions is detailed in the following letter. Finley was aware of the threat posed by football to baseball's revenue and the potential of television to expand baseball's attendance base. His solution was to play World Series games during prime time to increase viewership. He also pointed out the advantages of playing as many weekend games as possible, in direct competition with both college and professional football. At the time his ideas received no serious consideration, but in 1971

Commissioner Bowie Kuhn—later Finley's fiercest opponent—instituted the first night Series contests. Two years earlier baseball started the championship series and the World Series on a Saturday, following another Finley proposal. Other topics discussed by Finley below, including the importance of capturing and maintaining young fans, are still considered relevant today. On the other hand, now critics complain that too many postseason night games prevent children from becoming baseball fans.

Dear Mr. Frick:

For many years, going back to my childhood days, I had often wondered why America's Greatest Sport's Spectacle—"The World's Series"—was always staged at such an inconvenient and unreasonable time for the baseball fan. Since becoming an owner of a Major League Franchise, I naturally have become even more concerned over this situation.

It is my opinion the following facts will convince you and the Club Owners that we are "missing the boat" and something should be done immediately.

THE WORKING MAN

1. *Why does Major League Baseball play the majority of its games at night?*

For one reason only—greater attendance. We all know that baseball would rather play all its games during the day, but attendance-wise, this is economically impossible.

2. *Where does the vast majority of support come from for night games?*

The answer is very simple—from the working man. As a matter of fact, it is the working man who supports baseball throughout the entire season.

3. *Why does the working man support Baseball?*

The working man's income is limited and it is necessary for him to live on a very close budget. He must seek entertainment that will provide him and his family with the most entertainment at the least cost. This is the reason he comes to baseball. Please note I said, "he comes to baseball." We don't come to him—and this is my concern, and I am sure yours also.

4. *What made Sears Roebuck and Montgomery Ward so large over night?*

One thing only—They were quick to recognize that the working man was their life-blood—vital to their very existence and catered to him immediately.

5. Why do the *Breweries* and *Finance* Companies spend millions of dollars annually as Sponsors of Baseball?

They have always known that the working man was their best customer. They also knew the working man was a great baseball fan and sponsorship of baseball games on Radio and T.V. was the best, easiest and most economical way of entering his home many times during a ball game. The point is this—Breweries and Finance Companies are spending millions of dollars annually to reach the working man—their best customer. Baseball can reach untold millions of additional working people for *nothing*, and amazingly have done nothing about it.

We in baseball must appreciate the fact that the working man is also our "life-blood" and we should let him know we appreciate his support by doing everything possible in catering to him.

TODAY'S CHILDREN—TOMORROW'S FANS

Another very important factor to consider is that today's children are tomorrow's baseball fans, and we must do everything possible to cultivate the children's interest for tomorrow's support.

What are we doing to indicate our appreciation for the working man's support? What are we doing to attract and sustain the interest of today's children for their future support? What are we doing to attract NEW FANS to baseball? I am, of course, speaking exclusively of the present scheduling and televising of the World's Series. The answer is nothing—ABSOLUTELY NOTHING.

In essence, we have been saying for years to the working man, "Thanks, friend, we appreciate your support during the season and now that it's time to stage America's Greatest Sport's Spectacle, we are going to stage it at the most inconvenient and unreasonable time for you to see it. We are going to start it on a Wednesday afternoon when you are working at the steel mills, coal mines, factories, or offices. You can get the details when you get home from work." We are also saying to today's children, tomorrow's baseball fans, "Boys and girls, we love you too—we are starting the World's Series when you too can't see it—you are all back to school."

Baseball is fortunate in that its World's Series is considered "America's Greatest Sport's Spectacle." Therefore, we must make every effort to protect and to retain this outstanding and valuable recognition.

After considering the above facts, I can't help but continually ask myself, "Why do we continue staging the World's Series at such an inconvenient and unreasonable time?"

My suggestion is to end the season on Wednesday and play the first and second games on Saturday and Sunday afternoons. Travel on Monday. Play the third, fourth and fifth games at night—Tuesday, Wednesday and Thursday. Travel on Friday, and play the sixth and seventh games, if necessary, on Saturday and Sunday afternoons.

This arrangement would make it possible for almost everyone, including the working man, who supports us so generously during the season, and today's children—tomorrow's fans *to see the entire World's Series.* By what better way can we indicate to the working man and children that we not only need their support, but we also appreciate their support. This greater T.V. exposure will also help baseball tremendously in retaining fan interest and creating new fans.

Last year, 1962, according to NBC, 279,000,000 people viewed the seven game series, an average of 40 million per game. If this suggestion is adopted, by conservative estimate, at least 60 million fans would view each game.

One of the basic principles of selling *anything* is, "The more exposure—the more sales." We are selling baseball and if we are wise, we will do everything possible for the greatest exposure of America's Greatest Sport's Spectacle—The World's Series.

An objection to this suggestion may be, "Too cold to play at night in October." If this were true, we could still play the games as I have suggested, starting on Saturday eliminating the night games. However, cold weather in October cannot be used as an excuse for not playing games three, four and five at night. It is a fact, the weather at 8:00 P.M. in every Major League City is warmer from October 1 through October 10, than it is from April 9 through April 30. (See U.S. Weather Bureau temperatures for these periods enclosed.)

If baseball can play night games between April 9 and April 30, then there is no reason why we can't play three games at night between October 1 and October 10, when the weather is more favorable than most times during the year.

Some objections will also be that the different time zones would interfere. This can easily be resolved by starting the night games in the East and Midwest at 8:00 P.M. local time and at 5:00 or 6:00 P.M. local time on the West Coast.

I have not touched on the possibility of additional revenue from the sponsors with this type of schedule, but I am confident it would be considerably more. Not only would this benefit Baseball, it would also benefit the Players' Pension Fund.

PROFESSIONAL FOOTBALL

Professional Football is definitely gaining in popularity. Football would never think of playing its championship games on a Wednesday, Thursday or Friday afternoon. Football is too smart and aggressive to be so unwise. We should at least try to compete with football. At the present time, we are saying to football, "We will not try to compete with you—our present schedule of the World's Series games will take up only one weekend, even if we should play seven games."

Last March, I suggested we start the season on Saturday and gave good reasons for it. A copy of this suggestion is enclosed for your review. By starting the season on Saturday, ending on Wednesday, it will coincide perfectly with the suggestion to start the World's Series on Saturday.

I hope you will give this suggestion your serious consideration. We have everything to gain, as opposed to the possibility of *losing* the title "America's Greatest Sport's Spectacle."

Sincerely,

Charles O. Finley

77

Jim Bunning Throws First NL Perfect Game of Century (1964)

SOURCE: *Philadelphia Evening Bulletin*, June 22, 1964

The first time Tracy Stallard entered the consciousness of baseball fans was on the last day of the 1961 season, when the Red Sox rookie lost 1–0 on Roger Maris's sixty-first home run. Three seasons later, Stallard—now exiled to the New York Mets—gained footnote status for a second time by losing to Jim Bunning, who led the Philadelphia Phillies to victory by driving in two runs and pitching the first perfect game in the National League since 1880, when within a five-day span both John Lee Richmond and John Ward achieved the feat.

Bunning was also an exile. After earning five All-Star nominations in his nine-year career for the Detroit Tigers, he was traded to the Phillies, in large part because Tigers management did not appreciate his less-than-reverential attitude and his role as a leader in the MLBPA. Bunning exhibited his leadership by helping to appoint Marvin Miller— and reject Richard Nixon—as the union executive director in 1966. Bunning retired after the 1971 season as only the second man (after Cy Young) to win more than one hundred games in both the American and National Leagues. In the 1990s he earned election, in succession, to the U.S. House of Representatives, the U.S. Senate, and the Baseball Hall of Fame.

JIM BUNNING . . . PERFECT PITCHER

Defies Jinx By Talking Way Through Classic
By Ray Kelly

Jim Bunning, the Phillies' 32-year-old righthander who became the first National Leaguer to hurl a perfect game in the 20th century, did it while defying one of baseball's oldest superstitions.

He knew what was going on and talked about it—incessantly—yesterday in New York.

Throughout the late stages of his mound masterpiece in which he retired 27 straight to beat the Mets, 6–0, Bunning acted as his own cheerleader.

After each inning, he returned to the dugout and counted down for the Phillies: "Nine more to go, boys, let's get them!"

Then, "Only six to go now, boys, get going, dive for the ball . . . do something."

After the eighth inning, Jaunty Jim quieted down. All he said was: "Three more, that's all."

ENDS ON 2 STRIKEOUTS

He personally took care of that important detail, getting the no. 25 batter, Charlie Smith, on a popup, before striking out pinch-hitters George Altman and John Stephenson in a finishing flourish.

When Stephenson made his futile swing for the third strike, Bunning balled his right hand into a fist and pounded his glove in elation. Then, catcher Gus Triandos and the other Phillies swarmed over him.

"I really felt good," said Bunning, who hurled a no-hit, no-run game with the Detroit Tigers in Boston in 1958. . . .

Bunning, an off-season stockbroker with seven children, decided he was going to give himself a Father's Day present after the fifth inning. His wife, Mary, and daughter Barbara, 12, were at Shea Stadium yesterday.

"Sure I knew I had it going," he said. "Everybody does."

THANKS TAYLOR, ALLEN

The Mets hit only two balls solidly the entire game. In the fifth inning, second baseman Tony Taylor made a diving grab to knock down Jesse Gonder's line drive and in the seventh, third baseman Richie Allen turned Ron Hunt's smash into a putout.

"I'll tell you," Bunning said. "Taylor made a great play and so did Allen. But the guys on this team have been doing it all season."

Bunning didn't remember the ball that came closest to being a safety. In the fourth inning, Hunt reached and pushed a curving liner down the right field line. At the last instant, the ball sliced into foul territory.

"Guess I thought it was foul all the way," Bunning said.

THE METS? SO WHAT?

Somebody asked if the sheen was dulled by the fact that his game was against the hapless New Yorkers.

"I don't care who it was against," Bunning declared. "This is the big leagues and the Mets will be here long after I'm forgotten."

Despite the 91-degree weather drenched with humidity, Bunning appeared to get stronger as the game progressed. He racked up six of his 10 strikeouts in the last three innings and used up only 90 pitches, including 44 fast balls which provided 34 strikes. He went to a full 3-2 count on only two batters—Hunt and Bob Taylor.

"Everything was working—it has to be to get everybody out," the pitcher said.

Bunning explained his between-inning talkativeness thusly: "I always yap," he said. "I do it to take my mind off the heat and off being tired. It keeps me loose. What was the temperature, 95?"

The 6–3 right-hander is 7-2 as a Phillie and a prospect for the All-Star Team.

MAUCH OUT OF WAY

"I've seen a lot of no-hitters but this is the first time I saw a perfect game," said manager Gene Mauch. "All I did was sit back and stay out of the way."

"That Bunning was something," said outfielder Johnny Callison. "He was really stirring things up on the bench between innings. Once he told me: 'Shake yourself and dive if anything comes out there.'"

Catcher Triandos, who caught knuckleballer Hoyt Wilhelm in a no-hitter against the Yankees when he was with Baltimore, said the Bunning effort was much easier.

"He had the good curve and I kept calling for it."

Triandos felt no pressure in calling signals.

"The burden was on Jim," he said. "He had to get them out."

"He got downright silly one time. With two hitters to go, he called me out and says I should tell him a joke, just to give him a breather. I couldn't think of any so I just laughed at him."

Going out for the ninth inning, Bunning told himself: "I suppose Altman will be the last hitter."

He was wrong. Altman batted for Amado Samuel after Smith popped out, and struck out on three pitches. Here Casey Stengel sent up rookie Stephenson, another left-handed hitter, to bat for Tom Sturdivant.

"I figured I could get him if I could get three curves over the plate," Bunning recalled. The count went to 2-2 and then Stephenson struck out.

78

Dodgers to Experiment with Pay Television (1964)

SOURCE: *Sporting News,* August 1, 1964

Dodger owner Walter O'Malley had been intrigued with pay television for more than a decade before he had the opportunity to demonstrate to critics the effectiveness and profitability of the system. The men who made the experiment possible—Pat Weaver, former president of NBC, and Matthew Fox—were the executives of Subscription TeleVision, Inc. (STV). The Los Angeles area at this time boasted twenty-five hundred subscribers to STV, and it was hoped that the association with the Dodgers would encourage more Californians to embrace the rapidly expanding realm of cable television. A different Sporting News *article in the same issue noted that of those subscribers, 61 percent were watching the baseball game. The pay television trial appeared to have merit.*

The experiment, which O'Malley hoped would lead to games being available exclusively on pay television, was short-lived. At the insistence of Congress, baseball games remained on the public airwaves, but owners like O'Malley continued to dream of the potential of cable.

O'MALLEY TAPS NEW MOTHER LODE—FEE TEEVEE

Dodgers-Cubs Tilt Seen at Cost of $1.50
By Bob Hunter

LOS ANGELES, Calif.—Major league baseball's historic debut on a new electronic medium—pay television—staged a typical Hollywood premiere in the Los Angeles area the night of July 17.

There were 2,500 subscribers wired for sight, sound and a statement at the end of the month and they watched the Dodgers play the Cubs in another Walter O'Malley first.

The San Francisco area, featuring the Giants, makes its premiere on Subscription TeleVision, Inc., this month.

All fans were enthusiastic with the reception and most observers actually raved about the color, which was noticeably more accurate than the usual color. This oddity was explained by STV officials in this way:

Subscription television is by direct cable, while the free TV programs are reflected indirectly.

In addition to the one area in Los Angeles, in which some 4,000 sets have been wired by the television company, there were receivers in the Stadium Club at Dodger Stadium, the Press Room and in the offices of O'Malley and Buzzie Bavasi.

FRESCO THOMPSON TELECASTS

Frank Sims, who handled some of the Philly games and more recently did the broadcasting for the Dodger farm club at Albuquerque, was the play-by-play man, with Dodger Vice-President Fresco Thompson handling the color.

Installation for "charter" subscribers was a nominal $5, and the weekly $1 service charge was waived for one year in order to speed up interest.

The charge for a ball game is $1.50, with an electronic computer figuring each subscriber's tab by the month.

STV actually provided three different programs over three different channels on premiere night. In addition to the Cubs vs. Dodgers game, another channel offered the African dance drama, "Sponomo," taped on the Broadway stage, and a third offered the surfing film, "Gun Ho."

All "premieres" started at 8 o'clock and there were also "late" shows, including a travel film on ancient Egypt and a visit to the New York night club, Upstairs and Downstairs.

The surfing film tab was $1 and the archeological film was six bits.

FIRST 12 MINUTES ARE FREE

Each program offered the first 12 minutes free, as sort of an "invitation," then periodic checks were made on what people were watching via an electronic "interrogator."

President Pat Weaver of STV told writers at a "preview" the night before the actual showings that pay television was designed only as "a creative addition to family viewing, not as a replacement for serials, comedies and other presentations of sponsored commercial television."

Some subscribers reported that they utilized only the picture of the Dodger-Cub game, using the radio voices by Vin Scully and Jerry Doggett. . . .

Gene Autry, when asked what his position he would take with his Angels, answered that he will "just wait and watch what happens before doing anything."

The pay-television business faces a battle of the ballot in the November election, with motion picture interests leading a successful fight to place an initiative before the voters, hoping to make this new form of home entertainment illegal in California.

In San Francisco, City Attorney Thomas O'Connor said Horace Stoneham and the Giants may be sued for placing their games on pay television, claiming that the team's contract prohibits the club from doing anything to diminish attendance in Candlestick Park.

O'Connor contended that pay-TV would cut attendance at the park, thus affecting the parking, most of which goes toward paying off the bonds that financed the stadium construction.

79

"Phillies 6½ Up With 12 to Play" (1964)

SOURCE: *Philadelphia Evening Bulletin*, September 21, 1964

The Philadelphia Phillies, who had won only two National League pennants since the franchise joined the league in 1884, appeared to have clinched their third after defeating the Los Angeles Dodgers. Their closest competitors, the Cincinnati Reds and the St. Louis Cardinals, were both six and a half games behind the Phillies, who had been playing well down the stretch. The Phillies played the majority of their remaining games at home, while the opposite was true for their rivals. Their star pitcher, Jim Bunning, had thrown a perfect game earlier in the season and won again on September 20. Philadelphia seemed to be in control.

However, not even the most pessimistic Phillies fan could have predicted the collapse that would cost them a sure pennant. Starting with their September 21 game against the Reds, the Phillies lost ten consecutive games, often as a result of questionable strategy by manager Gene Mauch or uncharacteristically poor play. They ended the losing streak, and the season, with two wins against the Reds, which clinched the pennant for the Cardinals. The Phillies tied for second with the Reds. They would not win another pennant until 1980, when they won the only World Series in franchise history.

"PHILLIES 6½ UP WITH 12 TO PLAY"

Bunning's 18th, Callison's Throw Beat Dodgers
By Ray Kelly

With a six-and-half game lead and only 12 to play, the Phillies will do well to heed Wes Covington's advice about "not letting ourselves be carried away."

The younger folk will need reminding that in 1950 on this date the Whiz Kid Phillies had a seven-and-a-half game lead with 11 to play. Yet they lost eight of the next 10 and had to beat the Dodgers at Brooklyn on the last day of the season to avoid a pennant playoff.

There is no reason for the present Phillies to give the past a second morbid thought. They've reason to feel confident after getting through another rugged road trip with a favorable 6-4 balance that was tipped by Jim Bunning's 3–2 decision over the Dodgers at Los Angeles yesterday.

"It was a struggle—they all are," Bunning said of his 18th triumph. He had a shutout going into the ninth inning when the Dodgers scored two runs, one on a Vic Power error, and put the tying runner on base before John Roseboro struck out.

FOUR SQUEAKERS

Thus, all four series games were decided by one run and manager Gene Mauch was quick to point out: "These other clubs are not making it easy for us."

Mauch was generalizing. The Dodgers committed four errors and two of them were involved in the scoring. Moreover, rookie outfielder Derrell Griffith tested Johnny Callison's throwing arm twice on the same play. He got away with it only once.

A throwing error by Maury Wills on Cookie Rojas' infield single in the first inning, plus Tony Taylor's double and a single by Richie Allen gave Bunning a two-run working margin. After singles by Ruben Amaro and Gus Triandos in the fourth, the Phillies picked up their third run when Roseboro tossed Bunning's bunt into right field.

Bunning's worst moments in his first-time conquest of the Dodgers came in the fourth inning. That's when young Griffith got too frisky on the bases.

Wills led off with a single and was forced by Griffith. Willie Davis singled to right and Griffith raced into third ahead of Callison's high throw. At the same time, Davis took off for second and Allen's hurried throw went past Tony Taylor at second base—into right field.

CALLISON'S FOLKS SEE HIM

Griffith immediately broke for home and Callison, making like an infielder, took the ball on the run and threw out Griffith at the plate—with the help of a nice pick-up and tag by Triandos. This broke up a budding rally and gave Callison's mother and father, along with 1,000 friends and neighbors from nearby Bakersfield, something to cheer about.

Johnny, who received a batch of gifts from the townspeople before the game, followed custom after such doings and went hitless. He didn't seem to mind and made that corny "as long as we won" crack sound genuine.

The Dodgers stirred up considerable excitement for the 25,867 spectators in the ninth. With one out, Wills singled. Griffith went out and Wills made his 49th steal before coming home as Power mashed his thumb on W. Davis' hopper.

W. Davis stole second while Bunning was concentrating on the hitter and thus was in position to score on Tommy Davis' single to left. But Bunning, paying attention to the runner, went to a 2-2 count and then fanned Roseboro.

Although the teams played 16 innings Saturday night in a game that ended at 1:16 A.M., the players on both sides were reasonably alert, with the Phillies getting eight hits off Jim Brewer, Bob Miller and Ron Perranoski.

Ruben Amaro was the batting star for the trip. The Mexican dandy was 14 for 38 (.368) and he fielded like a master. Tony Taylor also turned in some plays that rocked the Los Angeles audiences.

"This is a .600 team," declared Mauch. "We're 12 over .500 on the road and 18 over .500 at home which is consistency."

It was also the Phillies' 90th victory. No team in Phillies history has ever won more than 91.

80

Draft Approved, Commissioners' Powers
Restored at Winter Meetings (1964)

SOURCE: *Houston Post*, December 4, 1964

After experimenting with a variety of "bonus baby" rules in the 1940s and 1950s, the major leagues finally approved an amateur draft on December 2, 1964. Eligible players included high school and college players whose class was scheduled to graduate in the spring of the draft year (to be drafted in January and June) and American Legion and sandlot players (to be drafted separately). Major league teams and their AAA affiliates would draft in reverse order of finish the previous season, alternating by league. Minor leagues of lower classification would draft according to a lottery system. Although the draft may seem like a natural development today, some teams—especially those with extensive scouting networks—were not enthusiastic about the innovation. The new rule governing the draft was published in Senate Subcommittee on Antitrust and Monopoly, Professional Sports Antitrust Bill—1965, 89th Cong., 1st sess., 1965, 162–68.

Another major decision made at the winter meetings was to restore, as a parting request of retiring commissioner Ford Frick, the powers stripped from the office in the aftermath of the death of Kenesaw Mountain Landis in 1944 (see document 1). The new commissioner would be able to act to counter a decision he felt was "not in the game's best interests," a broader standard than had been permitted in the previous twenty years. During his deposition in the State of Wisconsin v. Milwaukee Braves et al. case on November 12, 1965, Frick testified (on pages 16–21) that his inability to act in this regard was "a handicap." The transcript of the deposition can be found in the Ralph L. Andreano Papers, State Historical Society of Wisconsin, Box 1, Folder 10.

In addition, owners again forfeited their right to challenge the commissioner's deci-

sions in court. It is likely that the owners considered these developments prior to selecting the next commissioner.

Although, as the following article notes, the All-Star Game vote was returned to the fans, Frick overturned the decision. Fans did not regain the vote until 1971.

ALL-STAR GAME RETURNED TO FANS

More Aid for Expansion Clubs
By Mickey Herskowitz

The trade winds ceased to blow again Thursday, as baseball buried itself in an all-day orgy of law-making. In separate meetings, American and National League clubowners voted to:

1) Give the All-Star Game back to the fans.

2) Restored to the commissioner powers that had been missing since the reign of crusty, iron-fisted Judge Kenesaw Mountain Landis.

3) Tightened the rule governing the sale of any club.

4) Approved the pro-football type draft of high school and college players passed Wednesday by the minor leagues.

5) Moved to help the expansion teams, who are still trying to overcome their humble beginnings. The National League proposed that Houston, Washington, the Angels and the Mets be permitted to option two first-year players to the minors. This would be in addition to the so-called designated player, who can be farmed out but counts against the varsity roster.

All that feverish activity moved the convention a full day ahead of schedule, a development that caused no tears to be shed. The owners will ratify Thursday's separate votes at their joint meeting Friday at 11 A.M., then wing for home.

They may have to wrestle departing writers for airline space, however. Some of them checked out Thursday as it became apparent that no trades of any consequence were likely to be made.

"All hell is standing still," summed up Charles Maher of the Associated Press. Maher is also the originator of the famous line, "he received a sitting ovation."

Meanwhile, the moguls spent their day cleaning up some old business. In a morning session they added their endorsement to a plan first endorsed by the players to return the all-star vote to the fans.

But Commissioner Ford Frick, who steps down after the 1965 season, thought that the doing might be considerably harder than the saying.

"I'm not anti at all," he said, "but it seems to me that there are many problems in this thing. I understand they want to have ballots printed and passed out among the fans at the ball parks.

"I know from personal experience it is very expensive to distribute and count millions of ballots. A poll of this nature must have from six to eight million votes, or the public will laugh at you. . . .

"In the final analysis," said Frick, "the determination will have to be made by the commissioner. You've got to look at this realistically. There's the problem of printing, distributing, mailing, sorting and many other things."

Although Frick could veto the new All-Star plan, those sweeping powers restored to the commissioner's office Thursday won't be available until his successor is named.

The owners gave the commissioner vast new authority simply by rewording one troublesome phrase. Formerly, he could act only in the event of action deemed "detrimental to baseball." He is now empowered to veto any move that he feels is "not in the game's best interest."

The commissioner will interpret that phrase as he sees fit.

A second change provides that no one—owners, managers or players—penalized by the commissioner will have recourse to the courts. This is a power not now available to the President of the United States, and to non-baseball minds might seem to conflict with the right of every citizen to due process of law.

However, all this could be resolved simply by amending the Constitution—the country's, not baseball's.

The National League amended its by-laws to provide that controlling interest in any club may not be transferred without approval of three-quarters of all league members. Such approval must be given at a regular league meeting, and any club found violating the rule will forfeit its franchise—a penalty that seemed adequate. . . .

The rule would prohibit a club from obtaining approval of a sale by wire or telephone, as was the case in the recent sale of the Yankees to the Columbia Broadcasting System.

The amendment that most directly affected Houston is the one allowing the expansion waifs two "free" options of their first-year men. Last season they were allowed four, but that dispensation was to be in effect only one year.

The vote on the free agent draft was unanimous in the American League and 9–1 in the National, with Saint Louis believed to be the dissenter. The National League gave unanimous approval to the extension of the commissioner's powers, and this time the American went 9-to-1.

"Whenever there's one 'no' vote in our league," said an American Leaguer, "you're fairly safe in speculating that it was Charles O. Finley."

6

Baseball Confronts Modernity

The Houston Astrodome, which opened for business in 1965, was merely the most visible indication of the changes in the world of major league baseball in the mid-1960s. In the executive offices of the owners and the players, in the press box and the locker rooms, and on the field, transitions occurred that signaled an acceptance of (or a concession to) the cultural transformation of the 1950s and 1960s. It was unclear if any faction within baseball would benefit more than another in the new environment of the mid-1960s, and often positions changed rapidly or seemed contradictory.

Players embraced the new relationship they forged with owners in the first Basic Agreement between the MLBPA and the owners, even though many of them had to be convinced that the union's new leader, Marvin Miller, would not lead them to destruction instead. They resented the intrusive and seemingly irrelevant questions of a new breed of reporters, labeled "chipmunks" by offended traditionalist sportswriters, who advanced their own careers by celebrating the same sort of personal freedom later endorsed by Miller. However, one of the most beloved broadcasters in baseball history, Red Barber, fell victim to the reactionary Yankee management as he attempted to exercise his journalistic freedom.

Owners rang in the post–Ford Frick era by selecting General William Eckert as the new commissioner, but none ever claimed responsibility for orchestrating the event. Eckert's unwritten task was to weakly wield his newly enhanced authority, thereby allowing the owners to strengthen their influence over the commissioner's office which they had enjoyed under the cooperative Frick. The general fulfilled his destiny all too well, a failing immediately apparent but not magnified until several years later, when the owners faced threats they could not have imagined earlier in the decade. This lack of imagination would cost them dearly in the future.

81

Design Flaws in Houston Astrodome Revealed (1965)

SOURCE: *Houston Post*, April 8, 1965

Ambitious designers first envisioned a domed baseball stadium more than a decade earlier, but the construction of the Houston Astrodome astonished many inside and outside the game. In addition to air-conditioning and luxury skyboxes for wealthy spectators, the key element of the design was the dome itself. In order to allow grass to grow in the enclosed environment, over forty-five hundred specially designed skylights were installed. Unfortunately, it never occurred to the architects that in daylight the glass would produce a glare that made catching fly balls a dangerous endeavor. Team officials experimented with sunglasses and colored baseballs, but eventually they succumbed to common sense and painted over the skylights.

The inevitable result was that the grass died. The newly renamed Astros simply painted the field green for the remainder of the 1965 season, but in 1966 they responded by installing a synthetic surface that became known, generically, as Astroturf.

In his autobiography, Joe Morgan: A Life in Baseball *(New York: Norton, 1993), Morgan recalled that he was the first player to complain about the problem. Although the following* Houston Post *article does not mention Morgan at all, another article reported that he was the first Astro to hit a home run in the park, in an exhibition game against a minor league affiliate.*

FIELDERS FIND DOME FLIES HARD TO FOLLOW
By Mickey Herskowitz

Fresh from the beachheads of Florida, the Houston Astros tested their Domed Stadium Wednesday for the first time in force. They approached it with mixed feelings, both awed and uneasy, like a small boy entering a church.

In a two-hour workout the Astros satisfied themselves that the thrown and batted ball behaves much as it does outdoors. But catching it was something else.

The Astros haven't exactly had a perfect record in the past at capturing flyballs. But because of the unique character of the Domed Stadium, their problems Wednesday received more than casual attention.

The players had trouble tracking the ball against the grillwork of skylights and girders in the roof. The effect is like looking at a boiled marble.

It is an artistic design, but not exactly ideal for following the flight of a baseball.

Paul Richards, Houston's general manager, and field manager Luman Harris interviewed the players, but both felt the matter could be corrected without difficulty.

"We'll turn on the lights for the intrasquad game tomorrow afternoon," Richards said. "I think it will be all right."

Harris thought the problem a minor one. "If everyone had been wearing sun glasses," he said, "there would have been no problem."

But Luman is not by nature a worrier. "How's the grass?" he was asked. "Just like any other grass," he said. "Has chiggers in it."

Richards was concerned enough about the fly ball crisis to venture into the outfield, checking the action first with and then without sunglasses. Several players staggered under high flies, and one just missed being hit on the head.

When he rejoined reporters he inquired about the number of day games the Astros play. The writers, who are never at a loss for quick answers, told him 21.

"I didn't realize it was that many," said Paul, frowning. A year ago Houston limited its daylight appearances to four, because of the intense Texas heat.

The workout was conducted for the most part in available light, as they say in the photo department. The glare of the late afternoon sun complicated things for the fly chasers before twilight came on.

"I dropped two out there," said Ronnie Davis, the young outfielder who is attached to Oklahoma City. "Most of the guys said there were losing the ball in the girders. I was losing it in the glass and picking it up in the girders."

Jim Beauchamp came off the field shaking his head. "First you see it, then you don't," he said, "making it sound like the old shell game."

It may be necessary, as club officials have pointed out before, to keep the arclights on even during afternoon games. In the meantime the discovery of a flaw in the stadium—real or imagined—gave the players something to worry about. This made them happy.

"The park is fantastic," said catcher Ron Brand, seeing it for the first time. "But it may be hard to catch a flyball." He conceded that this would certainly make for an exciting, high scoring season.

"Any outfielder who catches a ball," recommended pitcher Ken Johnson, "should get a Distinguished Service Cross and a $50 raise."

After watching the veteran Nellie Fox, now a coach, misjudge several balls, Richards examined his watch, as if it might contain the secret. "It's this time of day (4:30)," he said, "that we may have problems."

82

Marichal Attacks Dodgers' Roseboro with Bat during Game (1965)

SOURCE: *San Francisco Chronicle*, August 23, 1965

All Dodgers-Giants games involve a certain amount of drama, but this late-August matchup generated more than usual. Not only were the Giants within one game of the league-leading Dodgers, but the game—the last of the four-game series—featured a matchup between Sandy Koufax and Juan Marichal. San Francisco fans had reason to expect fireworks, but not the kind they witnessed on August 22.

The pairing of aces did not produce the expected result. Los Angeles scored single runs in each of the first two innings, and San Francisco responded with one in the bottom of the second. When Marichal came to bat in the third, Koufax knocked him off the plate with his second pitch. When John Roseboro—who had angered the Giants earlier in the series by threatening outfielder Matty Alou—returned the ball to Koufax, the throw nicked Marichal in the ear. Enraged, Marichal proceeded to club Roseboro over the head with his bat. Both dugouts erupted, and Willie Mays played peacekeeper by protecting and restraining Roseboro, a close friend. After the furor died down, Mays stunned Koufax with a three-run home run that provided the Giants with the winning margin in the 4–3 contest.

Marichal was suspended for eight games and fined $1,750 by NL president Warren Giles. The Giants lost the pennant to the Dodgers by two games.

GIANTS WIN RIOTOUS GAME, 4–3

Mays' HR Off Koufax Big Blow
By Bob Stevens

What was supposed to have been a pitching duel between Sandy Koufax and Juan Marichal, the two greatest hurlers of their day, turned into a blood-splattered riot yesterday as the Giants beat the Dodgers, 4–3.

A three-run homer by the unbelievable Willie Mays—immediately after Marichal and Dodger catcher Johnny Roseboro provoked an ugly, insane, brutal riot around home plate—created a 2–2 series tie and a first division jam-up of spectacular proportions.

Their victory, bagged before 42,807 emotionally drenched fans, the largest non-field seats mob in Candlestick history, moved the Giants within half-a-game of the still league-leading Dodgers.

You could cover now the first three clubs with a small facial tissue as the standings today look like this:

Dodgers	73	53	.576
Giants	69	51	.575
Braves	70	52	.574

The bat-swinging melee followed after the Dodgers had scored single runs in the first and second innings and Marichal had flattened Dodger shortstop Maury Wills. When Marichal came to the plate, Koufax, now 21-5, whipped a called strike past him and then came high and inside on his next pitch.

On Roseboro's return throw to Koufax the ball nicked Marichal's ear and Juan turned and appeared to say something to the catcher.

Manager Herman Franks said Juan told him he asked Roseboro, "Why did you do that?" and nothing more. . . .

Koufax came down off the mound and Giant third base coach Charlie Fox dashed into the vortex of this violent cyclone, each trying to restrain his man as the crowd went out of its mind and the entire rosters of both teams spewed onto the field.

Plate umpire Shag Crawford, the bravest man on the field and caught in the middle of this violence, grabbed the now-berserk Marichal and hauled him to the ground as Dodgers furiously tried to get to Juan and Giants just as furiously tried to pull him away.

But before the Dominican righthander went down he lashed out at Roseboro with his bat and crashed it against the side of Johnny's head opening a wound from which poured a flow of blood.

Also in the middle of it with bat in hand, but not as a weapon of offense, was Giant rookie shortstop Tito Fuentes who, too, had to be pulled away as Juan disappeared under a wave of punching, mauling Dodgers.

The action took place just to the right of the plate and about 20 feet within foul territory, all the Dodgers knotted in one angry group and all but one of the Giants gathered in another blurring circle of hauling and tugging athletes.

The one Giant who was not with his group was captain Willie Mays. He rushed over to the stricken Roseboro, perhaps his best friend in baseball, and tried to push him away. At one point, Willie, now with his uniform spattered with the blood of his friend, placed his head gently on Roseboro's chest and cried, "Johnny, Johnny I'm so sorry."

Marichal eventually was hauled to the lip of the Giant dugout, Mays still restraining the enraged Roseboro, and police came down out of the stands. Juan was thrown out of the game and Roseboro had to leave, a blood-soaked towel pressed against his bleeding head.

It is possible Marichal, who was going for his 20th victory, could be suspended and fined by National League President Warren Giles. But before either happens provocation for the fight must be determined, and that will be determined by the reports of umpire Crawford, who should in turn deserve high praise for the physical risk he took in trying to stop the small but bitter war.

Koufax, a mild-mannered man, was so emotionally shook up by this incredible scene that after he struck out Marichal's pinch-hitter, Bob Schroder, and got Fuentes to fly to left, he completely lost his composure.

He went to a three-ball, no strike count on Jimmy Davenport then lost him on a full-count walk. He lost Willie McCovey on the same sequence, and Mays came to the plate.

Koufax' first pitch was high and Mays battered it as few balls have ever been battered. It chewed its way through the mild breezes, over the centerfield fence between the 365 and 410 markers, and crashed above the wall of the bleachers and into the temporary red seats.

It was Willie's 38th of the year, it was his 14th in the month of August, it was the 491st of his career, and the sixth in the last six games.

And it was the ball game.

83

Emmett Ashford Becomes First Black Major League Umpire (1965)

SOURCE: *Boston Globe*, September 16, 1965

The first African American to become an umpire in the major leagues earned the position with fifteen years of work in the minor leagues, but he was best known for his flamboyance. Emmett Ashford spent those fifteen years—including several years in the Southwest, where racial prejudice was especially strong—developing a singular style that perfectly reflected his extroverted personality. The umpiring profession, while demanding expertise, has always had room for a few colorful individuals, and it is possible that Ashford's style of umpiring, coupled with his talent, was required to allow Ashford to advance in his career.

Ashford retired from the American League after working the 1970 World Series, a fitting culmination to a five-year career. He was the only African American umpire throughout his career, and few blacks have followed in his footsteps.

ASHFORD CRACKS BARRIER AS FIRST NEGRO UMPIRE IN MAJORS
By Bob Holbrook

Eighteen years ago the Brooklyn Dodgers brought up a player who created considerable controversy. His name was Jackie Robinson.

Those were bitter baseball days. Some of the St. Louis Cardinals openly rebelled at playing against a colored player. Others grumbled. It was nasty business.

But that passed and later baseball men wondered when the day would come when there would be a Negro manager, or even a Negro umpire.

Well, there hasn't been a Negro manager yet, but there is a Negro umpire.

His name is Emmett Ashford. He is 47 years old, the umpire-in-chief of the Pacific Coast League. Ashford's contract was purchased by the American League Wednesday.

He will report to Florida training camps next Spring, thus creating another breakthrough in a game that two decades ago banned players because of their color.

How will Ashford find the majors? The same as the Negro players find it, just another baseball league where the opposition is more talented than any they played against before.

Yet there will be a difference. Ashford will be in a position of authority. He will be subjected to the usual bench riding that every umpire undergoes, rookie or otherwise.

Ashford, however, is not sensitive. He has been around. His 12 years in the Coast League served him well and he not only is a capable umpire, but one of the most entertaining personalities the umpiring ranks have seen in modern times.

Ashford fairly oozes personality. They love him in the Coast League and the players delight in some of his antics.

He alone may be enough to breathe some zip back into a league that has become overly sedate in recent years.

This writer had an opportunity to watch Ashford work an exhibition game between the Red Sox and their Seattle farm team.

The guy was impressive. For one thing, this blocky figure astounded the press box by doing warmup sprints, racing down the first base line into right field and back again. He can outrun some young players.

He has a voice that can be heard from Fenway Park to Hopkinton. And he makes a very fine speech.

The particular game between Boston and Seattle was underway for six innings when a torrential downpour hit the ball park.

After a suitable wait, with water filling the dugouts, a figure dressed in fisherman's foul weather gear emerged from the Red Sox dugout.

Towing an imaginary boat, the old salt made his way around all three bases, finally halting at home plate.

"Pretty funny groundskeeper," said the writer to a Seattle scribe.

"Groundskeeper? That's Emmett Ashford," came the reply.

Sure enough, the umpire-in-chief, doffed his rain hat, placed it over the heart and commenced the finest game-cancelling speech we ever heard:

"Because of the inclemency of the weather, and slender possibility of renewing the game, I, as umpire-in-chief of this here contest and because of the authority invested in me, have no alternative but to declare it cancelled. I thank you."

Yes, that's Emmett Ashford, first of his race to make the majors as an umpire.

84

William "Spike" Eckert Elected as New Commissioner (1965)

SOURCE: *Chicago Daily News*, November 17, 1965

Less than one year after strengthening the powers of the commissioner's office, major league baseball owners selected as the new commissioner a man unequipped to use them. Realizing that William D. "Spike" Eckert, a retired U.S. Air Force general, knew little about baseball—the game or the business—owners assigned Baltimore Orioles president Lee MacPhail to serve as Eckert's assistant and named four other men to aid Eckert in other capacities. These appointments counter the argument of Eckert's successor, Bowie Kuhn, that perhaps Eckert was chosen because his military training would help him keep the owners in line. The owners' efforts to lower expectations of their new leader were successful, but Eckert failed to meet even these standards of performance. Even sympa-

thetic writers like MacPhail have had difficulty identifying accomplishments achieved by Eckert. As a result, owners forced him to resign less than four years into his term. To this day, no owner has claimed responsibility for nominating Eckert for commissioner.

GEN. ECKERT NEW CHIEF OF BASEBALL

Major baseball league owners Wednesday chose William B. Eckert, a retired air force three-star general, to succeed Ford Frick as the new commissioner of baseball.

The owners also announced the appointment of Lee MacPhail, president and general manager of Baltimore as administrator in the commissioner's office.

It is a new post created as a result of a reorganization voted by the leagues in Chicago several weeks ago.

Eckert signed a 7-year contract of $65,000 and MacPhail signed a contract for three years at $40,000 annually.

Eckert was named at a surprise meeting of the major league owners in Chicago. The selection became known an hour before the scheduled formal announcement at 2 p.m. He has had no previous formal connection with organized baseball.

American League president Joe Cronin had been rumored to be a top contender for the post. But Cronin's elimination was signalled earlier Wednesday when the league announced he had been granted a seven-year extension of his present contract at a raise in pay.

Eckert praised the selection of MacPhail as his right hand man.

"I have had an opportunity to meet him and know his record as one of the best informed men in baseball," the new Commissioner said.

Eckert said that the next order of business was for him to visit Frick, Charles Segar and others in the Commissioner's headquarters in New York.

"I would like to schedule a fast tour to meet with the presidents of the American and National Leagues, the American Assn., and as many owners as possible throughout the nation before the December league meetings in Miami," said Eckert.

Eckert was a three star general and held the post of comptroller of the Air Force when he retired from the service in 1961.

Eckert was commissioned a second lieutenant in field artillery upon graduation from West Point in 1930. He was transferred to the army's flying branch and won his pilot's wings in October, 1931.

In September, 1938, Eckert went to Harvard University and in June, 1940, he received a master's degree from there in business administration.

He was named production executive at Wright Field, Ohio, and in January, 1944, was made commanding officer of the 452d bomb group in Europe. He was a lieutenant colonel at the time. Later Eckert was chief of maintenance and supply for the 9th Air Force Service Command.

In July, 1945, Eckert was named executive officer to the assistant chief of staff for materiel at Air Force headquarters in Washington and, in November, 1947, was assigned to the office of the Secretary of [the] Air Force. Two months later he became executive to the Undersecretary of the Air Force.

In April, 1949, Eckert was named comptroller of the Air Material Command at Wright Patterson Air Force Base, Ohio, and in October, 1951, was named deputy commander of that operation.

Eckert was transferred to Air Force headquarters in June, 1952, as assistant deputy chief of staff for materiel. In 1956, he was named deputy commander of the Tactical Air Force at Langley Air Force Base, Va. In February, 1960, he was named comptroller of the Air Force.

His decorations include the Distinguished Service Medal with Oak Leaf Cluster, the Legion of Merit with two Oak Leaf Clusters, and The Distinguished Flying Cross, The Bronze Star, The Air Medal and The Croix de Guerre.

In addition to his post with Aerospace Industries, he is president of the Ruletta Corp.

MacPhail started his baseball career at Reading, Pa., in 1941, and joined the Yankee organization with his father in 1946. He became co-director of the Yanks' farm system and in 1957 director of player personnel under George Weiss, then the general manager. He moved to Baltimore as general manager of the Orioles in 1958.

85

MLBPA Executive Director Position
Approved by Majors (1966)

SOURCE: *Miami Herald*, March 5, 1966

William Eckert and Marvin Miller, appointed to their new posts within four months of each other, were criticized by many as the wrong men for their jobs. However, aside from the fact that both men defeated Richard Nixon to earn their positions, they had nothing in common. Miller, after a difficult first month spent gaining the approval of the union membership, quickly convinced players and reporters alike that he was uniquely quali- fied to lead the players in their future dealings with the owners and Eckert. The owners underestimated Miller's skill and resolve throughout his sixteen-year career with the MLBPA, but they realized he was a formidable foe.

The office of executive director was approved and financed by the owners with the understanding that the office would be filled by Judge Robert Cannon, the union's unpaid legal consultant, who was friendly with owners. In fact, Miami Herald *reporter Luther Evans reported that Eckert and other baseball officials were manipulating the selection process. Although Cannon was actually named to the position in late January, he balked when he discovered that the players would not match his judicial pension or allow him to remain in Milwaukee. Only then did union leaders Robin Roberts and Jim Bunning nominate Miller for the position.*

MAJORS CLEAR WAY FOR NEW COORDINATOR

By Luther Evans

Herald Sports Writer

Major league player representatives will meet at 9:30 A.M. today in Miami to select a man for a $50,000 job as their liaison and coordinator with Commissioner William Eckert and club owners.

Way was cleared for the appointment of a successor to former unofficial advisor Robert Cannon in a "briefing" with Eckert and baseball's executive council of owners at the McAllister Hotel.

Judge Cannon recently turned down a five-year offer for the post at $50,000 per year.

Although Eckert insisted that neither he nor the executive council would have any say-so in the choice, there was reason to believe he had vetoed at least one of the names the players had under consideration.

At one point, Bob Allison, Minnesota outfielder and spokesman for the player representatives, left the council meeting and huddled for an agitated hallway conference.

Eckert, however, limited his announcement after the two-hour session to an innocuous statement that "we had a very satisfactory meeting with the players on matters of organization."

Allison said "we hope to pick our man tomorrow," but declined to identify anyone under consideration. The player representatives also will have to decide on the salary, length of tenure and official title for the position.

The commissioner's office underwrites the salary for the post.

Six owners and Presidents Joe Cronin of the American League and Warren Giles of the National League attended the session.

Representing American League players were Allison and Bob Friend, New York Yankees' pitcher, and Bob Rodgers, California catcher. The National League was represented by John Edwards, Cincinnati catcher; Jim Bunning, Philadelphia pitcher, and Robin Roberts, Houston pitcher.

After much verbal sparring in a vain attempt to ascertain exactly what had transpired in the meeting, a sports writer said, "I have no more stupid questions."

"But we've got lots more stupid answers," quipped Arthur Allyn, owner of the Chicago White Sox.

86

Baseball Press Release Costs Majors
in Wisconsin Antitrust Suit (1966)

SOURCE: Ford Frick, *Baseball—An Institution*, Box 9, Philadelphia National League Club
Records, Hagley Museum and Library.

*On April 13, 1966, Judge Elmer W. Roller surprised many when he ruled that the
Milwaukee Braves could not transfer their franchise to Atlanta as scheduled because the
move would violate Wisconsin antitrust laws. Attorneys for the state of Wisconsin argued
that baseball was exempt only from federal—not state—antitrust laws, and Judge Roller
concurred. They also maintained that the loss of the Braves to Milwaukee would cause
irreparable damage to the local economy unless countered by transferring an existing
franchise to the city or providing it with an expansion club. Some of the most convincing
evidence they presented was produced by organized baseball itself.*

In the document Baseball—An Institution, *Commissioner Ford Frick emphasized
the unique economic contributions of a major league team to its host city. He calculated
the amount of money expended annually on such expenses as hotel rooms, airplane
tickets, and taxes. Frick also promoted the wisdom of building community-financed
ballparks "when the community has a major league club or the assurance of getting one."
Since baseball's attorneys could hardly refute baseball's own figures, they could not
effectively counter Wisconsin's argument, and they lost the case. However, they immediately appealed to Wisconsin's Supreme Court, which overturned Judge Roller's decision
on July 27.*

*Excerpted below are sections from a chapter entitled "Baseball—In the Community,"
pages C1–C4.*

For a brief analysis of the legal significance of this case, see Lionel S. Sobel, Professional Sports and the Law *(New York: Law-Arts Publishers, 1977), pp. 505–12.*

MAJOR LEAGUE BASEBALL AS A MEMBER OF THE COMMUNITY

Major league baseball, as a business, is a pigmy among the collosi of American industry, but it is a giant in its contribution to the economy and in the
contributions of its clubs and its people to the welfare of the community.

For all its impact on the American public as the country's greatest spectator
sport, major league baseball's annual intake amounts only to somewhere around
$100,000,000. In one sense this is a lot of money, but it becomes rather small
potatoes when you realize that Macy's Department Store in New York in 1962 had
gross sales of more than $500,000,000!

And if you really want to talk about BIG BUSINESS, remember that the operating income of E. I. Dupont & Co. in 1962 was almost two and a half billion dollars
($2,436,351,631, to be exact). In the same year, the income of General Motors was

close to fifteen billions of dollars ($14,852,460,891). And these are but two of many billion-dollar corporations in the United States!

Still, no business compares with baseball as a generator of other business in the community in which a major league club is located, according to surveys made by the Chambers of Commerce of many cities.

For more than half a century, baseball has been the motivating factor in the construction of great stadiums, each the pride and showplace of its community when it was erected.

The baseball stadium is an essential part of a great city. There, some 70 or 80 times a year, the throngs assemble for baseball games, forgetting for a time differences and dissensions in their common love of the national game and their partisan support of one of the two teams on the field.

The baseball stadium provides an arena for other sports, and is the stage for many other spectacles, as diverse as the championship high school baseball game and a three-day assemblage of a religious group.

Most of the stadiums have been built by baseball capital, and 12 of the twenty major league clubs today play in privately-built and owned stadiums. The newest and finest stadium in the country is Chavez Ravine, built by the Los Angeles Dodgers.

The value of a baseball stadium to a city was recognized by civic leaders many years ago, when far-sighted Clevelanders built their mammoth Municipal Stadium, and Cleveland's example has been followed by other cities. As mounting costs of construction, maintenance and taxes make it difficult for private capital to finance a stadium, more communities are deciding that the value of a baseball stadium justifies construction with public funds, as in New York and Houston today. But community stadiums are built only when the community has a major league baseball club or the assurance of getting one. . . .

BASEBALL AS A FACTOR IN THE ECONOMY

Professional baseball is an important factor in the economy of major league cities, to an extent not usually realized.

Most people have a vague appreciation that a baseball club generates a considerable amount of business for the retail, entertainment and transportation companies, but few realize how much money is spent by the baseball clubs themselves in the course of a year.

Major league baseball probably is the best customer the commercial airlines of the United States have; no enterprise uses more hotel rooms than does baseball; and the tax collectors rejoice when the big league season gets under way each Spring.

A survey of 1962 travel shows that 19 big league clubs flew 19,030,176 passenger miles during the regular season, and paid $2,172,692.02 to the airlines. The total does not include the Los Angeles Dodgers, who did their flying in a company-owned plane.

If we make a conservative estimate of 1,000,000 passenger miles flown by the Dodgers, we get a total of 20,030,176 miles. Astronaut Gordon Cooper traveled 600,000 miles in his record setting 22 orbits around the earth. To equal the big leagues' one-year travel, he would have had to stay up for 738 orbits—or 46 days.

The 20 big league clubs spent 53,921 man days in hotel rooms on their regular-season journeys. Just think of how much work the laundries got out of those pillow slips, sheets and towels!

None of these figures include the travel done by executive and administrative personnel of the clubs, which in itself probably dwarfs the travel expense of our greatest corporations, since baseball people spend unbelievable hours in the air and on the road.

Nor do the figures include travel to and from and during Spring Training; travel during the World Series, nor travel by minor league baseball clubs—all of which would add at least another 2,000,000 passenger miles on planes, trains and buses. . . .

Recent studies by the Chamber of Commerce of San Francisco and Minneapolis–St. Paul demonstrate vividly the impact of a major league baseball club on the economy of its community. The conclusions drawn from the surveys are staggering.

The research department of the San Francisco Chamber of Commerce determined that in 1961, the almost incredible total of $326,860,000 turned over in the Bay Area as the direct result of the presence there of the San Francisco Giants!

In studies by the Minnesota Chamber of Commerce, it was determined that out-of-town visitors drawn by the Minnesota Twins games spent almost $15,000,000 in one season.

In San Francisco, the third-place Giants in 1961 drew 1,390,679 cash customers. According to Chamber of Commerce researchers, these people spent $11,271,000 directly and indirectly because they attended the baseball games. The Chamber used a formula devised by the Federal Reserve Banks in studies of bank deposits and debits, based on the fact that each dollar spent changes hands 29 times, to reach its estimate of $326,860,000 in business traceable to baseball's presence. . . .

Although the immediate effect of a baseball club's location in a community can pretty well be measured in dollars, the intangible benefits may be of even greater importance through the years.

Nationwide, indeed worldwide, recognition is accorded a city which holds membership in the major leagues. The very term, "major league city," carries its own accolade. Every action by the baseball club is carried in detail in newspapers, on radio and on television to every corner of the United States, and the city's name is mentioned hundreds of thousands of times each year.

The presence of a big league club adds to a city's qualifications as a convention site, and also as an attraction to new industry and investment.

87

"Chipmunks": New Breed of

Sportswriter Emerges (1966)

SOURCE: *Sporting News*, April 16, 1966

In 1934 Stanley Walker wrote that there were two schools of sportswriting: the "Gee Whiz" school, personified by Grantland Rice, and the "Aw Nuts" clique, led by W. O. McGeehan. He noted that writers like Rice, who saw athletes as heroes to be emulated, were being replaced by reporters who were more cynical about their subjects. Fourteen years later, veteran sportswriter Stanley Woodward updated the list to include "On-the-Button" writers, men who reported the facts without embellishment and left "the hooray-hooray business to the radio announcers." In fact, both men were describing the same situation: the confrontation between an older, more nostalgic generation and a younger group of sportswriters searching for their own style.

During the mid-1960s several veteran observers noted another generational transformation occurring within the field. Leonard Koppett, in the article below, describes the characteristics of the new wave of sportswriters, who were known as "chipmunks." Koppett and Frederick C. Klein, who wrote about this group in an October 6, 1967, Wall Street Journal *article, agreed that chipmunks like Larry Merchant and Leonard Shecter—who in 1970 edited Jim Bouton's irreverent book* Ball Four—*were energetic writers forever in search of different perspectives from which to launch their journalistic efforts, which never included obsequious odes to the athletes they covered.*

Among the observations made by Koppett is that the surprising popularity of the woeful Mets may be partially attributable to the presence of the chipmunks. Not only did they work primarily in New York, but they specialized in stories about unusual personalities whose comical ineptitude seemed tailor-made for writers like Merchant, who summed up the philosophy of the chipmunks as a belief in "fun and games vs. life and death."

EAGER BEAVERS + RAT PACK = CHIPMUNKS

Youth, Hustle, Irreverence Mark New Writing Breed

By Leonard Koppett

FT. LAUDERDALE, Fla.—We will now examine the latest addition to the natural history of baseball, small-creature species: the chipmunk.

All well-educated baseball fans have long been familiar with "gophers," the home-run balls thrown by pitchers; with the "rabbit" that resides in lively baseballs, making gophers proliferate; and with the "butterflies" tossed by knuckleball pitchers.

The chipmunk is different: the chipmunk is a writer, a particular type of writer.

Exactly which particular type of writer is hard to define, but fairly easy to recognize. The main outer characteristics of chipmunks are:

1. Youth.

2. Pre-occupation with off-beat angles, particularly humorous ones.

3. Hustle, in the form of endless questioning.

4. A constant concern with, and profound admiration for, the literary talents of himself and his fellow chipmunks.

5. Irreverence.

6. A "fun and games" philosophy of sports, in contrast to a "life or death" philosophy.

7. Beatnik tendencies in dress and manner.

8. Quick, if not always polished, wit.

It is apparent that the chipmunk's ancestry includes the Eager Beaver. It is a historical fact that the current chipmunk coterie grew out of a primitive "Rat Pack."

WILDLIFE SURVEY NEEDED

And just who are the chipmunks?

No formal census has ever been taken (although the next Fish and Wildlife Survey has been asked to include them) but they can be divided into several groups.

The "originals" include Stan Isaacs of *Newsday* (Long Island); Leonard Shecter, formerly of the New York *News;* Larry Merchant of the Philadelphia *News;* and Phil Pepe of the New York *World-Telegram and Sun.*

Other "self-confessed" chipmunks include: Maury Allen and Vic Ziegel of the New York *News;* Steve Jacobson, Joe Donnelly and George Vecsey of *Newsday;* John Crittenden of the Miami *News;* and perhaps a half-dozen others scattered around the country. . . .

It all started half a dozen years ago.

At that time, in the New York area, there was an above-average turnover in sports writers; a relatively large group of bright new minds came into the picture at the same time.

Among these, some strong friendships developed—a phenomenon as old as baseball writing, with its enforced close company, day in and day out. This particular group, which shared so many outlooks on life, admired probing questions, humorous writing, amateur psychoanalysis and the intimate human qualities of athletes with very little regard for statistics, victories, technical analysis or tradition.

Since they would hang around together socially, and invariably congregate in one corner of a press box or press room, and since they didn't feel much community of interest with older writers, they quickly became an identifiable group. Because the Frank Sinatra crowd was so much in the news, and so desirably hep by their standards, they became known as the "Rat Pack," or sometimes the "Mouse Pack" by those unwilling to grant them full status.

Not long afterward, a novelty musical record became popular, a high-pitched chorus of "chipmunks," led by one "Alvin." In the meantime, some older writer (the identity is in dispute), annoyed by a covey of them chattering and giggling while he was trying to think his own thoughts, christened them "chipmunks"— "little animals that chatter away, going chip-chip-chip."

CANDIDATES FOR THE HONOR

Some say it was Jimmy Cannon who first gave them that title, others say Tommy Holmes of the *Herald Tribune,* or Joe Trimble of the *News,* or Milton Gross of the *Post.* It is entirely possible that the same thought occurred in different mature minds at different times. And Pepe, a handsome, dashing fellow whose two front teeth suggest just a bare trace of Bugs Bunny, is convinced that his appearance contributed to the idea, perhaps subliminally.

At any rate, the name stuck, and promptly acquired two meanings: Good and bad.

To the older (and some not so older) writers who were irritated by noisy irreverence, "chipmunk" was a term of derision.

To the chipmunks themselves, it became a badge of honor. After all, the whole idea of calling them chipmunks was chipmunkery of the first order.

Among baseball people—players, managers, officials—the term was overheard and adopted. They, too, could see chipmunks—or at least chipmunkery—as a distinct phenomenon. Almost all chipmunks were columnists or afternoon paper writers, devoted to interviews and features; they were most active, and most in evidence, in locker rooms, especially after a trying game.

Chipmunks asked the "silliest"—by baseball standards—questions, the most personal, the most embarrassing and sometimes the most unwelcome.

One must understand, at this point, the attitude of baseball people toward writers in general; distaste. Most admit the necessity for writers, but consider them as necessary an evil as income taxes, and as unavoidable.

THE ATHLETE'S VIEWPOINT

To most athletes, anything less than adoring praise is a "knock"; a "good" writer is one who confines himself to the score and mentions the name of every man who got a hit—unless, of course he happens to "rip" someone the particular player dislikes. (For instance: if a player is being platooned, and a writer neglects to point out that the manager is an idiot for wasting that player's talent, the writer is "covering up" for the manager; but if the writer happens to print a statistic to show that our platooned hero is batting .076 against lefthanders, then he is a "ripper.")

Furthermore, even worse than "ripping" is the press' tendency to intrude on "private life." Thus, if a player is arrested in a drunken brawl, or if he does something rude in public, he feels his privacy has been invaded when this is written about. ("I don't mind if you say so when I make an error or strike out," is the stock complaint, "but don't get personal.")

This is the prevailing view, although there are plenty of exceptions—so many, in fact, that chipmunks find several soul mates among the players on every club. But orthodox people—writers and others—find chipmunkery hard to live with for any extended period. . . .

Every creature needs a favorable environment. The chipmunks found it in the advent of the Mets.

One big reason was Charles Dillon Stengel. "There is no question," declares one present chipmunk, "that if Stengel had been a writer, he would have been a chipmunk. He was all chipmunk."

Casey, perhaps, didn't love the chipmunks quite as madly as they loved him, but there was plenty of reciprocity.

Another factor was the bumbling, built-in ineptitude of the Mets. If there is any one animal for which the chipmunk feels the closest sympathy, it is the underdog. And no doggies ever got further under than the Mets.

THEY'RE REAL HUSTLERS

What can be said in summation, as an evaluation of the chipmunk as he has thrived in the seventh decade of the Twentieth Century?

On the positive side: They represent the hustle, energy and lively talents absolutely essential to journalistic health. They are the new blood that must be transfused, over and over, if reporting is to remain interesting and valid. Not all have equal writing ability, but the general level is high, and their concern with what's under the surface is the right concern.

On the negative side: They tend to be intolerant of viewpoints that differ from their own, and to get so bogged down in the search for the off-beat or inner-truth that their reliability for simpler truth is sometimes compromised.

And they cannot, of course, all be lumped together. They are as diverse in talents and in specific points of view as any other group of writers.

As a matter of fact, they are far more identifiable for their behavior—among other writers and at work—than for their writing. Those who are annoyed by them—and many people are—are annoyed socially rather than professionally. Irreverence, which can be a valuable intellectual quality, is hardly a social asset.

88

Koufax, Drysdale Agree to End Joint Holdout (1966)

SOURCE: *Los Angeles Herald-Examiner,* March 31, 1966

On February 28, 1966, star pitchers Sandy Koufax and Don Drysdale informed Dodger general manager Buzzie Bavasi that they were staging a joint holdout in order to earn multiyear contracts with six-figure salaries. They acted after learning that Bavasi had told each player that the other had asked for a lower salary than the first was requesting, thereby playing one off against the other. After missing all of spring training, Koufax and Drysdale signed one-year deals for $125,000 and $115,000, respectively. Although they did not get everything they had asked for, they got enough to scare O'Malley and the other *owners. Ten years later the owners insisted that the* MLBPA *agree to an anticollusion clause that would prevent similar actions in the future. They had no idea that the clause would come back to haunt them in the 1980s, when on three occasions federal judges would find them guilty of colluding against players in an attempt to reduce salaries.*

J. William Hayes, the players' agent, is quoted as saying that Koufax had surpassed Willie Mays as the major league's highest-paid player with his new contract, but this conclusion appears to be mistaken. In a separate article, attorney Morton Moss described his threat to institute an antitrust lawsuit against the Dodgers and major league baseball if his clients were unsuccessful in signing new contracts.

KOUFAX HIGHEST PAID EVER

$132,500 for Sandy; $105,000 for Don?
By Bud Furillo
Herald-Examiner Sports Editor

The Great Holdout Case is closed, paving the way today for the start of the Great Guessing Game on how much Koufax and Drysdale are getting to pitch for the Dodgers this year.

The boys have asked Dodger general manager Buzzie Bavasi not to divulge the terms they agreed to yesterday afternoon which ended a salary stalemate that lasted 32 days. Nobody knows the facts except Walter O'Malley, Bavasi, Koufax, Drysdale and J. William Hayes, a new star in the field of representing stars.

The signing makes Koufax the highest paid player in baseball according to Hayes. His attorney Morton Moss goes into this in detail on page two.

Based on all the evidence available today, it is believed that:

Koufax, baseball's greatest pitcher, will receive approximately $132,500, slightly more than the published $125,000 the Giants pay Willie Mays, baseball's greatest player.

Drysdale agreed to an estimated $105,000.

NICE NEIGHBORHOOD

It's a long way from a million dollars, but at least the boys are in a good neighborhood, and, there will be absolutely no need for Ginger Drysdale to go to work at Woolworth's.

There can be no question that the Dodgers have not only the first, but baseball's only two pitchers to ever sign for $100,000 or more. The old money mark was $85,000, which the gypsy Braves once handed over to Warren Spahn between stops.

Pitchers everywhere will always remember Sandy and Don for opening the door to the mint for them.

If Koufax is getting $132,500, and this looks pretty solid, it represents a raise of

$57,000 for him over a year in which he won 26 games. The last win raised the National League flag at Dodger Stadium a day before the season ended.

Then, he won the fifth and seventh games of the World Series to make everyone on the team $10,000 richer last October.

For Drysdale, $105,000 would mean a pay hike of $30,000, a just reward for 23 victories, another in the World Series, plus spectacular hitting in the games he pitched and many others in a pinch-role.

When the signing was announced, Las Vegas oddsmakers immediately reinstalled the Dodgers as National League pennant favorites at 5–2, with the Giants second at 3–1. It had been the other way around before Ballpoint Pen Day.

The boys expressed relief that the whole thing was over when they appeared at a mid-afternoon press conference in Bavasi's office yesterday.

"I'll be ready to pitch a couple of innings this weekend in Arizona if they'll let me," Drysdale said.

The boys will join the Dodgers in Mesa on Saturday.

"I can't say when I'll be ready," said Koufax, "but I hope Walt (Alston) will let me pitch in some exhibitions instead of just batting practice before the season starts. I wouldn't mind even if I got bombed in the few exhibitions that are left."

It's likely that Drysdale will pitch the first week of the season at Dodger Stadium, which the defending world champs open against Houston on April 12, then switch to the Cubs on the 15th before leaving town.

"I wish I could pitch against Durocher the first week of the season," Koufax said.

GOODBYE HOLLYWOOD

Asked for clarification, Sandy explained:

"I'd like to pitch against Leo, but not Banks, Santo and Williams."

Koufax's debut will probably be made in Houston during a series starting on April 18.

The boys won't miss more than one turn apiece, although it's possible Koufax may miss two.

Sandy hasn't been throwing, but Don has for 10 days.

"I've been running to get some soreness in my legs," Koufax said, in discussing the conditioning he undertook awaiting the start of his motion picture career.

That's out now. Paramount handed Koufax and Drysdale their unconditional release from "Warning Shot" yesterday. But the studio has had a couple of actors in the bullpen.

The Dodgers stressed that Koufax and Drysdale have signed individual contracts for separate sums. You may recall that in the beginning the boys wanted a million dollars for three years cut right down the middle.

BUZZIE'S TARGET DATE

It's possible that they will pool their money for the 1966 season. This we will never know unless they want to tell us.

Drysdale and Koufax floored Bavasi with their original request.

After taking the count, Buzzie got up and flew to Florida without the pitchers, who would have nothing to do with his proposal of $100,000 for Sandy and $85,000 for Don.

In Florida, Bavasi seemed unconcerned about their absence from spring training.

"I think we'll be all right if they sign before the first of April," he said in February. "Veterans don't need any more than 12 days of spring training. The first five weeks just give you an opportunity to look at kids like Jim Lefebvre, who was a great development last spring for us."

Bavasi swung into action as his personal deadline for the dynamic duo approached. He flew here with a new offer of $210,000 for the boys on Wednesday.

Hayes, the lawyer who was a valuable figure in the negotiations in Bavasi's mind, rejected that offer. Yesterday, Bavasi raised the ante to at least $237,500. The boys accepted.

It's a good thing it happened when it did. Nobody would have believed the signing if it had come tomorrow.

It will be April Fool you know.

89

Review of *The Glory of Their Times* (1966)

SOURCE: *World Journal Tribune Book Week* (New York), October 16, 1966, pp. 14, 21

Almost exactly ten years prior to the publication of The Glory of Their Times, *sportswriter Charles Einstein proved with the first volume of his anthology* The Fireside Book of Baseball *that baseball fans appreciated books that treated their appreciation for the history of their sport seriously. While Einstein celebrated the written word, economics professor Lawrence Ritter took a different approach by giving voice to twenty-two players, stars and journeymen alike, from the first quarter of the century. As the reviewer notes below, the genius of the book lies in Ritter's decision to remove himself from the text by excluding his questions and editing the players' responses so that they read like a seamless narrative. His decision is validated by the players, who were not only articulate but also cognizant of the passage of time and willing to admit—in some cases—that the modern era had produced players equal to, and better than, the stars of their era.*

JOYS IN MUDVILLE
By Red Smith

THE GLORY OF THEIR TIMES. BY LAWRENCE S. RITTER. ILLUSTRATED. MACMILLAN. 300 PP. $7.95.

Miss Pauline Whittington, as English as her ancestor ("Turn again, Dick Whittington, thrice Lord Mayor of London"), had the excellent taste to marry an American, Jack Tait, then stationed in London for the New York Herald Tribune.

On home leave one summer they visited Jack's folks in Seattle and when her husband returned to London Pauline stayed behind to become a naturalized citizen. With time on her hands, she took to attending Pacific Coast League games. By the time she got home to England, baseball had her hooked. A year later the Taits were in New York.

"You know," Pauline said during that visit, "last year I was made a citizen, but when I got back home I didn't talk about it with my friends. It was nothing I was ashamed of, but I had a strange feeling that it was somehow—well, incomplete."

"But this afternoon," she said, "at Yankee Stadium I saw Joe DiMaggio hit a home run—and now I'm an American citizen!"

Which seems to support Mr. Jacques Barzun, the philosopher, who is quoted in Mr. Ritter's preface and on the dust jacket to the effect that "whoever wants to know the heart and mind of America had better learn baseball."

Maybe the point is debatable. Perhaps in an age of H-bombs and Beatles, baseball does not occupy quite the same place in our lives that it had for earlier generations but it would be difficult to believe this while reading Mr. Ritter's fine book. Not when John McGraw and Christy Mathewson, Ty Cobb and Walter Johnson are stalking through the pages at least as large as life.

Few writers can capture and reproduce the flavor of the past so effectively, and in this case the author didn't rely on writing skills to accomplish his purpose. Instead he went to the men who were a part of the times he is dealing with and the events that illuminated those times, he took down their words on tape and he presents them with a minimum of editing. The result is a warm and wonderfully [*sic*] evocation of a day when a man playing second base for the inclement McGraw could exult, as Larry Doyle did exult, "It's great to be young—and a Giant!"

Between 1962 and 1966, Mr. Ritter traveled 75,000 miles to interview men who played in the major leagues from the closing days of the 19th century to the middle years of the 20th. (Tommy Leach and Wahoo Sam Crawford were the earliest, Paul Waner the most recent.)

Some whom he talked with made the Hall of Fame; the names of others would be strange to kids who think the game began with Mickey Mantle and will end with Sandy Koufax. But all "were honored in their generation, and knew the glory of their times."

90

Red Barber Fired by Yankees (1966)

SOURCE: *Saturday Review*, November 5, 1966, p. 12

On September 23, 1966, the New York Yankees, on their way to their first last-place finish in more than half a century, hosted the Chicago White Sox. Only 413 people—the lowest attendance in Yankees history—bothered to attend the meaningless contest. Recognizing that this was the most newsworthy story of the game, legendary broadcaster Red Barber directed his cameramen to pan the empty stands, but club officials forbade them to comply. Sensing that his credibility was at stake, Barber briefly described the scene he and the few spectators beheld.

Only three days later new Yankees president Mike Burke fired Barber, abruptly ending his distinguished thirty-three-year career. Neither Burke nor the Yankees initially provided a reason for the firing, but the truth was too obvious to be concealed. On October 9 the New York Times published an editorial excoriating not only the Yankees but broadcast journalism as a whole. The termination of Barber was the latest indication that baseball announcers were beholden to their teams first and their fans—and the game—afterward.

TOP OF MY HEAD

Seeing Is Disbelieving

The New York Yankee ball club is now owned by CBS—the Columbia Baseball System. Not only has the attendance at Yankee Stadium fallen off this year but the rating of the telecasts of the Yankee games has fallen below the rating for another New York team which also purports to play baseball: the Mets.

The CBS management has been sorely plagued to remedy this situation. First they tried what always works in TV shows—putting a laugh-track on the telecasts of Yankee games. The new baseball commissioner didn't think that was quite the thing.

So they did the next best thing—they fired Red Barber. Mr. Barber was one of the announcers. Not that I intend to hold up Mr. Barber, who often went too far afield from reporting the game, as the epitome of a baseball broadcaster. But Mr. Dan Topping, who was in charge of the club, said he used to watch the games at the stadium with a television and radio set at his side to hear what was going on. And what was going on and on was Mr. Barber.

Mr. Topping didn't seem to mind those expansive disquiparancies [ramblings] during all those years when the Yankees were winning. It's the old story of the poker game. When a player tells a funny story, the winners laugh and the losers say, "Deal the cards. What's holding up the game?"

Mr. Topping had figured to permit Mr. Barber to go on like that because it stood to reason that he would drive fans away from their TV sets to Yankee Stadium. But he didn't. At one of the games in late September there were some 400 rooters in the stands, a statistic about equivalent to the number of runs the team made all season.

Meanwhile, back at Shea Stadium, the Mets were pulling in fans by the trainloads. They gave away bats. So, in desperation, the Yankees gave away bats. It made the tots happy, but the fans squirmed because the Yankee pitchers gave away hits and runs. And especially this year. What a time this would have been to be in the World Series. But how could the Yankees have known that the Dodgers were going to lose four straight?

Of course the Mets kept losing too. But their fans had something special going for them. They flocked to the park to see in what new way their darlings could lose a ball game on any given day.

But as a Yankee fan I am not downhearted. And I have utmost confidence that the creative men who operate CBS can recapture the glory and popularity the Yankees once enjoyed. Any broadcasting company that can make *Gilligan's Island* popular—I'm for them. Unless CBS is so intrigued with having all its TV shows high in the Nielsen rating that its executives are overjoyed to find that their Yankees finished in the top ten.

Somebody ought to tell them about that tenth place in the American League.

Goodman Ace

91

Sandy Koufax Retires at Age Thirty (1966)

SOURCE: *San Diego Union,* November 19, 1966

The Notre Dame and Michigan State football teams, on the eve of playing the latest "game of the century," were displaced from the top of sports pages across the country by the stunning news that baseball's greatest pitcher, Sandy Koufax, had retired due to chronic pain in his invaluable left elbow. In the last four years of his career Koufax won ninety-seven games, four ERA titles, three Cy Young Awards, and one Most Valuable Player Award. During his final two seasons, when his arm hurt the most, he led the National League in both complete games and innings pitched—along with strikeouts and wins—both years. Although fans knew of Koufax's arm problems, given his historic performance during this period his retirement at such a young age baffled and disappointed many. However, none could question his courage, nor his status as one of the most dominant pitchers of all time, if only for a brief period.

The following article was written by Phil Collier, who was told by Koufax in August 1965, in confidence, that the 1966 season would be his last. Collier was credited with breaking the story on November 18, the day of Koufax's dramatic press conference.

KOUFAX QUITS BASEBALL

Confirms Collier Exclusive
Dodgers Shun Conference
By Phil Collier
San Diego Union Sports Writer

LOS ANGELES—The Los Angeles Dodgers let Sandy Koufax walk away from a meteoric pitching career yesterday without even bidding him farewell.

No one from the Dodger front office was present in Beverly Hills when Koufax startled a press conference with news that he is retiring from baseball rather than risk further injury to his arthritic left elbow. The 30-year-old strikeout sensation, a winner of 53 games the last two seasons, ignored general manager E. J. (Buzzie) Bavasi's plea that he delay making the move.

Bavasi inferred that Koufax' announcement has scuttled Dodger hopes of arranging a trade for a pitching replacement.

"I had hoped Sandy would wait until after the winter meetings early next month," said Bavasi. "Now it's going to be tough to make a trade there. When the other ball clubs get you down, they step on you."

"Buzzie had plenty of warning—I told him a month before the season ended that I was planning to retire," said Koufax, a three-time winner of the Cy Young Award and the only player ever to receive the honor more than once. "But I don't think he believed me."

Sandy was asked if his retirement was motivated by trouble with the front office.

"No," he said. "Buzzie and I have had a few arguments in the past but we're friends and I expect us to remain that way."

Koufax, the only major leaguer ever to hurl four no-hitters, said his retirement decision is final.

"I can't take the pain any more," he said, "and I've been advised (by Dr. Robert Kerlan) that the medication I've been taking in order to pitch could ruin my health.

"I might have been able to pitch one more season, but the risk is too great. I have a life to live and I don't want to spend it as a cripple."

He was willing to admit, however, that he could be quitting a year too soon.

The holder of most of baseball's strikeout records is turning his back on a 1967 contract that could have run $200,000. Sandy held out for $125,000 last spring and became the highest-paid pitcher in history.

"I started thinking about retirement in spring training last year (1965)," he said, "when the elbow swelled up and I had to fly back here from spring training. By the end of that season, I was pretty sure this would be my last year."

The sport's biggest drawing card was asked why he made the announcement yesterday, instead of heeding Bavasi's plea for another month delay.

"I don't like to be devious, I don't want to lie to people," he said. "Everyone wanted to know what my plans were and I couldn't tell them. I had three more phone calls from writers Thursday night and that's when I decided I couldn't wait any longer.

"I have no regrets about the 12 years I've been with the club, but I would regret it if I played one season too long. This thing (the elbow) gets a little worse every year. It hurt more this season than it did last season and it has hurt more this fall than it did last fall."

National League hitters have been scoffing for two years over stories about Koufax' ailments. One of Sandy's most vocal antagonists has been Roberto Clemente, the Pittsburgh outfielder who nipped Koufax earlier this week in balloting for the National League's Most Valuable Player Award.

But Sandy revealed for the first time yesterday the extent to which his doctors had gone to keep him on the firing line.

"There were 16 or 17 cortisone shots in the elbow this summer—so many I almost lost count," he said. "I was having to take codeine before I went out to pitch and I was taking some pills (butazoldin) that caused my stomach to be upset most of the time.

"I pitched only one game without pain this season."

After each mound assignment, Sandy would have to sit for half an hour with his left elbow in a bucket of ice. The treatment was designed to reduce hemorrhaging and swelling in the elbow.

He said the traumatic arthritic condition has even affected him off the field. "I've had to learn to do some things righthanded," he said, "because I've started dropping things with my left hand. And I've had to have the left sleeve taken up in all my jackets."

The strain of pitching more than 300 innings two seasons in a row and the effects of the arthritis have taken such a toll that Koufax can't come any where close to straightening his left arm.

Sandy said he has no plans for a new career. He said he has no future as an actor, despite several Hollywood offers, but said he might be interested in a job as a radio or television announcer.

Someone asked if he would like to remain in baseball.

"Not if it meant a lot of traveling," he said. "I always considered that the toughest thing about being a ballplayer."

Someone even asked Sandy about his financial condition.

"Well, there's enough left for lunch and dinner," he smiled.

It was suggested that he might have been able to help the Dodgers next year if he pitched only once a week.

"I'm not sure," he said, "that pitching once a week would be any easier than pitching every fourth day."

He was asked what his loss will mean to the Dodgers.

"Players come and go," he said. "When I came up, I replaced somebody. Now somebody will take my place. The Dodgers might not even need to trade for another starting pitcher if they can come up with another kid like Don Sutton."

Sutton was a rookie sensation this year.

Koufax said his only immediate plan is a vacation trip to the Bahamas early next month.

Though there had been speculation that the handsome bachelor might retire, his announcement brought disbelief to an adoring public.

"You can't quit, you just can't," pleaded one feminine admirer yesterday when she spotted Koufax in the Beverly Hills restaurant.

But he's gone for good and the Dodger dynasty of three pennants in the last four seasons seems definitely ended. There is no way to replace a pitcher who won 27 games and lost nine this season; a pitcher who twice has fanned 18 batters in one game; a man who hurled a perfect game against Chicago in 1965.

The Dodgers would never have won the pennant without him this year. Sandy had to toil the final game of the season, with only two days' rest to clinch the title at Philadelphia.

92

Red Sox Complete Miracle Season, Win AL Pennant (1967)

SOURCE: *Boston Globe*, October 2, 1967

The 1967 American League pennant race, by any measure one of the greatest in baseball history, came down to three games on the final day of the season. The Minnesota Twins and the Boston Red Sox, tied for first place, met at Fenway Park, while the Detroit Tigers hosted the California Angels for a doubleheader. If the Tigers swept the Angels they would tie the Twins–Red Sox winner for first place. If that wasn't enough to excite baseball fans, Red Sox left fielder Carl Yastrzemski—who had carried the Sox almost single-handedly with his extraordinary performance over the past three weeks—had a chance at winning the Triple Crown. His only obstacle was the Twins' formidable slugger Harmon Killebrew, who entered the final game tied with Yastrzemski for the league lead in home runs with forty-four. The Red Sox, who had not played in the World Series since 1946 and who avoided last place in 1966 by only half a game, were counting on Yastrzemski and starting pitcher Jim Lonborg, who was trying for his twenty-second victory, to end this exhilarating season on a high note.

In his column, Bud Collins, better known today for his reportage on tennis, barely mentions that the Red Sox clinched the pennant by defeating the Twins 5–3, thanks to Yastrzemski's 4-4 performance. However, he does cite Karl Marx, Chiang Kai-shek, and country singer Bobbie Gentry's hit song "Ode to Billy Joe."

RED SOX TAKE PENNANT AS HISTORIC SEASON ENDS

Sox Barely Escape Screaming, Streaming Fans
By Bud Collins

As the ball came down in Rico Petrocelli's glove for the last-and-final out, the town went up in the air like a beautiful balloon. Perhaps it will never come down; Red Sox euphoria is a gas that can keep you higher than helium. Or pot.

For an instant Petrocelli looked at the baseball. Then he began to run as though he were Chiang Kai-shek in Peking because he could hear the shrieking mob behind him.

It was the Red Sox Guard charging across the Fenway playing field Sunday afternoon, and the old ball park suddenly became a newsreel from Hong Kong; the Red Guard storming the British embassy. These were the zealots, thousands of them from the congregation of 35,770 at Fenway Park, which was packed tighter than the Black Hole of Calcutta.

They leaped the fences and streamed onto the field, screaming the Red Sox Guard oath—"We're No. 1!"—and displaying their banners. . . .

Respectable people who had left their homes placidly, if nervously, to attend the pennant-deciding rites indulged in by Our Old Town team had become fanatics celebrating a holy war triumph.

"Is Yaz God?" asked one of the banners.

It was an interesting theological question in the light of the miracles achieved by Carl Yastrzemski. Certainly he and his fellows are the children of the gods in this year of 1967.

Karl Marx, who said religion is the opiate of the people, would have revised himself had he watched the Red Sox unite to throw off their ninth place chains. The Red Sox are the opiate right now, Karl, baby, although you might classify them as a religion.

"Just like '46!" proclaimed another banner. "Next Stop St. Louis!" "Spirit of '67!" "Go Sox!" "Wipe out Cardinals!"

The banners were waving and the mob advanced, and pitcher Jim Lonborg stood on the mound savoring it all, ready to be hailed as a conquering hero.

"Then it became a mania—and I was scared to death," Lonborg recalled. He didn't mind being raised to the sky by admirers—but not by 5000 of them, each wanting a piece of him as a relic of their religious experience. He was sucked into the crowd as though it were a whirlpool, grabbed, mauled, patted, petted, pounded and kissed.

"This made Roxbury look like a picnic," said Patrolman John Ryan, a riot veteran who was one of Lonborg's rescuers. "Jim could have been hurt bad. We barely got him out of there."

Lonborg emerged nearly in tatters. His buttons were gone, and though his uniform shirt was still on his back his undershirt had disappeared. Nevertheless his right arm still dangled from the shoulder and his fingers were intact. He would pitch and win again, although his 5–3 decision over Minnesota seemed enough forever at that moment.

Growing more fervent, the crowd split into platoons. One attacked the scoreboard, ripping down signs and everything else that could be lifted for souvenirs. Others looked elsewhere for loot. The fervor had begun to degenerate into the ugliness of vandalism. And the fever in some had become a mood of recklessness that endangered. Twenty or so kids climbed the screen behind the plate like monkeys. Several nearly fell to the concrete 40 feet below. The screen sagged ominously beneath their weight as the people in the seats below looked up helplessly.

Nobody seemed to want to leave the park. A few firecrackers went off, and horns blew endlessly. On the field, most of the Red Sox Guard had settled into a milling pattern, wandering about the diamond, dazed at the wonder of it all, ecstatic to be treading the hallowed ground.

Joe Tierney led a group of ushers who stood on the mound, protecting that rise from the human bulldozers. A man named Ray Copeland from Wellesley stooped at the edge of the mound, scooped up a palmful of dirt and poured it into a small box. "Going to take this back to England," he said. "I've been working in Boston a year, became a Red Sox fan, but when I go back, some of the soil of Fenway goes with me to London."

Kris Becker, a college girl from Worcester, plucked a handful of grass from along the third baseline. "Not sure what I'll do with it yet. Maybe frame it," she said.

Only the cops prevented the mob from removing the left field wall.

Last year on the last day of the season the Red Sox choked; they won and blew 10th place by a half-game. Sunday it was altogether something else. "You respond differently when you're in first place than when you're in ninth," said Yastrzemski.

Lonborg set the faithful to chanting and clapping with his bunt single that opened the sixth. The Red Sox, behind 2–0, devoted 24 minutes to their half of the inning and the Minnesotans began to feel the mysterious power of Our Old Town Team. They threw to the wrong base, made wild pitches, an error, and put the ball over the plate to Yastrzemski. It meant five runs for Boston, the team that is today's American Dream. The inning ended with John Kiley, the Fenway organist, playing "The Night They Invented Champagne." It was a hymn to the day, and to the evening to come when Uncle Tom Yawkey poured for Our Old Town Team.

They drank champagne the way people drink it when it is free, and many of them probably have heads resembling the Goodyear blimp today.

The players will sober up by Wednesday, but it will take the town much longer to get over its Red Sox high.

And now, on this day of revelation, we know what Billy Joe and his chick were throwing off the Tallahatchie Bridge; World Series tickets printed in Detroit, Minneapolis and Chicago.

93

MLBPA, Owners Sign First Basic Agreement (1968)

SOURCE: 1968 Basic Agreement, from National Baseball Hall of Fame Library

In his first two years as the executive director of the Major League Baseball Players' Association, Marvin Miller negotiated promotional contracts with Coca-Cola and Topps and an improved pension plan, and earned the trust of the players—and the hatred of the owners—in the process. Miller earned another triumph when he gained a number of significant concessions in a Basic Agreement between the owners and the union, the first such pact in American professional sports. Among the improvements were an increased minimum salary (from $7,000 to $10,000), increased meal money, and an agreement not to institute major rules changes without the prior approval of the MLBPA. However, *the most important component of the Basic Agreement was the establishment of a formal process for the hearing of player grievances relating to disciplinary or contractual issues. Although the ultimate arbiter was the commissioner, the inclusion of the grievance procedure was a key step in the owners' eventual acceptance of an independent arbitrator in the 1970 Agreement.*

Printed below is the procedure to be followed for one or more players or a team to enter the arbitration process.

SCHEDULE C

Grievance Procedure

B. PROCEDURE.

Step 1. Any player who believes that he has a justifiable Grievance shall first discuss the matter with a representative of his Club designated to handle such matters, in an attempt to settle it. If the matter is not resolved as a result of such discussions, a written notice of the Grievance shall be presented to the Club's designated representative, provided, however, that for a Grievance to be considered beyond Step 1, such written notice shall be presented within (a) 45 days from the date of the occurrence upon which the Grievance is based, or (b) 45 days from the date on which the facts of the matter became known or reasonably should have been become known to the Player, whichever is later. Within 10 days following receipt of such written notice, the Club's designated representative shall advise the Player in writing of his decision and shall furnish a copy to the Players Association. If the decision of the Club is not appealed further within 15 days of its receipt, the Grievance shall be considered settled on the basis of that decision and shall not be eligible for further appeal.

Step 2. A Grievance, to be considered in Step 2 shall be appealed in writing by the Grievant or by the Players Association to a designated representative of the Player Relations Committee within 15 days following receipt of the Club's written decision. The Grievance shall be discussed within 10 days thereafter between representatives of the Player Relations Committee and representatives of the Players Association in an attempt to settle it. Within 10 days following such discussion, the designated representative of the Player Relations Committee shall advise the Grievant in writing of his decision and shall furnish a copy to the Players Association. If the decision of the Player Relations Committee representative is not appealed further within 15 days of its receipt, the Grievance shall be considered settled on the basis of that decision and shall not be eligible for further appeal.

Grievances which involve (a) more than one Club, or (b) a Player who is not under contract to a Club which is party to the Grievance, may be filed initially in Step 2, provided that written notice of the Grievance shall be presented to the designated representative of the Player Relations Committee within (a) 30 days from the date of the occurrence upon which the Grievance is based, or (b) 30 days from the date on which the facts of the matter became known or reasonably should have become known to the Player, whichever is later.

Step 3. In order for a Grievance to be considered further, it shall be appealed in writing by the Grievant or by the Players Association, within 15 days of receipt of the Step 2 decision, to the president of the Club's League, for his consideration. Upon receipt of the notice of appeal, the president of the League shall designate a time and place for an informal hearing, which hearing shall be commenced as soon as practicable but no later than 20 days from the date of receipt of the appeal. The League president shall render a written decision within 10 days following the conclusion of such hearing, and may affirm, modify or reverse the decision appealed from. If the decision of the League president is not appealed further within 15 days of its receipt, the Grievance shall be considered settled on the basis of that decision and shall not be eligible for further appeal.

The Parties may, by mutual consent, waive the necessity of the Step 3 procedure and permit the appeal of a Grievance from Step 2 directly to Arbitration.

Grievances which relate to League disciplinary action and which are not covered by the procedure set forth in Section C, below, may be filed initially in Step 3, provided that written notice of the Grievance shall be presented to the League president within 30 days following the date on which the Player receives written notification of the discipline.

Arbitration. Within 15 days following receipt of the decision of the League president (or, in the event the Parties have agreed to waive the Step 3 procedure, within 15 days following receipt of the Step 2 decision), the Grievant or the Players Association may appeal the Grievance in writing to the Commissioner for impartial arbitration. Upon receipt of the notice of appeal, the Commissioner shall set a time, date and place for hearing the appeal, which hearing shall be commenced as soon as practicable but no later than 20 days following receipt of the notice of appeal. Such hearing shall be conducted in accordance with the Rules of Procedure attached hereto as Appendix A. The Commissioner shall render a written decision as soon as practicable following the conclusion of such hearing, and may affirm, modify or reverse the decision appealed from. The decision of the Commissioner shall constitute full, final and complete disposition of the Grievance appealed to him.

With regard to the arbitration of Grievances, the Commissioner shall have jurisdiction and authority only to interpret, apply or determine compliance with the provisions of agreements between the Players Association and the 20 Clubs or any of them, and agreements between individual Players and Clubs. The Commissioner shall not have jurisdiction or authority to add to, detract from, or alter in any way the provisions of such agreements.

Grievances shall be presented initially to the Commissioner for Arbitration when (a) the Parties mutually agree to submit a Grievance directly to the Commissioner, or (b) the Grievance arises out of discipline imposed upon a Player by the Commissioner pursuant to action by him under Article I of the Major League Agreement, provided that written notice of the Grievance shall be presented to the

Commissioner within (a) 30 days from the date of the occurrence upon which the Grievance is based or (b) 30 days from the date on which the facts of the matter became known or reasonably should have become known to the Player, whichever is later.

Nothing contained in this Grievance Procedure or in the Rules of Procedure attached hereto as Appendix A shall in any way impair or limit the functions of powers of the Commissioner under the Major League Agreement. This Grievance Procedure and said Rules of Procedure are intended to implement the functions of the Commissioner under the Major League Agreement by providing the exclusive procedure and rules applicable to Grievances as defined herein. Any dispute arising hereafter to which a Player is a Party and which is not covered by this Grievance Procedure shall be processed in accordance with procedures heretofore provided and continuing. . . .

F. MISCELLANEOUS

4. In any discussion or hearing provided for in the Grievance Procedure, a Player may be accompanied by a representative of the Players Association who may participate in such discussion or hearing and represent the Player. In any such discussion or hearing, any other Party may be accompanied by a representative who may participate in such discussion or hearing and represent such Party.

5. The Parties recognize that a Player may be subjected to disciplinary action for just cause by his Club, League or the Commissioner. Therefore, in Grievances regarding discipline, the issue to be resolved shall be whether there has been just cause for the penalty imposed.

6. Nothing contained in this Grievance Procedure shall excuse a Player from prompt compliance with any discipline imposed upon him. If discipline imposed upon a Player is determined to be improper by reason of a final decision under this Grievance Procedure, the Player shall promptly be made whole.

7. In the event a vacancy occurs in the office of Commissioner, the Players Association and the Clubs will attempt to agree on an arbitrator to serve until a successor to the Commissioner takes office. If they are unable to agree, the time in which appeals may be made to the Commissioner will be extended until a successor takes office.

7

The Era of Labor Unrest Begins

The first half of Commissioner Eckert's first term in office was relatively peaceful and not without accomplishments, among them the signing of the first Basic Agreement between the owners and the players' union, the successful (if controversial) reconfiguration of each league into two divisions and the subsequent creation of the championship series to determine the World Series combatants, and the reduction of the pitcher's mound following the non-offensive 1968 season. Nevertheless, the owners were so embarrassed by Eckert—even though they had sought such a functional nonentity for the position—that during the 1968 winter meetings they informed the general of his resignation.

In February 1969, while continuing to search for a better candidate, the owners designated National League attorney Bowie Kuhn as an interim commissioner, but during the summer they made the appointment permanent. Their decision was applauded by the press, and with some reason. Kuhn was knowledgeable about baseball's backroom politics, was a fan of the game, and was not reluctant to speak to reporters. Within a few months the new commissioner acted to defuse several controversies, including two trades in which the primary players involved decided to retire rather than report to their new clubs. Kuhn intervened in each case, and the players rescinded their retirements after receiving significant salary boosts. Kuhn's willingness to exercise the powers of his office to the fullest extent so early in his term earned him both allies and enemies in quick order.

During the World Series a third prominent player, known for being outspoken, announced his retirement after being traded. Under the circumstances the player was not believed, and the commissioner responded to the player's anger with a firm but cool-headed reaffirmation of the reality of the trade—the player could retire or report to his new club. No other options were available. Kuhn had no way of knowing that the events spurred by the intransigence of this one player—Curt Flood—would forever change the world of professional baseball by helping to create another option.

94

Major Leagues Agree on Divisional Play, Playoffs (1968)

SOURCE: *Houston Post,* July 11, 1968

The American and National Leagues agreed to expand to twelve teams each for the 1969 season, but they could not agree on a common format for adjusting their regular-season schedule. On May 28 the AL voted to split the league into two six-team divisions and to play a 156-game schedule. The NL preferred to retain its traditional structure and the 162-game schedule it had adopted in 1962. During the All-Star Game break the two leagues compromised, much to the displeasure of several teams. The AL's divisional scheme, which concluded with a playoff between the regular-season champions, was accepted, and the 162-game season was preserved with the institution of an unbalanced schedule. Each club would play divisional foes eighteen times, while contesting other teams only twelve times. A key feature of the new alignment in the NL, which incongruously placed Atlanta in the West and St. Louis in the East at the insistence of clubs that feared the reduction of visits from popular teams like San Francisco and Los Angeles, is described from a different perspective in the following article.

NL SPLITS, SCHEDULE THE SAME
By Rush Wood

A day-long series of meetings Wednesday of the National and American League baseball club owners ended in the predicted compromise for a uniform formula between the two leagues.

The National League held to its stand of playing a 162-game schedule in 1969 but consented to realigning itself into two, six-team divisions as a result of the recent expansion from 10 teams to 12.

The American League won its position on splitting into divisions, while it relinquished its plans of playing a 156-game schedule.

This bit of arbitration was announced by baseball commissioner William Eckert late Wednesday at the Shamrock-Hilton Hotel, where the owners spent almost nine hours debating their problems.

Originally the National League, which recently voted expansion franchises to San Diego and Montreal, had announced the operation of a 12-team league over a 162-game schedule. And the American League, with the addition of Seattle and Kansas City, had made adjustments calling for two, six-team divisions and a 156-game schedule.

A meeting of the executive council of the two major leagues in New York two weeks ago suggested the compromise to which the two groups finally consented Wednesday.

"I am happy to report that both leagues adopted the resolution of the executive council," Eckert said to a press conference after meeting shortly with league presidents Warren Giles (National) and Joe Cronin (American) following the respective loop meetings.

"It is a great step forward, showing uniformity and cooperation," Eckert said.

The National League's divisional lineup announced by Giles throws Houston in one group with San Francisco, Los Angeles, San Diego, Cincinnati and Atlanta. New York, Montreal, Philadelphia, Pittsburgh, Chicago and Saint Louis will make up the other group.

"They're neither east or west, nor south or north yet," Giles said in explaining that names for the divisions will be decided at a later date.

Under Wednesday's announced plans, which Giles stressed "are for the 1969 season only," teams in the same division will play each other 18 times each season, and will oppose teams in the other division 12 times a year.

Judge Roy Hofheinz seemed quite pleased with the idea of divisional play.

"It's a fine move and a great day for Texas," Hofheinz said. "It is going to give us two races, and the Astros should be able to battle strongly for the championship of our division next season.

"We have with us two of our most attractive road teams—the Dodgers and the Giants—plus the great talent on the Reds and the Braves—all of which should make our fans very happy."

The Judge couldn't resist adding, "I hated to lose a game or two against the Cardinals, but in the long run it may be beneficial not to play them too often."

Unlike the judge, not all of the club owners left the bargaining table in good humor. Arthur Allyn, owner of the Chicago White Sox, was one of these.

"We are strongly opposed to the increase in games and the makeup of our division," Allyn said. "We (Calvin Griffith of the Minnesota Twins shared Allyn's views) plan to appeal to the commission [sic] and will abide by his decision."

The White Sox have been placed in the same division with Minnesota, Oakland, Kansas City, California and the new Seattle team.

"The National League is depriving us of the privilege of equality at the gate," Allyn told newsmen.

"I'm at a loss as to just what compels both leagues to have the same number of games," said Allyn, disputing Eckert's plea for uniformity.

Allyn disclosed that he thought the National League's divisional alignment to be "far superior to ours."

In announcing that "the league is very much pleased with the progress being made by San Diego and Montreal," Giles told of the Canadian city's plans of providing a domed stadium by 1972.

Until that time the Montreal club, which is yet unnamed, will play in the Autostade, which is due to receive a face-lifting that will increase its seating capacity from the present 26,000 to 37,000 by next April and also lengthen the distance to the foul poles to 330 feet.

Tentative plans regarding the erection of a domed covering for the Autostade were discussed Giles said, but were not included in "the commitments that the two new teams must fulfill."

Asked what precautions were taken to assure that a domed stadium will be built in Montreal, Giles answered, "We are taking the word of the mayor, the word of the city and the word of the team's sponsors. It is being done completely in faith of these."

According to Eckert, the two leagues will begin play next season on Monday, April 7 and conclude Thursday Oct. 2. Division playoffs in each league would start on Oct. 4 with the World Series scheduled to begin on Oct. 11.

"These dates are subject to change," Eckert said.

95

McLain Wins Thirty-First Game while Allowing Mantle's 535th Home Run (1968)

SOURCE: *Detroit Free Press*, September 20, 1968

During the 1960s, an era dominated by pitchers, few hurlers were as dominant as Denny McLain. In 1965, his third season, the twenty-one-year-old right-hander established himself as a future star by winning sixteen games for the Detroit Tigers. In the following two seasons McLain won thirty-seven games and appeared in one All-Star Game, but his remarkable performance in 1968 still stunned his contemporaries. His thirty-one victories led the Tigers to the pennant they just missed the previous season, when McLain was hampered by injuries, and earned him the Cy Young and Most Valuable Player Awards. McLain became the first—and last—pitcher since Dizzy Dean in 1934 to win thirty or more games in a season.

In sharp contrast, Mickey Mantle was suffering through the final season of his sterling career. Although he finished third in the AL in on-base percentage, his .237 batting average and eighteen home runs were disappointing to his fans and especially to

Mantle. He entered the September 19 game with the Tigers—who had already clinched the pennant—tied with Jimmie Foxx with 534 career home runs. According to both McLain and Mantle, the eccentric pitcher fed Mantle a number of batting-practice-quality pitches, the last of which Mantle slugged for the second-to-last home run of his career.

Joe Falls
Sports Editor

WHO'LL EVER FORGET THE MICK'S 535TH?

How many "magic moments" can there be in one week?

We had Denny McLain's 30th victory last Saturday. Then we had the Tigers' pennant-clinching Tuesday night. And finally there was Mickey Mantle's home run on Thursday . . . and this may have been the most touching moment of them all.

It was something I'll never forget. Nor will The Mick. Nor will McLain. Nor will any of the 9,000-odd fans who turned out for the game on this bleak Thursday afternoon.

It was, in some ways, the most amazing home run I have ever seen.

McLain, you see, let him hit it. He threw it right down the pipe, smack across the plate, squarely in Mantle's power and The Mick rode it out.

"Tell Denny thanks," Mantle smiled later in the Yankee clubhouse. "He's made a fan of me for life."

And we thought we'd had all the drama any city could see in one baseball season.

This may have been the only time in baseball history that a rival team stood up and applauded one of the enemy after he crashed one into the seats.

That's exactly what the players in the Detroit dugout did as Mantle rounded the bases.

Everybody was applauding. The Yankees, the Tigers, and the fans. Even McLain threw a salute over to Mantle when he got back to the dugout.

That's what they think of this guy.

MIGHT BE LAST VISIT TO DETROIT

The incident unfolded in the eighth inning. The game itself was of little consequence. McLain was breezing to his 31st victory behind a 6–1 lead.

Mantle was the second batter in the inning.

As he walked to the plate, the fans started to rise and give him a hand. Soon everyone in the stadium was standing and applauding.

It was not a wild kind of ovation but one that was warm and sincere. They knew this might be the last time they would ever see Mantle play ball in Tiger Stadium.

They wanted him to know how they felt about him.

The home plate umpire called time so Mantle could receive the full measure of applause. Mantle stood there, with his head slightly bowed, feeling embarrassed and awkward.

Later, he said: "The chills were running through my body."

McLain threw two quick strikes over to The Mick. He fouled the third one back. The crowd started that rhythmic applause, imploring Mantle to get a hit.

As catcher Jim Price walked back to the plate after chasing the foul ball to the screen, Mantle looked out at McLain and made a motion for Denny to throw the next one chest high. The Mick was grinning.

McLain threw and the pitch, with nothing on it, came in chest high. Mantle uncoiled that frightening swing and the ball screamed toward the seats in right. It crashed into upper deck, fair by inches.

Now the place was in an uproar. All of the players in the Detroit dugout were applauding. As Mantle turned for home, he nodded to McLain and said: "Thanks, Denny."

McLain looked at him and grinned.

WAITING FOR IT ALL SEASON

Mantle was mobbed when he got back to his dugout. This was his 535th home run, breaking his tie with Jimmie Foxx and putting him into third place on the list of all-time home run leaders. Only the Babe with his 714 and Willie Mays with 585 rank ahead of the Yankee muscle man.

They retrieved the ball out in rightfield. Umpire Hank Soar picked it up and made Mantle come out of the dugout to catch it. The fans applauded some more.

The organist was playing "East Side, West Side, All Around the Town. . . ."

McLain threw a wave over to Mantle. Joe Pepitone, next up, walked to the plate and was signalling for McLain to throw another one chest. "Me, too," Pepitone yelled out to the pitcher's mound.

Afterwards, Mantle sat in front of his locker smiling like the farm boy that he really is. "How about that guy—just laying it in for me?" he was saying. "Everybody knew he was doing it. I looked at the Tigers in the dugout and there were all in there laughing."

Mantle shook his head.

"It seems like I'd been waiting all year for that one. It sure feels good. I know Hank Aaron is going to pass me next year, but this feels good now."

They asked him about next year. He said he didn't know yet. He said he felt good but hadn't made up his mind whether he'd play again. If he doesn't return this will be a perfect ending to an exciting career of playing in Detroit.

As Mantle started for the shower, he said: "Be sure to tell Denny thanks."

And down the hall, Dennis D. McLain grinned that innocent, choir-boy grin of his and said: "Thanks? Thanks for what? I was trying to get him out."

96

Two AL Umpires Fired after Planning Union (1968)

SOURCE: *Cleveland Plain Dealer*, September 17, 1968

On October 7, 1963, the Association of National Baseball League Umpires (ANBLU) was incorporated in Chicago in an effort "to improve the general conditions pertaining to the relationship of [umpires with the NL] and to further aid in the constructive improvement of the game of National League Baseball." The following season, after threatening a general strike, the ANBLU signed a five-year contract that resulted in a higher average salary, double the daily expense money, and a better pension plan than their AL counterparts received. As the 1968 season wound down, AL umpires Al Salerno and Bill Valentine worked clandestinely to organize their own union. On September 16, AL president Joe Cronin, shortly after learning about their plan, fired the two men, claiming that they were incompetent.

Outraged, the remaining eighteen AL umpires and the ANBLU made plans to form a larger union, eventually called the Major League Umpires Association, at a September 30 meeting in Chicago. Several New York congressmen threatened to begin another investigation of baseball, and journalists openly questioned Cronin's explanation of his action. Nevertheless, the firing remained in effect, and Valentine and Salerno never umpired in the major leagues again.

UMPIRES FIRED; TALK STRIKE

By Russell Schneider

The possibility of a strike by major league umpires was raised yesterday by the firing of two of their members by American League president Joe Cronin.

Summarily dismissed and immediately replaced by two rookies from the Southern Association were veterans Al Salerno and Bill Valentine.

Salerno and Valentine, along with partners Emmett Ashford and Jim Honochick, were in Cleveland to work tonight's game between the Indians and Washington Senators at the Stadium.

Replacing the two deposed men in blue are former New York Yankee pitcher Bill Kunkel, and Jake O'Donnell.

If a strike is called, it probably couldn't be done before the end of the current season, however, because of the impossibility of all 40 umpires meeting prior to that time.

According to Salerno, "Yes, I'd say there is a good possibility of a strike—if the other guys think we're worth fighting for.

"I hope they support us for the betterment of all umpires, but it's up to them now. If they don't support us, I guess it's all over," added the 37-year-old veteran of seven years in the American League.

Valentine, 35, has been an A.L. umpire for six years.

Salerno and Valentine immediately retained two Cleveland lawyers to fight their dismissal. Representing the arbiters are Jerry Milano and Harry Hanna.

Hanna told The Plain Dealer, "We're not making any strike threats, but if the other umpires want to support these guys through their association, that's up to them."

Ironically, it was the formation of the American League Umpires Association which, it was charged by Salerno and Valentine, led to their dismissal.

"There's no doubt we were released from our jobs because of our activities," said Valentine during a news conference in the Carter Hotel last night.

But Cronin denied that was the case.

Cronin, in fact, said he knew nothing about the formation of the A.L. union, and further insisted he had no knowledge of a National League Umpires Association [sic], which has been in existence for some time.

"A union?" asked Cronin when he was finally reached at his home in Boston by The Plain Dealer.

"It's all news to me. I don't know anything about an umpires' association," he added.

Cronin readily admitted he had fired Salerno and Valentine earlier in the day, but was reticent about giving any reasons.

"Was it because you were dissatisfied with their work?" he was asked.

"Yeah, go ahead and say it that way," replied the president.

"It was this way," Cronin elaborated. "We (the A.L.) bought the contracts of three minor league umpires this year, and had three others optioned to the minors from last year.

"We were planning to make a change at the end of the season so we decided to do it now. That's why I called Salerno and Valentine and replaced them with Kunkel and O'Donnell."

Isn't that unusual, considering there are only 13 days left in the season?

"Yes," Cronin agreed. "But I'm anxious to see these guys (Kunkel and O'Donnell) under fire. Besides, we (Cronin and supervisor of A.L. umpires Cal Hubbard) had made up our minds to replace Salerno and Valentine—so why not right away?"

Another discrepancy in the stories as related by the umpires and Cronin concerned the severance pay Salerno and Valentine are to receive.

"He gave me 10 days severance pay," said Salerno, "and he gave Valentine 30 days."

Cronin, however, claimed he had promised both men they'd get "about one-fourth of their full annual salary."

Cronin added, "Another reason for releasing them now was to give them the opportunity to latch on with one of the new minor leagues that are sure to begin operations next year."

All of which brought only scorn from the two umpires.

"There's only one reason we were canned," said Salerno. "That's because of our activities. Hell, it was just last Thursday that we met in Chicago with the National League umpires and they agreed to accept us (the American Leaguers) in their association.

"Their head man is an attorney named John J. Reynolds. Call him. Ask him if that's not true," continued Salerno.

The two umpires said they began their union organizational efforts in Oakland several months ago. "We contacted an attorney there named Wayne Hooper," Salerno revealed.

"All the American League umpires were aware of our plans—and they all gave us the go-ahead. But we (Salerno and Valentine) did it.

"We later found out the National League was interested in combining with us through one of their umpires, an officer in their association, and we went to their meeting. It was at the Pick-Congress Hotel.

"That's when they voted unanimously to include us," declared Salerno.

"It's a funny coincidence that four days after that meeting we get fired by Cronin," he said without a smile.

Valentine said cards were sent to the 20 American League umpires asking each man for authorization to be represented by the new association.

"All the cards haven't been returned yet, but we already have a majority," said Salerno.

Apparently it was through the dissemination of the authorization cards that Cronin or another league official learned of the unionization efforts, figured Salerno.

"Somebody must have called Cronin and told him what was going on, so he moved in and fired us," added Salerno.

"It's rotten, but I don't care if I never umpire another game, just so that these things are brought into the open. I hope it will improve conditions for other umpires."

Primary complaints of the American League umpires, according to Salerno and Valentine, concern salary and pension.

Both said they earn only $12,000 per year, but that the National League umpires' starting pay is $9,500.

To qualify for a pension—which provides $2,750 a year at age 55—they must work a minimum of 10 years in the American League, compared to only five years in the National League.

"Hell," snorted Salerno. "My wife is a school teacher and she makes more money than I do.

"They want us to live good . . . to uphold the image of the American League," he continued sarcastically. "But how can we—how can anybody—on $12,000 a year?

"It's all the fault of umpires long ago for not fighting for themselves.

"That's what we're trying to rectify now," said Salerno.

97

Changes in Rules, Pitcher's Mound Approved
at Winter Meetings (1968)

SOURCE: *Sporting News, December 21, 1968*

Baseball officials at the San Francisco winter meetings realized that the spectacular performances of pitchers like Denny McLain and Bob Gibson, among many others, reflected an imbalance between offense and defense that displeased many fans. In response to this threat, several significant changes were made to assist batters. The height of the pitcher's mound relative to home plate was reduced from fifteen to ten inches. In addition, the strike zone was slightly reduced. In the first of two articles reprinted below, different pitchers and pitching coaches suggest that the changes might not have the desired effect.

On the same day (December 3), baseball officially acknowledged the save, a statistic advocated by Chicago sportswriter Jerome Holtzman since 1960 and first suggested as early as 1924. The new save rule had problems, as writer Harry Jupiter noted in the second article. The definition of a save was changed several times until the current definition was approved in 1975.

RULES ALTERED; NOW IT'S UP TO SWINGERS
By Harry Jupiter

SAN FRANCISCO, Calif.—The strike zone will be smaller, the mound will be lower and the men who run baseball hope the hitters will finally realize there is somebody up there who likes them.

"As far as I'm concerned, it's a psychological thing," said Bill Rigney of the Angels. "At least the hitter is going to know we're thinking about it."

"The pitcher won't be looking down his throat. I think the rules changes are good. Let's try it. I'd rather do this than move the mound back."

The top of the pitchers' mounds will be ten inches higher than plate level in 1969. They had been 15 inches high.

The strike zone will be from the top of the batter's knees (after he has assumed his stance) to his armpits. It had been from the knees to the top of the shoulders.

The National League hit .243 this year. The American League walloped a composite .230, with only one man, Carl Yastrzemski, cracking .300, and barely, at .301.

It's high time, the rules makers say, that they get some more hitting back into baseball.

"Anything that works a hardship on the pitcher has got to be beneficial to the hitter," said Montreal's Gene Mauch.

Stu Miller, the former relief ace with Baltimore and San Francisco, isn't at all convinced the new rules will make it tougher on the pitchers.

"The lower mound will give pitchers better control," said Stu. "The higher the mound, the higher pitchers throw.

"I always had better control off lower mounds."

Miller, of course, was never noted for a blazing fast ball. He wasn't the kind of pitcher who reared back, gave it a high kick and fired with everything he had.

For the guys with the super hummers, though, Miller acknowledged there could be a psychological difference.

Walter Alston of the Dodgers, ever the realist, gave it his characteristic shrug and said, "The good hitters are still going to hit and the rotten hitters are still going to strike out."

More important than the reduced strike zone or the height of the mound, in Alston's opinion, is the new rule calling for uniform slopes of the mound.

This is designed to eliminate even the illusion of greater mound heights in some parks.

"Uniformity is good," said Alston. "Pitchers won't be able to complain about mounds when they are the same in every park. But the conforming is going to be a tricky thing. When they work out the uniform slope, or grade, who are they going to favor?

"There are pitchers with long strides, and pitchers with short strides. That's where the slope will be important."

Clyde King, the new skipper of the Giants, said, "Some guys don't seem as fast from a lower mound, but the good pitchers always seem to adjust."

SLOPE IS IMPORTANT

King, a scholarly pitching teacher, said, "The slope of the mound is more important than the height. A pitcher can do better off an eight-inch mound with a 20-degree slope than a 15-inch mound with a five-degree slope."

Paul Richards of the Braves explained the importance of the slope this way: "If the pitcher's foot hits the ground too quickly, it can hurt him.

"All this stuff is trial and error anyway. If it works, let's do it. I'm all for finding out if it works."

Richards has been campaigning to move the mound back two feet.

"I can't get an audience for it," Paul said with a sigh. "Nobody wants to listen to an idea about changing the mound's position."

Now Richards was warming up. He snorted, "It's like Ponce De Leon when he set up shop in St. Augustine, the oldest city in the United States. Old Ponce told the city fathers, 'Don't do anything until you hear from me.' They ain't heard from him. And they ain't changed St. Augustine."

FIREMEN WILL GET CREDIT FOR SAVES IN THE BOX SCORE
By Harry Jupiter

SAN FRANCISCO, Calif.—Baseball has finally officially acknowledged the importance of saves. They're going into the Official Rule Book and they'll be listed in box scores and official statistics, starting next season.

Under the new rule (10.20), only one pitcher can be credited with a save in any game, but the provisions for it will be very liberal.

The rule states: "Credit a save to a relief pitcher who enters the game with his team in the lead if he holds the lead the remainder of the game, provided he is not credited with the victory."

So a man can qualify for a save whether he pitches to one batter or 20, and whether the score at the time he comes in is 1–0 or 20–0.

The rule further states: "A relief pitcher cannot be credited with a save if he does not finish the game, unless he is removed for a pinch-hitter or runner.

"When more than one relief pitcher qualifies for a save under the provisions of this rule, credit the save to the relief pitcher judged by the scorer to have been the most effective. Only one save can be credited in any game."

98

Teams to Experiment with "Wild-Card" Hitter in Spring Training (1969)

SOURCE: *Sporting News,* February 15, 1969

Pitchers have long been criticized for their inability to hit. As early as 1929, baseball officials proposed that permanent pinch hitters bat for pitchers. The Pacific Coast League attempted to adopt a similar rule for the 1961 season, but it was overruled by the Playing Rules Committee. After the moribund offensive performance of the 1960s, however, some baseball men were willing to set tradition aside for the sake of improving the game.

The Baseball Rules Committee agreed to use the pinch hitters in four minor leagues for the 1969 season. In addition, major league teams would experiment with the new rule during spring training, but they would not implement the rule during the regular season. The American League, whose batters suffered more in recent years than their National League counterparts, was more willing to try the innovation. A March 29, 1969, Sporting News *article revealed that three* NL *teams refused to cooperate with the experiment. The leagues' respective positions would remain intact in future years.*

The experiment was terminated after the 1969 season, despite its popularity with the minor leagues. A January 31, 1970, Sporting News *editorial revealed that several major league teams instructed their affiliates to vote against reinstating designated pinch hitters, and noted that they complied with great reluctance.*

WILD-CARD HITTER TO GET TRIAL IN FOUR MINORS— MAJORS WATCH CLOSELY
By Jack Lang

NEW YORK, N.Y.—Baseball continues to search for a way to put some punch back into the game. While it may not be the solution to the problems, the Major

League Playing Rules Committee has taken a giant step forward in authorizing several liberal rule changes for selected minor leagues this season. This could lead to adoption by the majors in 1970.

That in itself would be quite a concession. Baseball hasn't changed a major batting rule in 66 years. The last time they made a radical change was 1903, when it was decided to call the first two foul balls strikes.

But the rules committee met at the Americana Hotel January 31 and decided to give four minor leagues permission to experiment officially with "wild card" pinch-hitters who, presumably, will add some sorely needed hitting to the game.

It also authorized the American League to experiment with certain changes in spring training and will give the National League the same privileges when it applies. As of now, the N.L. isn't sure what it wants to do.

That's about par for the course. One league never knows what the other is doing.

FOUR LOOPS SOUGHT OKAY

The four leagues which petitioned for permission to experiment and were granted the right are the International League, Texas League, Eastern League and New York–Pennsylvania League.

Others may ask for permission provided the requests are received by March 1. The rules committee expects several more to seek the rights to experiment.

Basically, the big change agreed upon in the four experimental leagues is a "wild card" pinch-hitter. In each league, however, the "wild card" will be played differently and it is hoped that baseball will determine from the experiments which is the best plan. When that decision is reached, it probably will be legalized for use in the majors and all other leagues for the 1970 season.

Here are the four plans authorized by the rules committee and the leagues in which they will be used.

International League: A wild-card hitter for the pitcher will be permissible, but the manager of each team must designate that wild-card pinch-hitter prior to the game and list his name at the bottom of the lineup card. He can bat only for the pitcher and there is no limit as to how many times he can go to bat.

If the manager decided to put in a pinch-hitter for the wild-card hitter at any time in the game, the substituted hitter becomes the wild-card hitter. The manager has no alternative once he has designated the wild-card hitter prior to the start of the game. He must bat for the pitcher. He cannot bat for any other player in the lineup.

EASTERN NOT SO STRICT

Eastern League: It will not be necessary in this league to designate the wild-card hitter before the start of the game. He may be designated at any time. That's the only departure from the rule permitting wild-card pinch-hitters in the International League.

Texas League: A pinch-hitter shall be allowed to bat more than once provided the man he's replacing leaves the game. The wild-card pinch-hitter cannot bat for more than one man in any inning.

If the manager wants the wild-card pinch-hitter to stay in the game, he must place him in the field in the half inning following the inning in which he has batted. In other words, he could not bat in the seventh and go in for defense in the ninth.

NYP: The pinch-hitting specialist may be designated before the game and must be listed on the lineup cards. He will be permitted to hit only twice in the game and never more than once in any inning. He can bat for any man in the lineup, and the man he bats for may remain in the game.

If the manager uses a second pinch-hitter for the designated pinch-hitting specialist, the second hitter becomes the specialist and the first man cannot re-enter the game. Also, he can go in the field only in the half-inning after which he has batted.

A.L. CHANGES OPTIONAL

Changes suggested by the American League will be used in intraleague games in spring training, but are not mandatory. It has been suggested, however, that they be given a whirl. It is up to the N.L. club to approve if any of the changes are to be used in interleague games.

The four rules that the A.L. will experiment with are as follows:

1. Basically the same as the NYP League rule except that the pinch-hitter may not appear in the field.

2. Pinch-hitting specialists may be used if designated prior to the start of the game. They may not be used more than twice in any game and more than once in any inning. The man he replaces can remain in the game.

3. Wild-card pinch-hitter rule same as in the International League, but manager cannot pinch-hit for wild-card hitter unless he has been hurt.

4. The four pitches necessary for an intentional base on balls are waived. An intentional walk can be issued by merely waving the man to first base.

The final rule may prove the least popular with the fans. It will, as Connie Mack once said, deprive them of four opportunities to boo.

99

Bowie Kuhn, NL Lawyer, Elected as Interim Commissioner (1969)

SOURCE: *Miami Herald,* February 5, 1969

*At the end of the 1968 winter meetings, William "Spike" Eckert announced his resigna-
tion as baseball commissioner. The resignation resulted from pressure applied by owners*

who realized soon after Eckert's selection that he was not at all suited for the position. However, the owners could not agree on his successor. Candidates supported by different factions included Montreal Expos president John McHale, New York Yankees president Mike Burke, and former MLBPA leader Judge Robert Cannon. None could earn the eighteen votes, or three-quarters of the total cast, necessary for election.

In desperation, an owner (whose name was not recorded) suggested Bowie Kuhn, a lawyer for the National League. The closest Kuhn had come to public attention was when he served as lead lawyer for the NL in the antitrust lawsuit filed against baseball by the state of Wisconsin over the departure of the Braves. For that reason he was well known to the owners, who agreed to appoint Kuhn to a one-year term as commissioner pro tem. They had reason to believe that Kuhn would place the interests of baseball (in other words, the owners) above those of the players.

Despite his interim status, Kuhn quickly asserted himself as an activist commissioner. His accomplishments included reorchestrating a trade between the Astros and the Expos when one of the players threatened to retire and stepping in to avert threatened strikes by the MLBPA (over pensions) and the umpires (over the Salerno-Valentine firing). The owners were sufficiently impressed to make Kuhn's appointment permanent on August 12. Their decision was anticipated by columnist Edwin Pope, who lauded Kuhn's selection and predicted—correctly—that Kuhn would be a long-term commissioner.

BOWIE KUHN

An Interim Choice, But He Could Be There a Long Time
By Edwin Pope

I have an idea big-league baseball got lucky and smart at the same time Tuesday. In the basement of the Americana Hotel, a few yards from where a loser named Hubert Humphrey was purchasing some outlandish tropical togs, baseball picked what looks like very much a winner in Bowie Kuhn, who will serve as commissioner for at least a year.

Never heard of him? You're in the majority. Most outside of baseball never have. His counseling of the National League through the years has received a minimum of ink. But baseball knows him and obviously has an immense regard for him. Cruel though it may be, much of this is based upon his direct oppositeness from the recently deposed Commissioner William Eckert.

The New York lawyer at 42 is far younger than his predecessor. Standing in the blinding lights of a press conference just before 6 P.M. Tuesday, he conveyed other contrasts.

He is poised; Eckert was not. He is forceful where Eckert had been bland. He is tall (6–5½), and heavy (230); Eckert was, and is, a small man physically. Kuhn is blunt and articulate, where Eckert often groped for words and avoided direct statements whenever possible.

Kuhn's title is commissioner pro tem. He is an interim choice. But he could be there a long time. When someone asked if Kuhn might still be commissioner 10 years from now, American League President Joe Cronin blurted: "I've dealt with this man, and the answer to that is a very emphatic 'yes!'"

This was supposed to be a catch-as-catch-can match for the commissionership between supporters of the New York Yankees' Mike Burke and the San Francisco Giants' Chub Feeney.

The first hint of a possible compromise came at mid-afternoon. Bill Bartholomay, president of the Atlanta Braves, left the meeting for a few minutes. Two writers buttonholed him for his opinion. "I don't know who it's going to be," Bartholomay said slowly, "but I think we're going to end up with an interim man."

Burke and Feeney had seen the light some time before. "It was becoming obvious," said Burke, showing no disappointment, "that neither Feeney nor I could get enough votes, and that someone else would have to be it. I'm not crushed or anything. You have to be practical. There's no sense in just battling it out when neither side can win."

The same thing happened a few hotels north of the Americana some years ago when National Football League owners hassled for days over a commissioner to succeed the late Bert Bell, and finally came out with the longest sort of compromise shot in Pete Rozelle.

Late Tuesday, a lot of the baseball owners were looking upon their selection in the same fashion as the NFL later came to view its own.

"Kuhn's a strong man," said Frank Cashen, executive vice-president of the Baltimore Orioles. "He handles himself well."

"Quite a guy," said John McHale, boss of the new Montreal Expos of the National League. "He has a clever mind and a sense of humor. I'm very pleased."

So baseball has come almost full-circle in naming a man from the legal profession to its highest office.

Owners first tried the judiciary with Judge Kenesaw Landis, whom no later commissioner ever even came close to rivaling for effectiveness. Baseball dipped into politics for Happy Chandler. It tried a man from its own ranks in Ford Frick. Owners then turned to the military for Gen. William Eckert.

Now it has a lawyer in charge, which is getting back pretty close to a judge, and the good Lord knows baseball can use a man acquainted with legalities.

One of the first things Kuhn must face is the players' militantly emphatic threat to strike unless owners meet their pension-plan demands.

Kuhn enters upon the challenge with optimism. "Elston Howard asked me the other day if I thought this thing could be settled," said Kuhn. "I told Elston I thought it would be. And Elston said, 'If that's what you think, Bowie, it's good enough for me.'"

Clearly the owners feel the same way.

100 _____

Baseball Encyclopedia Research Adds
715th Home Run to Ruth's Total (1969)

SOURCE: *Sporting News,* May 10, 1969

Starting in 1965, researchers for Information Concepts Inc., with the endorsement of Major League Baseball, undertook a massive project to produce the most accurate, detailed statistical history of baseball yet compiled. In order to resolve conflicts and controversies regarding inconsistent information or the applicability of obsolete scoring procedures, a Special Baseball Records Committee (SBRC) was appointed. After meeting twice in 1968, the committee agreed on a number of guidelines by which they would operate. Their most controversial decision was to apply a change in the 1920 scoring rules retroactively—specifically, that all balls hit over the fence would be scored as home runs, regardless of the game situation. Prior to 1920, if such a hit was made in the bottom of the last inning, the batter was credited with the number of bases necessary to drive in the winning run. For instance, if the winning run was on first, a batter slugging a ball over the fence would be credited with a triple.

The researchers discovered that that scenario took place on July 8, 1918, and the batter "robbed" of a home run was none other than Babe Ruth. Therefore, Ruth would be given a home run instead of a triple and his lifetime total would be raised to 715. When this adjustment of the most revered number in baseball was announced, fans reacted angrily. Several weeks later the SBRC reversed its decision, and The Baseball Encyclopedia *preserved Ruth's traditional lifetime home run total.*

ANOTHER HOMER FOR THE BABE? DEBATE GROWS HOT, HEAVY
By Bill Fleichman

NEW YORK, N.Y.—Babe Ruth hit a home run the other day, in a manner of speaking, and it hiked his career total to 715. But it isn't about to go into the record books if some baseball officials have their way.

What started as a routine official report by the Baseball Special Records Committee has not turned into a nightmare of sorts—over one home run.

The committee was formed, with the authorization of the major leagues, to "correct obvious errors and establish ground rules" for long-published records. When everything is assembled and approved, it will go into a new Baseball Encyclopedia, a 2,400 page effort to be published in September by Macmillan.

The word got out the other day, in a story by Leonard Koppett in the New York Times, that Ruth would be credited with another homer, one he hit in 1918 under a rule that was changed two years later.

But at least three members of the committee—Joe Reichler of the Commissioner's Office, Dave Grote, director of public relations for the National League, and Jack Lang, secretary of the Baseball Writers' Association—won't go along with homer No. 715. The Bambino's record is being impounded at 714 as far as they are concerned.

The other members of the committee are Lee Allen, historian for the Hall of Fame and a columnist for THE SPORTING NEWS; Bob Holbrook, assistant to American League President Joe Cronin.

They, too, have some views on the matter.

"UNANIMOUS" VOTE UNDER FIRE

When a vote was taken some time ago, it was unanimous that the Babe and others involved would get credit for homers under the newer rule. Reichler, however, was out of the country at the time and Jim Gallagher of the Commissioner's Office voted for him.

Grote said he now has a change of heart and won't give the Babe No. 715. "A woman has the prerogative of changing her mind," Grote laughed, "and so do I."

But before the homer of homers gets too involved, here's the incident that is causing the furor, real or imagined:

In a game between the Indians and Red Sox at Fenway Park in Boston on July 8, 1918, with no score in the bottom of the tenth, Amos Strunk singled for the Red Sox and Ruth followed with a drive into the right field bleachers.

According to the rule at the time, this wasn't a homer. The game was considered ended, with the score, 1–0, as soon as Strunk crossed the plate. Ruth was credited with a triple—the number of bases required to advance the winning run. Had the runner been on third, the Babe would have been given credit for only a single.

Ruth wouldn't be the only one to have an increase in homer output. All the others, at least 35, uncovered by a team of 22 researchers for Information Concepts, Inc., would have the same data put into their records.

While Reichler, Lang and Grote are solid foes of tampering with the old rules in such situations, Allen is just as firm for giving the Babe and all the others their due.

BABE WOULD PREFER A BEER

The jovial Holbrook refuses to get too excited, although he thinks it might be a good idea to award the Babe with No. 715 and plaster the now-popular asterisk after the total.

"Frankly, I think the Babe would rather have a cold beer," said Holbrook.

"It's all kind of interesting, but I'm not going to get too excited as long as Ruth can have 715 somewhere, even with footnotes."

Reichler, who has demanded another meeting and another vote, said he "absolutely will not approve" the Ruth rule.

"It wasn't in the original concept of the committee to change rules," said Reichler. "The idea was to correct obvious errors and establish ground rules. When you carry this a little further, what do you want to do about hits that bounced into the stands and were declared homers?" A good question. They now are doubles.

Lang can see no reason for turning back the hands of time.

"Records that were made under the rules of the times should stand," Lang declared. "It just doesn't make any sense to go back 50 years and alter rules that were in force then.

"It's the same with civil law today. You wouldn't think of trying a person under an old law when a new one is in force, would you? These things can't be retroactive."

As for Allen, there's no doubt how he will vote in any new balloting.

"I'm all for the Ruth deal," he said. "It would be in the interest of consistency in the records."

Actually 17 rulings originally were approved by the committee, but most of the others are minor and at least didn't create any uproar.

An innocent bystander in all the heavy traffic is Dave Neft, the scholarly director of research for Information Concepts, Inc.

A THOROUGH RESEARCH JOB

"Our job was to assemble information for use in the book," he said, "and present it to baseball. It was up to the committee to decide what to do.

"We researched every game from 1876 and our men traveled all over the country. It wasn't difficult to assemble data since 1920. That's when more elaborate and accurate records were kept."

What alarms Grote is that the Ruth situation could open a "Pandora's box" for other rules revisions. "Just where would you end this thing?" he asked.

Reichler was high in his praise for Information Concepts, Inc., which did a thorough job of research into many types of records, not just homers. The firm's team used private collections of records, newspaper files and other sources to unearth data almost from baseball's inception.

And from the past came a voice of the man who first proposed the new rule, the one that says a homer is a homer when it is hit out of the park.

He is Fred Lieb, veteran correspondent of THE SPORTING NEWS and a former New York writer.

Lieb, a member of the rules committee in 1920, first proposed the change. He met strong opposition from N.L. Umpire Hank O'Day, also a committee member, who contended "there is no way you can score a run after a game is over."

But Lieb's proposal was adopted, 5 to 1, with only O'Day casting a negative ballot.

"For a long time I felt it was unfair to a batter if he drove the ball out of the playing area under the old rule and did not get credit for a homer," said Lieb.

"In 1919, Frank Baker of the Yankees hit a ninth-inning drive into the stands at the Polo Grounds with the score tied and the bases full. All he received credit for was a single and one run batted in."

101

Curt Flood Threatens to Retire
after Being Traded (1969)

SOURCE: *St. Louis Globe-Democrat,* October 9, 1969

In his autobiography The Way It Is *(New York: Trident Press, 1971), Curt Flood and Richard Carter acknowledge that Flood was known for bluntly expressing his opinions and was considered a controversial figure in St. Louis. As a result, Flood, who had been a regular with the Cardinals for a dozen years, was not shocked when he was informed that he had been traded to the Philadelphia Phillies for Dick Allen, an even more controversial—and talented—player. For the same reason, Cardinals and Phillies officials were not surprised to learn of Flood's declaration that he would retire rather than report to Philadelphia and abandon his photography studio businesses in St. Louis. Nevertheless, they expected that Flood, like countless other disgruntled players before him, would soon succumb to reality and report to his new club.*

CARDS GET ALLEN IN 7-MAN DEAL

Bing Grabs Broom, Starts to Clean House
By Jack Herman

Bing Devine and Red Schoendienst began their housecleaning Wednesday of the disappointing Cardinals. And while Manager Schoendienst says he won't pre-judge Richie Allen and his bad-boy reputation, the general manager indicated "you ain't seen nothing yet."

At a hurriedly-called press conference, Devine announced that the Red Birds had traded two front-liners, catcher Tim McCarver and centerfielder Curt Flood; ace lefty reliever Joe Hoerner and spare outfielder Byron Browne to the Philadelphia Phillies for the slugging Allen.

The 27-year-old Allen was the principal figure in the seven-player transaction disclosed at Busch Stadium. Utility performer Cookie Rojas and righthander Jerry Johnson, who sometimes pitched like Walter Johnson against St. Louis, also will be here in '70.

That is, if Flood doesn't carry out his threat to retire.

The 32-year-old defensive whiz issued a statement, in which he said: "With my playing days nearing an end due to physical considerations," he feels he should devote more time to his studio franchise enterprises and oil portrait commissions.

Consequently, effective immediately, Flood says he'll focus his energies on his business interests here.

Neither Devine nor his Phillie counterpart, John Quinn, expressed undue concern over Flood's bombshell. "Before I make any comment," Quinn informed The Globe-Democrat, "I'll want to talk to Flood and McCarver."

Flood isn't the first to say he'll hang it up following a trade, as witness Donn Clendenon and Ken Harrelson during 1969. He won't be the last, either.

Commissioner Bowie Kuhn finally adjudicated the Clendenon–Rusty Staub deal in which the Houston Astros wound up with a couple of other players instead of Clendenon and cash.

"I'll cross that bridge," remarked Devine, "when I come to it." . . .

After a two-year reign as National League champions, the Red Birds qualified for the "flop of the year" in '69.

They hit more homers (90–73) than a year ago, but still ranked last. Even the expansion teams, San Diego (99) and Montreal (125) hit with more power without scoring as often. The Cardinals scored 595 runs, compared with 582 for the Expos and 468 for the Padres.

"Yes," Devine conceded, "from the players involved, I guess this is the biggest trade I've made."

McCarver, 28, and Flood were members of the 1964–67–68 league champions and World Series kingpins in '64 and '67.

IT'S A CHALLENGE

McCarver, a big bonus investment, agreed: "It's going to be a challenge to me to make the Phils a winning club. I don't like to lose. We are paid to win games. If I can help to do that, then that is my aim and desire."

Hoerner had been the St. Louis staff's most reliable bullpen operative for three years. He slumped off somewhat the past season, but still stood out with 15 saves. The entire staff had only 26.

"I thought we gave up too much for Allen," noted Hoerner, "although he's probably as fine a hitter as there is. Still, I couldn't believe it. I hope I can do as good a job for the Phillies as I thought I did here." . . .

Allen is in the $80,000 salary neighborhood, a fashionable vicinity for any laborer. McCarver earns $60,000 and Flood, after leading the Cardinals in batting in 1967–68, jumped to $90,000.

Flood was the first player Devine got in a trade, 12 years ago, after succeeding Frank Lane as G.M. when the latter jumped to the Cleveland Indians.

Flood became incommunicado after release of his statement and was said to be out of town. Allen said he's looking forward to coming to St. Louis, "even if I have to stay in the YMCA."

Whether the Cardinals will be "overjoyed" with their new slugger next year, is another matter. But [Lou] Brock has no qualms about playing right field. He'd been rated a butcher there when with the Chicago Cubs.

"I see no problem," said Brock, who led all St. Louis regulars with a .298 average in '69, along with 195 hits and 53 stolen bases. "As for Allen, he's championship material."

102

New York Mets Stun Baseball,

Win World Series (1969)

SOURCE: *New York Post*, October 17, 1969

Few teams have evoked a stronger reaction from winning the World Series than did the New York Mets in 1969. Ever since the franchise entered the National League in 1962 it captured the hearts of New York fans, including some former Yankee rooters. As the Bronx Bombers started a rapid descent to the second division in 1965, the Mets—though still one of the worst teams in baseball—inherited even more Yankee fans. This myste- rious state of affairs attracted the attention of a group of young baseball writers known as "chipmunks" for their irreverence and peskiness. These writers, including columnist Larry Merchant, celebrated the Mets and watched their fortunes rise along with those of their chosen club. When the Mets beat the seemingly unbeatable Baltimore Orioles in five games, it seemed, however, that even the chipmunks were justified in terming the victory a "miracle."

FUN AND GAMES

Believe

Larry Merchant

They say baseball is a religion, not a game. Believe. Believe, brothers and sisters, sinners and losers, you must believe. The Mets are champions of the world.

And they have angels in the outfield, good angels in the infield, gods on the mound, a prophet in the dugout, and shoe polish on their saintly feet. If that won't make you believe nothing will.

The Mets are champions of the world and Shea Stadium is their Lourdes and yesterday was their day of all days, of all miracles.

It will be writ in the good book, Gil Hodges version. Hear this one and fall to your knees.

It is the sixth inning of the World Series and the faithful—the ever-faithful and the new faithful, the old looking for old answers and the young looking for new answers—are being put to one last test. The Orioles, bloody great baseball team, symbol of pagan excellence are striking in this game 3–0 on two blasphemous home runs. Those who have not yet accepted the Mets deep in their souls may envision a defeat, a shift to the Baltimore playground and the flood.

Cleon Jones leads off. Dave McNally's pitch is in the dirt. Jones lifts his foot, a reflex to keep from being hit. The ball skips exactly as high as his foot and hits him. Then it caroms into the Mets' dugout between home and first.

Believe.

The umpire, Lou DiMuro, rules that the ball did not hit Cleon Jones. Which is heresy. The ball had to hit someone and since it didn't hit anyone else around there, DiMuro or catcher Andy Etchebarren, it had to hit Jones.

Gil Hodges thinks so too. He comes out of the dugout with the ball in his hand, spinning it slowly, studying its symmetry, its smudges. There is an inch of black shoe polish on the ball. Hodges walks the walk of the wise, deliberately, judiciously. He shows the ball to the umpire not in anger but in evidence.

"I believe," the umpire says, and he waves Jones to first base.

There is an other-worldliness about this seeing-of-the-light. Umpires change decisions about as often as they see visions of Casey at the bat. And just an inning before in a similar situation, DiMuro refused to change his decision in favor of the Orioles.

Frank Robinson said he was hit and Frank Robinson is a brutally honest man. He said he was hit high on the left leg. He offered as evidence a bad bruise. What he needed was shoe polish. What he said, basically, was that the umpire couldn't polish. Frank Robinson was the last agnostic.

The Orioles are frantic about Jones. They know that Jones was hit, but they want to know how the umpire suddenly knows it, how he knows the ball Hodges gave him was the ball that hit him. What this is is railing at the fates. The Orioles would insist later that the Mets were not helped by occult forces, but their appeal for justice is really a cry for an even break, for some small favor from above. It is apparent even to them that this is the beginning of the end.

Believe.

A bolt of lightning reveals the truth. Donn Clendenon, the very next batter, fired a home run into the left field seats. The score is 3–2. It is clear that the Mets have set the Orioles up for a spiritually uplifting finish.

It comes in the seventh inning. The meek are going to inherit a championship and Al Weis is the meekest of the meek with a bat. Sometimes you don't know if he's swinging it or if it's swinging him. He hits a fly ball to left field, just a fly ball.

The left fielder, Don Buford, takes a step in, then drifts back toward the fence. Suddenly over the starched flag in centerfield there's someone in the sky—a bird? a plane? No, a fat fellow with cheeks puffed and lips puckered. And a heaven-sent wind carries the ball over the fence. It is Al Weis's first home run in Shea Stadium. The score is 3–3 and all you can think about is that conversation between Sandy Koufax and Tom Seaver.

"Is God a Met?" asks Sandy Koufax.

"No," says Tom Seaver. "But he has an apartment in New York."

The most Met-like Met of them all is chosen to deliver the biggest Met run of the ages. Cleon Jones doubles to lead off the eighth inning. Ron Swoboda drives home with another double. The Mets are champions of the world and there are only believers.

"We are the saints of lost causes," Ron Swoboda said. "This season has been one high after another. We've gone higher and higher until you can't go any higher."

Until you are up there with the angels and good fairies.

103

National Labor Relations Board Rules Baseball Subject to Its Jurisdiction (1969)

SOURCE: *Decisions and Orders of the National Labor Relations Board* 180 (1971): 190–94

On December 15, 1969, the National Labor Relations Board (NLRB) issued a landmark ruling that dramatically affected the relationship between major league baseball and the unions—representing players and umpires—with which it must coexist. Following the firing of AL umpires Al Salerno and Bill Valentine in September 1968, allegedly for their advocacy of the formation of a union for AL umpires, the umpires of both leagues formed the Major League Umpires Association (MLUA). After the AL refused to recognize the organization (the NL had recognized the MLUA's predecessor in an 1964 agreement), the union filed a petition with the NLRB to certify that the union was legally established.

The AL argued that the NLRB had no jurisdiction because of baseball's antitrust exemption and because the umpires were supervisors and therefore not entitled to appeal to the NLRB, among other reasons. By a 4–1 margin the board rejected the AL's position and ruled that since the antitrust exemption was a legislative and judicial accident rather than the intended result of a specific decision, the business of major league baseball was subject to the jurisdiction of the NLRB.

Although Valentine and Salerno ultimately lost their case in federal court, the NLRB ruling gave baseball unions leverage they had lacked previously. Now unions and union members had an outside, impartial arbitrator to whom they could appeal. Not only did the decision play a role in baseball's decision the following year to accept independent arbitration in specified circumstances, but in the following decades the union benefited by its access to the NLRB to overturn unjust actions against it by baseball.

All footnotes have been deleted from the following excerpt. The decision can also be found in House Select Committee on Professional Sports, Inquiry into Professional Sports, *94th Cong., 2nd sess., 1977, 456–64.*

THE AMERICAN LEAGUE OF PROFESSIONAL BASEBALL CLUBS *AND* ASSOCIATION OF NATIONAL BASEBALL LEAGUE UMPIRES, PETITIONER. CASE 1-RC-10414 DECEMBER 15, 1969

DECISION AND DIRECTION OF ELECTION

The Board's jurisdiction under the [National Labor Relations] Act is based upon the commerce clause of the Constitution, and is coextensive with the reach of that clause. In 1922 the Supreme Court in *Federal Baseball Club of Baltimore v. National League of Professional Baseball Clubs,* 259 U.S. 200, although characterizing baseball as a "business," ruled that it was not interstate in nature, and therefore was beyond the reach of the nation's antitrust laws. However, subsequent Supreme

Court decisions appear to proceed on the assumption that baseball, like the other major professional sports, is now an industry in or affecting interstate commerce, and that baseball's current antitrust exemption has been preserved merely as a matter of judicial *stare decisis*. Thus, in both the *Toolson* and *Radovich* decisions the Supreme Court specifically stated that baseball's antitrust status was a matter for Congress to resolve, implying thereby that Congress has the power under the commerce clause to regulate the baseball industry. Since professional football and boxing have been held to be in interstate commerce and thus subject to the antitrust laws, it can no longer be seriously contended that the Court still considers baseball alone to be outside of interstate commerce. Congressional deliberations regarding the relationship of baseball and other professional team sports to the antitrust laws likewise reflect a Congressional assumption that such sports are subject to regulation under the commerce clause. It is, incidentally, noteworthy that these deliberations reveal Congressional concern for the rights of employees such as players to bargain collectively and engage in concerted activities. Additionally, legal scholars have agreed, and neither the parties nor those participating as *amici* dispute, that professional sports are in or affect interstate commerce, and as such are subject to the Board's jurisdiction. Therefore, on the basis of the above, we find that professional baseball is an industry in or affecting commerce, and as such is subject to Board jurisdiction under the Act. . . .

We have carefully considered the positions of the parties, and the *amicus* briefs, and we find that it will best effectuate the mandates of the Act, as well as national labor policy, to assert jurisdiction over this Employer. We reach this decision for the following reasons:

Baseball's system for internal self-regulation of disputes involving umpires is made up of the Uniform Umpires Contract, the Major League Agreement, and the Major League Rules, which provide among other things, for final resolution of disputes through arbitration by the Commissioner. The system appears to have been designed almost entirely by employers and owners, and the final arbiter of internal disputes does not appear to be a neutral third party freely chosen by both sides, but rather an individual appointed solely by the member club owners themselves. We do not believe that such a system is likely either to prevent labor disputes from arising in the future, or, having once arisen, to resolve them in a manner susceptible or conducive to voluntary compliance by all parties involved. Moreover, it is patently contrary to the letter and spirit of the Act for the Board to defer its undoubted jurisdiction to decide unfair labor practices to a disputes settlement system established unilaterally by an employer or group of employers. . . .

We can find, neither in the statute nor in its legislative history, any expression of a Congressional intent that disputes between employers and employees in this industry should be removed from the scheme of the National Labor Relations Act. In 1935, 1947, and again in 1959, Congress examined the nation's labor policy as reflected in the National Labor Relations Act; and Congress has consistently affirmed the Act's basic policy, as expressed in Section 1, of encouraging collective bargaining by "protecting the exercise by workers of full freedom of association, self-organization, and designation of representatives of their own choosing." Nowhere in Congress' deliberations is there any indication that these basic rights are not to be extended to employees employed in professional baseball or any other professional sport. We do not agree that Congress, by refusing to pass legislation subjecting the sport to the antitrust laws when it considered the regulation of baseball and other sports under the antitrust statutes, sanctioned a government-wide policy of "non-involvement" in all matters pertaining to baseball. Indeed, to the extent that Congressional deliberation on the antitrust question has reference to the issue before us, it indicates agreement that players' rights to bargain collectively and engage in concerted activities are to be protected rather than limited.

There is persuasive reason to believe that future labor disputes—should they arise in this industry—will be national in scope, radiating their impact far beyond individual State boundaries. As stated above, the Employer and its members are located and conduct business in 10 States and the District of Columbia. The stipulated commerce data establishes that millions of dollars of interstate commerce are involved in its normal business operations. The nature of the industry is such that great reliance is placed upon interstate travel. Necessarily, then, we are not here confronted with the sort of small, primarily interstate employer over which the Board declines jurisdiction because of failure to meet its prevailing monetary standards. Moreover, it is apparent that the Employer, whose operations are so clearly national in scope, ought not have its labor relations problems subject to diverse state labor laws. . . .

The Employer contends that the petition should be dismissed on the ground that the umpires sought to be represented are supervisors as defined in Section 2(11) of the Act. It is not contended that umpires have authority to hire, fire, transfer, discharge, recall, promote, assign, or reward. We think it equally apparent that umpires do not "discipline" or "direct" the work force according to the common meaning of those terms as used in the Act.

The record indicates that an umpire's basic responsibility is to insure that each baseball game is played in conformance with the predetermined rules of the game. Thus, the umpire does not discipline except to the extent he may remove a participant from the game for violation of these rules. Testimony shows that after such a removal the umpire merely reports the incident to his superiors, and does not himself fine, suspend, or even recommend such action. As the final arbiter on the field, the umpire necessarily makes decisions which may favor one team over another, and which may determine to some extent the movements of various players, managers, and other personnel on the ball field. The umpire does not, however, direct the work force in the same manner and for the same reasons as a foreman in an industrial setting. As every fan is aware, the umpire does not—through the use of independent judgment—tell a player how to bat, how to field, to work harder or exert more effort, nor can he tell a manager which players to play or where to play them. Thus, the umpire merely sees to it that the game is played in compliance with the rules. It is the manager and not the umpire who directs the employees in their pursuit of victory.

Accordingly, we find that the umpires are not supervisors, and thus the Employer's motion to dismiss on this ground is hereby denied. We further find that the following employees of the Employer constitute a unit appropriate for the purposes of collective bargaining within the meaning of Section 9(b) of the Act:

All persons employed as umpires in the American League of Professional Baseball Clubs, but excluding all other employees, office clerical employees, guards, professional employees and supervisors as defined in the Act.

104

Flood to File Antitrust Suit against Baseball (1969)

SOURCE: *St. Louis Globe Democrat*, December 31, 1969

Just two weeks after the NLRB concluded that baseball's fabled antitrust exemption was nothing more than an accident of jurisprudence, a defiant Curt Flood—acting with the support of Marvin Miller and the MLBPA—prepared to test that interpretation in federal court. Denying allegations that the suit was part of a ploy to force the Philadelphia Phillies—whose acquisition of Flood from the St. Louis Cardinals triggered the dispute— to increase his salary, Flood maintained that he was fighting on principle alone. If Bowie Kuhn and other baseball officials had thought that the dawn of a new decade would bring a period of relative tranquility, they now knew better.

KUHN FLATLY REJECTS PLEA, SUIT LOOMS

Flood Told He Can't Become Free Agent

A court battle over baseball's reserve clause appeared in the making when commissioner Bowie Kuhn rejected St. Louisan Curt Flood's plea to be permitted to negotiate his 1970 contract as a free agent.

Flood, dealt by the Cardinals to the Philadelphia Phillies after the 1969 season, reportedly plans a federal court suit challenging the reserve clause, which binds a player to his club until it releases him.

The 31-year-old veteran wrote to the commissioner in New York requesting he be allowed to make a deal for himself and said Monday night he would make no comment on a court suit until he received a reply.

Copies of Flood's letter also were sent to Marvin Miller, executive director of the Major League Players Association, and John Quinn, the Phillies' general manager.

In New York, Kuhn made public Tuesday afternoon Flood's letter and his own answer, which expressed sympathy with the player's position but did not comply with his wish to be made a free agent. . . .

Flood says he will contest the reserve clause, last challenged unsuccessfully—in 1952, in a federal suit and that Arthur Goldberg, former U.S. Supreme Court justice, would file the challenge early in 1970.

Flood said: "Until I receive a reply I cannot comment." He said he would "react to what Commissioner Kuhn does."

Kuhn, the former National League legal counsel who was elected commissioner last winter, said he received Flood's letter, dated Dec. 24, Monday. The commissioner said he telephoned the player at his St. Louis home before releasing both the letter and his reply to the news media.

The text of the Flood letter:

"After 12 years in the major leagues, I do not feel that I am a piece of property to be bought and sold irrespective of my wishes. I believe that any system which produces that result violates my basic rights as a citizen and is inconsistent with the laws of the United States and of the several States.

"It is my desire to play baseball in 1970, and I am capable of playing. I have received a contract offer from the Philadelphia club, but I believe I have the right to consider offers from other clubs before making any decisions. I, therefore, request that you make known to all the major league clubs my feelings in this matter, and advise them of my availability for the 1970 season.

"Sincerely Yours,

"Curt Flood"

And the Commissioner's reply:

"Dear Curt:

"This will acknowledge your letter of Dec. 24, 1969, which I found on returning to my office yesterday.

"I certainly agree with you that you, as a human being, are not a piece of property to be bought and sold. That is fundamental in our society and I think obvious. However, I cannot see its applicability to the situation at hand.

"You have entered into a current playing contract with the St. Louis club, which has the same assignment provision as those in your annual major league contract since 1956. Your present contract has been assigned in accordance with its provisions by the St. Louis club to the Philadelphia club. The provisions of the playing contract have been negotiated over the years between the clubs and the players, most recently when the present basic agreement was negotiated two years ago between the clubs and the Players' Association.

"If you have any specific objection to the propriety of the assignment, I would appreciate your specifying the objection. Under the circumstances, and pending any further information from you, I do not see that action I can take and cannot comply with the request contained in the second paragraph of your letter.

"I am pleased to see your statement that you desire to play baseball in 1970. I take it this puts to rest any thought, as reported earlier in the press, that you were considering retirement.

"Sincerely yours,

"Bowie K. Kuhn."

Counting Numbers, Dollars, and Rights

With the Curt Flood federal lawsuit now a reality, major league baseball struggled to reclaim the attention and affection of its fans. After a decade of offensive dormancy, new stars like Johnny Bench, Rod Carew, and Reggie Jackson took advantage of the more liberalized rules and launched their careers in impressive fashion. Similarly, pitching sensations like Tom Seaver, Nolan Ryan, and Steve Carlton made assaults on the record book throughout the 1970s. Seymour Siwoff, who headed the Elias Sports Bureau, kept track of the records and publicized them to a growing number of fans preoccupied with baseball statistics. One small group, based in the sociology department of the University of Michigan, used statistics as a means to create the Baseball Seminar—their own "fantasy" league. By the early 1980s a direct descendant of their game, Rotisserie Baseball, became a sensation, with thousands of adherents reveling in their ability to manage statistical versions of the flesh-and-blood players they so admired.

In the early 1970s many players and umpires felt like abstractions. Their struggle for expanded rights was fought by owners and Commissioner Bowie Kuhn. Attempts by players like Flood and Jim Bouton to inform the public of the realities of major league life were met with outrage and denial by baseball officials, large segments of the sports media, and even other players. Kuhn grudgingly endorsed an effort to open a back door of the Hall of Fame to Negro League stars, but many remained unsatisfied with the compromise. The umpires, who, like the players, were demonstrating a growing solidarity and a willingness to fight for their principles, staged the first union-organized strike during the 1970 League Championship Series, and the owners quickly acceded to most of their demands.

The Major League Baseball Players' Association (MLBPA) actively supported Flood's suit, and executive director Marvin Miller convinced Kuhn to join him on a three-man board, headed by an independent arbitrator, to settle certain disputes between players and clubs. The owners saw this concession as insignificant; the players, however, realized that for the first time their arguments would be heard by an objective judge and that true reform could be achieved as a result. Even the Supreme Court decision in the Flood case, which left intact the antitrust exemption and the reserve clause, failed to dampen their optimism that change was just ahead on the horizon, no matter how intransigent the owners proved to be.

105

"Baseball Seminar": The First Fantasy Baseball Game? (1970)

SOURCE: Ralph L. Andreano Papers, Box 3, Folder 10, State Historical Society of Wisconsin

In the spring of 1960, sociologist William Gamson introduced a new game to some of his fellow social scientists and baseball fans at the Harvard School of Public Health. In the game, called the "Baseball Seminar," participants bid on the rights to major league players in a mail auction, monitored key statistics of their players throughout the season, and declared winners based on their players' performance. When Gamson became a professor at the University of Michigan, he brought his game to his department, where it became so popular that several variants were quickly developed, some of which still may be active. One sociologist even recruited Tigers broadcaster Ernie Harwell to play, and Harwell in turn reportedly enticed Roger Angell to join him. Another Michigan professor, film historian Robert Sklar, also became a "student" in the Seminar for several years in the late 1960s.

The significance of Sklar's involvement is that Daniel Okrent, the inventor of Rotisserie Baseball—the model for fantasy baseball today—has credited Sklar with inspiring him to create Rotisserie in 1979. In a March 31, 1981, Inside Sports article, Okrent noted that "using 'imaginary money' (whatever the hell that is), Sklar and a few sociologists and historians selected various major league players at the beginning of each season, and their performance—batting average for hitters, ERA for pitchers—determined the winner, who got a blue ribbon, or something." It seems likely that the game Okrent recalled was the Baseball Seminar, and as such it deserves recognition as the progenitor of fantasy baseball. The Seminar is still active, and many of the original players from the early 1960s still participate.

Apparently, Ralph Andreano, an economist then at the University of Wisconsin, played and helped coordinate the player draft for the 1970 season. Andreano, author of No Joy in Mudville *(Cambridge MA: Schenckman, 1965), was also an expert witness for the state of Wisconsin in its lawsuit against the Milwaukee Braves in 1966. His collected papers at the State Historical Society of Wisconsin focus on his preparation for his testimony.*

SEMINAR RULES—1970

1. Each bidder has $100,000 to use for each league. Each league is a separate contest. Money from one league cannot be applied toward bidding in the other.

2. Minimum bid for any player is $2,000. Bid in denominations of $100 only, e.g.: $10,200 but not $10,250.

3. Only one bid is allowed on each player, and all bids must be received on or before the deadlines designated below. Fines of $1,000 per day will be assessed against late bids. Bids received after the results have been tabulated will not be fined, but will not be accepted for that round. In order to facilitate tabulation, players electing not to bid in a given round should so notify me.

4. Each player will be assigned to the two highest bidders. In case of ties, players will be assigned to the tied bidders whose ballots were received earliest. Ties among bids received simultaneously will be resolved by the toss of a coin.

5. A ballot listing probably [*sic*] player rosters will be provided for each set of teams. Bids will be recorded in the order shown on the ballot, reading down by column from left to right. Bids for players not included on the rosters are welcomed and encouraged. These write-ins will be recorded at the end of each team's listed roster in the order received. In the event of a trade or the mistaken assignment of a player to a former team, he will be considered at the point at which he is listed on the ballot, even if this is now his incorrect team or league.

6. The leagues are divided into three randomly determined sets with the following bidding deadlines for each set:

Set One (Deadline March 10): AL: Baltimore, Kansas City, Detroit, Boston
  NL: Cincinnati, Philadelphia, San Francisco,
  Pittsburgh
Set Two (Deadline March 24): AL: Seattle, Chicago, Cleveland, Minnesota
  NL: Los Angeles, St. Louis, Chicago,
  Montreal
Set Three (Deadline April 7) AL: California, New York, Washington,
  Oakland
  NL: Los Angeles, St. Louis, Chicago,
  Montreal

7. After each deadline, bids will be opened and the players assigned to the highest two bidders. You will be notified of the results before the next bidding

stage. A complete record of all bids by all players (both successful and unsuccessful), will be provided. Unsuccessful bids cost nothing; however, any portion of the $100,000 for either league unused after Set Three will simply be considered wasted.

8. If insufficient funds remain to cover a bid, that bid will be reduced to the amount remaining in the bidder's treasury. For example, you may make bids totalling $350,000 (anticipating that many of your bids will be insufficient). You are a successful bidder (first or second high) on $75,000 worth of players, and your next bid is $40,000. This bid is reduced to $25,000 (your remaining capital), and if it is successful (one of the two high bids), all your subsequent bids are reduced to 0. You should anticipate that many of your bids will be insufficient.

9. Players once purchased may not be traded, rejected, or resold.

10. Awards.

A. Awards are stated in terms of shares where there are 100 shares and the value of each share is ¹⁄₁₀₀ of the total pool. Share values will be announced as soon as the total number of participants is known (probably after the tabulation of Set One). In 1969, there were 19 participants, and preliminary estimates for this year are in the 20–25 range. The management can offer no guarantees as to the number of participants until the first round of balloting is completed, and bidding miscalculations in Set One must be accepted as one of the hazards of the Seminar.

B. Grand prizes awarded at the end of the season:

First:	AL 25 shares	NL 25 shares
Second:	AL 12 shares	NL 12 shares
Third:	AL 6 shares	NL 6 shares
Fourth:	AL 3 shares	NL 3 shares

C. These awards are made on the basis of the owner's point total for each league, where points are awarded as follows: 10 for first place, 9 for second place, . . . 1 for tenth place, on each of the following criteria:

1) Batting Average (must have at least 450 official times at bat).

2) Runs Batted In.

3) Games Won (by pitcher).

4) Earned Run Average (must have at least 162 innings pitched).

Only players owned by at least one participant will count in the rankings. Thus, if an unowned player leads the league and your player is next, you will receive 10 points.

D. Lap Leader prizes.

One share for each league will be awarded for the highest point totals according to records published on the first Sunday in June, July, August, and September. Authority will be the New York Times, supplemented by wire service data from the Detroit Free Press or Toledo Blade.

Total: 8 shares.

106

Seymour Siwoff and the Statistics Revolution (1970)

SOURCE: *New York Post,* April 23, 1970

Statistics have been important to baseball players, executives, and fans ever since Henry Chadwick created the first box scores in the 1850s. It can be argued, however, that interest in baseball statistics accelerated dramatically during the 1960s. New statistics (the save) and statistical compilations (The Baseball Encyclopedia) were introduced in 1969. Unheralded statisticians like George Lindsay, Earnshaw Cook, and brothers Eldon and Harlan Mills produced studies offering new ways to analyze existing statistics and devised new measures of their own that influenced future "statistorians," some of whom founded the Society of American Baseball Research in 1971.

Much of the credit for this development belongs to Seymour Siwoff, owner of the Elias Sports Bureau. Founded in 1913, Elias soon convinced both major leagues to designate it as their official statistical organization. Siwoff joined Elias in the late 1950s, and through public relations and hard work he helped advance awareness of statistics. Proof of the success of his efforts are seen in the article below, in which Larry Merchant uses Tom Seaver's record-breaking nineteen-strikeout performance as an excuse to profile Siwoff and the movement he helped foster.

THE RECORD BUSINESS

Larry Merchant

The thing that Seymour Siwoff loves more than anything else in this world is "a nice quiet day when somebody breaks a record." It is practically a religious experience for him, like a good souffle for a gourmet. Yesterday was such a day.

Seymour Siwoff owns the Elias Sports Bureau, which assembles statistics for baseball and football and puts out record books. Records are to statistics as a good souffle is to a soft boiled egg.

"I'd like to see a guy hit five homers on a nice quiet day," Seymour Siwoff said. "Five homers—wham! Headlines. Everybody talking. Wham! On a nice quiet day."

So yesterday, Earth Day, a day of some meaningful quietude, the Mets played the Padres at Shea Stadium, and Tom Seaver went wham!

Seaver struck out 10 batters in a row, breaking the modern record by two, and 19 overall, tieing Steve Carlton. He did it with a dramatic flourish, getting the last 10 men to face him. In those moments, as a crowd of 21,000 cheered him on, Seaver seemed all alone, as though he were playing catch with himself in a vacuum. He threw the ball and it came back to him, he threw it again and it came back to him again.

It was, in the ninth inning, a game between Tom Seaver and that great record recorder in the sky, Seymour Siwoff. At his office on 42nd St., said Siwoff, "there was a mighty roar" when Seaver got Al Ferrara to end the game. Siwoff and his six assistants, whom he calls "my busy bees," conjuring visions of Disneyesque dwarfs skidaddling over columns of numbers, watched it on television.

"I don't care who or what," said Siwoff, "a record, any record, is a triumph. The other day Steve Whitaker struck out five times and hit a sacrifice fly. Holy mackerel! All he needed was one more. Nobody ever struck out six times in a game. I have nothing against the player, but what a record."

Seaver's records give him a small piece of immortality and a few lines of type in the record books and goodness knows what else. He is not the strikeout phenom that Feller and Koufax were (although, additionally, ugh, he broke their "day game" record of 18), but he is a Met and he has a Cy Young Award and the glamour of yesterday may project him into their status of super celebrity.

To Seymour Siwoff, the meaning of the records is clear. Max Surkont, Johnny Podres, Jim Maloney and Don Wilson, who struck out eight in a row, will be stricken from the 1971 record book. More important to Siwoff so too will Michael Welch be banished. "The 10th strikeout was the big one," Siwoff said. "I hate those old-time records." Welch, pitching for the Mets of antiquity, struck out nine in a row in 1884.

With baseball's preoccupation with contrived trivia, Siwoff has one major concern now. "If Seaver strikes out one or two guys at the start of his next game, they're going to ask if there's a strikeout record for two games. There isn't. You don't want to inundate people with meaningless statistics. Oddities detract from real records, records of value. Records should be cherished."

This promises to be a big season for Seymour Siwoff in the records-to-be-cherished department. Hank Aaron and Willie Mays will become the ninth and 10th players to get 3000 hits.

"We're on the brink of a real breakthrough," Siwoff said. "We're going to see how great modern players are. There's a possibility that Aaron (567 homers) will catch Ruth (714). He definitely could catch Musial in hits (3630) and come in second to Cobb (4191). He can break Musial's National League records in runs (1949) and RBIS (1724).* In 1968 Aaron drove me crazy. He needed 100 runs to break a tie with Lou Gehrig for scoring 100 runs in consecutive seasons (13). I said to myself, 'Oh, my God, how can you do this to me.' It killed a streak for me. I went to Musial one year and told him I needed some doubles and stolen bases from him. He looked at me kind of funny. It was like I was ordering off a shelf."

But records are more than numbers. "They're people," Seymour Siwoff said. "The human element. What gets into a Roger Maris? How does he get psyched to hit 61 homers? How does Dale Long hit homers in eight consecutive games? Why him suddenly? And Jim Gentile. He hit grand slam homers in consecutive innings. I remember it so well. It was a nice quiet day."

*Musial's career RBI total was 1,951—Ed.

107

Owners Grant Players Independent Arbitration in New Basic Agreement (1970)

SOURCE: 1970 Basic Agreement, from National Baseball Hall of Fame Library

The second Basic Agreement, signed on May 21, 1970, elevated the status of the MLBPA and set the stage for the arrival of free agency in 1976. The majority of the new clauses dealt with salary issues, including specified minimum salaries and maximum annual salary cuts, but the most important addition was a change in the grievance procedure. In 1968 players earned the right to appeal a decision by their club to the commissioner, who served as the arbitrator (see document 93). Marvin Miller and the union complained that Kuhn, as an employee of the owners, was incapable of impartiality, an accusation that offended Kuhn. Nevertheless, Kuhn and the owners granted the players the right to have an independent arbitrator vote on disputes as a part of a three-man committee, with Miller and Kuhn serving as the representatives of the union and the owners, respectively. The other elements of the grievance procedure were unchanged.

Kuhn soon regretted his acquiescence to the independent arbitration option. In December 1974 and December 1975 arbitrator Peter Seitz voted along with Miller to grant Jim "Catfish" Hunter and Andy Messersmith (respectively) free agency under different circumstances. After fighting the decision in federal court and exercising their right to unilaterally fire Seitz immediately after the Messersmith decision, the owners included limited free agency in the Basic Agreement signed in 1976. Arbitrators also ruled, on three separate occasions in the 1980s and 1990s, that the owners had colluded against the players, decisions that cost them hundreds of millions of dollars in damages.

Reprinted below are the official recognition of the MLBPA, new salary specifications, and the definition of the role of the independent arbitrator.

ARTICLE II—RECOGNITION

The Clubs recognize the Association as the sole and exclusive collective bargaining agent for all Major League Players, and individuals who may become Major League Players during the term of this Agreement, with regard to all terms and conditions of employment except (1) individual salaries over and above the minimum requirements established by this Agreement and (2) Special Covenants to be included in individual Uniform Player's Contracts, which actually provide additional benefits to the Player. . . .

ARTICLE V—SALARIES

Individual Player salaries shall be those as agreed upon between a Player and a Club, as evidenced by the execution of a Uniform Player's Contract, subject to the following:

A. MINIMUM SALARY

During the 1970 championship season, the minimum rate of payment to a Player for each day of service on a Major League Club shall be at the rate of $12,000 per season. During the 1971 championship season, said minimum shall be at the rate of $12,750 per season. During the 1972 championship season, said minimum shall be at the rate of $13,500 per season.

B. MAXIMUM SALARY REDUCTION

No Player's contract shall be renewed pursuant to paragraph 10(a) of the Uniform Player's Contract in any year for a salary which constitutes a reduction in excess of 20% of his previous year's salary or in excess of 30% of his salary two years previous.

C. REPRESENTATION DURING INDIVIDUAL SALARY NEGOTIATIONS

A Player may be accompanied, if he so desires, by a representative of his choice to assist him in negotiating his individual salary with his employing Club. . . .

ARTICLE X—GRIEVANCE PROCEDURE

A. DEFINITIONS

10. "Arbitration Panel" shall mean the tripartite panel of arbitrators empowered to decide Grievances appealed to Arbitration. One arbitrator shall be appointed by the Association, one arbitrator shall be appointed by the Clubs and the impartial arbitrator, who shall serve as the Chairman of the Panel, shall be appointed by agreement of the two Party arbitrators. In the event the Party arbitrators are unable to agree upon the appointment of the impartial arbitrator by September 1, 1970, they jointly shall request that the American Arbitration Association furnish them a list of prominent, professional arbitrators. Upon receipt of said list, the Party arbitrators shall alternate in striking names from the list until only one remains. The arbitrator whose name remains shall be deemed appointed as the impartial arbitrator.

Following any decision of the Arbitration Panel, either of the Party arbitrators may discharge the impartial arbitrator by serving written notice upon him and the other Party arbitrator. Within 30 days thereafter, the Party arbitrators shall either agree upon a successor impartial arbitrator or select a successor from an American Arbitration Association list, as set forth above.

Decisions of the Arbitration Panel shall be made by majority vote or, with the agreement of the Party arbitrators, by the impartial arbitrator alone.

108

Reaction to Jim Bouton's *Ball Four* (1970)

SOURCES: *Houston Post,* May 24, 1970

During the 1969 season, Jim Bouton, an outspoken and unconventional player who was attempting to resuscitate his pitching career with the expansion Seattle Pilots and the Houston Astros, recorded his views on his comeback and his career as a whole. During the off-season Bouton and his editor, sportswriter Leonard Shecter, edited the transcript. Excerpts from the resulting book, Ball Four, *were first published in two installments in* Look *magazine in early June 1970. The reaction was strong and immediate.*

Many sportswriters applauded Bouton's efforts to provide a rare look at the reality of baseball life in and out of uniform. Influenced by the "chipmunk" school of sports journalism—pioneered in part by Shecter—which emphasized offbeat and humorous perspectives of sports, these supporters saw the book as invaluable, and fun. Older sportswriters like Jimmy Cannon, sometimes credited with coining the nickname "chipmunk," attacked Bouton and especially Shecter for violating the privacy of the players and the sanctity of the locker room. Cannon endorsed the action of Commissioner Kuhn, who summoned Bouton to his office shortly after the first Look *article and afterward condemned the book as inaccurate and dangerous.*

Ball Four *seems quite tame today, but in 1970 news of players taking amphetamines (or "greenies"), going to great lengths to spy on women in various states of undress ("beaver shooting"), or rudely rejecting children in search of autographs stunned many who wanted to believe that major leaguers were heroes worthy of emulation. Another book released the next year, Curt Flood's (and Richard Carter's)* The Way It Is, *was far more bold in its attack on baseball orthodoxy. Both authors committed sins in the eyes of the baseball world; Bouton revealed too much of life inside baseball, while Flood made clear that players had lives outside baseball.*

EX-YANKEES BURNING OVER BOUTON'S BOOK

Excerpts causing furor in East
By Joe Heiling
Post Sports Writer

Excerpts from Jim Bouton's book, "Ball Four," have caused a furor in the East.

"That's what Joe Garagiola told me," said the Astros' knuckleballing pitcher, "when he called for a taped interview on Monitor, the week end radio program."

Look Magazine is running a two-part series on Bouton's book, and the first installment included a segment in which he discusses the two sides of Mickey Mantle's personality.

It has brought a strong reaction from a few of Mantle's former teammates, especially from the ex-Yankee slugger's sidekick, Whitey Ford.

"Whitey was quoted as saying that I shouldn't have written such stuff," Bouton said, repeating Garagiola's words, "and that I was the most disliked player on the team in his 18 years with the Yankees."

This brought a smile from Bouton, a 21-game winner with the Yanks in 1963.

"Well, I knew I ranked up there among the top five," he chuckled.

Of Ford, Bouton remarked that the great lefthander did have a couple of trick pitches up his sleeve in the waning years of his career—the mud ball and the ring ball.

"It's a lie," Ford's one-time batterymate, Elston Howard, bellowed over the charge.

In answering this, the Astro veteran said:

"I really didn't know what the response would be to my book. People in baseball may not like it, and if you have heroes and illusions about ballplayers I don't advise that you read it. I thought baseball people would say, 'Well, he shouldn't have done it,' but would accept it.

"Really, it's a funny book and a true look at baseball. It is filled with anecdotes about the players and the game. And everything I've written is true.

"If Elston doesn't think so, he can always sue me. But I know that everything I've written is the truth, and Elston knows it, too."

Bouton has heard nothing from Mantle, and really didn't expect to, anyway.

This doesn't mean they won't bump into one another somewhere along the line, however.

"If that happens," laughed Jim, "I don't know what Mantle will do. I might get a punch in the mouth in some airport lobby."

You've got to admit, Jim Bouton speaks his mind.

109

Rose Crushes Fosse to Win All-Star Game for NL (1970)

SOURCE: *Cincinnati Enquirer,* July 15, 1970

To celebrate the construction of Riverfront Stadium and the return of the All-Star vote to the fans (originally stripped from them following a 1957 ballot box–stuffing incident in Cincinnati—see document 47), the 1970 All-Star Game was awarded to Cincinnati. Local fans again responded with fervor in electing two of their hometown heroes— Johnny Bench and Tony Perez—to the starting lineup. Two other Reds, pitcher Jim Merritt and outfielder Pete Rose, were also named to the team. Prior to the twelfth inning, the representatives of the newly dubbed "Big Red Machine" had performed poorly, with only Merritt making a positive contribution to the National League squad.

The conclusion of the game ensured its place in baseball history. The image of Pete Rose, who led off the inning with a single, barreling through catcher Ray Fosse as he scored the winning run on a Jim Hickman single has been replayed thousands of times as an example of Rose's hard-nosed, aggressive style of play. It also captured the supposed end of the promising career of Fosse, who held his starting position through 1972 and continued playing until 1979. Interestingly, the article below mentions that Rose was injured in the play and says nothing about Fosse's condition.

FOR WINNING RUN

Pete Moved a Mountain
By Bill Ford
Enquirer Sports Reporter

"All I could see when I went in there," said Pete Rose on the training table in the victorious National League dressing room Tuesday night, "was this big mountain."

So Pete Rose, the darling of the Cincinnati Reds, hit the mountain. Because of it, the National League had their eighth straight victory in the All-Star series and Pete's manager Sparky Anderson almost had a heart attack.

The crashing pile into mountainous Ray Fosse, the bulking 205-pound American League catcher, damaged Rose's left knee. To what extent could not be determined immediately.

Pete says "It's all right." Trainer Bill Cooper believes Pete is right.

"It was the only way I could get in there," said Pete, stretched out on a table with an ice pack on the knee. "The throw had me beat, I think."

The situation was this: With the score tied, 4–4, and two out in the 12th inning, Rose lit out for home from second when Chicago's Jim Hickman singled to centerfield.

"I could hear Leo (third base coach Leo Durocher) holler 'you gotta go, you gotta go,'" recalled Pete.

"He had the plate blocked and I knew I couldn't get in with an ordinary head-first slide. I had to try to hit his glove and reach in."

That Pete did. So hard did he slam into Fosse that the ball went completely through to the backstop.

"But I think," said Rose, "I hit a mountain."

Until Rose began the rally with a two-out single, the Cincinnati contribution to the cause of the Nationals was a complete bust, pitcher Jim Merritt excepted.

It got so bad that American League writers scoffed, "Big Red Machine? That's a laugh. Big Red Mirage, that's what you mean," said one.

The man from the east was right too. Tony Perez, the starting third baseman who is the majors' chief home run hitter and run producer, had three at bats, no hits, two strikeouts. John Bench, the starting catcher and no. 2 to Perez in homers, showed three at bats, no hits, three strikeouts; Rose, two-time NL batting champion, had two previous official at bats, no hits, two strikeouts. That totalled to seven strikeouts in eight at bats. In fact, before Pete did his thing, the only favorable Reds angle was Bench's throw out of American speedster Tommy Harper attempting to steal in the fifth inning and Merritt's solid two-inning stint.

"I think," said Pete afterwards, "that they had some good pitching. Another thing you don't get to see those guys that much."

Although Rose says he responded to Durocher's pleading with his go for broke daring, he admitted also he was going to try anyway.

He did, in fact, glance over his left shoulder toward centerfield[er] Amos Otis to size up the eventuality.

"I knew it was going to be a hell of a close play," said Nationals manager Gil Hodges.

Dick Dietz, the San Francisco Giants catcher who replaced Bench, was mobbed by newsmen. It was his home run in the ninth inning that started the Nationals on the comeback after they had been embarrassed on three hits for eight frames.

Dietz, who wasn't even nominated on the All-Star ballot, flashed a big smile and just muttered, "It was quite a treat."

And then there was Hickman whose game-winner off Clyde (No-Hit) Wright did in the Americans.

"All I tried to do," he explained, "was just meet the ball. I wasn't looking for any particular pitch. This one was a fast ball, down low."

110

Umpires Strike during League Championship Series (1970)

SOURCE: *Pittsburgh Press*, October 5, 1970

Major league umpires capped a tumultuous two-year period by staging a strike for the first game of the League Championship Series (LCS) in both leagues in 1970. Tensions that flared up with the firing of umpires Bill Valentine and Al Salerno and the subsequent formation of the Major League Umpires Association in September 1968 (see document 96) remained unresolved. At issue during the LCS were payment for postseason and All-Star Game appearances. According to Shag Crawford, a leader in the union, following the two-game strike the umpires received generous raises in exchange for their return to the diamond. See The Men in Blue: Conversations with Umpires, ed. Larry Gerlach (Lincoln: University of Nebraska Press, 1994), pp. 211–12.

The Press Box

Ump's Life Boo-tiful
By Roy McHugh, Sports Editor

CINCINNATI—For the television cameras, Al Barlick tore up his sign. It said, "major league umpires on strike for wages," and the major league umpires had just wrenched an agreement from their employers to resume negotiations. Otherwise, there wouldn't have been a ball game at Three Rivers Stadium in Pittsburgh yesterday, for several hundred union members—the ground crew and the vendors, the ushers and the ticket sellers and turnstile men, the porters, janitors and maids—were refusing to cross the picket line.

Smiling, looking into the camera, Al Barlick ripped the cardboard in half. "We want to thank the wonderful people of Pittsburgh," he said.

That was at noon. One hour later, when six of Al Barlick's associates walked on the field to umpire the championship playoff game between the Pirates and the Reds, the wonderful people of Pittsburgh booed them.

Mudcat Grant, to the accompaniment of an organ, a trapdrum and a trombone, sang the national anthem and at a dignified lope the umpires went to their positions—Stan Landes behind the plate, Paul Pryor at first base, Doug Harvey at second, Bob Engel at third, Harry Wendelstedt and Nick Colosi the foul lines. The wonderful people of Pittsburgh booed them again.

Pittsburgh may be a union town, but sympathy for the working man does not extend to umpires, it would seem. Bill Klem once said of the job, "You can't beat the hours." The boos at Three Rivers Stadium yesterday said that the compensation isn't all that bad, either.

THE UNION TEAMWORK

In the umpires' dressing room after the Reds won, 3–1, that was not the common interpretation. "Ever hear an umpire get cheered?" Stan Landes demanded. "That's welcome home when they boo. That's music to our ears—it means payday."

Bent over his suitcase, he was folding a blue shirt for the trip to Cincinnati. He straightened up. "Let me ask you a question," he said. "How can you feel not wanted when nobody walks into the ball park until they find out you're there?"

If that was why nobody had walked into the park before noon, it was indisputable logic. A more cogent reason may have been the fact that two of the Three Rivers unions—508 Service Employees International and Teamsters Local 250—had shut the place down.

Early yesterday morning, while 13 umpires walked the picket line outside, Presidents Jeep DePasquale of the Service Union and Sam Montano of the Teamsters Local talked with National League President Chub Feeney at Three Rivers. "We made him know that if the pickets remained we wouldn't go to work," said DePasquale.

On Saturday they had gone to work because the pickets were not out until almost game-time. The umpires Saturday were from the American Association and the International League. Yesterday, to make sure no one missed them, the major league umpires got up and started picketing at 8.

Jeep DePasquale and Sam Montano gave the umpires the same assurance they had given Chub Feeney. The picket line would not be crossed. "Then we urged the umpires and Mr. Feeney to sit down and talk things out," said DePasquale.

The umpires and Mr. Feeney took the hint. By 11:55, the umpires had agreed to call off the strike on the promise that negotiations would continue "as soon as possible," any settlement to be retroactive.

Said John Reynolds, the umpires' attorney, "The labor unions did a magnificent job for us and we can't thank them enough."

The major league umpires will be paid for the game they didn't work and the minor league umpires who did work it will be paid at the scale previously offered the major league umpires instead of at last year's lower scale.

They were worth it. In Saturday's game, there was not a single complaint about a call and catcher Johnny Bench of the Reds made a point of congratulating the plate umpire, Bob Grimsley. Stan Landes received only beefs—a total of six.

From Pirate third baseman Jose Pagan, who drew a diagram in the dirt with his bat after a called third strike in the seventh inning and who pawed the ground like a stallion when Landes called a strike on a three-and-nothing pitch in the ninth, came an aphorism about umpiring. "It makes no difference who the umpires are," he said, "if they're wrong, they're wrong."

Roberto Clemente knew what the trouble was yesterday. The umpires, he said, were tired. They'd been picketing too early in the morning.

111

Hall of Fame Establishes Negro Leagues Committee (1971)

SOURCE: *New York Amsterdam News*, February 13, 1971

During the induction ceremony at the Baseball Hall of Fame in 1966, Ted Williams commented that it was unfortunate that stars of the Negro Leagues could not join him in Cooperstown. Ever since that speech, pressure had been mounting on major league baseball and the Hall of Fame to make Negro Leaguers eligible for election. On February 3 baseball announced the establishment of a special committee whose purpose was to elect one Negro League player per year to be commemorated in a special exhibit dedicated to the Negro Leagues. Six days later, Satchel Paige was chosen to be the first such player inducted into the Hall of Fame.

In spite of the conciliatory tone of the committee members quoted in the press, the method by which players were to become members of the Hall of Fame was criticized by many. They concurred with Commissioner Kuhn—a strong supporter of the new committee—who acknowledged that "technically, you'd have to say [Paige is] not in the Hall of Fame." On July 7 the Hall of Fame agreed to enshrine Paige and future committee selections alongside other inductees. Paige entered the Hall of Fame through the front door on August 9.

The Special Committee was dissolved in 1977, its duties taken over by the Veterans

Committee. Starting in 1995, the Veterans Committee held a special vote for one Negro Leaguer per year for five years, a term later extended after complaints.

Printed below is a column on Paige's selection in the Amsterdam News, New York's *preeminent African American newspaper. This issue also included a brief editorial and a cartoon on the subject.*

SORT OF SPORTY
By Howie Evans

Baseball was, and still is, my father's favorite sport. His love for athletics did much to stimulate the same desires in me. As a little guy, I recall the Sundays we spent watching the black baseball stars of the day.

There were those exciting double headers at Yankee Stadium and Dexter Park. On special occasions, I was rewarded with a trip over to Jersey City, another spot where the white establishment permitted the blacks to play when they had nothing going.

The best part of the day was missing church. I sang in the junior choir of Mount Sini [sic] Baptist Church. I can only imagine now—but I am sure they never missed me.

I always used to ask my father (William Howard Evans), why these men didn't play with the white guys I read about every day in the papers. His answer was always the same. "They're not allowed because they are colored."

Well, I really couldn't understand that, because I was playing on a baseball and softball team that had a lot of white guys. Maybe, I thought then, they were not good enough to play with the white guys.

As I grew older, I no longer had to ask my father questions of that nature. The answers were right there for me to see. My old man always said guys like Satchel Paige, Josh Gibson, Dan Bankhead, and Roy Campanella were good enough to play in the majors.

When he heard Jackie Robinson was getting a shot, it seemed then that all those hot Sundays at the stadium had not been spent in vain. My mother became an immediate baseball fan because of the presence of Robinson in the big leagues. Today, some 20 odd years later, we can say, Jackie Robinson, breaking baseball's color line, has more meaning now, than it did then—when the nation's blacks were emotionally overwhelmed.

Jackie is in the Hall of Fame, so is Roy Campanella. After all these years of near perfect public oblivion, the men they toiled with in the Black Leagues are being given the opportunity for recognition and immortality.

But just like it was in the old days of baseball, another wall is being erected. This is a 1971 wall covered not with ivy, but with layers of separatism.

Through the persistent urging of Bowie Kuhn, Commissioner of baseball, the Hall of Fame people have seen fit to create a special section for players of the black age of professional baseball. That being the Negro Baseball Leagues of 20 years ago.

A special committee has been formed of men who played with, wrote about them, and promoted their contests. There are no records at all to speak of. Sam Lacey [*sic*], a member of the committee, and sports editor of the Baltimore Afro-American, commented: "we have a lot of stuff in our files at the paper, but it's not like records."

Monte Irvin, also a member of the ten man selection committee said that the committee would be advertising through the various mediums for people to bring in anything they have on the old time Black stars.

Other members of the committee are Roy Campanella, Eddie Gottlieb, Eppy Barnes, Frank Forbes, Judy Johnson, Wendell Smith, Alex Pompez and Bill Yancey.

These men to be named in years to come will not actually be Hall of Famers, and that in itself is a pity. There is no reason in the world players from the black leagues should be separated. I am against the special section to be included at Cooperstown. Certainly Paige, Gibson and the others proved that they could play baseball with anyone.

Back then, white super stars like Babe Ruth, Walter Johnson, Gabby Hartnett and others barnstormed against the best of black baseball. The black stars were never overwhelmed. On days that Satchel pitched, the big white hitters got nothing.

The other night, Eddie Gottlieb said that Josh Gibson was perhaps one of the greatest ever to play the game. He went on to say that Gibson, had he been permitted to play in the majors, might have broken Ruth's homerun record.

Then he said the ten years a player must have in the majors before he can be considered should remain as a criterion for admission to the Hall.

All I know is that the Hall of Fame people will break their own rules if they choose. In the case of the stars from the black leagues, the rules should be extended to include these greats. The Black baseball leagues are as American as any item in Cooperstown now.

112

Washington Senators Forfeit Franchise's Final Game (1971)

SOURCE: *Washington Star,* October 1, 1971

Although the official decision by the American League to approve the transfer of the expansion Washington Senators to Arlington, Texas, was not made until September 20, Senators fans knew long before that their club was destined to be taken from them. As early as 1969 the Senators (thanks to a last-second schedule change) played a pair of preseason exhibition games in Arlington. Owner Bob Short, who previously owned the Los Angeles Lakers and sold it to Jack Kent Cooke for a sizable profit, had engaged in a campaign of alienating local fans by raising ticket prices to the highest in major league baseball while cutting expenses drastically and criticizing the city and the fans at every opportunity. In spite of these efforts, the Senators nearly matched the AL *average attendance totals in 1969 and 1970—before the threats to move became real—and generated a greater profit than the rival Baltimore Orioles, who won the pennant all three years—despite their poor performance on the field.*

At the final Senators game the fans reacted to the loss of the franchise with fury and hatred for Short. Banners were hung throughout R.F.K. Stadium attacking Short, who ordered their removal. After the Senators staged a comeback and entered the final inning with a 7–5 lead, fans swarmed the field in search of souvenirs. The New York Yankees were awarded a 9–0 forfeit victory, but all statistics—including a home run by local hero Frank Howard—were official.

An outstanding book on the last years of the Senators is Shelby Whitfield, Kiss It Goodbye *(New York: Abelard-Schuman, 1973).*

IT WAS A WHOLE NEW BALLGAME!

Howard Homers
Fans Go Bananas
Senators Forfeit
By Merrell Whittlesey
Star Staff Writer

Those die-hard fans who never leave the game until the last man is out can always say in their hearts that the Senators never left town.

After 71 years in the Nation's Capital, a charter member of the American League, the Senators never did get the last man out.

So now it's on to Texas—Dallas, Fort Worth, and Arlington. And if the people of that state do not get to see Frank Howard, they will have been cheated, not unlike the way Senators' owner Bob Short has shortchanged the citizens of this city.

Yes, Howard probably will play for the new Texas franchise next year. Be that as it may, seldom has an athlete ignited a crowd the way he did with an unforgettable home run leading off the sixth inning last night at RFK Stadium. And regardless of whether the pitch was purposely grooved by New York Yankees' left-hander Mike Kekich, Howard was the man who hit it out, who smacked a trademark shot high over the leftfield screen, and that is the main thing people came to see.

HYSTERIA BUILDS

Howard's blast built up mass hysteria, emotions that could not be controlled until the last man was out. With the Senators one out from their last victory ever in their home for 71 years, the Senators leading 7–5, hundreds spilled onto the field and the game was forfeited to the Yankees 9–0.

The forfeiture was the first in the majors in 17 years.

Howard's homer and all the records except a winning and losing pitcher will count. If the Senators' officials really care they can join the Yankees today in asking President Joe Cronin to overrule the mandatory decision of umpire-in-chief Jim Honochick, who had no alternative but to award the game to the Yankees.

President Mike Burke of the Yankees said he did not want the forfeit, and has the authority to join the Senators in asking for a reverse ruling from Cronin.

For the first time in seven years here Howard raised his cap, not for a tip but a twirl. When the 14,460 paid and the estimated 4,000 gate crashers continued a din that threatened the game at that point, Howard threw his helmet to the crowd and then a kiss as a curtain call.

The big man's 237th home run as a Senator was "Utopia," in his word, his greatest thrill ever, one he will "take to the grave."

ERRORS CONTRIBUTE

The Senators had come from four runs back to take their two-run lead with the help of four Yankee errors, but their victory was never completed. The mob that leaped the fences as though they were croquet wickets rushed for the bases, tore up the mound, climbed to the roof of the bullpen, took letters from the scoreboard, dug up the turf, danced and romped and it was obvious in seconds that the game would never be completed.

Extra police were on hand, but they were helpless. Relief pitcher Paul Lindblad cared—it cost him a victory—but nobody else really cared who won or lost.

It had been a loud, anti-Short crowd from the first pitch. Obscene banners were hauled down. There was a roar for a "Bob Short Stinks" sign that was quickly yanked down, an even louder roar for a hastily printed "Bob Short Still Stinks" sign that replaced it.

LOSS DIDN'T COUNT

Howard was the hero and Short was the villain. The city was losing its team and the fans were alternately ugly and spirited as they vented their frustrations or paid their last respects. They were carried away with their affections for Howard, the gentle giant who had provided more excitement for long-suffering Washington baseball fans than any player since Walter Johnson. The evening was a bitter wake, a joyous circus, a shouting match with an absentee offender named Bob Short. . . .

Howard said the response to the homers he hit with the Dodgers in the World Series and in the All-Star game paled in comparison to the thunderous reception he received last night. And for the rest of his career any baseball feat of his will be anticlimactic, he said.

In his modest way he did not want to go back out and face the crowd but Manager Ted Williams and the players insisted on it. "I'm not a showboat," Howard said, "but I went back because this was their game."

The umpires would never have permitted the game to be continued past Howard's homer on an ordinary night. The outfield was covered with confetti. Trash littered the field. But this night was something special. A faithful American League city was losing its team. As long as the fun was relatively clean, the umpires were patient. . . .

Most of the Senators were not concerned with the game records. Dick Billings had three hits but said he was more concerned with saving his life when the mob rushed afield.

Only the surprise size of the crowd kept the Senators hanging around the clubhouse longer than most final games of a season. They did not want to fight the traffic.

Their farewells were brief as they scattered quickly for their homes, school or winter ball. Sentiment is short on the players' side in baseball. Except for Howard, Casey Cox, [Dick] Bosman and a couple of others Washington was just another stop.

They'll talk about the pandemonium of their last game here over the winter, laugh about it, and head for Florida next spring as the American League entry from Texas.

Washington said a tumultuous goodby. Bob Short is due in today on bank business. Best he come in disguise.

113

Cardinals' Owner Lectures Players on Virtues of Proposed Pension Plan (1972)

SOURCE: March 24, 1972, statement by August A. Busch Jr., Major League Baseball Players' Association file, National Baseball Hall of Fame Library

After the start of spring training, MLBPA executive director Marvin Miller learned that the owners would not consider his request that they increase pension and health care costs to match the rise in the cost of living since the previous agreement—which was to expire on March 31—was reached in 1969. Miller and union general counsel Dick Moss asked the players to conduct a strike vote. By March 30 the results were in—the vote supported a strike by a margin of 663–10, with 2 abstentions.

Major league officials did their best to condemn Miller's actions and portray their position on the issue as fair and reasonable. In his autobiography A Whole Different Ball Game, *Miller noted that the majority of the press, with the exception of New York* Times *writer Leonard Koppett and columnist Red Smith, backed the owners. Notably, Koppett, along with New York Daily News sportswriter Red Foley, noted the apparent backlash against team player representatives by the teams following the strike, which lasted from April 6 through April 13. In the end the owners accepted the terms initially proposed by Miller.*

Printed below is a speech given by St. Louis Cardinals owner and president August Busch at the club's spring training facility in St. Petersburg, Florida.

Gentlemen, there has been a lot of talk and comment about baseball's health, welfare, and pension plan.

We believe you are entitled to hear from us—face to face—just how we see the present situation. That is why I have asked for a meeting with all of you this morning.

Wednesday, after hearing a report from our baseball representatives, the presidents of all the major league clubs unanimously agreed on the following statement:

> ". . . The clubs offered to pay—in either a one year or four year agreement—the increased cost of the excellent life insurance, hospital, and dental care coverage.
>
> "We will continue the current contributions to the pension plan.
>
> "These additional costs will amount to an increase of approximately $400,000 a year of the clubs' contribution of $5,450,000 per year."

That is what we offer—to add $400,000 a year to what is already the best welfare and pension plan to be found elsewhere.

That goes for any plan in business, in the professions, or in sports.

Most of you already know about the plan, but I would like to review some of the important features for a few minutes.

The plan provides for outstanding dental and medical coverage for you and your family.

It provides for disability pay.

It provides for a life insurance policy on each of you for $50,000.

It provides generous widows' benefits.

The pension plan—which I mention—is without equal.

We have had several examples recently of how the plan works:

When one member of the Cardinal organization accidentally lost his life, his family received insurance benefits of $100,000.

Another Cardinal player—in recent years—became ill during the season, and the plan provided income for himself and his family.

Now, about the pension plan itself:

We know of no other plan which allows an employee—with only four years of service—to start to collect pension payments at as early an age as 45 . . . if he chooses to do so.

If a player waits to collect his pension when most people do—at age 65—he will get $7,400.

And that's with only four years as a player!

If a player has ten years of service, he can collect $18,500 a year for life after age 65.

He can start drawing a pro-rated amount at age 45 if he desires.

With twenty years' service, a player can draw $23,000 at age 65 . . . and so it goes through the entire range of service in baseball.

These pension payments are in addition to what other pension plans a player may get into when he goes into private industry.

They are also in addition to any social security programs.

That is our proposal for increasing the payments into the health, welfare, and benefit program . . . namely, to pay an additional cost of $400,000 a year to meet the additional expenses of that program.

It is our position that this is a very fair and equitable program.

Mr. Miller does not think so, and he has proposed a strike.

Such threats as those we have heard of—such as refusal to play in the All Star Game or any other punitive action—can only serve to alienate the fans.

If we destroy the enthusiasm for baseball shared by millions of fans—both young and old—we will have lost everything!

I don't need to remind anyone that all of us rely on the support of these fans for the future of baseball.

By alienating them, we believe that the players—present and future—are certain to be the biggest losers.

Without the enthusiastic support of the people who pay to see you play, I suggest to you there won't be any pension plan.

There won't be any health and welfare plan!

And, there won't be any baseball. It is that serious!

Let me make it very clear that we are not seeking a "showdown" with Mr. Miller—or with you—or with anyone else.

We are taking our position because we believe it is the only one we can take to guarantee the future of baseball.

Since most of you are away from home—here in St. Petersburg—it is only fair to tell you our plans in the event of a strike . . . as Mr. Miller has threatened.

You are entitled to know our procedure in order for you to make your own plans accordingly.

We will provide airplane tickets for each of you to return to your respective homes. Our traveling secretary will help you to make your travel arrangements.

Gentlemen, I want to thank you for giving me this chance to discuss this very important matter with you . . . and to give you our point of view.

And now, Dick Meyer, Bing Devine, and I will be glad to try to answer any questions you may have.

The floor is open.

114

Comment on the Supreme Court Ruling against Curt Flood (1972)

SOURCE: *Washington Star,* June 22, 1972

The 5–3 Supreme Court decision against the case brought by Curt Flood surprised few in baseball. Although there were numerous cases dating back to 1882 in which the reserve clause had been declared invalid, the courts were reluctant to overturn it, a reluctance fueled in part by players' failure to actively seek such a resolution. After the Supreme Court ruled in 1922 that baseball was exempt from the Sherman Antitrust Act, judges made clear to plaintiffs that they should seek relief through Congress, not through the justice system. As Justice Harry Blackmun made clear in his colorful decision, Congress had numerous opportunities to pass legislation stripping baseball of its unique legal status, but declined to do so.

The following article by Tom Dowling attacks the decision by questioning the logic of the justices who openly doubted the validity of the previous Court decisions on the antitrust issue yet failed to overturn them. He also attacks the apparent behind-the-scenes politicking by the justices, a point also stressed by Bob Woodward and Scott Armstrong in The Brethren: Inside the Supreme Court *(New York: Simon and Schuster, 1979). Downing's article and his June 25 article in the* Washington Star *are reprinted in* Congressional Record, 92nd Cong., 2nd sess., 1972, 118, pt. 17:22282–83.

Blackmun's decision is in Supreme Court Reporter *92 (1972): 2099–2119, and is reprinted in Waller, Cohen, and Finkelman, eds.,* Baseball and the American Legal Mind, *pp. 120–40.*

Tom Dowling

FLOOD VERSUS KUHN: NOT THE COURT'S FINEST HOUR

When the players themselves sound glum and apologetic for the game they've just played, you have to figure the sport involved is baseball. And sure enough that's the way the Supreme Court sounded in its 5–3 decision Monday siding with baseball in the Curt Flood case. It was the third time this century the court has had its fling with the National Pastime and it has yet to get the hang of the game.

Essentially, the issue before the court was whether baseball's reserve clause violates antitrust law because it imposes restraint of trade by denying ball players the right to sell their services on the open market.

An ancillary consideration was why baseball should be the sole American professional sport to be granted the special privilege of antitrust immunity as a result of the High Court's decision in Federal Baseball Club of 1922 and Toolson of 1953.

ASTOUNDING RULING

Monday's ruling was astounding on several counts.

In the first instance, all knowledgeable observers, including baseball's own lawyers, assumed that the court had agreed to hear Flood vs. Kuhn last October because it had distinct reservations over the wisdom of its earlier decisions conferring antitrust immunity on a game that becomes more business oriented with each passing year.

Secondly, there is no clear evidence that the present court is markedly less vigilant in upholding antitrust statutes than its predecessor, the Warren Court.

Finally, the five justices who voted to reaffirm baseball's unique status were at best tepid in defense of their votes.

Writing for the majority—though two of his colleagues pointedly snubbed two-fifths of his opinion—Justice Harry Blackmun termed baseball's reserve clause exemption "an exception and an anomaly . . . an aberration." In a concurring opinion, Chief Justice Burger's most ringing defense of his own position was to note he had "grave reservations as to its correctness."

CHARITABLE INTERPRETATION

You would think that with friends like this the reserve clause hardly requires an enemy. Yet the indefensible carried the day, the unlikely and the illogical retains its age-old privileged sway. The obvious and disquieting explanation for baseball's triumph is that the court did not regard the clear if lucrative servitude of ball-players as a very serious public issue.

In substance, Burger's opinion argues that the reserve clause is an awkward but hallowed custom best left to Congress to rectify.

Blackmun, on the other hand, asserts that Congress' "positive inaction" over baseball's anomalous antitrust position implies legislative satisfaction with the status quo. This is surely one of the most charitable possible interpretations to account for Congress' characteristically dropsical inactivity, a torpor that extends to almost every issue of public policy. Indeed, by a 5–2 majority the court repudiated Blackmun's thesis on this point. In sum, both the Blackmun and Burger opinion are copouts.

This is all the more disappointing since the chief institutional difference between the Supreme Court and the Congress is that the former is alive and working, while the latter has long ago forfeited any public confidence in its capacity to take decisive action.

While it is possible to make a persuasive case that inequities and even chaos might result should baseball be shorn of its reserve clause, the fact is that such consequences are no concern of the Supreme Court, which commands considerable respect for rigorously deciding matters on the basis of the law. Sadly enough, by its own acknowledgment the court eschewed that responsibility with Curt Flood. True, he is only an individual, but then the rights of a single man are the special majesty of the law.

CONSIDERABLE CONFUSION

Because the court's deliberations are held in secrecy it is impossible to determine exactly how the Flood decision was reached. However, some details have come to light, which may help explain why Flood vs. Kuhn was not the High Court's finest hour, was indeed a matter of considerable confusion.

Justice Lewis Powell, who heard the oral arguments last March, promptly disqualified himself from the case, apparently because he owns 880 shares of Anheuser-Busch stock, worth approximately $44,000 at the time Powell was appointed to the court. Since Gussie Busch owned not only the Budweiser brewery but also the St. Louis Cardinals, Powell clearly felt that his active participation in the Flood case would raise a possible conflict of interest.

That left eight votes. Informed sources close to the court say that the eight justices originally were split in conference 5–3, with Chief Burger on Flood's side and Justice Thurgood Marshall on baseball's side. This is entirely plausible since the Star has learned that Justice Potter Stewart assigned the majority opinion to Blackmun. This could only happen in the event the Chief Justice and the next two justices senior to Stewart, William Douglas and William Brennan, were in the minority, as was, in fact, the case.

So, after the opinion for the majority had been given to Blackmun, either Burger or Marshall switched his position on the case. That change would have meant a 4–4 deadlock, which in turn would mean that the court could render no decision whatsoever in the case. Given the considerable publicity surrounding Flood vs. Kuhn, such a standoff doubtless would prove embarrassing to the court. After all, why go to the lengths of reopening baseball's antitrust immunity only to leave the matter up in the air? For if the court failed to speak to Flood vs. Kuhn, another baseball player could test the legality of the reserve clause again in the courts.

RULING INSURED

The cost of the Flood litigation was around $100,000. This is a fair sum of money for the Major League Baseball Players Association to spend on still another suit against baseball with the possibility that the issue ultimately would return to the Supreme Court only to be left dangling again in irresolution.

Therefore, whichever justice—Burger or Marshall—abandoned the majority to create the 4–4 standoff, the remaining one then reportedly defected from the minority side to create the final 5–3 vote. Internal evidence would suggest that Burger, who as Chief Justice has a special concern if not proclivity for preserving the court's public image of efficiency, was the last switch, thus insuring a ruling even if it were of an intellectually disagreeable nature.

Such switches are by no means an uncommon practice at the court, where decisions frequently are the result of consensus politicking and independent re-examination of views. Yet, these reported shifts certainly imply a confused, even a Byzantine approach to the relatively cut and dried antitrust issue involved in Flood vs. Kuhn.

Perhaps the explanation lies in the almost mythical grip of baseball on the national consciences, especially among the generation now old enough to sit on the Supreme Court. How else can you view Monday's curious decision with its extralegal, sentimental qualities?

More on that Sunday.

Bibliography

The history of baseball in the third quarter of the twentieth century has been from countless perspectives by hundreds of writers. The best general history of the period is still David Quentin Voigt, *American Baseball: From Postwar Expansion to the Electronic Age* (University Park: Pennsylvania State University Press, 1983), although it is beginning to show its age. Veteran sportswriter Leonard Koppett, in *Koppett's Concise History of Major League Baseball* (Philadelphia: Temple University Press, 1998), takes advantage of his press box seat to offer a unique combination of description and analysis. Other recent histories include John P. Rossi, *The National Game: Baseball and American Culture* (Chicago: Ivan R. Dee, 2000), and Jules Tygiel, *Past Time: Baseball as History* (New York: Oxford University Press, 2000), a chronologically arranged collection of essays. Still valuable are Benjamin G. Rader, *Baseball: A History of America's Game* (Urbana: University of Illinois Press, 1992), and Charles C. Alexander, *Our Game: An American Baseball History* (New York: Henry Holt, 1991). Geoffrey C. Ward and Ken Burns, *Baseball: An Illustrated History* (New York: Knopf, 1994); Daniel Okrent and Harris Lewine, eds., *The Ultimate Baseball Book* (Boston: Houghton Mifflin, 1979); and Lawrence Ritter and Donald Honig, *The Image of Their Greatness: An Illustrated History of Baseball from 1900 to the Present* (New York: Crown, 1979) are attractive, if somewhat basic, summaries of baseball history. An invaluable compilation of arcane and essential baseball information can be found in Jonathan Fraser Light, *The Cultural Encyclopedia of Baseball* (Jefferson NC: McFarland, 1997).

In recent years more writers have chosen to focus on one particular season or era. The most comprehensive analysis of this type is William Marshall, *Baseball's Pivotal Era: 1945–1951* (Lexington: University Press of Kentucky, 1999), in which Marshall—who oversees the papers of former commissioner Albert "Happy" Chandler—mines these papers and scores of interviews with Chandler's contemporaries to create a masterful examination of these years. John P. Rossi, *A Whole New Game: Off the Field Changes in Baseball, 1946–1960* (Jefferson NC: McFarland, 1999), competently summarizes his time period. Philip Baste, *Dog Days: The New York Yankees' Fall from Grace and Return to Glory, 1964–1976* (New York: Random House, 1994), succeeds in capturing his colorful subject. Historian Bruce Kuklick takes a different tack with his nostalgic evocation of the impact of baseball on the neighborhood around one of Philadelphia's major league stadiums in *To Everything a Season: Shibe Park and Urban Philadelphia, 1909–1976* (Princeton: Princeton University Press, 1991). Brent Kelley, *Baseball's Biggest Blunder: The Bonus Rule of 1953–1957* (Lanham MD: Scarecrow Press, 1997), is an invaluable examination of a misguided experiment at midcentury. Accounts of single seasons—each of which claims its season to be superior to any other—include two books by David Halberstam praised for the quality of writing and criticized by some players and historians for inaccuracy, *Summer of '49* (New York: William Morrow, 1989) and *October 1964* (New York: Villard Books, 1994). Roger Angell's first collection of his superb baseball essays, *The Summer Game* (New York: Popular Library, 1978), describes the early ineptitude of the New York Mets, among other topics. Single-season accounts written immediately after the year in question include Charles Einstein, *A Flag for San Francisco* (New York: Simon and Schuster, 1962), which may have been a year premature but is wonderful nevertheless. Other books in the genre include David Kaiser's superb *Epic Season: The 1948 American League Pennant Race* (Amherst: University of Massachusetts Press, 1998); Jeff Miller's *Down to the Wire: The Thrilling Inside Story of the Greatest Pennant Chase Ever—The 1967 American League Race* (Dallas: Taylor, 1992); Rick Talley's *The Cubs of '69: Recollections of the Team That Should Have Been* (Chicago: Contemporary Books, 1989); and Shelby Whitfield's biting analysis of the final season of the expansion Washington Senators, *Kiss It Goodbye* (New York: Abelard-Schuman, 1973).

A variation on this theme is the oral history. Upon perusing the literature it seems that few major leaguers from the mid–twentieth century have escaped the notice of the growing legion of writers—mostly amateur historians—with tape recorders. Easily the most comprehensive oral history of baseball is *We Played the Game: Sixty-Five Players Remember Baseball's Greatest Era, 1947–1964*, ed. Danny Peary (New York: Hyperion, 1994), whose decision to organize his book chronologically rather than biographically pays dividends for baseball historians. Larry Moffi's *This Side of Cooperstown: An Oral History of Major League Baseball in the 1950s* (Iowa City: University of Iowa Press, 1996) and Phil Pepe's *Talkin' Baseball: An Oral History of Baseball in the 1970s* (New York: Ballantine Books, 1998) are two of the better oral histories available. The best book on umpires is Larry Gerlach's oral history *The Men in Blue: Conversations with Umpires* (1980; rpt., Lincoln: University of Nebraska Press, 1994). A fascinating collection of firsthand accounts of men in different baseball-related professions was amassed by Harold Rosenthal in *Baseball Is Their Business* (New York: Random House, 1952).

Many players and baseball officials of this era have published autobiographies. The most famous player autobiography is Jim Bouton's *Ball Four: My Life and Hard Times Throwing the Knuckleball in the Big Leagues,* ed. Leonard Shecter (New York: World, 1970), which generated a storm of controversy upon its publication. Nearly as controversial—and more provocative—is Curt Flood with Richard Carter, *The Way It Is* (New York: Trident Press, 1971). Some other player autobiographies include Don Drysdale with Bob Verdi, *Once a Bum, Always a Dodger: My Life in Baseball from Brooklyn to Los Angeles* (New York: St. Martin's Press, 1990); Sandy Koufax with Ed Linn, *Koufax* (New York: Viking Press, 1966); and Joe Morgan and

David Falkner, *A Life in Baseball* (New York: Norton, 1993). *The Hard Way: Writing by the Rebels Who Changed Sports,* ed. Will Balliett and Thomas Dyja (New York: Thunder's Mouth Press, 1999), collects selections from the autobiographies of, among others, Flood, Bouton, Bill Veeck, Dock Ellis, Marvin Miller, and Jackie Robinson.

Useful player biographies are far less numerous than autobiographies, even though compelling subjects like Mickey Mantle, Willie Mays, and Joe DiMaggio have inspired many writers to interpret their significance to American society. I chose not to examine many biographies for this book because the information I sought was readily available elsewhere. Jackie Robinson has been the subject of several biographies, but the most complete is Arnold Rampersand, *Jackie Robinson: A Biography* (New York: Knopf, 1997), thanks to the cooperation of the Robinson family. Also important is a collection of essays by Jules Tygiel, *The Jackie Robinson Reader: Perspectives on an American Hero* (New York: Dutton, 1997). The best book on Willie Mays is Charles Einstein's *Willie's Time: A Memoir* (New York: Lippincott, 1979), which was nominated for a Pulitzer Prize. Another insightful biography is David Cataneo's *Tony C: The Triumph and Tragedy of Tony Conigliaro* (Nashville: Rutledge Hill Press, 1997). A recent, controversial deconstruction of one of the most beloved players ever is Richard Ben Cramer's *Joe DiMaggio: The Hero's Life* (New York: Simon and Schuster, 2000).

Baseball officials, perhaps because they are better-educated than players, have produced many worthwhile books. Most of the commissioners in the post–World War II era have defended their terms in print. Happy Chandler, with Vance Trimble, demonstrates his colorful personality in *Heroes, Plain Folks, and Skunks: The Life and Times of Happy Chandler* (Chicago: Bonus Books, 1989). His successor, Ford C. Frick (a former sportswriter), wrote his own book—*Games, Asterisks, and People: Memoirs of a Lucky Fan* (New York: Crown, 1973)—as did Bowie Kuhn with *Hardball: The Education of a Baseball Commissioner* (1987; rpt., Lincoln: University of Nebraska Press, 1997). Jerome Holtzman, *The Commissioners: Baseball's Midlife Crisis* (New York: Total Sports, 1998), is an unsatisfactory examination of each of baseball's top executives. Kuhn's fiercest rival, Marvin Miller, discusses his differences with the commissioner in *A Whole Different Ball Game: The Sport and Business of Baseball* (New York: Birch Lane Press, 1991). Other baseball officials who have contributed to the literature include Buzzie Bavasi with John Strege, *Off the Record* (Chicago: Contemporary Books, 1987); Walter Alston and Si Burick, *Alston and the Dodgers* (Garden City NY: Doubleday, 1966); Dick Williams and Bill Plaschke, *No More Mr. Nice Guy: A Life of Hardball* (San Diego: Harcourt Brace Jovanovich, 1990); and Bobby Bragan as told to Jeff Gunn in the superb *You Can't Hit the Ball with the Bat on Your Shoulder: The Baseball Life and Times of Bobby Bragan* (Fort Worth: Summit Group, 1992). One of the only biographies of a major figure in baseball management is Murray Polner, *Branch Rickey* (New York: Atheneum, 1982).

A rapidly growing body of texts on African Americans in baseball has begun to venture beyond the confines of the Negro Leagues. Jules Tygiel, *Baseball's Great Experiment: Jackie Robinson and His Legacy* (New York: Oxford University Press, 1983), remains the definitive examination of the tortured process of integration. Bruce Adelson, *Brushing Back Jim Crow: The Integration of Minor-League Baseball in the American South* (Charlottesville: University Press of Virginia, 1999), is a fascinating examination of the sociological and legal ramifications of integration. Larry Moffi and Jonathan Kronstadt, *Crossing the Line: Black Major Leaguers, 1947–1959* (Jefferson NC: McFarland, 1994), offers brief biographical sketches of the first generation of black major leaguers. Steven A. Riess and Donn Rogosin's entry on "Baseball" in *The Information Now Encyclopedia of the African-American Experience,* ed. Jack Salzman (New York: Macmillan Library Reference U.S.A., 1998), provides a brief summary of this complicated subject. Alfred Dennis Mathewson, "Major League Baseball's Monopoly Power and the Negro Leagues," *American Business Law Journal* 35 (Winter 1998): 291–318, suggests an alternative legal strategy that might have eased the transition to integration. An important book on a different minority, Hispanics, is Samuel O. Regalado, *Viva Baseball! Latin Major Leaguers and Their Special Hunger* (Urbana: University of Illinois Press, 1998).

One of the most significant developments in professional sports in the post–World War II era was the involvement—some would say interference—of the U.S. Congress in the administration of the industry. Starting in 1951, nearly every Congress convened hearings to discuss baseball's antitrust exemption, broadcast regulations, gambling, and other issues. The published hearings included not only the testimony of players, officials, and other experts, but also dozens of significant documents otherwise unavailable to historians. The first, and most important, of these hearings was held by the House Subcommittee on Study of Monopoly Power, *Study of Monopoly Power, Serial 1, Part 6: Organized Baseball* (82nd Cong., 1st sess., 1951), better known simply as *Organized Baseball.* Two years later the Senate Subcommittee on Interstate and Foreign Commerce staged a hearing on *Broadcasting and Televising Baseball Games* (83rd Cong., 1st sess., May 1953) that collected testimony and documents on the growing controversy of television and baseball and its impact on the minor leagues. Between 1957 and 1960 both the House and the Senate held hearings published separately as *Organized Professional Team Sports,* which analyzed the changing conditions in which modern pro sports were contested. Several books discuss these and other congressional hearings. Stephen R. Lowe, *The Kid on the Sandlot: Congress and Professional Sports, 1910–1992* (Bowling Green OH: Bowling Green University Popular Press, 1995), summarizes the hearings in a satisfactory manner. More insightful is Jerold J. Duquette, *Regulating the National Pastime: Baseball and Antitrust* (Westport CN: Praeger Press, 2000).

The attention paid baseball and other professional sports by Congress reflected a realization that sport was a business with a unique legal status. Scholars have in recent years showered attention on these aspects of baseball history. The most valuable book addressing baseball and the law is *Baseball and the American Legal Mind*, ed. Spencer Weber Waller, Neil B. Cohen, and Paul Finkleman (New York: Garland, 1995), which includes not only original documents such as legal decisions in landmark cases but also articles by legal scholars. Roger Abrams has written a pair of books, *Legal Bases: Baseball and the Law* (Philadelphia: Temple University Press, 1998) and *The Money Pitch: Baseball Free Agency and Salary Arbitration* (Philadelphia: Temple University Press, 2000), which explain in layman's terms many complicated legal and business related issues. An older but still valuable examination of sports law is Lionel S. Sobel's *Professional Sports and the Law* (New York: Law-Arts, 1977).

It is difficult to keep up with the flood of books addressing the baseball industry from a business or economic perspective. One of the first such books, *Government and the Sports Business*, ed. Roger G. Noll (Washington DC: Brookings Institution, 1974), collects some of the earliest analyses of the subject. Eighteen years later the same think tank issued an updated volume edited by Paul M. Sommers, *Diamonds Are Forever: The Business of Baseball* (Washington DC: Brookings Institution, 1992). Two straightforward guides to baseball economics are Gerald W. Scully, *The Business of Major League Baseball* (Chicago: University of Chicago Press, 1989), and Andrew Zimbalist, *Baseball and Billions: A Probing Look Inside the Big Business of Our National Pastime* (New York: Basic Books, 1994). The foremost account of the battles between the MLBPA and the owners is John Helyar, *Lords of the Realm: The Real History of Baseball* (New York: Villard Books, 1994). Several academic examinations of the business of baseball include Paul D. Staudohor, *The Sports Industry and Collective Bargaining* (Ithaca NY: ILR Press, 1986); Eric M. Leifer, *Making the Majors: The Transformation of Team Sports in America* (Cambridge MA: Harvard University Press, 1995); Michael N. Danielson, *Home Team: Professional Sports and the American Metropolis* (Princeton: Princeton University Press, 1997); and Jamie Quirk and Rodney Fort, *Hard Ball: The Abuse of Power in Pro Team Sports* (Princeton: Princeton University Press, 1999). Works on the phenomenon of franchise transfers include Neil J. Sullivan, *The Dodgers Move West* (New York: Oxford University Press, 1987); Glen Gendzel, "Competitive Boosterism: How Milwaukee Lost the Braves," *Business History Review* 69 (Winter 1995): 530–66; and Frank P. Jozsa Jr., and John J. Guthrie Jr., *Relocating Teams and Expanding Leagues in Professional Sports: How the Major Leagues Respond to Market Conditions* (Westport CN: Quorum Books, 1999).

Another development critical in baseball's history was the emergence of television as the dominant broadcast medium. The best general history of television in this era remains Erik Barnouw, *Tube of Plenty: The Evolution of American Television*, 2nd rev. ed. (New York: Oxford University Press, 1990), which includes data on the rise of sports on television. Benjamin G. Rader, *In Its Own Image: How Television Has Transformed Sports* (New York: Free Press, 1984), though somewhat dated, retains its value. Curt Smith has written two fascinating books on radio and television broadcasters featuring interviews with seemingly every important baseball announcer, *Voices of the Game: The Acclaimed Chronicle of Baseball Radio and Television Broadcasting—from 1921 to the Present* (New York: Simon and Schuster, 1987) and *The Storytellers: From Mel Allen to Bob Costas—Sixty Years of Baseball Tales From the Broadcast Booth* (New York: Macmillan, 1995). Of the many broadcasters who have written books, two of the best are Red Barber, *The Broadcasters* (1970; New York: Da Capo Press, 1985) and Curt Gowdy with John Powers, *Seasons to Remember: The Way It Was in American Sports, 1945–1960* (New York: Harper-Collins, 1993). Books on radio which I found helpful include Susan Douglas, *Listening In: Radio and the American Imagination, From Amos 'n' Andy and Edward R. Murrow to Wolfman Jack and Howard Stern* (New York: Times Books, 1999), which includes a chapter on sports broadcasting, and David J. Halberstam (a basketball broadcaster, not related to the noted journalist), *Sports on New York Radio: A Play-by-Play History* (Chicago: Masters Press, 1999).

Journalists continued to play a vital role in reporting the game and shaping its history. One of the most beloved baseball books of all time, Roger Kahn's *The Boys of Summer* (1972; New York: Harper and Row, 1987), explores the world of sports journalism in New York City at length. Kahn has expanded on this theme in two other books, *The Era: 1947–1957: When the Yankees, the Giants, and the Dodgers Ruled the World* (New York: Ticknor and Fields, 1993) and *Memories of Summer: When Baseball Was an Art, and Writing About It a Game* (New York: Hyperion, 1997), which serve equally as sentimental yet accurate histories of 1950s baseball. One of the most acclaimed baseball writers and editors of the period, Stanley Woodward, explains his profession in *Sports Page: The Story behind Newspaper Sports Writing* (New York: Simon and Schuster, 1949). Other veteran baseball reporters were given a chance to describe their life's work by Jerome Holtzman in his oral history *No Cheering in the Press Box*, rev. ed. (New York: Henry Holt, 1995). Another fine oral history of baseball writers—essayists and historians as well as journalists—is Mike Shannon, *Baseball: The Writers' Game* (South Bend IN: Diamond Communications, 1992). Richard Orodenker analyzes the evolution of baseball writing in *The Writers' Game: Baseball Writing in America* (New York: Twayne Press, 1996). Orodenker also edited an invaluable collection of biographies of many legendary baseball reporters, *Twentieth-Century American Sportswriters* (Detroit: Gale Research, 1996). The evolution of one of the most important sports periodicals is chronicled in Michael MacCambridge, *The Franchise: A History of Sports Illustrated Magazine* (New York: Hyperion, 1997).

Acknowledgments

"Ashford Cracks Barrier as First Negro Umpire in Majors" (doc. 83) and "RED SOX Take Pennant As Historic Season Ends" (doc. 92) courtesy of *Boston Globe*.

"Change Is Made in All-Star Cast" (doc. 47) and "For Winning Run/Pete Moved a Mountain" (doc. 109) used with permission from *The Cincinnati Enquirer/Bill Ford*.

"Fun and Games/Believe" (doc. 102) and "The Record Business" (doc. 106) courtesy of *New York Post*.

"History Is Made in Series Classic; Larsen Hurls Perfect Game, Wins 2–0" (doc. 39) and "NL Latin Stars Pin 5–2 Loss On AL Aces" (doc. 75) © *New York Daily News*, L.P. reprinted with permission.

"House Asks Baseball to Reinstate Jackson" (doc. 17) courtesy of *The State* (Columbia SC).

"Juan, Spahn 16 Inning Duel; Mays HR Wins It" (doc. 73) and "With Willie At the Bat" (doc. 74) courtesy of *San Francisco Examiner*.

"Koufax Quits Baseball" (doc. 91) courtesy of *San Diego Union*.

"Majors Clear Way for New Coordinator" (doc. 85) and "Bowie Kuhn: An Interim Choice, But He Could Be There a Long Time" (doc. 99) courtesy of *Miami Herald*.

"Named to 5-Year Term; Retiring Chief Honored" (doc. 7); "Necciai Whiffs 27 in Bristol No-Hitter" (doc. 23); "Minors Reject Moves to Loosen Major Ties; Veeck's Surprise Proposals Create Convention Tumult" (doc. 25); "DeWitt Sees Minors' Fund Job as 'Challenge'" (doc. 42); "Rules Makers Take Toehold on Spitter, Beat it Down, 8–1" (doc. 70); "22 Clubs, Only 20 Tieups, Add Up to Headache" (doc. 72); "O'Malley Taps New Mother Lode—Fee Teevee" (doc. 78); "Eager Beavers + Rat Pack = Chipmunks" (doc. 87); "Firemen Will Get Credit for Saves In the Box Score" (doc. 97); "Wild-Card Hitter to Get Trial in Four Minors—Majors Watch Closely" (doc. 98); and "Another Homer for The Babe? Debate Grows Hot, Heavy" (doc. 100) courtesy of *The Sporting News*.

"Reading for Pleasure: Grand Slam" (doc. 40) courtesy of the *Wall Street Journal*.

"The Responsibilities of a Team Statistician" (doc. 22) from *Baseball Is Their Business* by Harold Rosenthal. Copyright © 1952 and renewed 1980 by Harold Rosenthal. Reprinted by permission of Random House, Inc.

"Review of *Baseball: The Early Years*" (doc. 63) courtesy of *American Historical Review*.

"Rookie Performs 'Impossible' Task" (doc. 10) © 1948 *The Plain Dealer*. All rights reserved. Reprinted with permission.

"Score's Accident Jeopardizes Career of Baseball's Most Talented Youngster" (doc. 46) © 1957 *The Plain Dealer*. All rights reserved. Reprinted with permission.

"Seminar Rules—1970" (doc. 105) courtesy of William Gamson.

"S.F. Wins Pennant on Wild Four-Run Rally in 9th, 6–4" (doc. 71) and "Giants Win Riotous Game, 4–3" (doc. 82) © *San Francisco Chronicle*. Reprinted by permission.

"Sort of Sporty" (doc. 111) courtesy of *New York Amsterdam News.*

"Umpires Fired; Talk Strike" (doc. 96) © 1968 *The Plain Dealer.* All rights reserved. Reprinted with permission.

"Who'll Ever Forget The Mick's 535th?" (doc. 95) reprinted by permission of the *Detroit Free Press.*

Index

franchise relocation, xviii, xx, 41, 65–67, 77, 114–16, 119

Frank, Jerome, 32

Frankfurter, Felix, 105

Franks, Herman, 198

free agency, 182,

Frick, Ford, xvi, xvii, xix, xx, 7, 9, 11, 25, 26, 27, 41, 52, 60, 80, 90–91, 99, 100, 109, 110, 111, 129–31, 141, 143, 155, 159, 161, 162, 163, 164, 167, 168, 169, 183, 192, 193–94, 195, 202, 205, 242

Friend, Bob, 153, 204

Fuentes, Tito, 199

Fullmer, Gene, 109

Furillo, Carl, 53, 95, 146, 148

Galbreath, John, 80

Galehouse, Denny, 29

Gallagher, Jim, 168, 169, 244

Gallo, Bill, 94

Gamson, William, 256

Ganung, Bob, 59

Garagiola, Joe, 26, 263, 264

Garcia, Mike, 109

Gardella, Danny, xvii, 32, 33, 42

Gehrig, Lou, 260

Gentile, Jim, 260

Gibson, Althea, 165

Gibson, Bob, 236

Gibson, Josh, 269, 270

Giel, Joe, 59

Giles, Warren, 6, 8, 9, 10, 62, 110, 111, 116, 138, 140, 162, 169, 198, 199, 204, 229, 230

Gilleandeau, Joseph A., 12

Gillette Safety Razor Co., xvi, 78

Gilliam, Jim, 172, 173

Gimbel, Bernard F., 120, 121

Glennon, Eddie, 73

"Glory of Their Times," 214–15

Glynn, Bill, 85, 88

Goldberg, Arthur, 253

Gonder, Jesse, 187

Gonzalez, Tony, 182

Goodale, George, 112, 113

Goodman, Billy, 37, 38

Gordon, Joe, 182

Gottlieb, Eddie, 270

Grabiner, Harry, 11

Grant, Jim "Mudcat," 267

Grant, M. Donald, 115, 141, 156

Grasso, Mickey, 85

Greenberg, Hank, 80

grievance procedure, 222–25

Griffith, Calvin, 229

Griffith, Clark, 71, 74

Griffith, Derrell, 191

Griffith Stadium, 19, 71, 72

Grimes, Burleigh, 118, 169

Grimsley, Bob, 268

Grissom, Marvin, 86, 88

Groat, Dick, 153

Gross, Milton, 210

Grote, Dave, 243, 244

Haddix, Harvey, 138–40, 152, 153

Hall of Fame. *See* National Baseball Hall of Fame

Hammond, Bobby, 59

Hamner, Granny, 53

Handley, Gene, 103

Haney, Fred, 140, 148

Hanna, Harry, 234

Hannegan, Robert, 7, 9, 10, 11

Harder, Mel, 21

Harlan, John, 105

Harlem Satellites (basketball team), 145

Harper, Tommy, 266

Harridge, William, 110, 111

Harris, Bucky, 71

Harris, Luman, 197

Harrisburg (pa) Senators, 60

Hartnett, Gabby, 270

Harwell, Ernie, 56, 256

Harvey, Doug, 267

Hayes, J. William, 212, 214

Heath, Tom, 50

Hegan, Jim, 85, 88

Henderson, Robert, 150

Henrich, Tommy, 37, 38

Herman, Billy, 21

Heymans, Bill, 112

Hickman, Jim, 265, 266